COMPETITION POLICIES IN EUROPE

CONTRIBUTIONS TO ECONOMIC ANALYSIS

239

ELSEVIER
Amsterdam – Lausanne – New York – Oxford – Shannon – Singapore – Tokyo

COMPETITION POLICIES IN EUROPE

Edited by

Stephen MARTIN
Centre for Industrial Economics
Institute of Economics
University of Copenhagen
Copenhagen K, Denmark

1998

ELSEVIER
Amsterdam – Lausanne – New York – Oxford – Shannon – Singapore – Tokyo

ELSEVIER SCIENCE B.V.
Sara Burgerhartstraat 25
P.O. Box 211, 1000 AE Amsterdam, The Netherlands

Library of Congress Cataloging in Publication Data
A catalog record from the Library of Congress has been applied for.

ISBN: 0 444 82673 4

♾ The paper used in this publication meets the requirements of ANSI/NISO Z39.48-1992 (Permanence of Paper).

Printed in The Netherlands

INTRODUCTION TO THE SERIES

This series consists of a number of hitherto unpublished studies, which are introduced by the editors in the belief that they represent fresh contributions to economic science.
The term 'economic analysis' as used in the title of the series has been adopted because it covers both the activities of the theoretical economist and the research worker.
Although the analytical methods used by the various contributors are not the same, they are nevertheless conditioned by the common origin of their studies, namely theoretical problems encountered in practical research. Since for this reason, business cycle research and national accounting, research work on behalf of economic policy, and problems of planning are the main sources of the subjects dealt with, they necessarily determine the manner of approach adopted by the authors. Their methods tend to be 'practical' in the sense of not being too far remote from application to actual economic conditions. In addition they are quantitave.
It is the hope of the editors that the publication of these studies will help to stimulate the exchange of scientific information and to reinforce international cooperation in the field of economics.

The Editors

Contents

Competition Policies in Europe - S. Martin (Editor)

Chapter 1

Introduction

Stephen Martin

The methodical erecting of the Single Market — in an economic rather than a legal sense — generates an ongoing series of laboratory experiments that test the theories economists develop to explain behavior in imperfectly competitive markets. It also provides a testing ground for different approaches to competition policy — inherited corporatist approaches that historically played roles in several Member States, more recent approaches that seek to promote national champions within the EU, and EU policies aimed at maintaining (in appearance and in fact) a level playing field for market competition. All of this makes it an exciting time to be an industrial economist in the European Union.

The chapters of this book, which were presented at meetings of the Competition Policy Working Group of the Centre for Industrial Economics in 1995 and 1996, survey the broad range of issues raised the development of EU competition policy. These include collusion, vertical restraints, the role of competition policy with respect to regulated industries, and the implementation of competition policy, for the first time in many Member States, in a framework of subsidiarity.

The picture that emerges is one of change in the direction of maintaining workable competition over as broad a segment of EU markets as possible, to the benefit of consumers and of the integration process. This movement is evident in

- policies toward collusion, which evolve in the direction of prohibition rather than abuse control;

- policies toward vertical restraints, which evolve in the direction of allowing efficiency-generating restraints while disallowing those that have the effect of dividing markets;
- policies toward competition in regulated industries, which tend to limit the scope of derogations from competition policy to the narrowest range consistent with the regulatory mandate; and
- in the role of independent Competition Authorities, in several Member States, as promoters of the market system of resource allocation.

Much institutional detail about these general trends, and exceptions from them, is contained in the chapters that follow. It is a rich documentation of the state of competition policy in the European Union

1.1 Collusion

A practical man with some responsibility for interpreting U.S. competition policy once wrote[1]

> The defendants cannot be ordered to compete, but they properly can be forbidden to give directions or make arrangements not to compete.

This is also the policy embodied in Article 85 of the Treaty of Rome, but this policy was not chosen because the EU Founding Fathers were convinced of the desirability of competitive markets in a narrow economic sense.[2] Their motivation lay in political economy rather than in economics: the appearance of a level playing field was seen as essential if economic integration in the European Community was to make any headway at all, and this led the drafters of the Treaty of Rome to adopt constitutional provisions toward collusion in particular and competition policy in general that were tougher than those of any single Member State, with the possible exception of Germany.[3]

[1] Justice Holmes, *Swift and Co.* v. United States 196 US 375 (1905).

[2] Nor was this the reason why such a policy was adopted in the United States. But that is another story.

[3] See the Spaak Report (1956, p. 53). As Manfred Neumann makes clear in Chapter 3, German competition policy was a postwar grafting onto an older tradition that had much in common with the cooperative approach to competition policy.

Before the Treaty of Rome, the European approach to collusion and less intimate forms of cooperation between independent firms was quite different. The historical view of collusion in many EU Member States was that it was a normal and unavoidable type of firm conduct in modern industrial markets, which it would make no sense to forbid. Rather, the appropriate public policy was held to be control of cartels to ensure that behavior contrary to the public interest did not take place.[4]

The first portion of this book deals with the transition, at the Member State level, from the view that cartelization is normal and to be controlled rather than prohibited to the view embodied in Article 85 of the Treaty of Rome.

The experience of the Netherlands is characteristic. Brusse and Griffiths trace the origins of the Dutch pro-cartel policy to misguided measures adopted in hopes of avoiding economic collapse during the 1930s. The Netherlands established a cartel register during World War II, under the occupation government. It was continued after the war — in the reconstruction period, governments found it convenient to deal with organized trade associations rather than unorganized mobs of individual firms.

Legislation put into effect in 1958 continued the cartel register, and also allowed the government to publicize the activities of offending firms. The new law was not effective in promoting good market performance, as Brusse and Griffiths document by drawing on information contained in the cartel register. The control approach was abandoned reluctantly and after several false starts that were scuttled by the unwillingness of the administrative infrastructure to implement legislation that made life difficult for cartels. The desire to harmonize the Netherlands' practice with that of the EU was a major factor behind change when it did come, as was the feeling that tough domestic competition was essential if firms were to survive in the Single Market. The latter reflects a recognition that a tough competition policy promotes efficiency — competitiveness — at the firm level, although like many effective medicines, it is one the patient cannot be expected to like.

The Danish experience, discussed in institutional detail by Albæk et al and from an abstract point of view by Martin, has much in common with that of the Netherlands. Denmark long embraced the publicity approach

[4]For an explicit statement of this view, see the resolution on The Control of International Trusts and Cartels of the 26th Conference of the Interparliamentary Union (London, 1930).

to motivating desirable business behavior — in essence, the idea that businesspeople can be depended upon to do the right thing if they believe that doing the wrong thing will get their names into newspaper headlines. This view was popular for short periods in the United Kingdom and the United States (both discussed by Martin). Leaving grudging *noblesse oblige* aside, the mechanism by which publicity must be thought to work is that fear of publicity-induced entry will induce profit-maximizing businesspeople to behave in ways that avoid publicity, and that if this does *not* work, then actual entry, induced by publicity, will eliminate bad market performance. A chain is only as strong as its weakest link, and the Danish experience (reviewed by Albæk et al) does not suggest that potential or actual entry can be relied upon to function as the publicity theory requires. Danish economists have actively called for modifications in Danish competition law to bring it more in line with that of the EU, and such changes are under active consideration at this writing.

The German and the UK approaches to collusion involved episodes of acquiescence toward collusion, each however with its own distinctive elements. In the UK, as discussed by George Symeonidis, the 1956 Restrictive Trade Practices Act marked a toughening of cartel policy, although this was not immediately clear. It became so only after negative decisions in initial cases where firms sought to defend cartel agreements. Symeonidis outlines later changes in UK law, and analyzes the impact of cartel policy on market structure. He suggests that the toughening of competition policy was one factor inducing a simultaneous weeding-out of less efficient firms and increased concentration of sales in the hands of larger firms. By implication, the abandoned approach of tolerance toward interfirm cooperation had protected inefficient firms and impaired the competitivity of UK firms, at least as measured by world standards.

Manfred Neumann documents the emergence of cartels and a cartel monitoring policy in industrial Germany. It is interesting to speculate that this approach might have died a natural death, which is at least suggested by some of the policy changes that took place in the 1920s, but events intervened. Cartels were adopted by the Nazi government as an integral element in the administration of the German economy. Occupation authorities introduced US-style antitrust rules to postwar Germany. German versions of these rules were introduced in the late 1950s, and enforcement of these rules by the Federal Cartel Office has been vigorous.

Neumann also provides a theoretical analysis of the costs and benefits of adopting a *per se* rule against cartels, coming down in favor of such a rule.

1.2 Vertical Restraints

Vertical restraints are a persistently contentious issue for competition policy. Ulrich Kamecke discusses the reasons behind differences in the German treatment of resale price maintenance and other vertical restraints, and outlines the pressures for harmonization that arose when the Bundeskartellamt was given the authority to enforce Treaty of Rome competition rules as well as their not entirely consistent German counterparts. The treatment of vertical restraints under German competition law is related to the treatment of abuse of a dominant position.

Paul Seabright offers a general analysis of the policy treatment of vertical restraints, taking into consideration not only the impact of such restraints on performance but also enforcement considerations and the desirability of clarity in public policy. He puts forward the proposition that a vertical restraint should be presumed to be acceptable unless it can be shown to injure some third party — either customers, competitors, or potential entrants. This approach leads to a workable rule that is proposed for use by competition authorities.

1.3 Implementing Member State Competition Policies

One of the distinctive characteristics of competition policy in the European Union is the adaptation by Member States of their own competition policies for consistency with those of the European Commission. Such adaptations are part of a wider series of changes that are needed to make the subsidiarity principle of the Maastricht Treaty a working reality.

1.3.1 Belgium

Leo Sleuwaegen and Patrick Van Cayseele discuss the Belgian experience, that of implementing a national competition policy for an open economy that is also subject to EU competition policy. The Belgian economy is characterized by substantial openness to trade flows and by leading positions of multinational firms in many sectors. This openness means that foreign competition limits the exercise of market power in tradable sectors; there remains a substantial role for domestic competition policy with respect to nontradables.

They describe the gradual disenchantment of policymakers with a policy of price regulation, which was ineffective in controlling inflation and worsened market performance at the micro level, and the implementation, from 1993, of a Belgian competition law with provisions that generally parallel those of the European Union. There are differences, however: the Belgian law permits an efficiency defense in merger cases. How important this option will be in practice remains to be seen.

1.3.2 France

Saïd Souam documents the deeply rooted French tradition of government intervention in the economy and the slow but steady progress that understanding of the efficiency aspects of market processes has made in the post-World War II period. Protectionist themes (for example, abuse of a state of economic dependency) remain an element of French competition policy, and this chapter gives the impression that official willingness to accept the constraints implied by a market system (perhaps even to recognize that a market mechanism implies constraints) remains limited. Support for intervention remains strong, despite its dismal track record.

1.3.3 Ireland

Frank Barry and Francis O'Toole note that a mercantilist slant to Irish government policy has impeded the development of an effective national competition policy, while at the same time underlying what is in effect discrimination against the service and non-traded sectors. This mercantilist approach seems to be rooted in a belief that trade promotion creates jobs while domestic competition policy destroys jobs. General equilibrium considerations, Barry and O'Toole argue, suggest the contrary: more competitively priced imported inputs generate a number of jobs in purchasing sectors that more than make up for any jobs lost in import-competing sectors. They also make the argument that a protectionist approach increases labor-market rigidities.

As with many other EU Member States, prohibition-based competition policy has come only recently to Ireland, and has harmonized the principles of Irish competition policy with that of the EU. 1996 legislation that amends Irish competition law increases the resources and the mandate of the Irish Competition Authority, which may now be in a stronger position to advocate a market-oriented approach to resource allocation.

1.3.4 Italy

The early experience of Italy's Autorità Garante, which is outlined by Fabio Gobbo and Massimo Ferrero, involved establishing a secure position in a governmental infrastructure that lacked confidence in the market as a mechanism of resource allocation. The Autorità's activity has gone forward on two levels.

On a practical level, the Autorità has implemented the new Italian competition law, which broadly parallels that of the European Union. A notable distinction is that the Autorità Garante is an independent enforcement agency, which administers laws but does not make them. The activity of the Autorità has included actions against collusion, against abuses of dominant positions, and the control of mergers.

On a different level, the Autorità has assumed the task of defending the market mechanism, peppering legislative and regulatory bodies with reports that emphasize the shortcomings associated with attempts to short-circuit market processes. The Autorità's advice has often been followed, and sometimes not, but it has always been present in the policy debate.

1.3.5 Portugal

Successive right-wing and left-wing regimes in Portugal largely rejected a market system, the former in favor of a corporatist organization of the economy and the latter in favor of state ownership. The result, as indicated by Pedro Barros and José Mata, was that competition policy effectively appeared in Portugal only in anticipation of entry into the European Union.

The provisions of Portuguese competition law generally follow those of the European Union. Barros and Mata discuss a rich menu of cases illustrating the application of the law to business behavior, covering collusion, predation, vertical restraints, and merger control. They also examine conflicts between competition policy, industrial policy (which aims to promote large firm size and competitiveness), and trade policy. Regarding the latter, the place of export cartels in the economy is distinctive; an example of a government-organized export cartel for Port wine is given. Barros and Mata argue that competition from foreign producers is not a satisfactory substitute for domestic competition policy, even in small EU Member States.[5]

1.4 Competition Policy Toward Regulated Sectors

1.4.1 Italy/energy

The overlap of competition policy with other public policies that concern the functioning of specific markets is a topic of continuing interest. In the first of two chapters that confront such overlaps, Paola Valbonesi examines issues raised by the privatization of the energy sector in Italy. She reviews the alternative regulatory schemes that have been put forward, and argues that the public interest requires that exceptions made for this sector from the general rules of competition policy should be made a small as possible.

1.4.2 Spain/para-pharmaceuticals

Aurora García, Nikolaos Georgantzís, and Maria Petit model cross-subsidization in the Spanish para-pharmaceutical sector. The possibility of such cross-subsidization arises from the combination of regulated pharmacy locations and the adoption of distribution schemes by manufacturers of non-pharmaceutical products that restrict retail outlets to pharmacies. Although regulations restricting the distribution of non-pharmaceutical products have been relaxed, changes in distribution schemes have not followed. This illustrates the remark of Justice Holmes, quoted in Section 1.1, that while the law can forbid firms to make arrangements not to compete, it cannot compel them to compete.

The chapter includes a spatial model that allows for vertical as well as horizontal differentiation among retail outlets. The model is calibrated using data from a survey of distribution outlets, and results suggest that allowing

[5]Barry and O'Toole reach a similar conclusion with respect to Ireland.

for additional non-pharmacy outlets will improve welfare, even if the quality of service at such outlets is perceived as being lower than at a pharmacy.

1.5 Convergence

Laraine Laudati's contribution closes the volume with an overview of the interaction of EU competition law and the competition laws of the various Member States. The EU-Member State relationship creates substantial pressures for harmonization of Member State laws with that of the EU. Member States without indigenous competition law traditions have tended to adopt laws patterned after those of the EU; Members States with divergent approaches have modified them, at varying speeds, in the same way. The result has been a general expansion of the prohibition approach at the expense of "abuse control." Convergence in the area of merger control is also evident, although it seems clear that the desire to retain the ability to promote national champions seems to maintain a certain influence at the Member State level.[6] Laudati notes the spread of independent competition authorities at the Member State level, authorities that are more insulated from political pressures than is the European Commission. Just as the substantive elements of EU competition law have created pressure for modification of Member State law, so this institutional aspect of competition law in some Member States has led to calls for institutional reform, in the direction of greater independence, at the EU level.

1.6 References

Comité Intergouvermental créé par la Conférence de Messine *Rapport des Chefs de Délégation aux Ministères des Affaires Etrangères* (Spaak Report), Bruxelles, 21 avril 1956.

[6] As, indeed, the desire to maintain the ability to promote European champions retains a certain following at the EU level.

Competition Policies in Europe - S. Martin (Editor)

Chapter 2

Paradise Lost or Paradise Regained? Cartel Policy and Cartel Legislation in the Netherlands

Wendy Asbeek Brusse
Richard Griffiths

2.1 Introduction

In March 1990, the Dutch economist and competition policy expert, Professor H.W. de Jong, published a path-breaking article entitled: 'The Netherlands: Europe's cartel paradise' (de Jong, 1990). This article broke the 'taboo' around public discussion on cartels in the Netherlands (van der Zwan, 1992) and inspired at least the title of the conference 'The end of the cartel paradise,' although, in fairness, the substance of the conference drew heavily on the changes in Dutch competition legislation being discussed at the time. Therefore, despite the similarity between our title and John Milton's famous epic poems, we acknowledge Professor de Jong as the more direct inspiration.

Dutch cartel policy, having been mired in apathy and indifference for several decades, has been moved higher up the political agenda in the last ten years. In 1987, the Ministry of Economic Affairs announced that it was planning a more rigorous enforcement of the provisions of the virtually dormant 1958 Economic Competition Law. This was rapidly overtaken by a series of amendments to that legislation and subsequently by an entirely new law. At the time of writing this article, this new Competition Law has passed through all the major legislative stages and is expected to take effect early in 1998 (Economische Zaken, 1997).[1]

This paper will divide the evolution of Dutch policy towards cartels into three phases stretching back virtually sixty years:

— the pro-cartel phase (1935-1956)

— the phase of indifference (1956-1987)

— the current anti-cartel drive (1987-1997)

It will demonstrate how the framing and implementation of legislation was determined by the political and economic climate of the times. This, rather than shortcomings in the legal apparatus, explains the tolerance towards collusive business behavior that has characterized much of the history of various governments' cartel policies in the Netherlands.

2.2 The Pro-Cartel Period

The first Dutch national legislation, the Business Agreements Act (*Ondernemersovereenkomstenwet*) of 1935, was conceived in the depths of the Depression. Its main aim was to curtail the deleterious effects of excessive (domestic) competition on prices and employment. As a result, it tended towards the endorsement of restrictive producer agreements and the government even took powers to force cartel membership upon dissenting firms, if necessary. In the same way as the early New Deal had been in the United States, so the Dutch government was sympathetic to the argument that cartels maintained profits and therefore helped stem the rash of business collapses that had characterized the early years of the Depression.

This motivation was reinforced by the introduction of higher tariffs and, more especially in the Dutch case, quotas on national frontiers in an effort to prevent the erosion of the balance of payments and the destruction of

[1] In March 1997, the legislation passed through the Dutch parliament's Second Chamber and it is currently awaiting approval by the First Chamber.

employment. Since such restrictions would also diminish the impact of foreign deflationary forces in undermining domestic prices, their introduction was somewhat at odds with a deflationary policy aimed at realigning Dutch prices with international price levels without recourse to currency depreciation. Nevertheless, these trade controls were intended to keep the home market for home producers, and the effects would obviously be lost if murderous foreign competition were simply replaced by murderous domestic competition. Moreover, where quotas served to create artificial shortages, national trade and producer associations served a useful allocative function.

All of these aspects were absorbed into the 1941 Cartel Decree (Kartelbesluit), imposed by the Nazi government of occupation. The law also incorporated many of the principles inherent in corporatist fascist ideology. In addition, the Decree established a compulsory confidential cartel register, albeit without stipulating any sanctions for non-compliance, and created an independent commission to advise on any measures to be taken. It is interesting to note that 1941 Cartel Decree remained intact for the following ten years. This situation is not really surprising, since like many European governments, post-war Dutch administrations retained a pro-cartel stance and embraced a neo-corporatist philosophy in relations with organized business and labor.

The factors encouraging a sympathetic attitude towards cartels, that we have mentioned above, were reinforced by the exigencies of war-time planning and post-war reconstruction. First, the war effort had centered around national industrial boards that had encouraged the standardization of products and the diffusion of techniques. This, together with the sharing later of captured German patents, eroded one of the props of domestic competitive advantage and, therefore, inhibited governments in making subsequent demands for more competition. Second, post-war reconstruction elevated government priorities from the *sectoral* protection of the 1930s to *national* reconstruction, whose benefits were for the nation as a whole and not for any individual firms within it. Moreover, with domestic priorities directed towards maximizing output, for economic and political ends, governments had little time for American concerns of increasing productivity. If marginal firms needed the protection of restrictive arrangements to allow them to add to the national cake, it was a small price to pay. Thirdly, the universal situation of shortages and trade deficits intensified the use of quantitative frontier controls, and therefore the need for means of domestic allocation. This task was often left to national trade associations which, in effect, became the executive arm of government policies. In addition, when these frontier controls were dismantled from 1949 onwards, there was little official inclination to have the 'gains' of reconstruction wiped out by foreign competition, and so these trade associations were expected, and encouraged, to take care of matters for themselves (Asbeek Brusse and Griffiths, 1996).

Apart from these general considerations, there are two specifically Dutch elements that reinforced this tolerant attitude towards cartels. The first was the commitment of successive Dutch coalition cabinets towards neo-corporatist institutions. At its peak was the Social Economic Council (*Sociaal-Economische Raad*, SER) that formalized continuous tripartite discussion between representatives of employers, employees and government on virtually all aspects of economic and social policy. At a lower level, the Ministry of Economic Affairs cooperated closely with sectoral, horizontal national business organizations in the planning and implementation of its industrialization policy (van Zanden and Griffiths, 1989), its policy of import restraint and its regional development schemes. The second factor, that enhanced the effectiveness of this system of regular consultation, was the high priority given by the governments, until deep into the 1950s, to the implementation of formalized prices and incomes policies. In exchange for a system of national wage restraint, this policy required from industrialists the observation of price ceilings and price controls which could only happen if businesses were allowed to cooperate in this area (Windmuller and de Galan, 1979). Given such arrangements, it would clearly be difficult for a government, even if it were so inclined, to act against industries engaged in collusion on prices, a practice common in most cartel agreements.

Despite a broadly tolerant attitude towards cartels, the government became increasingly concerned to establish a greater degree of supervision and control over restrictive practices. In 1951, in anticipation of new legislation, the parliament passed the Suspension of Business Regulation Act, for use against cartels operating against the public interest. Over a period of six years, under the terms of this interim legislation, the government proceeded against 36 cartels. In 14 cases it had declared certain provisions of the agreement to be unenforceable while in a further 19 cases it recognized that the cartel had been amended satisfactorily (Wijsen, 1956). This achievement, however, needs to be put against the context of virtually 200 cartel agreements registered with the Ministry of Economic Affairs, a number that underrepresented the full extent of cartel practices (Barendregt, 1991).

2.3 Indifference

A new Economic Competition Law (*Wet Economische Mededinging*) was passed by parliament in 1956 and became operative in 1958. It kept the cartel register but extended its coverage to embrace banking, insurance and transport. However, the liberal professions were excluded from the provisions of the Act. The definition of cartel was a broad one, intended to cover all 'competition agreements,' whether designed to restrict markets or not. In keeping with the earlier legislation of 1935 and 1941, the Law still allowed the minister to impose a cartel agreement on the industry as a whole but only on condition:

— that members of the agreement request this (i.e. the government cannot initiate such a step),

— that members to the agreement represent a 'substantial majority' of the industry,

— and that the interests of the industry and the public interest require such an extension to the agreement.

It was in allowing action *against* cartels that the new law differed most from its predecessors. Among the new powers it granted the Minister were the ability to declare any agreement that was considered against the public interest non-binding, either provisionally (which would allow the cartel time to amend itself) or definitively. He could also suspend an agreement whilst coming to a decision. In addition, the Minister could chose to publicize the contents of an agreement considered to be against the general interest (thereby allowing public opinion to force the cartel to amend itself). Most importantly, he could declare certain types of restrictive practices non-enforceable. This last provision implied that the government no longer had to judge each case individually and on its own merits.

Another important facet of the new legislation was that it allowed the government to act against "positions of economic power" involving a "predominating influence" over the Dutch market. In such cases, the government could publish the relevant data and, for a maximum of five years, it could compel the bodies concerned to meet certain, specified supply conditions.

The procedures established by the law for prosecuting cartels left the initiative for starting any investigation into competition agreements with the

Ministry of Economic Affairs. It could act on complaints or on its own initiative, presumably on the basis of information submitted to the cartel register. This was a provision maintained from the 1941 Decree but, somewhat out of line with the accent on the beneficial effect of publicity elsewhere in the Law, the register was kept confidential. However the action was started, officials in the Ministry were bound first to consult with the parties of the agreement under investigation. In this way, should there be grounds for complaint, both parties would attempt to arrive at an acceptable solution. Should they still consider the outcome unsatisfactory, they could then refer the matter to the Minister who then decided whether to begin formal proceedings. At this stage the matter would pass to the hands of an independent advisory body, the Commission on Economic Competition (*Commissie Economische Mededinging*, CEM), another survival from the 1941 Decree. The CEM could hear any sides involved in the case, but the judgement it reached was in the form of a non-binding advice to the Minister. It was for the Minister to take the final decision of whether the agreement contravened the "general interest." There was no definition given in the law itself for criteria of what constituted the 'general interest.' In the subsequent explanation on the 1956 act submitted to parliament it was defined as ensuring that the general economic and social policy of the government was not subverted by alternative practices (Barendregt, 1991).

In looking at the implementation of the new legislation, we have to consider the background of the cartel phenomenon. The cartel register affords some insight into the scale of the cartel phenomenon, although it grossly underestimates the scale of 'competition agreements.' Even so, there were 198 agreements registered in 1958 and, after the register had been 'cleaned' to remove those agreements that had lapsed, there still remained 201 in 1988. These were not necessarily the same as those registered thirty years earlier, although de Jong does demonstrate that Dutch cartels were remarkably resilient. Of the 109 horizontal price cartels for which information was released in 1988 (included within the total of 201), over half had existed for more than a decade and no less than 16 cartels had been in force for more than thirty years (the record being held by the bicycle trade cartel formed in 1920 and eventually forbidden in 1992) (de Jong, 1992).

Against this backdrop, the activity under the 1956 Law is not at first sight particularly impressive. Over a span of thirty years, only eight agreements had (some of) their provisions dissolved (2 cases in the first decade of the working of the Law and 6 cases in the 1980s). It is possible that the informal consultation procedures incorporated in the legislation were successful in achieving the dissolution of pernicious cartel practices, but the qualitative evidence suggests that this is unlikely. In the period 1978–1987 some 22 horizontal price agreements were voluntarily withdrawn after such consultations but this represented only a fraction of the many national, regional and local price and market division arrangements still remaining within the cartel register (de Jong, 1990).

This leaves five cases of general prohibition of certain restrictive practices to consider (3 in the first decade of the Law's operation and 1 each in the subsequent decades).

In 1964, in line with the trend in much of Western Europe at the time, the government introduced the Law to prohibit collective resale price maintenance. However, the effect of these measures was largely undone by allowing for exemptions in over half the cases where these were requested by producers. That same year, with more success, another ban was imposed on resale price maintenance agreements involving some durable consumer goods (radios, televisions, household electrical goods, automobiles and photographic goods). In 1965, the Ministry attempted to prohibit certain practices inherent in exclusive dealership and price and loyalty rebates, but after a juridical challenge, it was forced later to withdraw the measure. In the interim period, only one case of administrative action in this respect was announced. After this flurry of activity, the Ministry settled into a pattern of almost total inertia for virtually two decades (with the single exception of a proscription of race discrimination) until, in 1986, it issued a general ban on certain tendering practices in the building industry (a ban initially proposed in 1953). This last action, however, can be considered a prelude to the more active stance announced the following year.

In his memoirs, the author of the 1956 legislation, ex-minister of Economic Affairs Jelle Zijlstra considered that as an exercise it had been 'intellectually satisfactory,' but he admitted that it could not be called effective (Zijlstra, 1992). In its advice on the new legislation, the Social Economic Council argued that the 'formal policy was - at least until the recent general prohibitions of some heavy cartel forms - of little significance.' Rather more dubiously it suggested that 'the most important contribution was made by informal policy, which was founded on consultations with firms about possible adaptations in cartel agreements before employing legal instruments.' Yet, it was forced to concede that (Sociaal-Economische Raad, 1994):

> In the past, Dutch competition policy has proved to have had little impact. Already in the early seventies, the minister of Economic Affairs observed that "the means to follow an effective control of abuse on the basis of the Economic Competition Act have been more limited than people generally have assumed."

The ex-Secretary of State for Economic Affairs, Yvonne van Rooij, also quoted Zijlstra and wrote that (van Rooij, 1992) "In view of the policy history, that conclusion cannot be denied. The practice of Dutch case by case cartel policy is doubtless unimpressive."

Part of the explanation for the failure of the authorities to prosecute restrictive practices more vigorously lies with the nature of the legislation itself. First, the Law is based on the assumption that cartels are good, unless proved otherwise, and it is left to the government to demonstrate that the agreement constitutes an abuse of the general interest leaves the burden of proof up to the government (Sociaal-Economische Raad, 1994). This requires a labor-intensive 'policing' since each cartel has to be judged individually against each specific market situation. Second, the term 'general interest' is not specified within the law itself and the intention described in the explanation of the Law to the effect that it constitutes action thwarting the goals of government policy seems unnecessarily restrictive. Legally, however, the term is no more than 'relatively vague norm that offers little guidance in concrete situations.' (Sociaal-Economische Raad, 1994). The result is that the Ministry is left a large margin of judgement and, therefore, freedom in the implementation, or non-implementation of policy. Third, although there is a cartel register, the law did not really make provisions for uncovering unregistered cartels, or for sanctions against non-registration. Thus, the register has always been inadequate, and de Jongsuggests at least doubling the figures it contained to obtain a more accurate impression (de Jong, 1990). At a conference 'Enterprise and Brussels, national versus European competition policy' in June 1989, the Christian Democrat MP Schartman summed up his judgement as follows (Schartman, 1990):

> More than thirty years of Dutch competition policy on the basis of the Economic Competition Law has taught us the following:
>
> — The aims and ideals of the Economic Competition Law are wonderful

— The criteria are too abstract; a concrete and clear policy is hard to pursue

— Modifying the Act is not really reconcilable with its character

— For some decades, policymakers have unsuccessfully tried to introduce prohibitive elements into its abuse system

— Active policy on the basis of the existing law is hardly productive and, in view of deregulation, undesirable

— We are ready for an entirely new Act.

Whilst the law may have had its shortcomings, most of the failure can be attributed to a reluctance to use its provisions. Officials in the Ministry had gradually forsaken the prosecution of cartels (whether by searching for non-registered agreements or by evaluating newly registered agreements). The policy had been purely reactive, 'driven' by complaint and subsequently resolved within the internal discussion rounds between civil servants and business (Sociaal-Economische Raad, 1994). Given the tight relations between government and business, it might have been unrealistic to expect otherwise. The government relied on the cooperation of the organized business community for its macro-economic policy goals whether it was in the form of price controls as part of a prices and incomes policy in the 1950s and 60s, or its industrialization and regional policies, or through the increasing web of industrial subsidies that spread in the wake of the first oil crisis. Officials at the Ministry of Economic Affairs worked closely with business on an almost daily basis. Given their dependence on the goodwill of business, they were therefore not in a strong position to take an independent stance towards undesirable forms of business cooperation.

We could expect that a domestic legislative climate that posed little threat to cartel practices, would stimulate cartel formation. On the other hand, the trade dependence of the Dutch economy may be expected to have inhibited cartel formation. At this juncture, therefore, we should ask the question: Where were there cartels in the Netherlands? We cannot answer this question completely, nor can we say whether the Netherlands had more or fewer cartels than elsewhere in Western Europe. However, as part of the discussions on renewed legislation, the Ministry of Economic Affairs has released (some) more details from its, admittedly incomplete (and still confidential) cartel register.

In 1989 the Ministry of Economic Affairs released details on the 109 horizontal price agreements still active in September 1988 (Ministerie van Economische Zaken, 1989).[2] Despite the received wisdom that such agreements are fragile constructions, especially in times of cyclical upheaval, those captured in the Dutch register proved to have been remarkably resilient. Judging by their date of first notification, 40 per cent had survived for more than two decades and a further 19 per cent had already celebrated their tenth anniversary.

These agreements occurred most frequently in the building sector (building materials 28 per cent, construction 12 per cent and finishing 5 per cent). Next in importance followed the metal industry (11 per cent), transport, storage and communication (10 per cent) banking and insurance (7 per cent) agriculture and fisheries (6 per cent) and the food drink and tobacco sector (also 6 per cent). There were 3 instances of agreements in business services, two each in the chemicals and the instruments and optics sectors, and one each in clothing, electronic articles and apothecaries.

The most common provision in these agreements was joint tendering, which occurred in 36 per cent of cases. Virtually all operated on a national scale (only 7.5 per cent were local). They tended to be fairly simple constructions and almost two thirds contained no other provision. Among the remaining one third the most common additional measures were exclusivity clauses (57 per cent) and conditions criteria (36 per cent). Almost all fell either in the metal industry (31 per cent) or the building industry[3] (66 per cent).

Fixed price agreements (29 per cent of cases) were the next most common category in the register but 42 per cent of these were of purely local significance. These agreements were also the most complicated, with 87 per cent including other provisions, usually in combination.[4] The most common additional clauses were for market sharing (66 per cent), production, sales or marketing quotas (55 per cent), conditions criteria (48 per cent), exclusivity clauses and centralized purchasing and sales agencies (30 per cent each). Half of the recorded agreements were in building materials (but, aside from two instances in the food and drink sector and one in the instruments and optical industry (together 10 per cent), they were further entirely absent from the

[2] This is not the same as the total number of competition agreements, that numbered 240.

[3] Including materials, construction and finishing.

[4] Each agreement included, on average three other categories of restrictions.

manufacturing sector.

Minimum price agreements constituted 27 per cent of the agreements in the register, and 73 per cent of these operated on a national scale. In 86 per cent of cases they were also supplemented by other measures but were slightly less complex in structure. Quotas played a less prominent role in these agreements (12 per cent) whilst market sharing, exclusivity clauses and conditions criteria were equally represented (35 per cent each). Unlike the other horizontal price agreements, the building sector was not particularly prominent (building materials accounting for 13 per cent of cases). The most common sectors were transport, storage and communications (27 per cent), followed by agriculture and fisheries and by food, drink and tobacco (with 13 per cent each).

In 1992, the Ministry of Economic Affairs published information on the 201 market sharing agreements that were registered in existence in September 1991 (Ministerie van Economische Zaken, 1992). Compared with the horizontal price agreements analyzed two years earlier, these were generally younger. Only 14 per cent had been on the register for more than twenty years and a further 17 per cent had survived on the records for more than a decade. By contrast, almost half were striplings that had yet to reach their fifth anniversaries. The classification of these agreements is enormously complicated because even within the general description of 'market sharing' 68 per cent of these agreements combined more than one practice. Of these, the most common combinations were territorial agreements and limitations on product mix (58 per cent) linked in turn with obligations not to engage in certain brand sales after the ending of the agreement (43 per cent): a mixture that features regularly in commercial cooperation agreements involving franchising, joint purchasing and exclusive dealership. Moreover, 94 per cent of market sharing agreements also embraced other forms of restrictive practices.

One fifth of the market sharing agreements involved quantitative restrictions on output, sales or capacity. They were by far the most tenacious. Half of the agreements over thirty years old were found in this category, sixty-five per cent of those aged between twenty and thirty and thirty-five per cent of those aged between ten and twenty years. They were overwhelmingly concentrated in the building sector (76 per cent) and in transport (17 per cent).

Output quotas were rare. The four instances were all national in their impact. One involved agriculture (silver onions) and the other three building materials (paving stones, bricks and sandstone products). Sales quotas occurred in 21 agreements, all but two involved building materials and most were on a regional/local basis. Most were also complemented by horizontal price agreements. The remaining 16 instances all included clauses of distribution of sales, usually in the form of a central bureau that coordinated orders and fixed prices. Sixty per cent had a national coverage. In contrast with the strict quota arrangements, this form of cartel prevailed where large numbers of small concerns 'competed' for orders. Half of these involved building materials, but the remainder were in the transport sector (shipping, road transport and courier services). In framing its request to the Committee for Economic Competition for advice, the Ministry could not refrain from making plain its disapproval of such market sharing agreements that 'never made up part of more intensive, and positive, forms of cooperation.' More often than not, such measures were accompanied by (ibidem) 'more intense restriction of commercial freedom without there being any countervailing productive gain.'

The register also captured 5 cases of agreements focussed primarily upon capacity limitations (2.5 per cent of the total) though most included other marketing restrictions. All were concentrated in the building sector. Only in one case did the Ministry recognize the existence of a 'crisis cartel' of limited duration involving the reduction of capacity and the sharing of losses, in order to rid the national market of a supply overhang. The others it condemned as being part of arrangements to control local markets for the mutual benefit of the participants.

The remaining practices captured by the inventory mostly formed part and parcel of commercial cooperation agreements. Generally, these agreements have been smiled upon by the Ministry for embodying sales and management economies. These practices included:

- territorial distribution (included in 66 per cent of total)
- qualitative restrictions (included in 51 per cent of total agreements)
- end of agreement clauses (included in 34 per cent of total).
- normalization/standardization (included in 17 per cent of total)
- distribution of clients (included in 7 per cent of total)

Because of overlap, if we concentrate on the two most common practices we obtain a far wider sectoral distribution than we found in the case of quantitative restrictions. The largest concentrations are textiles, leather and furniture (17 per cent) automobiles and food, drink and tobacco (13 per cent each) do-it-yourself articles (11 per cent) and household goods (8 per cent). The building industry accounted for only 7 per cent of the cases, and the most restrictive forms at that.

Territorial distribution usually involved geographical restrictions on the establishment of sales outlets. Franchise agreements accounted for 66 per cent of such cases, exclusive dealership for 17 per cent and central purchasing accords for 5 per cent. The remaining 12 per cent appear to have formed part of the regional restrictions prevailing in the building industry which we have discussed above (and to have been utterly disapproved of as a result).

Most of the qualitative restrictions (98 cases) involved limitations on the assortment of goods that had to be purchased, running from minimum sales percentages for certain goods to 100 per cent determination of the sales composition. Franchising accounted for 84 per cent of these cases, and joint purchasing accords and exclusive dealership contracts for the rest. The register also caught 7 specialization agreements, mostly combined with horizontal price agreements. One case involved joint venture production for a highly specialized market whilst the remainder defined sub-specialties within a sector (projection tables, bibles, porcelain) or specialized sales (flowers, films). In contrast with their overall incidence, these agreements were relatively young - 60 per cent of agreements less than 5 years old and 55 per cent of those between five and ten were found in this category.

The Ministry was fairly sanguine about end-of-agreement clauses which limited freedom of purchase once a contractual agreement had been terminated. The time limit of the restriction was relatively short, and the clauses were mostly attached to franchise or dealership agreements (80 per cent of cases) whose primary purpose lay elsewhere.

Normalization/standardization clauses appeared in dealership contracts (49 per cent) (usually for automobiles) and, to a far lesser extent, in franchise agreements (14 per cent). A further 14 per cent were associated with product definition in the context of quantitative restrictive agreements already condemned by the Ministry. The remainder imposed quality definition for personnel, protection of trade-marks or uniform sales conditions. However, the Ministry drew attention to the fact that these could unnecessarily limit competition or could be employed to support horizontal price agreements.

The distribution of clients was not particularly common. In 4 cases, client sharing occurred within the context of joint commercial agreements but, even then, the Ministry judged the provision as 'not an essential or necessary part of this potentially positive form of economic cooperation.'(ibidem). In the other 11 cases, it usually involved obligations not to deal with the 'fixed clients' of another member of the cartel and. again for this reasons, they were thoroughly condemned. Seven of these cases made up part of wider restrictive agreements within the building industry.

2.4 Changes

The first concrete attempt to change the Act were initiated in 1971, after growing dissatisfaction among policymakers and civil servants that the limited scope for pursuing an active anti-cartel policy inhibited the fight against inflation. The then Minister of Economic Affairs asked the SER for advice on whether a new law was required or whether the existing measures could be made more effective, either by streamlining the procedures or by general prohibitions instead of case by case action (Uitermark, 1990). Moreover, he asked the SER to consider giving the public access to the hitherto confidential cartel register. Although in its advice delivered in 1973 the SER initially rejected the option of a prohibition on price cartels, the criticism of current policy stimulated further debate. In 1977, the new minister of Economic Affairs, Ruud Lubbers, suggested amending the existing Law to refine the abuse principle and, against the advice of the SER, to prohibit vertical and horizontal price agreements. In addition, the amendment would allow the government to impose price ceilings on certain goods. This proposal, too, met strong criticism from business circles and within the SER and it eventually came unstuck when a special governmental committee charged with examining deregulation (the Commissie Van der Grinten, named after its chairman) concluded that the existing Act already provided all the means necessary for promoting competition and suggested that new regulations were therefore undesirable. The initiative was shelved when a new cabinet took office (t'Gilde and Haank, 1985).

A decade later, forced by pressure from the EC's active anti-cartel policy which had led to repeated clashes with Dutch cartels at the national levels, the Secretary of State for Economic Affairs Evenhuis (whose motto was 'Less government, more market') launched a so-called 'Plan of Activities' aimed at bridging the gap between Brussels and The Hague on matters of cartel policy. In line with the pronouncement of the Commissie Van der

Grinten, he eschewed an overhaul of existing legislation. In his view, the Economic Competition Law itself 'offered adequate instruments for an active competition policy' (Schartman, 1990). The powers to outlaw swathes of undesirable cartel practice (article 10 of the 1956 Law) afforded ample scope for a stricter policy, and one that was in line with article 85 of the Treaty of Rome (Schartman, 1990; Sociaal-Economische Raad, 1994).

Nonetheless, the Dutch government subsequently chose for a gradual transition towards a more restrictive, anti-cartel policy through a 'two-track' approach. The first track implied a strengthening of anti-cartel policy within the existing framework. Apart from a more alert policy of dealing with cartel complaints, this embraced a series of general prohibitions against:

— vertical price agreements (a new Order in 1991, replacing the failed effort of 1964)

— horizontal price agreements (effective from July 1993)[5]

— market sharing agreements (effective from June 1994)

— collusive tendering agreements (also effective from June, 1994) (van Rooij, 1992).

The second track involved new legislation.

The government was forced to legislate amendments in 1992. The decision was closely linked to the embarrassment surrounding the EU's condemnation of a construction cartel, an agreement between building firms that the Dutch law had previously sanctioned (Kat, 1995). To avoid this type of intervention in future, the Dutch had to adapt their legislation to European norms. The revised cartel legislation of 4 November 1994 (to take effect on 1 September, 1995) officially aimed merely at increasing the effectiveness of the old Economic Competition Law, pending its replacement in 1997. Nevertheless, it introduced several changes in substance (Tweede Kamer, 1993:2).

Unlike the previous Law which related to legally binding competition agreements, the 1994 amendment also prohibited all types of collusive behavior having the same effect as practices that had already been prohibited

[5]Unlike in 1964, the government did not receive many requests for exemptions (OECD, 1994:1). The more recent requests and decisions are discussed in the annual competition reports to parliament (Ministerie van Economische Zaken, 1995).

under the Law.[6] Moreover, whereas the old legislation was only applied to a restricted list of 'liberal professions,' the amendment extended the Law to cover *all* 'liberal professions and those participating independently in the economic process' (Tweede Kamer, 1993:1).[7] In addition, the amendment abandoned the rule under the old Act whereby the implementation of a government order against a cartel was automatically suspended in the event of an appeal, and it also clamped down on exemptions agreed under the old legislation. Finally, it increased the maximum fine from Dfl.25,000 to Dfl 100,000 (still pathetically low by international standards) but, by considering violations a criminal rather than an civil offence, it effectively extended the duration of any order under the Law from two years to six.

The amended Law also increased the scope for controlling the observation of any prohibitions<. It was particularly concerned to guarantee the effectiveness against so-called 'heavy cases' of cartel practices that had been generally prohibited (such as horizontal price, market sharing and tendering agreements). The 1956 Law had only empowered civil servants of the Economic Control Service (Economische Controle Dienst) to act in cases where they had a 'reasonable suspicion' that the Law had been violated. This provision had led to complaints, both by officials and by injured parties complaining against non-observation, that it was usually impossible to find concrete evidence sustaining such 'reasonable suspicion.' The amended Law provided for a more active 'policing' role for the Service, and also stipulated that the party under investigation was obliged to cooperate with any investigation (Tweede Kamer, 1993:1).

Despite a streamlining of existing legislation and a demonstrable determination to increase its enforcement, the government nonetheless introduced an entirely new Act to govern its competition policy. It argued that a new law was necessary to adapt Dutch legislation to the aims of European competition policy. Thus, in contrast to the parsimonious definition of 'general interest' that motivated the 1956 Law, it now accepted that legislation should 'ensure effective competition in order to allocate resources efficiently and to create the best possible climate for fostering innovation and technical progress.' Moreover, the government accepted the need to ensure the completion of the EC's internal market. At the EC level, the Single European

[6] Again, this runs parallel to EC Law.

[7] With this definition, the authorities wanted to follow the EC's concept of enterprise as meaning every entity participating in economic activities, irrespective of its legal form or financial structure.

Market Programme strengthened European competition policy in parallel with the '1992' package with the argument that 'the expected benefits of the single market, including increased productivity, lower prices and greater employment opportunities cannot be realized unless free and fair competition is fully maintained in the post-1992 Community' (European Commission, 1989). This aim was further enshrined in the Maastricht Treaty, which subjected EC economic policy to 'the principle of an open market economy with free competition' and that any new provision on industrial policy may not 'lead to a distortion of competition' (European Community, 1994).[8] At a European level, these aims can be summarized as:

— promoting cost efficiency, both in the long and short run

— promoting flexibility and innovation

— protecting the workings of the market mechanism

— guaranteeing free market access to new competitors and protecting competitors against competitive agreements

— protecting consumers against restrictions on competitiveness and abuse of power

The motivation underlying the Dutch government's wholehearted endorsement of a more dynamic market policy, and its wish to adapt to it, was described as structural. It was based on an increasing perception that the long run viability and international competitiveness of the Dutch economy depended upon a flexible, competitive home market. The Dutch domestic market, it was argued, had for a long time lacked such flexibility. This awareness had slowly dawned through the inability to cope with economic recessions since 1973. It was expressed in the declining international competitiveness of Dutch industry, growing structural unemployment, sluggish growth rates and a structural imbalance of the economy (OECD, 1994:2). It was, moreover, argued that these problems would be aggravated by the EC's internal market programme, which would increase competition not only internationally, but also within the national and regional market. Ex-Secretary of State Yvonne van Rooij warned that if Dutch conditions for determining

[8]See Article 130(3)EC.

	Netherlands	Belgium	Luxembourg	Italy	Germany	France
Horizontal price and reduction agreements	7	6	3	2	4	1
Market sharing agreements	5	4	2	2	1	—
Collective exclusive dealing	6	4	2	1	—	—
Collective resale price maintenance	3	1	1	—	—	—

Table 2.1: Incidence of serious restrictions to competition of a predominantly national character that have been the subject of an Order under article 85,1 by the European Commission (1970-1989)
Note: the table embraces 27 Orders, but since each one of these may involve several different practice and more than one country, the total number of agreements is much higher, i.e. 55. Source: de Jong (1990).

locational decisions for new investment or for the establishment of new business deviated too far from European norms, they would 'eventually translate themselves into a shift in the spread of economic power bases in an open European market.' She therefore concluded that 'well functioning national and regional markets are of vital importance for the locational climate and the entrepreneurial climate in the Netherlands' (van Rooij, 1992).

Aside from this structural motivation, there were almost certainly also tactical considerations influencing this decision to align Dutch competition policy with European legislation. The government could not ignore the effect of the country's increasing isolation within Europe in this area. The Dutch were among the last to maintain legislation that did not prohibit cartels outright. Not only did this enhance the Netherlands' reputation as Europe's cartel paradise, it also meant that Dutch cartels were increasingly under siege by the European Commission, who found some of them to be in conflict with article 85 of the Treaty of Rome. It was no coincidence that by far the larger part of the EU's Orders relating to national competition agreements was directed against Dutch cartels.

Table 2.1 shows that 21 of the total of 55 serious competition infringements involved the Netherlands and that the Dutch also scored the highest for each type of agreement considered separately. This situation was undesirable in that it created judicial inequality and insecurity for firms that had to cope with differential systems at the European and the national level. Moreover, the subsidiarity principle required that national governments have the instruments to implement the EU's competition policy aims at a national level. If such instruments were missing, frequent EU intervention at the national level, as in the case of the builders cartel, would be the result.

The new Dutch competition legislation presented to parliament prohibits in principle horizontal and vertical agreements and abuse of economic power.[9] It amended the unsatisfactory situation whereby these measures are proscribed by administrative regulation in the framework of a law whose guiding principle is the judgement of individual cases for abuse of 'general interest' in specific situations. The core components of the EU's article 85 and 86 provide the main elements of this prohibition (Ministerie van Economische Zaken, 1995). The law includes a system of exemptions for R&D and franchise agreements based on EU legislation, whereby specific national interpretation and implementation are limited to those practices to which Community policy does not apply. Exemptions have also been made for those competition agreements (mainly in small and medium size businesses) whose influence on the market is marginal (so-called bagatelles). Cartels in commerce are exempt as long as no more than eight firms are involved and the combined turnover is below Dfl. 10 million. For all other cartels the ceiling is Dfl. 2 million (Ministerie van Economische Zaken, 1997).[10] Unlike EU legislation, it does not include a market share criterion (Tweede Kamer, 1996). Also allowed are certain practices in the retail sector, such as joint purchasing agreements and short-term joint advertising campaigns involving joint price discounts.

One of the law's most controversial components has been its system of enforcement. In the original draft, responsibility for competition surveillance, for granting exemptions and for penalizing infringements was placed with a new civil service operating within the Ministry of Economics Affairs and supposedly working independently. However, since the Ministry retained the

[9]The law also contains concentration clauses, but these have not been dealt with in this article.

[10]In the original draft law these ceilings were much lower, i.e. Dfl. 5 and 1 million respectively, but they were raised at the insistence of parliament.

right to give the service guidelines, both general and specific, many critics argued the service would be vulnerable to special pleading and would fail to gain credibility. de Jong, for one, maintained that during his 14 years as a member of the 'independent' advisory Commission on Economic Competition, he had seen too much log-rolling to believe in the new body's future immunity to such pressures (Snoep, 1996). Others criticized the fact that a single organization would be responsible for investigating, judging and punishing a cartel (Biesheuvel et. al., 1996; van der Ploeg, 1996). The amended law accepts this service, known as the Dutch Competition Authority (Nederlandse Mededingingsautoriteit, NMa) and its position within the Ministry, subject to two main provisos. First, that all general and specific interventions by the Ministry be published in the annual competition report to parliament and, second, that the entire construction be reviewed after three years with a view to making it still more independent (Ministerie van Economische Zaken, 1997).

2.5 Conclusion

We entitled this article, with a stunning lack of originality, 'Paradise Lost or Paradise Regained?' We could have put question marks by both parts of the title.

Paradise Lost? Was the Netherlands ever a cartel paradise? Did it really deviate so much from European practice? Of course we will never know for certain. It is doubtful whether restrictive agreements were unfailingly registered (who would, if they were going to be declared illegal?) and there has been no systematic disclosure of those agreements that were. Moreover, the fact that we can now castigate the old Dutch law as being weak in its formulation and lax in its persecution means very little in itself. There has been a great deal of sanctimonious humbug written about cartel legislation, much of it derived from close reading of the legal texts. These tell us very little about enforcement. For example, the famed independence of the German Bundeskartellamt in the heyday of Erhard's free market experiment could not prevent over half of the 1,000 largest German firms surveyed in the early 1960s being tied into international cartels (Bundesrepublik Deutschland, 1964). Similarly, recent research into the famous anti-trust measures written into the European Coal and Steel Community Treaty (and which the Americans would have liked to have seen in the Treaty of Rome) has confirmed their crashing failure to tame the main cartel and collusive abuses in the coal and steel markets (Spierenburg and Poidevin, 1994). We would even be reluctant to accept that the relatively high rate of prosecution of Dutch firms by DG IV was evidence of much more than an (astonishingly naive) willingness to take part in the original round of cartel registrations. Our own research into the history of cartels in postwar Europe suggests that until the late 1950s and early 1960s, when a new wave of legislation was enacted, anti-cartel policy was rarely pursued rigorously in Europe. Even when legal provisions against cartels were tightened (and the main beneficiary was the widespread abolition of resale price maintenance) it is far from clear whether competitive conditions were improved as a result. The new wave of legislation coincided with (and perhaps contributed to) a wave of mergers and consolidations within the business community and the increasingly widespread recourse of governments to subsidies and non-tariff barriers to maintain uncompetitive branches of the economy.

Nor does the data in the Dutch register reveal much of a paradise to be lost. Numerically, most of the serious restrictions lay in the clubby, chummy world of local building contractors and the less than ferociously competitive transport sector. It is unlikely that competition in these areas is much more fierce elsewhere. Of course, the register did not contain evidence of the cozy world of estate agents, solicitors and conveyancers, whose squeals of protest echoed through the press when the definition of 'liberal professions' covered by the law was extended. But this, too, represents an area of self-regulation that is only now being broken open elsewhere. And, of course, the register will not reveal the really large horizontal international agreements between major industrial concerns.

Paradise regained? A free world of dynamic competitive firms that will propel countries like the Netherlands back up the ladder of relative economic performance? We can question this assumption at several levels. First, we can observe (again) that legislation is only as good as its enforcement and this depends both on the political economy of the country concerned and on the specific context. Without a commitment to ensure compliance, no amount of legal fine tuning will change a prevailing situation. Second, it is doubtful whether an injection of competition (even assuming that it can be encouraged by legislative means) will be a panacea for the Dutch economy. Although more balanced reviews of the Dutch economy avoid the trap, it is amazing how often the demand for increased competition is associated with monocausal explanations of economic malaise (based, naturally, on the lack of such competition). It was not so long ago that 'Dutch disease' was synonymous with a complex of causes centered around a positive balance of payments forcing up the exchange rate, eroding competitiveness and undermining the industrial base. There is no evidence that such an approach has lost any of its explanatory power with the passing years. Finally, it is worth reflecting in the context of the new orthodoxy that the golden age of European economic growth in the 1950s and 1960s was not accompanied by free market behavior but occurred in the context of widespread government regulation in the economic sphere and by a tolerance of business cooperation, self-regulation, collusion and cartels (Asbeek Brusse and Griffiths, 1996).

Explaining (differences in) economic performance is a complex task, and the phenomenon is only vaguely understood. It is certainly not susceptible to radical change by grafting legislation onto the economy. Undoubtedly a more competitive climate will help ameliorate the current situation. But even if it were possible to emulate these circumstances in the high-growth new industrialized nations (assuming that governments would even want to, and that electorates would tolerate it) we feel that, at best, an effective competition policy will remain a necessary but not sufficient condition for improved economic performance.

2.6 References

Asbeek Brusse, W. and Griffiths, R.T. " L'European Recovery Program' e i cartelli: una indagine preliminare," *Studii Storici*, Volume 37, 1996, pp. 41–68.

Barendregt, J. "Het Mededingingsbeleid in Nederland: conjunctuurgevoeligheid en effectiviteit." Research memorandum 1991/17 Faculteit der Economische wetenschappen en Econometrie, Vrije Universiteit Amsterdam, 1991.

Biesheuvel, M. B., Mok, M. R. and Sevenster, H. G. "Van ordening naar marktwerking. Kanttekeningen bij het ontwerp-Mededinging swet." Pre-advies voor de Vereeniging "Handelsrecht" en de Vereeniging voor Mededingingsrecht, The Hague, 1996.

Bundesrepublik Deutschland (German Federal Republic), Deutscher Bundestag, 4. Wahlperiode, Zu Drucksache IV/2320, "Bericht über das

Ergebniß einer Untersuchung der Konzentration in der Wirtschaft," October 1964.

European Commission (1989) *EEC competition policy in the single market.* European Documentation, 1, 1989.

European Community, Directorate General for Economic and Financial Affairs (1994), *European economy,* Volume "Competition and integration. Community merger control policy," Brussels, 1994.

Gilde, P. t' and Haank, D.J. "De praktijk van de Wet Economische Mededinging," *Onderzoeksrapporten,* nr. 37, Stichting Wetenschappelijk Onderzoek Konsumentenaangelegenheden, The Hague, 1985.

Jong, H.W. de "Nederland: het kartelparadijs van Europa?," *Economisch-Statistische Berichten,* 14 March, 1990.

Jong, H.W. de "Het kartelparadijs: de punten van bezwaar," *Economisch-Statistische Berichten,* 23 September 1992.

Kat, M. de "Nederland wordt braaf jongetje in de Europese kartelklas," *NRC Handelsblad,* 12 September 1995.

Ministerie van Economische Zaken (Ministry of Economic Affairs) (1989), Bijlage bij adviesaanvraag betreffende horizontale prijsregelingen, 8 March.

Ministerie van Economische Zaken (1992), Bijlage bij adviesaanvraag inzake marktverdelingskartels, 7 April.

Ministerie van Economische Zaken (1995), Jaarverslag mededinging 1994-1995, The Hague.

Ministerie van Economische Zaken (1997), "Meer concurrentiekracht door nieuwe Mededingingswet," *EZ Informatie,* 22 March.

OECD, *Competition policy in OECD countries 1991-1992.* Paris 1994:1.

OECD, *OECD Economic Surveys 1992-1993: Netherlands.* Paris, 1994:2.

Ploeg, R. van der "Mededinging. Vijf kanttekeningen bij de nieuwe mededingingswet," *Economisch-Statistische Berichten,* 31 July 1996.

Rooij, Y. van "Het einde van het kartelparadijs," *Economisch-Statistische Berichten*, 23 September 1992.

Schartman, H.J. "De deur wijd open voor het Europese mededingingsbeleid" in: VNO, NCW, *Ondernemen en Brussel. Nationaal versus Europees mededingingsbeleid*, The Hague, 1990.

Sociaal-Economische Raad (Social Economic Council) *Advies nieuwe mededingingswet. Advies inzake de nieuwe mededingingswet uitgebracht aan de minister van Economische Zaken.* Publikatie nr. 13, 21 October 1994.

Snoep, T.M. "Mededingingswet zal tot cultuuromslag leiden," *NRC Handelsblad*, 13 December 1996.

Spierenburg, D. and Poidevin, R. *The History of the High Authority of the European Coal and Steel Community. Supranationality in Operation.* London, 1994.

Tweede Kamer der Staten-Generaal "Wijziging van de Wet economische mededinging (vergroting van de effectiviteit)," *Memorie van Toelichting.* Kamerstukken II 1992-1993, 23306, nr 3, 1993:1.

Tweede Kamer der Staten-Generaal "Wijziging van de Wet economische mededinging (vergroting van de effectiviteit)," *Memorie van Antwoord.* Kamerstukken II 1992-1993, 23306, nr 5, 1993:2.

Tweede Kamer der Staten-Generaal "Nieuwe regels omtrent de economische mededinging (Mededingingswet)," *Voorstel van Wet. Kamerstukken II* 1995-1996, 24707, nr 2, 1996.

Uitermark, P.J. *Economische Mededinging en algemeen belang. Een onderzoek naar de economisch-theoretische fundering van de Mededingingspolitiek.* Rotterdam, 1990.

Windmuller, J.P. and Galan, C. de *Arbeidsverhoudingen in Nederland.* Utrecht, Antwerpen, 1979.

Wijsen, J.F. "Cartel legislation in the Netherlands," *Cartel* Volume 6, 1956.

Zanden, J.L. van and Griffiths, R.T. *Economische geschiedenis van Nederland in de 20e eeuw.* Utrecht, 1989.

Zijlstra, J. *Per slot van rekening.* Amsterdam, 1992.

Zwan, A. van der "Verboden vrucht," *Economisch-Statistische Berichten,* 23 September 1992.

Competition Policies in Europe - S. Martin (Editor)

Chapter 3

The Evolution of Cartel Policy in Germany

Manfred Neumann

3.1 Introduction

Cartel policy in the Federal Republic of Germany has been embodied in the "Law against restraints of competition" (Gesetz gegen Wettbewerbsbeschränkungen, henceforth abbreviated "GWB"), which was enacted in 1957 and which, in the meantime, has been amended several times. The pattern underlying the regulations of the GWB made a substantial imprint on the EC law regarding cartels since drafting Article 85 of the Treaty of Rome was heavily influenced by representatives of Germany.

German cartel policy itself underwent a long and painful history. It began in 1897 when the Imperial Court of Law held cartels to be lawful devices to organizing industry. In 1923 a law intending to prevent abusive behavior of cartels was enacted, and the Nazi government used cartels as an instrument of a centrally planned economy. After the war the military government of the Allied Forces applied US antitrust regulations to West Germany until in 1957 it was replaced by German legislation.

In this paper the evolution of cartel policy in Germany beginning around the turn of the century will be depicted in more detail. In particular the opposing principles of *per se* prohibition of cartels and monitoring cartels with regard to abuse of market power will be discussed. Section II will be devoted to the experience prior to the enactment of the GWB and section III will be concerned with the experience with those regulations contained in the GWB. The final section IV will provide some afterthoughts regarding the respective merits of *per se* prohibition and control of abuse of market power.

3.2 The Pre-war Experience

3.2.1 Emergence and proliferation of cartels in pre-war Germany

Although collusion among businessmen can be traced far back into history and seems to have been widespread also during the Industrial Revolution in England (Ashton 1964, p. 89f.) cartels as a major kind of industrial organization came to the forefront of public interest and economic analysis only during the later decades of the nineteenth century. The Austrian economist Kleinwächter (1883), who provided the first systematic treatment of cartels, considered them to be "children of distress." He deemed them to be indispensable to avoid chaos and to adjust supply to fluctuating demand in an orderly way.

Upon an accelerated increase in the number of cartels during the later decades of the nineteenth century the Imperial Court of Justice ruled in 1897 that cartels are legal since freedom of business activity, according to the view of the Court, is deemed to encompass freedom to enter contracts which regulate prices in particular industries. According to later critics (Böhm 1948, Möschel 1972), the legal reasoning of the Court is somewhat questionable. Still, the ruling itself was in accord with the opinion of a large majority of economists of the late nineteenth century in Germany. Some of them refused to consider cartels as organization exploiting consumers but viewed them in a romantic light as being regulators of an otherwise chaotic environment. The leading German socialist of that time, August Bebel, in a parliamentary debate alluded to the emergence of cartels as a welcome step towards socialism (Möschel 1972, p. 15). Thus, for different reasons, cartels were welcomed by a majority of economists and politicians.

After the Court had put aside all legal obstacles cartels proliferated tremendously. Cartels numbered 137 in 1890, 364 in 1910, and 1539 in 1925 (Feldenkirchen 1985, p. 154). According to other sources the number of cartels in 1925 has been estimated as lying between 2000 and 2500 (Fischer

1954, p. 443). So Germany became a country of cartels.

The emergence of cartels in industries characterized by huge fixed costs and fluctuating demand may be explained by the fact that particularly during business cycle depressions prices are driven below average costs and a competitive equilibrium may not exist, as suggested by Bittlingmayer (1982) for the emergence of trusts in the U.S.A. Thus cartels in such a situation may indeed be "children of distress." This reasoning cannot, however, be invoked to explain the drive to cartelization in general. Whereas in 1890 the bulk of cartels were to be found in coal mining and in the iron and steel industry, in chemical industry and cement industry, for which the aforementioned reasoning may have some merit, later on both prior to World War I and during the twenties cartels proliferated into various labor intensive consumer goods industries. Hence cartels more and more assumed the character of monopolistic organizations. The market power of cartels was enhanced by trade protection which, not only in Germany, had been introduced during the later decades of the nineteenth century. Whereas in the seventies of the past century the power of cartels was held at bay by competition from foreign suppliers, later on protective tariffs created a wall behind which cartels could proliferate.

The evaluation of cartels as being monopolistic organizations accords with the finding of one of the leading German economists of the time, Werner Sombart, who stated (Sombart 1921, p. 316) that it is not during a time of deep depression when enterprises are prepared to cooperate with regard to prices but it is during business cycle upswings that prices are elevated above the costs of production. More recently this view has been challenged by Rotemberg and Saloner (1986) who advanced a game theoretic model to show business cycles upswings to give rise to price wars. This conclusion, however, rests on the assumption that demand shocks are independently and identically distributed over time. This assumption is clearly violated in case of business cycle fluctuations where time series are typically serially correlated. If strong demand today signals strong demand tomorrow and vice versa, collusion has been shown by Haltiwanger and Harrington (1991) to be more difficult to sustain during recessions and collusive pricing tends to be procyclical (Bagwell and Staiger, 1997). Empirically in a study pertaining to export cartels in the US from 1918 to 1965 Dick (1996) came to the conclusion that "cartels were more likely to collapse during actual demand downturns in the export markets." In a cross section analysis of West German industries covering the time from 1965 to 1977 Neumann, Böbel, and

Haid (1983) found the positive impact of concentration on the price-cost margins to be statistically significant only during business cycle upswings and to be insignificant during recessions. Thus the conclusion ofSombart (1921) appears to be vindicated both by theory and by more recent empirical evidence. In fact, during the twenties, in the public opinion pricing by cartels gave increasingly rise to concern and demands for a legislation against abuse of market power.

3.2.2 The act of 1923

In 1923, towards the very height of the hyperinflation, a law against abusive conduct of cartel ("Verordnung gegen Mißbrauch wirtschaftlicher Machtstellungen") was enacted. It contained two main provisions. The first one was directed against unreasonable pricing. Since the legal preconditions for applying this provision of the law were very demanding, but also for more fundamental reasons to be discussed in section IV of the present paper, the law remained completely ineffective in this respect (Bremer 1985, p. 124). The second aim of the act was to inhibit undue restrictions of freedom of cartel members, such as threats against defecting members. But even this provision fell short of what it was expected to achieve (Bremer 1985, p. 125).

3.2.3 After 1933

After 1933 the Nazi regime found it expedient to declare membership in a cartel as mandatory, and finally, ten years later, the cartels were simply changed into government agencies of a centrally planned war economy.

After World War II cartels were declared illegal by the Allied Military Government the legislation of which was guided by the principles of U.S. Antitrust policy. This legislation remained valid until in 1957 it was replaced by the Act against restraints of competition (GWB). The regulation of the GWB were inspired both by the experience of U.S. Antitrust and the teaching of a group of German economists and lawyers which became known as the Ordo-liberal School. The most prominent persons were Walter Eucken, an economist, and Franz Böhm, a lawyer, respectively. The principles developed by these people, later on, were politically sold under the label of "Social Market Economy" (Soziale Marktwirtschaft), a term coined by Alfred Müller-Armack, and implemented under the leadership of Ludwig Erhard, the first Minister of Economics of the Federal Republic of Germany.

3.3 Competition Policy in the Social Market Economy

3.3.1 Principles

The Ordo-liberal School holds that competition to be maintained requires the government to establish a legal framework which inhibits restraints of competition. This view is opposed to the notion that freedom alone will guarantee a competitive environment. The development of cartels in Germany convincingly refutes the view that restraints of trade set up by private contract are swept away by the forces of competition once individual freedom exists.

In the parliamentary debate about the appropriate legislation the Ordo-liberal School favored an outright prohibition of cartels. On the other side, mostly representatives of industrial interests were in favor of government supervision over cartels to inhibit abusive exercise of market power. The legislation of 1957 which took effect in 1958 turned out to be a political compromise. It contained two elements. First, it established a *per se* rule against cartels. This rule, however, is attenuated by a number of exemptions to be discussed below in some detail. Second, the GWB provided for dominant firms, legal cartels and vertical agreements to be subject to supervision with regard to abusive exercise of market power. The administration of the law has been assigned to a Federal authority, i.e., the Federal Cartel Office, and appropriate authorities of the Federal States (*Länder*) as far as local violations of the law are concerned.

3.3.2 The *per se* rule against cartels

Horizontal contracts of both private and public enterprises aiming at restraining competition, i.e., cartels, are disallowed. Those contracts are null and void, and participants in such agreements are subject to be fined. Originally, only explicit contracts aiming at influencing the terms of market transactions were illegal. Only after the Federal Cartel Office failed to successfully prosecute dyestuff producers for tacit collusion an amendment to the GWB was enacted in 1973 which outlawed tacit collusion as well. This amendment put the German regulation regarding domestic cartels on an equal footing with rules laid down in Article 85 of the Treaty of Rome.

3.3.3 Exemptions from the *per se* rule

There are three kinds of exemptions from the general rule against contractual restraints of competition.

First, some sectors of the economy are completely or partially exempt, namely, telecommunication, which until recently has been under the exclusive control of the Federal Post Office and still is subject to supervision by a Federal Ministry; traffic, agricultural producer co-operatives and their contractual relationships with individual farmers, banking and insurance, public utilities, and associations engaged in the administration of patent rights of individuals. Traffic, banking and insurance as well as public utilities, in particular, are subject to specific regulations exercised by public authorities. As far as horizontal or vertical contractual restraints of competition in these sectors are concerned, which are exempt from the general ban, an additional supervision by the Federal Cartel Office applies. These exemptions account for about one fifth of gross value added of all German enterprises. It might also be noted that coal mining and the iron and steel industry are exempt from the national law against restraints of competition since they are subject to regulation at the European level.

Second, particular types of cartels are either exempt *per se* or can be exempted by decree of the Federal Cartel Office.

Exemption *per se* obtains for pure export cartels, i.e., those cartels which do not affect the domestic market. If the agreement also affects the domestic market the Federal Cartel Office may permit the cartel, provided the side effect is indispensable to ensure the success on foreign markets.

Cartels which exclusively pertain to terms of contract with customers or rebates which do not entail an unjustified discrimination between customers have to be notified to the Federal Cartel Office. The agreement becomes valid unless the Federal Cartel Office raises objections within three months.

Cartels set up for the purpose of facilitating rationalization and specialization between firms may be allowed by the Federal Cartel Office. Such cartels may be permitted even if the agreement also pertains to prices and distribution outlets, provided rationalization is deemed to serve the public interest and the agreement does not unreasonably restrain competition. Similarly, in the case of specialization, a substantial degree of competition must be maintained. Cooperations of the aforementioned type may, in particular, be allowed by the Federal Cartel Office if they do not substantially lessen competition and enhance competitiveness of small and medium sized firms.

Third, in the case of a structural crisis the Federal Cartel Office may allow a cartel to be set up if it is necessary to ensure a systematic reduction of productive capacity and if the arrangement is in the public interest (§4 GWB). Such a permission shall be granted only for a limited time span, subject to prolongation if necessary.

Finally, the Federal Minister of Economics may allow a cartel if it is deemed necessary to further general welfare (§ 8 GWB). This part of the law has been applied regarding limitations of TV advertising for cigarettes and pharmaceutical products (Schmidt 1996, p. 106).

All cartels with the exception of pure export cartels and all recommendations of trade associations regarding technical norms, general terms of business transactions and rules of fair conduct are registered with the Federal Cartel Office. The register is public and thus accessible to anybody. In 1990 276 cartels were in existence, the bulk of which were agreements about rationalization and specialization, 60 pertained to general terms of contract and rebates, 2 were export cartels affecting the domestic market. Among the agreements about rationalization and specialization there were 147 cooperations between small and medium sized firms which have been actively propagated by the Federal Government as part of a policy that aims at compensating disadvantages of smaller firms vis-à-vis large firms. It is remarkable that only a single cartel (for synthetic fibers) existed which was formed to cope with a structural crisis.

The bulk of rationalization and specialization agreements are to be found in the quarrying industries and building trades, in metalworking and machine-building industries, independent suppliers for the automotive industry and food processing. Cartels pertaining to terms of contract are mostly found in textile and clothing industries. On the whole it is noteworthy that most cartels and recommendations given by trade associations exist in industries where small scale firms abound and where the degree of industry concentration is relatively low.

3.3.4 Prosecution of violations of the *per se* rule

A substantial number of cases of violations of the *per se* rule against cartels has been successfully prosecuted by the Federal Cartel Office and the respective authorities of the Federal States in Germany. For example, during 1985-1986 the Federal Cartel Office brought to a close by imposing a fine 74 proceedings against violations of the *per se* prohibition of cartels, and the respective number of cases handled by the authorities of the Federal States was 78. Although quite a few violations will remain undetected the active prosecution by the authorities entails a substantial risk which can be expected to reduce the number of violation.

3.3.5 Control of abuse of market power

Dominant firms and cartels which are permitted due to general exemption or by decree of the Federal Cartel Office must not their market power. Here, we again find the same principle which was postulated by the previous law of 1923. Two kinds of abuses are distinguished, i.e., charging unreasonable prices and infringement upon the freedom of action of competitors, for example, by discrimination, exclusive dealing, boycotting, and bribing to induce anticompetitive behavior. The authorities may disallow abusive practices, which thereupon become legally invalid, and impose fines on violators.

In actual practice prosecution of abusive pricing turned out to be extremely difficult and almost ineffective. Although most actual proceedings of the Federal Cartel Office applied to dominant firms the problems encountered by the authorities are the same for cartel. The basic requirement for a proof of excessive prices consists, first, in finding a comparable market, or, second, to construe a fictitious situation of effective competition, and, third, to establish that prices are substantially in excess of competitive prices. All these proofs are extremely difficult to produce.

The authorities were more successful in prosecuting abusive practices which infringe upon the behavior of competitors. For example, in quite a few cases rebate schemes of dominant firms were found to entail an exclusion of newcomers by granting a rebate on the basis of total purchases during a full year.

So when it comes to assess the effectiveness of supervision with regard to abusive practices, on the whole, the experience has been similarly disappointing as the experience with the law of 1923. In fact the number of proceedings of the Federal Cartel Office against abusive practices, which amounted to 314 during 1973-1975, decreased to a mere 14 during 1990-1991. That may witness resignation on the part of the Federal Cartel Office in view of almost insurmountable difficulties. This experience alone makes a strong case against only monitoring abuses and in favor of a *per se* rule against cartels.

3.4 Some Afterthoughts Regarding a *per se* Rule vs. Monitoring Abusive Practices

As pointed out before, cartels have been attributed some merits in industries with increasing returns to scale because a competitive equilibrium where price equals marginal cost does not exist. However, this claim, although formally correct, is misleading, because an oligopolistic equilibrium does exist (Novshek 1980). Consider the simple model of linear inverse demand

$$p = a - bQ, \tag{3.1}$$

where Q is the sum total of individual supplies of a homogeneous product. Let all producers have identical cost functions

$$C(q) = cq + F, \tag{3.2}$$

where F are fixed costs. Then at a Cournot equilibrium

$$p = c + \frac{a - c}{n + 1}, \tag{3.3}$$

and individual production is

$$q = \frac{1}{n+1} \frac{a - c}{b}. \tag{3.4}$$

Given free entry into the industry, and disregarding the fact that the number n must be an integer, at a zero profit equilibrium, the surviving number of producers is given by

$$n^* + 1 = \frac{a - c}{\sqrt{bF}} \tag{3.5}$$

and the equilibrium price is

$$p = c + \sqrt{bF} = c + \frac{a - c}{n + 1}. \tag{3.6}$$

The price thus exceeds marginal costs and still profits are zero.

It can moreover be shown that free entry into a cartelized industry gives rise to an excessive number of firms the supply of which falls short of what would be expected in a Cournot equilibrium.

Proof: Let n_K and n_C denote the equilibrium number of identical firms under cartelization and Cournot competition, respectively. Let $b = 1$. Thus zero profits imply

$$n_K = \frac{1}{F}\left(\frac{a-c}{2}\right)^2 \tag{3.7}$$

$$n_C = \frac{a-c}{\sqrt{F}} - 1 \tag{3.8}$$

Hence

$$y = n_K - n_C = \frac{1}{F}\left(\frac{a-c}{2}\right)^2 - \frac{a-c}{\sqrt{F}} + 1. \tag{3.9}$$

Define

$$x = \frac{a-c}{\sqrt{F}}. \tag{3.10}$$

Then

$$y = \frac{1}{4}(x^2 - 4x + 4) = \frac{1}{4}(x-2)^2 \tag{3.11}$$

Thus $y > 0$ unless $x = 2$.

Now as $n_C + 1 = (a-c)\sqrt{F}$, if $n_C \geq 2$, $x = (a-c)/\sqrt{F} \geq 3$. Therefore, if $n_C \geq 2$ it follows that $n_K \geq n_C$.

Given this result, as $p_C = c + (a-c)/(n_C+1)$, $p_K = c + (a-c)/2$, and $n_C + 1 > 2$, $p_K > p_C$. Consequently, $Q_K < Q_C$.

Problems arise if demand decreases, for example, during a business cycle downturn. Upon a shift of the demand schedule to the left (lowering the intercept a of the inverse demand curve) all firms incur losses unless supply is curtailed. To maintain equilibrium the number of operating plants, n, must be reduced. In this case the price p^* remains unchanged. In the short-run, however, if costs are sunk and the number of plants cannot be reduced, Bertrand competition applies. Firms may lower prices in order to capture demand at the expense of competitors. Alternatively cartels or mergers which yield a reduction of supply, may appear as the appropriate remedy.

Although the model is theoretically correct and conducive to some valuable insights the assumption that all firms are alike, disregards the very essence of competition. As emphasized in particular by Hayek (1973), competition is the most powerful way to discover new ways to do things. Therefore, at a particular point in time, given sunk costs and longevity of equipment, firms with differing cost functions will operate side by side. The more recent methods of production will be characterized by lower marginal costs and ordinarily be a higher level of fixed costs. If under these conditions demand decreases during a recession, or otherwise, in the short-run firms with modern plants can survive when prices fall below total average cost. Older plants with higher average costs are driven out of business once the price falls short of their average variable costs. By contrast, under the protection of a cartel they are likely to survive because all members of the cartel are cutting down production. The industry will thus enter a new business cycle upswing with excess capacity and firms with modern plants will be reluctant to invest in order to expand capacity. Consequently, technical progress will be slowed down. For this reason, in the U.S., Mr Justice Stone, in the famous Trenton Potteries case in 1927, was right when he stated (as cited in Neale, 1966, p. 36) that reasonable prices of today may become unreasonable in the future once a cartel has been established.

Since competition affects costs in a way which cannot be foreseen with any degree of precision it is simply impossible for a supervising authority to know the price which would apply under undistorted competition. It therefore lacks a standard to identify abusive exercise of market power. The difficulties encountered by the Federal Cartel Office, alluded to above, are thus not attributable to deficiencies of the administrative procedure. They are fundamental ones and cannot be overcome by any efforts whatsoever.

Therefore, even if the *per se* rule against cartels may, in the short-run, yield apparent losses, in the long-run it is the only appropriate policy to keep the competitive process going.

3.5 References

Ashton, T.S. *The Industrial Revolution 1760-1830.* New York: Oxford University Press, 1964.

Bagwell, K. and R.W. Staiger "Collusion over the business cycle," *Rand Journal of Economics* Volume 28, 1997, pp. 82–106.

Bittlingmayer, George "Decreasing Average Cost and Competition: A New Look at the Addyston Pipe Case," *Journal of Law and Economics* Volume 25, 1982, pp. 201-229.

Böhm, F. "Das Reichsgericht und die Kartelle," ORDO-Jahrbuch Volume 1, 1948, pp. 197-213.

Bremer, K.J. "Die Kartellverordnung von 1923: Entstehung, Inhalt und praktische Anwendung," in: H.Pohl, editor, *Kartelle und Kartellgesetzgebung in Praxis und Rechtsprechung vom 19. Jahrhundert bis zur Gegenwart.* Stuttgart: Franz Steiner Verlag Wiesbaden, 1985, pp. 111-126.

Dick, A.R. "When are Cartels Stable Contracts," *Journal of Law and Economics* Volume 39, 1996, pp. 241-283.

Feldenkirchen, W. "Das Zwangskartellgesetz von 1933. Seine wirtschaftliche Bedeutung und seine praktischen Folgen," in: H. Pohl, ed., *Kartelle und Kartellgesetzgebung in Praxis und Rechtsprechung vom 19. Jahrhundert bis zur Gegenwart.* Stuttgart: Franz Steiner Verlag Wiesbaden, 1985, pp. 145-164.

Fischer, C.E. "Die Geschichte der deutschen Versuche zur Lösung des Kartell- und Monopolproblems," *Zeitschrift für die gesamte Staatswissenschaft* Volume 110, 1954, pp. 425-456.

Hayek, F.A. von *Der Wettbewerb als Entdeckungsverfahren.* Kiel 1968.

Haltiwanger, J. and J.E. Harrington, Jr., "The Impact of Cyclical Demand Movements on Collusive Behavior," *Rand Journal of Economics* Volume 22, 1991, pp. 89-106.

Kleinwächter, F. *Die Kartelle. Ein Beitrag zur Frage der Organisation der Volkswirtschaft.* Innsbruck 1883.

Möschel, W. *70 Jahre Deutsche Kartellpolitik: Von RGZ 38,155 "Sächsisches Holzstoffkartell" zum BGHZ 55,104 "Teerfarben."* Tübingen: J.C.B. Mohr (Paul Siebeck), 1972.

Neale, A.D. *The Antitrust Laws of the United States of America.* Cambridge: Cambridge University Press, 1966.

Neumann, M., I. Böbel and A. Haid "Business Cycle and Industrial Market Power: An Empirical Investigation for West German Industries, 1965-77," *Journal of Industrial Economics* Volume 32, 1983, 187-196.

Novshek, William "Cournot Equilibrium with Free Entry," *Review of Economic Studies* Volume 47, 1980, pp. 473-486.

Rotemberg, J.J. and G. Saloner "A Supergame-Theoretic Model of Price Wars during Booms," *American Economic Review* Volume 76, 1986, pp. 390-407.

Schmidt, I. *Wettbewerbspolitik und Kartellrecht.* 5. Aufl., Stuttgart: Luzius.

Sombart, W. *Die deutsche Volkswirtschaft im neunzehnten Jahrhundert und im Anfang des 20. Jahrhunderts.* 5th ed., Berlin: Bondi, 1921.

Competition Policies in Europe - S. Martin (Editor)

Chapter 4

The Evolution of UK Cartel Policy and Its Impact on Market Conduct and Structure

George Symeonidis[1]

4.1 Introduction

Like competition policy in general, UK cartel policy developed gradually over several years since the second world war. Although it dates initially from the late 1940s, the first major piece of legislation on restrictive agreements was the 1956 Restrictive Trade Practices Act. The Act required the registration of most types of restrictive agreements between firms on goods. Registered agreements were presumed to be against the public interest unless shown otherwise.[2] The Act was subsequently amended and extended, partly in the light of its impact on competition. Information agreements on goods and agreements on most types of services, to both of which the 1956 legislation

[1]I would like to thank Stephen Martin, Paul Seabright, John Sutton and workshop participants at the Centre for Industrial Economics, University of Copenhagen for helpful comments on an earlier draft.

[2]Hunter (1966) and Wilberforce et al (1966) describe in detail the structure of the 1956 Act. Subsequent developments in UK cartel policy are discussed in the various reports of the Registrar of Restrictive Trading Agreements (until 1972) and the annual reports of the Director General of Fair Trading (since 1972) and also in Swann et al. (1974) and Borrie (1986). A general introduction to UK competition policy is Frazer (1992).

did not apply, were brought within the scope of the law. These various amendments were consolidated in the 1976 Restrictive Trade Practices Act, which has remained the main instrument of UK cartel policy for the past twenty years. Government proposals to effect fundamental changes in the law were put forward in the late 1980s and, after a long delay, a draft bill was published in 1996. The proposed changes would have the effect of bringing UK cartel policy very close to EU policy.

The first part of this paper describes the evolution of UK cartel law and its implementation. The second part focuses on the impact of the law on market conduct and structure. The economic impact of cartel policy has been significant. Horizontal agreements between firms were widespread in the UK in the 1950s. As a result of the 1956 legislation, nearly all restrictive agreements were abandoned and the intensity of price competition increased in the large majority of the previously cartelized industries. In addition, there were important repercussions on market structure: the intensification of price competition following the 1956 Act caused a significant rise in concentration. This suggests that firms' conduct, which itself partly depends on the climate of competition policy and possibly other institutional factors, is an important determinant of market structure.

4.2 The evolution of UK cartel policy since the 1950s

The 1956 Restrictive Trade Practices Act was based on the principle that restrictive agreements are in general adverse to the public interest unless shown otherwise. The Act required the registration of restrictive agreements between firms on goods, where the restrictions related to prices, quantities and qualities supplied, conditions of sale, persons to or from whom goods could be supplied or acquired, and areas where goods could be supplied or acquired. The definition of "agreement" included both formal, written undertakings, as well as informal, verbal or even implied arrangements. It also included cases where a trade association made recommendations to its members. The Act also prohibited the collective enforcement of resale price maintenance. (Individual resale price maintenance was abolished in the mid-1960s.) On the other hand, agreements on services or relating only to exports, most types of bilateral vertical arrangements, and agreements to simply exchange information on prices, quantities supplied, and so on were not registrable.

A key feature of the Act was the adoption of a judicial procedure for assessing the impact of restrictive practices on the public interest. The Restrictive Practices Court was created, consisting both of High Court judges and qualified lay members. In addition, a new officer within the Board of Trade, the Registrar of Restrictive Trading Agreements, was given responsibility for keeping a Register of agreements which was open to public inspection, referring all but insignificant cases to the Court, and investigating for any unregistered but registrable agreements. Registered agreements were presumed to be against the public interest, and should therefore be abandoned, unless they were successfully defended in the Court or considered by the Registrar as not significantly affecting competition. There was no outright prohibition of restrictive practices: an agreement could be upheld if the Court was convinced that it had benefits for the public interest, of a kind defined in the Act, which offset the presumed detriment.

The Act set out a number of headings, known as "gateways," by reference to which the parties of an agreement could defend it in the Court. These related to such things as the protection of the public against injury, the need to counteract anticompetitive behavior by other firms, the need to counterbalance monopoly or monopsony power, the avoidance of serious adverse effects on employment in a specific area of the country or on exports, and, more generally, the provision of "specific and substantial" benefits to the public. Even if an agreement passed through one or more of the gateways, however, it should also be shown to be in the public interest "on balance" if it was to be upheld.

By the end of 1959 some 2200 agreements had been registered, about a third of which were national agreements between manufacturers containing price restrictions. Since the attitude of the Court could not be known for certain until the first cases had been heard, the large majority of the existing restrictive agreements were registered rather than being immediately abandoned or secretly continued. The adoption of a system whereby an agreement is not illegal *per se*, and the Court is expected to examine possibly complex economic issues in assessing the balance of benefits and detriments in any particular case, has been a matter of considerable debate. It has not been a major issue in practice, however, since the hard line taken by the Court, especially in its initial decisions, induced most cartels to voluntarily terminate their agreements. Of those which were brought before the Court and defended by the parties, only a few were upheld. Still, some of the decisions, especially those to allow the continuation of certain agreements, were much criticized, so the issue of whether the Court is in a position to evaluate particular agreements has been relevant in a small number of cases.[3]

One of the most interesting cases heard in the Court concerned the agreement between the members of the Yarn Spinners' Association. This provided for a minimum selling price for cotton yarn and for standard terms and conditions of sale. The case was significant for several reasons: it was the second case to come before the Court, and the size and historical significance of the industry meant that the Court's decision would be of considerable importance for industry in general. Moreover, this was the one case where the debate largely focused on the issue of the impact of the removal of the minimum price scheme on the structure of the industry. The Registrar, arguing against the restrictions, pointed out that the agreement had resulted in prices higher than would be the case under competition, and had allowed the survival of high-cost producers and the maintenance of excess capacity in the industry. The Court accepted that all these effects were not in the public interest. At the same time, it was convinced by the Association that the removal of the price restrictions would be detrimental for employment in specific areas of the country. In the event, the Court struck down the agreement on the grounds that its beneficial effect on employment was outweighed by the detriments to the public, including the fact that it might have delayed what seemed to be the necessary restructuring of a declining industry.

Another significant Court case concerned a series of bilateral agreements between steel producers and a common marketing company which the steel firms had formed to sell basic slag, a by-product of steel manufacture used as a fertilizer. Each of the steel producers appointed one director to the Board of the marketing company and had an independent agreement with the company about the terms on which it supplied it with basic slag, including the obligation to sell the whole of its output of basic slag to the company. These

[3] Some price-fixing agreements were upheld because they were thought to be beneficial for exports or for technical cooperation and development, with the benefits outweighing the detriment of higher prices. In some other cases, the arguments were much more dubious. For example, one agreement was upheld partly because it was said to result in cost savings for purchasers since there was no need to "shop around." Another was thought to promote product standardization. And still another was upheld because the Court accepted the argument that the restrictions helped maintain prices below the competitive level by reducing uncertainty and hence the return on capital required by firms in the industry.

bilateral agreements were all identical and, although there was no explicit arrangement between the steel producers themselves, the Court was persuaded that there was an implied arrangement between these firms, because none of the directors of the marketing company would have agreed to that company entering into an agreement with a steel firm which was different from the one his firm was going to execute.

In fact, the question of what constitutes an "arrangement" was settled in the context of the Basic Slag case. It was pointed out by the Court that an arrangement between A and B exists if "(1) A makes a representation as to his future conduct with the expectation and intention that such conduct on his part will operate as an inducement to B to act in a particular way, (2) such representation is communicated to B, who has knowledge that A so expected and intended, and (3) such representation or A's conduct in fulfillment of it operates as an inducement, whether among other inducements or not, to B to act in that particular way" (see the third report of the Registrar of Restrictive Trading Agreements, published in 1964).

The 1956 Act laid the basic framework for UK cartel policy. Subsequent legislation, introduced in 1968, made a number of amendments. Early studies of the economic impact of the Act showed that in many industries the agreements had been replaced by informal arrangements having the same effect on competition. These were typically "information agreements," i.e. they involved the exchange of information on prices, price changes, quantities or conditions of sale, usually through a trade association. Two such cases came before the Court in the mid-1960s. In both cases prices and price changes had consistently been notified in advance of their coming into effect, and the prices of different firms had always been identical. The Court found against the parties to the respective arrangements on the grounds that these amounted to the same effect as explicit price-fixing. Moreover, the 1968 Restrictive Trade Practices Act sought to strengthen the law by making information agreements registrable. It was recognized, however, that some types of information exchange, for example cost comparisons and exchange of technical information, were beneficial, so it was left to the Department of Trade and Industry to decide which types of information agreements should be called up for registration. Only agreements on the exchange of prices and conditions of sale were subsequently called up.

A second deficiency of the 1956 legislation related to illegal non-registration of agreements. The 1956 Act provided for only moderate powers of discovery. In contrast to US and EC law, the Act did not allow unexpected raids and seizing of company documents. In addition, there were no penalties for non-registration. The 1968 Act sought to reduce the incentives not to register by allowing injured parties to sue participants to an unregistered agreement for damages. However, this provision has very rarely been used. On the other hand, the 1956 Act did provide for penalties if the secretly colluding firms had been parties to any agreement that the Registrar had referred to the Court and the Court had struck down, including agreements which had not been defended by the parties, and considerable fines have in fact been imposed in some cases. However, while many voluntarily abandoned agreements were nevertheless referred to the Court and struck down, a large number were not referred, so this provision would be irrelevant (as it would be for firms who had not been parties to any registered agreement). In any case, the detection of collusion was not facilitated by these provisions. The problem of illegal non-registration has therefore remained as one of the weaknesses of UK cartel law.

The 1968 Act also increased the flexibility of the system by making it easier for the Registrar to allow the continuation of agreements of little significance for competition, subject to the consent of the Secretary of State for Trade and Industry. The single largest group of agreements that were thus cleared (sometimes after the removal of more significant restrictions) were agreements involving the recommendation by trade associations of standard terms and conditions of sale or contract, such as terms of guarantee, provisions as to contractual liability for loss or damage, formulas for contract price adjustment to cover costs when delivery does not take place until some time after the contract is made and costs have changed in the meantime, etc. The view of the Registrar was that such provisions may often be beneficial to all parties involved and have no effect on competition, provided that they are "fair" to both buyers and sellers and are optional rather than compulsory.

Additional legislation was introduced in the 1970s. The 1973 Fair Trading Act reorganized UK competition policy in general and created the Office of Fair Trading (OFT), so the powers of the Registrar of Restrictive Trading Agreements were transferred to the Director General of Fair Trading (DGFT). Also, agreements on commercial, as distinct from professional, services became registrable, and were called up for registration in 1976. As with goods agreements two decades earlier, the large majority of restrictive agreements on commercial services were voluntarily abandoned in the 1970s and early 1980s. Very few were brought before the Court, and were nearly all struck down. Finally, the 1976 Restrictive Trade Practices Act consolidated the various amendments made to the 1956 legislation and has remained for the past twenty years the main instrument of UK cartel policy.

In summary, the policy currently works as follows. Most types of restrictive agreements must be registered at the OFT. Moreover, if the DGFT has reasonable grounds to believe that a secret agreement exists, he can require firms to give details of the agreement. When the OFT uncovers a secret agreement, this is almost always referred to the Restrictive Practices Court. When the OFT receives an agreement, there are two possibilities. If the restrictions are not significant or the firms agree to abandon all significant restrictions, then, subject to the consent of the Secretary of State, the agreement is allowed to operate and the procedure ends (this is what typically happens nowadays). If, however, the restrictions are significant, then the DGFT refers the case to the Court. When a case comes before the Court and the Court decides that the restrictions are against the public interest, the agreement must be abandoned and the OFT monitors the implementation of the Court's decision. In the event of a favorable decision, the agreement is allowed to continue (although this has never occurred in the past few years).

While UK policy was very effective in breaking down the previously legal cartels in manufacturing during the 1960s, and apparently also in the services industries during the 1970s, it could be less well suited to present-day conditions, where collusion may often be tacit and difficult to detect. Two official reviews of cartel policy were undertaken since the mid-1970s, the first in 1979, the second in 1988. The major weaknesses of the law were identified and detailed proposals for reform were made.

The first weakness is the exemption from the legislation of certain sectors of the economy. The most important exemption relates to professional services, including lawyers, doctors and dentists, architects, surveyors, accountants and auditors, etc. A second shortcoming has already been mentioned above: the law does not sufficiently deter the formation of restrictive agreements. On the one hand, the penalties for illegal collusion are not very effective: either firms are not liable to any fines or the fines are not thought to be sufficiently heavy. On the other, the powers of investigation of the Director General of Fair Trading are not sufficiently severe. Under the present system, he can only send a formal notice to a company asking whether it is a party to an unregistered restrictive agreement (in which case there are penalties for failing to reply or for giving a false reply). Moreover, he can do this only if he already has some evidence of the probable existence of an agreement, i.e. mere strong suspicions are not enough.

The adoption of a "form-based" rather than an "effects-based" approach may constitute another weakness of current UK cartel policy. The law requires the registration of all agreements of a specified form rather than covering all agreements which have an effect on competition. In general, an agreement is registrable if it is between two or more firms operating in the UK and more than one party accepts "restrictions," i.e. some limitations on the freedom to make decisions. This implies that, despite the fact that certain types of agreements are exempt from registration, a large number of obviously harmless agreements must nevertheless be registered. Actually, the Court is little used nowadays, since the large majority of registered agreements are insignificant and the rest are modified to remove all significant restrictions by negotiation with the Office of Fair Trading.[4]

Finally, it has been suggested that the whole procedure of registration and evaluation of agreements is slow and expensive, although the implications of this are not entirely clear. Some commentators have argued, in line with the 1979 Review of Restrictive Trade Practices Policy, that this may lead to the abandonment of beneficial agreements and hence amount to a *per se* prohibition, which may be undesirable, at least as long as the form-based approach remains in place. Others have suggested that the procedure is possibly a waste of resources, given the very small number of agreements upheld by the Court since the 1950s, and that a move towards a *per se* system might be desirable.

In contrast with the moderate reforms proposed in the 1979 Review of Restrictive Trade Practices Policy, the changes in UK cartel policy proposed in the 1988 Review were fundamental (see DTI 1988). The main proposals were to replace the current system with an effects-based system, to introduce a general prohibition of restrictive agreements (with the possibility of exemption for specific types of agreements or for agreements having certain countervailing benefits, but not for specific sectors), and to strengthen enforcement powers. Progress with the implementation of these proposals has been slow, for a variety of reasons (see Wilks 1996). A consultation on the proposed reforms was finally launched in early 1996 and a draft bill was pub-

[4]It has also been argued that another consequence of the adoption of a form-based system is that an agreement with significant effects on competition may sometimes be drafted in a way that makes it not registrable. For instance, Sharpe (1985) and the 1972 report of the Director General of Fair Trading provide details on a case where the Court decided that an agreement which seemed to involve explicit market-sharing between two firms was not registrable. Such cases are probably unusual, however.

lished for comment in August 1996 (DTI 1996). However, the draft bill did not come before Parliament before the 1997 general election, which brought about a change of government in the UK.

The draft bill provided for a general prohibition of restrictive horizontal agreements, including concerted practices, which have a "significant" effect on competition. The requirement that the effect be significant implied that the prohibition would be somewhat narrower than Article 85 of the EC Treaty. Vertical arrangements, with the exception of those involving price-fixing and resale price maintenance, would be excluded from the scope of the legislation. Finally, agreements which have certain countervailing benefits would be exempt, the criteria for individual or block exemptions being based on those set out in Article 85. In particular, the agreement should contribute to "improving production or distribution" or to "promoting technical or economic progress," while also providing consumers with a "fair share" of the benefits and not eliminating competition in respect of a substantial part of the products in question.

The Director General of Fair Trading would have the prime role of investigation, issuing of exemptions and enforcement. He would be able to enter and search business premises and take documents, and also to impose substantial fines on firms (up to the higher of 10% of total UK turnover of the business involved or 350,000). Finally, parties to agreements would have the right to appeal against any decision by the Director General to an independent Tribunal, and further to the High Court "on a point of law." Overall, these changes, if implemented, would bring UK cartel policy very close to EU policy.

4.3 The impact of cartel policy on market conduct and structure in UK manufacturing

The economic impact of UK cartel policy on manufacturing industry has been examined in a number of studies. The impact of the legislation on the services industries, on the other hand, is less well known. This section largely draws on recent work on the impact of the 1956 legislation on market conduct and structure in British manufacturing (Symeonidis 1997a, 1997b).

At the time the 1956 Act was passed, nearly half of UK manufacturing industry was subject to agreements significantly restricting competition. Although they were not illegal, these agreements were not enforceable at law. Most of them provided for minimum or fixed producer prices, maximum or fixed discounts to distributors, and standard conditions of sale such as cash settlement discounts, packing and delivery charges etc.; some also specified ancillary restrictions such as collective exclusive dealing or the maintenance of common resale prices. In certain other cases, especially in some differentiated product industries, prices were individually set but there were common maximum discounts to distributors, retail price maintenance and sometimes specified conditions of sale or exchange of information on individual prices and price changes. In general, there were no restrictions on media advertising or R&D expenditure. In most cases, there were also no restrictions on entry.

Were the agreements effective? This depended, first, on the extent to which the parties conformed to the agreement or accepted the recommendations, and, second, on the extent of competition from outside firms, domestic or foreign. The evidence suggests that in most industries the agreements had been operated honorably before cancelation. There were also a number of factors that limited the effectiveness of outside competition in many industries. First, the cartels tended to contain most or all of the largest and best known domestic firms. Second, practices aimed at discouraging distributors from buying from outside firms were common. Finally, competition from imports was often limited because of tariffs and quantitative controls, transport costs or international restrictive agreements.

To what extent did the intensity of price competition increase following the abolition of cartels? Some of the evidence on this issue comes from a detailed study of the impact of the 1956 Act carried out in the early 1970s (Swann et al. 1974). The authors conducted case studies of 40 industries, including 34 with terminated agreements and 6 with agreements upheld by the Court. They found, first, that price competition increased in the short run in some, but not all, of the 34 industries. The intensification of competition took the form of a fall in list prices or an increase in trade discounts. In many cases, however, information agreements replaced the former restrictive arrangements and were usually successful in restricting competition. Second, in many industries with information agreements, price competition emerged after these were abandoned or changed into post-notification (rather than pre-notification) arrangements in the mid-1960s, following the two Court cases mentioned in the previous section. Hence in these industries competition did not break out until nearly a decade after the 1956 Act came into force. Overall, the evidence from Swann et al. (1974) and other sources suggests that the majority of the cartelized industries did experience, sooner or later, an increase in the intensity of price competition as a result of the 1956 legislation.[5]

The impact of UK restrictive practices policy on market structure has remained until recently an unresolved issue. The argument that more price competition would lead to higher concentration was used in some Court cases by associations defending their agreements and became a topic of debate during the early discussions of the effects of the 1956 legislation. However, there was little evidence at the time either for or against this view (Wilson 1962). In later years, the hypothesis of a link between the introduction of cartel laws and changes in concentration has also been advanced by economic historians who have claimed that differences in the evolution of market structure between the US and the UK since the late 19th century could be partly attributed to the different competition policy regimes in the two countries. Hannah (1979) and Freyer (1992) have argued that the prohibition of cartel practices in the US in the 1890s has been a key factor in the great turn-of-the-century merger wave and the early rise of the corporate economy in that country. On the other hand, the UK permissive policy towards cartels has helped maintain a more fragmented structure until the 1960s, when the reversal of the policy greatly contributed to the UK merger wave that closed the gap in industrial organization between the two countries. However, Hannah has also warned against any simplistic interpretation of the link between cartel policy and market structure by highlighting the case of Germany, where despite the significant increase in the degree of cartelization in the early 20th century, the predominance of large firms was more noticeable than in Britain.

More systematic evidence on the impact of the 1956 Act on the evolution of market structure in the UK was examined in two early studies that compared those industries which were affected by the legislation with a group of industries in which no restrictive agreements had existed prior to the Act. However, the results of these studies were mixed. Elliott and Gribbin (1977) examined some 700 manufacturers' restrictive agreements of nationwide applicability registered before 1960. They found that the rise in the 5-firm sales concentration ratio between 1958 and 1968 was, on average, signifi-

[5] This is so despite the fact that parallel pricing was quite common in the early 1970s. In particular, the Monopolies Commission 1973 report on parallel pricing listed approximately 60 industries in which the witnesses thought that parallel pricing occurred. In most of these industries, however, this was probably not the result of collusion.

cantly greater in industries with terminated agreements than in industries without agreements, and that nearly all of the differential effect occurred between 1963 and 1968. They also noted, however, that market size was growing much faster for industries in the latter group throughout the period, so the cause of the difference between the two groups is not clear. Moreover, the exact criteria used to classify industries in one or the other group were not made explicit.

On the other hand, O'Brian et al. (1979) examined merger activity over 1959-1972 for a sample of about 30 industries split into four groups, namely a group whose restrictive agreements were upheld by the Court, another with agreements struck down by the Court, a third group comprising industries which voluntarily abandoned their agreements, and, finally, a control group of industries which, according to the authors, had not been directly affected by the 1956 Act. Three different variables were used to measure merger activity: the ratio of expenditure on acquisitions to total assets, the proportion of firms in an industry taking over other firms, and the proportion of firms in an industry being themselves acquired. O'Brien et al. found no statistically significant difference in the ratio of expenditure on acquisitions to total assets between the four groups during the period under study, and they also found that the control group had the highest proportion of both acquirers and acquired firms. They concluded that there was no evidence that industries affected by the legislation had been relatively more merger-intensive during the 1960s. It may be the case, however, that their sample was not sufficiently large to be representative. Moreover, the criteria used to construct the control group are not clear, since parts of some of the industries included in this group had in fact been subject to restrictive agreements before the introduction of the 1956 Act.

The effect of price competition on concentration was first studied in the context of a formal theoretical model by Selten (1984). His model predicted that a switch from collusive to non-collusive behavior in a homogeneous goods industry would result in a higher level of concentration. More recently, a general theory of market structure, emphasizing the role of firms' conduct, was proposed by Sutton (1991). The theoretical framework for the analysis of the competition-concentration relationship in Symeonidis (1997a) is based on Sutton's theory. An important distinction within this theoryv is between exogenous and endogenous sunk cost industries. In industries where the only important sunk costs are the exogenously determined costs of setting up a plant of minimum efficient scale, concentration is expected to increase with the intensity of price competition. In industries where endogenous sunk costs, such as advertising or R&D, are significant, the effect of price competition on concentration may, in principle, be in any direction.

The concept of the "intensity of price competition" does not relate to the size of the price-cost margin, which is endogenous, but is intended to capture the idea that, for any given market structure, the price-cost margin will depend on firms' pricing strategies, which will in turn partly depend on exogenous institutional factors such as the climate of cartel policy or the degree of economic integration. In circumstances where the key determinant of changes in firms' pricing behavior is an exogenous change in the institutional framework, as was clearly the case in British manufacturing industry during the 1960s, it seems justifiable to regard the intensity of price competition as an exogenous variable.

The intuition behind the above predictions is as follows. An increase in the intensity of price competition reduces the price-cost margin, given the initial level of concentration. As a result, firms, especially high-cost firms, can no longer cover their fixed costs at the initial free entry equilibrium. In an exogenous sunk cost industry, this will inevitably lead to mergers and exit until the gross profit of each of the remaining firms rises sufficiently to cover its fixed costs.[6] Note that since the output of each remaining firm has increased and fixed costs (and therefore also equilibrium gross profits) are unchanged, the price-cost margin will now be lower than at the initial equilibrium. In an endogenous sunk cost industry, on the other hand, the intensification of price competition may affect the incentive of firms to spend on advertising or R&D. If advertising or R&D fall, then the decrease in the fixed costs that each firm must cover at equilibrium may or may not offset the fall in gross profits due to increased price competition, and hence concentration may decrease or increase.[7] An implication of this framework for the study of the impact of UK cartel policy on market structure is that exogenous and endogenous sunk cost industries should be analyzed separately.

Some descriptive statistics on changes in concentration in industries with

---

[6] In the short run, the competition effect on concentration may be weaker the higher the proportion of fixed costs which are sunk. However, the difference between sunk and fixed costs should not be overemphasised, since in the longer term capital stock depreciates and has to be replaced.

[7] See Symeonidis (1996, 1997b). The latter study also contains an analysis of the impact of the intensification of price competition on advertising intensity in the UK during the 1960s.

	$\Delta C5$ 1958–1975
39 industries with change of competition regime	0.149
70 industries without change of competition regime	0.074
26 industries with change of competition regime and with ADS < 1% and RDS < 1%	0.159
34 industries without change of competition regime and with ADS < 1% and RDS < 1%	0.118
8 industries with change of competition regime and ADS > 1%	0.120
28 industries without change of competition regime and with ADS > 1%	0.033
7 industries with change of competition regime and RDS > 1%	0.134
18 industries without change of competition regime and with RDS > 1%	0.036

Table 4.1: Average Change in C5, 1958–1975 (109 industries with unambiguous state of competition and available observations for both 1958 and 1975)

and without a change in competition regime are reported in Table 4.1. The classification of industries in one or the other group is here based on a number of criteria, including the types of restrictions contained in each particular agreement, and the proportion of an industry's total sales covered by products subject to terminated significant agreements as opposed to products not affected by the 1956 legislation. Industries where the state of competition was thought to be ambiguous, e.g. because the restrictions would have an uncertain effect on competition or because the proportion of industry sales subject to significant agreements was neither substantial nor negligible, have been excluded.

Table 4.1 seems to suggest that the 1956 legislation has had a significant impact on market structure. For example, the average change in the 5-firm sales concentration ratio C5 between 1958 and 1975 in industries affected by the Act and for which observations are available for both these years was

14.9 percentage points. This compares to 7.4 percentage points for industries which were not cartelized and were therefore not affected by the legislation. The table also provides statistics for three sub-samples of industries defined on the basis of advertising-sales ratios (ADS) and R&D-sales ratios (RDS). In all cases, the change in C5 was quite larger for industries with a change in competition regime.

Of course, other factors have also influenced the evolution of concentration during this period. For example, the data show that, except for exogenous sunk cost industries, market size was growing faster in industries without a change of regime. Also, changes in the tax system in the mid-1960s that are thought to have encouraged mergers, the progressive opening of the British economy and other factors may have contributed to the rise in concentration during the 1960s. A proper test of the hypothesis that cartel policy has led to a rise in concentration in those industries which were subject to significant restrictive agreements would have to involve the estimation of an econometric model that controls for these various other influences. This exercise has been carried out in Symeonidis (1997a).

The results of the above study support the hypothesis of a positive and strong effect of price competition on concentration both in exogenous and endogenous sunk cost industries. The results suggest that the increase in the intensity of competition following the 1956 legislation has, on average, raised the 5-firm sales concentration ratio by about 5 percentage points in exogenous sunk cost industries. The impact in advertising-intensive and R&D-intensive industries does not appear to have been any smaller. This is strong evidence that the emergence of price competition following the successful implementation of cartel policy should be expected to have important repercussions on market structure.

Two final remarks are in order. It has been argued in this paper that the rise in concentration following an intensification of price competition is the result of a structural mechanism that involves a movement between two free entry equilibria: gross profit, which falls when price competition intensifies, has to rise in order to cover again fixed costs, and this is achieved through a reduction in the number of firms. A view sometimes expressed in discussions of the impact of the 1956 Act is that restrictive practices policy has caused firms in previously cartelized industries to try to restore market power through mergers (see, for example, Curry and George 1983). While it is difficult to see this latter view as an alternative theory of the competition-concentration relationship, since it provides no general account of how market structure is determined, it may be a valid description of managerial behavior, and as such it is perfectly consistent with the structural mechanism outlined in this paper.

The second remark concerns the relationship between cartel policy and merger policy and in particular the implications of the endogeneity of market structure for merger and antitrust policies. An underlying theme in much of the recent literature on market structure is the notion that, for any given set of values of the measurable and systematic exogenous factors, there is a multiplicity of possible outcomes. Sutton (1991, 1995) has therefore advocated the use of a "bounds" approach for the study of market structure. This approach involves placing bounds on the space of outcomes and thus excluding certain outcomes as either impossible or unlikely. For example, in Sutton (1991) a lower bound to concentration is proposed, as a function of demand, cost and market conduct variables, which corresponds to a situation where each of a number of symmetric single-product single-plant firms operates at a level of output equal to the minimum efficient scale level. While actual concentration cannot be lower than this bound, it can be higher to the extent that an industry comprises asymmetric multi-plant or multi-product firms or firms operating above the minimum efficient scale level. Within this approach, an intensification of price competition should be seen as causing an upward shift of the lower bound to concentration. The implication for policy is that merger and antitrust policies are constrained by the existence of the bound, although they can be freely used to influence market structure within the space of possible outcomes.

4.4 Concluding remarks

UK cartel policy developed gradually over several years since the second world war. Legislation on restrictive agreements on goods was introduced in 1956 and resulted in the abolition of cartels across a wide range of manufacturing industries. Legislation regarding services was introduced in the 1970s and again resulted in the termination of restrictive agreements in a large number of services industries. Despite its considerable success in promoting competition, UK cartel policy has been subject to shortcomings, including the exemption of certain sectors of the economy and insufficient provisions for the detection of collusion. A move toward a legislative framework similar to that of the EU, which has been on the political agenda for nearly a decade, may be currently under way.

An important lesson from the British experience of the 1960s is that the intensification of competition following the successful implementation of cartel policy should be expected to result in higher levels of concentration. This must be seen as a natural consequence of the initial fall of gross profits to a level where firms, or high-cost firms, can no longer cover their fixed costs. Higher concentration will in this case be associated with more, rather than less, competition.

There seem to be two implications of this result for competition policy in general. First, high concentration and mergers may often be a consequence of the intensification of price competition, whether this is brought about by the successful implementation of cartel policy or otherwise. This means that there are important economic constraints in the exercise of merger and antitrust policies. In particular, these policies cannot be used to impose a market structure so fragmented that it is not sustainable once competition intensifies.

The second implication is that higher concentration need not be associated with higher profit margins, increased allocative inefficiency and lower welfare; in fact, the opposite may be the case. Therefore, concerns with the level of market concentration need not take precedence over the need to ensure that competition remains effective, i.e. firms do not engage in collusive practices and no barriers to entry are created. This seems to strengthen the case for a competition policy that focuses more upon the regulation of conduct than of market structure, as has, in fact, always been the approach taken both in the UK and the EU.

4.5 References

Borrie, G. "Restrictive Practices Control in the United Kingdom," *Journal of Business Law*, 1986, pp. 358–371.

Curry, B. and George, K. D. "Industrial Concentration: A Survey," *Journal of Industrial Economics* Volume 31, 1983, pp. 203-255.

Department of Trade and Industry *Review of Restrictive Trade Practices Policy: A Consultative Document*, Cm. 331, London: HMSO, 1988.

Department of Trade and Industry *Tackling Cartels and the Abuse of Market Power: A Draft Bill*, London: DTI, 1996.

Director General of Fair Trading *Annual Reports*, various years covering the period after 1972, London: HMSO.

Elliott, D.C. and Gribbin, J. D. "The Abolition of Cartels and Structural Change in the United Kingdom," in A. P. Jacquemin and H. W. de Jong, eds, *Welfare Aspects of Industrial Markets*, Leiden: Martinus Nijhoff, 1977.

Freyer, T. *Regulating Big Business: Antitrust in Great Britain and America, 1880–1990.* Cambridge: Cambridge University Press, 1992.

Frazer, T. *Monopoly, Competition and the Law.* London: Harvester Wheatsheaf, 1992.

Hannah, L. "Mergers, cartels and concentration: legal factors in the US and European experience," in N. Horn and J. Kocka, eds, *Law and the Formation of the Big Enterprises in the 19th and Early 20th Centuries.* Göttingen: Vandenhoeck and Ruprecht, 1979.

Hunter, A. *Competition and the Law.* London: George Allen, 1966.

Monopolies Commission *Parallel Pricing.* London: HMSO, 1973.

O'Brien, D. P., Howe, W. S., Wright, D. M., and O'Brien, R. J. *Competition Policy, Profitability and Growth.* London: MacMillan, 1979.

Registrar of Restrictive Trading Agreements *Report for the Period 1st July 1961 to 30th June 1963*, Cmnd. 2246, London: HMSO, 1964.

Selten, R. "Are cartel laws bad for business?," in H.Hauptmann, W.Krelle and K.C. Mosler, eds, *Operations Research and Economic Theory.* Berlin-Heidelberg: Springer-Verlag, 1984.

Sharpe, T. "British Competition Policy in Perspective," *Oxford Review of Economic Policy* Volume 1, Number 3, 1985, pp. 80-94.

Sutton, J. *Sunk Costs and Market Structure*, Cambridge, Massachusetts: M.I.T. Press, 1991.

— "The size distribution of businesses, Part I: a benchmark case," STICERD Working Paper no. EI/9, London School of Economics, 1995.

Swann, D., O'Brien, D. P., Maunder, W. P. J., and Howe, W. S. *Competition in British Industry.* London: George Allen, 1974.

Symeonidis, G. "Price and non-price competition with endogenous market structure," mimeo, London School of Economics, 1996.

— "Price competition and market structure: the impact of restrictive practices legislation on concentration in the UK," STICERD Discussion Paper No. EI/18, London School of Economics, 1997a.

— "Cartel policy, non-price competition and market structure: theory and evidence from the UK," STICERD Discussion Paper no. EI/19, London School of Economics, 1997b.

Wilberforce, R. O., Campbell, A. and Elles, N. *The Law of Restrictive Trade Practices and Monopolies.* London: Sweet and Maxwell, 2nd edition, 1966.

Wilks, S. "The Prolonged Reform of United Kingdom Competition Policy," in G. B. Doern and S. Wilks, eds, *Comparative Competition Policy: National Institutions in a Global Market.* Oxford: Clarendon Press, 1996.

Wilson, T. "Restrictive practices," in J. P. Miller, ed., *Competition, Cartels and their Regulation.* Amsterdam: North-Holland, 1962.

Competition Policies in Europe - S. Martin (Editor)

Chapter 5

The Danish Competition Act and Barriers to Entry

Svend Albæk
Peter Møllgaard[1]
Per B. Overgaard

> 'All limitations of free and equal access to trades that are not motivated by the common weal must be annulled by law.'
>
> Section 74 of the Danish Constitution (Act No. 169, June 5, 1953)

5.1 Introduction

The current[2] legal antitrust regime in Denmark is somewhat of an outlier in several respects, when compared with antitrust policies in the European Union and the United States. The legislation is based on an *abuse-control* principle, with the creation of improved market *transparency* as the main weapon in the arsenal of the competition authorities. Within this general framework, the authorities have so far focused on the creation of transparency as the means of promoting competition generally, and hence, according to the logic of the law-makers, efficiency. The underlying motivation is that in

[1] Corresponding author. Thanks are due to Niels Blomgren-Hansen for comments on an earlier draft.

[2] At the time of editing, new prohibition-based legislation had just passed Parliament (on May 30, 1997), to come into force on January 1, 1998.

transparent markets above-normal profits will be bid away by customers and competitors. Recently, the competition authorities seem to have changed their focus to add emphasis and resources to the dismantling of *barriers to new competition*. As a result of this, the reliance on the creation of market transparency as the main instrument of policy has decreased somewhat, and other instruments available under the current legislation have been played more frequently. As we argue below, this is a natural change, since transparencymay often be too impotent or insufficiently fine-tuned as an instrument against barriers to entry. The question remains, however, whether the other instruments available form a potent force against such barriers.

To emphasize the apparent change of focus by the Danish competition authorities we note that in the latest annual report (1995) from the Competition Council (CC in the following), the Director takes stock of the first six years of competition policy practice under the 1989 Danish Competition Act (DCA in the following). In this account, mention of the positive effects of the transparency principle – prominently expounded in the five previous annual reports – is strangely absent. Instead the Director maintains that (CC, 1996, p. 2)

> *Central to the endeavour* [i.e. to promote competition] *has been the removal of barriers to competition.*

The purpose of this paper is, *initially*, to present the instruments of the CC vis-à-vis entry barriers, and, *more importantly*, to comment on how effectively they can be brought to bear.

5.2 An Inquiry into the Nature and Origin of the Danish Competition Act

This section briefly outlines the principles of the DCA and traces its roots. Based on abuse control and the transparency principle, the act differs from most other European and American antitrust legislations that are typically based on prohibition. It turns out that, except for a short period just before the Second World War, Danish competition legislation has been inspired by the 1930 London Resolution of the Interparliamentary Union that was favorable to horizontal agreements.

The first attempt at making an act regarding monopolies and restraints of trade was made in 1919.[3] The 'Extraordinary Commission' that supervised and administered restrictions during the First World War recommended that a provisional act be proposed concerning supervision with such undertakings or combines within production and sale that might be able to exercise a dominating influence on price determination. The 'Extraordinary Commission' included members from various industries. The reason that it recommended a *provisional* act was that it considered its own experiences during the war insufficient to decide on permanent legislation. The proposal only concerned *supervision* of undertakings and combines – direct intervention was ruled out: The proposed Supervisory Council would have to approach the Minister of the Interior who, in turn, would have to propose an intervention to Parliament. For political reasons, the proposal never passed through Parliament even though it passed through the lower chamber. However, two Danish competition law principles find their root in this proposal: First, industry representatives were active participants in the creation of the antitrust legislation. Second, Danish competition law was to be based on supervision.

The second attempt and the first piece of antitrust legislation that passed Parliament was the so-called 'Gaol Act' of 1929. Its real name was 'Act regarding the protection of the liberty of trade and the freedom to work.' This act, passed by a liberal government, was aimed as much at unions as at restraints of trade. According to this act, agreements attempting to limit the individual's free entry to trades or jobs in an inappropriate manner would not be legally binding. Furthermore, any personal or economic persecution – including boycotting – of an individual with the aim at limiting its free entry to trades or jobs or its right to be a member (or not to be a member) of an organization would be *prohibited*. Transgressors should pay damages, fines up to DKK100,000, and could go to gaol. The Act was revoked in 1937 by a labor government after several attempts that were blocked by the liberal/conservative majority in the upper chamber of Parliament. This was the first Danish experience with an antitrust legislation based on a prohibition principle, and it is widely agreed that the Gaol Act proved ineffective vis-à-vis agreements in restraint of trade amongst undertakings.

Danish competition legislation has since then primarily been based on a *principle of abuse control*. The origin of this principle, according to which no restraint of trade is *per se* illegal but may become illegal if the authority de-

[3]The source of much of the following is Trustkommissionen (1953, pp. 47-64).

cides so, may be traced to the London Resolution of the Summer meeting of the Interparliamentary Union in 1930. The main reasoning of the Resolution is: Cartels, trusts and other combines are natural phenomena in the economy, and legislation should, as a matter of principle, not be unsympathetic to these. However, regulation is called for, as these phenomena may possibly be harmful. Regulation should not jeopardize the natural evolution of the economy, but be limited to abuse control. The recommended measure is a principle of publicity, based on an obligation to notify and publicly register agreements etc. Such agreements etc. should be null and void unless notification had been made. Individual firm names in a cartel, a trust etc. should be made public, but agreements should only be made public insofar as abuse had been established. The control should be carried out by an independent cartel commission that might approach the appropriate ministry publicly. The ministry might then go to court.

It is thus interesting to note that a basic premise of existing Danish legislation is a principle based on a large amount of sympathy with horizontal agreements.

Parallel with the Gaol Act, in the years 1931-1937 the Danish Competition regime included the control-based 'Act on price agreements,' that was clearly inspired by the London Resolution: A three-member Price Agreement Committee (one Supreme Court justice, one High Court justice and one member appointed by the President of the Maritime and Commercial Court) should on request investigate price agreements in trusts, cartels and other combines having monopoly character, insofar as these agreements led or could lead to excessive prices on commodities that were part of a general consumption pattern. If the agreement was found to lead to unreasonable prices, it could be brought before the High Court. The High Court could annul the agreement and fine the participants to the agreement. Complaints according to this Act were only filed six times during its existence, and in three cases the complaints were immediately dismissed. Two cases were still pending before the Price Agreement Committee when the Act was revoked, and only one case was in the process of being brought before the High Court. Thus, the early enforcement of a control-based antitrust legislation was not very intensive, to say the least.

The Gaol Act and the Price Agreements Act were replaced in 1937 by a new 'Act on Price Agreements etc.' that combined the protection of liberty of trade found in the Gaol Act and the consumer protection found in the previous Price Agreements Act. Wage and working conditions were excluded from the domain of the Act. The central section of the new act *prohibited* agreements, insofar as they led to excessive prices or restraints of trade. A nine-member Price Control Council, which, as far as possible, should be independent of industry, was empowered to initiate investigations and should be notified about agreements etc. that led or could lead to market power. If it found unreasonable conditions, the council could seek to terminate these by negotiation or, if necessary, by means of an order to cease and desist.

During the Second World War, the Act on Price Agreements was replaced by a Price Act empowering the Price Control Council to directly regulate prices. After the war, in 1952, a new Price Agreements Act was introduced that was built on the same principles as the 1937 Act. However, some of the extra powers vested in the Price Control Council during the war were upheld. The main elements were: 1) The Council should be notified of agreements; 2) These notifications should be made public; 3) The relationships in question should be under the supervision of the Council; 4) Unreasonable agreements etc. were prohibited; 5) If the prohibition was violated, the Council should first attempt to terminate the offence by means of negotiation; 6) If negotiations failed, the Council could issue an order to cease and desist *or* directly regulate prices or margins. The Act did not pertain to undertakings owned or regulated by state or municipality.

The Price Agreements Act was replaced by the Monopolies and Restrictive Practices Act in 1955. This Act remained in force until replaced by the current Danish Competition Act in 1990.[4] The Monopolies Act was based on a report from the Trust Commission (1953). The purpose of the act was to prevent unreasonable prices and business conditions as well as to ensure the best possible conditions for the freedom of trade through public supervision of monopolies and of restraints of trade. The act only applied to private undertakings. The Monopolies Control Authority (MCA) consisted of a Council with 15 members, the chairman and majority of which should be independent of business interests, and of a Directorate under the management of a director. The Act was, as the previous and subsequent acts, based on notification and registration of agreements and regulations that affected or could affect price, production, sale or transportation in the country as a

[4]From 1974, the Act on Prices and Profits also regulated pricing behaviour. However, the purpose of this act was to contribute to the economic stabilization and to regulate earnings in accordance with the general incomes policies. Part of the *raison d'etre* of this act was the battle against inflation: The act provided an analogous measure to the direct regulation of wages.

whole or in a given region. Resale price maintenance was prohibited. The MCA was empowered to initiate negotiations and subsequently issue orders to desist, in order to counter restraints of trade. Furthermore, the MCA could issue orders to supply, cf. sections 2.5 and 3.2. The act also included provisions according to which the MCA could gain access to the information it needed, to reduce an undertaking's future prices in response to previous excessive margins, to make public its investigations and decisions and to take offenders to court.

The existing Danish Competition Act (Act No. 370, June 7, 1989) came into force on January 1, 1990. The Act is based on a proposal contained in a report (Ministry of Industry, 1986; in the following referred to as 'the Report') by three independent experts (two economics professors and a law professor). The Report was commissioned by the Danish Parliament and provides the 'theoretical basis' against which competition law practice may be measured. The main change from the Monopolies Act to the Competition Act was that it was foreseen that direct intervention in the price formation should be replaced by furthering of competition, i.e. the new act should primarily rely on 'market forces' rather than regulation, cf. Albæk, Møllgaard and Overgaard (1996).

5.2.1 An Overview of the Danish Competition Act

The DCA is divided into seven chapters covering twenty-three sections. The seven chapters concern:

1. the purpose and scope of the Act;
2. the Competition Council;
3. transparency;
4. measures against harmful effects of anti-competitive practices;
5. appeal;
6. penalty provisions and other powers;
7. commencement and transitional provisions.

The seven chapters are discussed briefly in turn.

5.2.2 Purpose and Scope of the Act

Section 1 of the Act states that 'the purpose of the Act is to promote competition and thus strengthen efficiency of production and distribution of goods and services etc. through the greatest possible transparency of competitive conditions and through measures against restraints of the freedom of trade and other harmful effects of anti-competitive practices. Accordingly, in step with the increasing internationalization, the aim is to ensure a development of the market structure based on competition and efficiency'.

Thus, Section 1 has three elements: First, it states that the purpose of the Act is to actively promote competition, thus embodying the belief that intensified competition will always lead to improved efficiency. Second, it indicates that the foremost measure to further competition should be the rather ill-defined concept of 'transparency', cf. below, and that other provisions come second.[5] Third, it indicates that the industrial structure should be allowed to evolve according to market forces. The reasoning behind these three elements is discussed at more depth in Albæk, Møllgaard and Overgaard (1996).

DCA Section 2 explains that the Act pertains to commercial enterprises and associations of such enterprises. Furthermore, it applies to public or publicly regulated undertakings, but Sections 11-14 (provisions against harmful effects of restraints on trade) do not apply to these.[6] This means that the CC is restricted to the use of Section 15, empowering it to publicly and formally address the relevant public authority in case it wishes to affect the public and quasi-public sector, cf. Sections 2.4 and 3.3 below.

DCA Section 3 stipulates that the Act does not apply to wages and labor relations, effectively excluding the labor market from its jurisdiction.

5.2.3 The Competition Council

The second chapter of the DCA consists of Section 4 explaining that the Act is administered by the Competition Council made up of a chairman

[5] That this has indeed been the interpretation may be seen from the following quote from p. 7 of the CC's annual report of 1992: "Transparency has in the Danish Competition Act been assigned the rôle as the most important means to further competition and thus strengthen efficiency. Neither in the competition law of the E.E.C. nor in that of other countries does transparency occupy a similar position."

[6] In the case of publicly regulated firms, Sections 11-14 may actually apply if the relationship in question is not regulated.

and fourteen members. The chairman is appointed by the King (i.e., by the government), and the other members are appointed by the Minister of Industry for a period of four years. The composition of the Council should ensure a comprehensive knowledge of business conditions, and a majority of members (the chairman and seven members) should be independent of business interests. The Council is serviced by a Secretariat managed by a director. The exact rules regarding the activities of the Council are left at the discretion of the Minister of Industry.

5.2.4 Transparency

The transparency chapter covers six sections (5-10) of the DCA. It is, as indicated, the central chapter of the Act, since transparency is the foremost weapon against dormant Danish competition.

DCA Section 5 explains that the CC must, within fourteen days, be notified of agreements and decisions (and changes in these) leading to a dominant position. The agreements or decisions are not valid unless notified within the prescribed deadline.[7]

According to DCA Section 6, the CC may demand all information it judges necessary to its activities or to find out whether a mode of conduct falls under the regulations of the act.

DCA Section 7 then empowers the CC to request that undertakings etc. notify the CC about specified types of information such as prices, profits, discounts, bonuses, business conditions, financial and organizational relations etc. The CC may also specify how invoices or price tags should be made or how prices should be posted.

Section 8 is central to the transparency principle: The CC *must* carry out, and *may* make public, investigations suitable for promoting transparency regarding competitive situations. Undertakings etc. that are included in an investigation must be notified about the content before publication and may have possible remarks to the investigation published with it.

Another important transparency section is Section 9: The CC may, when this is judged suitable to promote competition and thus strengthen efficiency, publish information regarding prices, discounts, and bonuses etc.

In the original DCA, Section 10 basically stated that anyone could gain access to all information collected according to Sections 5-8, except informa-

[7]A similar formulation is found is the 1930 London Resolution.

tion about technology or individual bank-client relationships. In subsequent amendments, however, this access to CC files has been restricted somewhat.

The transparency principle and its effects have been thoroughly described in Albæk, Møllgaard and Overgaard (1996, 1997). In brief sum, the ideas behind this principle may be two: First, if buyers are given information that suppliers charge different prices, they will demand to get the lowest price and this will bid down prices. Second, if potential suppliers are made aware of large profit margins, this will induce either entry into the market or lower prices (thus make for a contestable market), cf. Section 3.1. The problem is, of course, that in oligopolistic markets, improved information about e.g. prices may facilitate coordination of the suppliers' actions, i.e. assist tacit collusion, by making deviation from a collusive agreement detected with more ease and/or sooner than would otherwise have been the case. In a recent case, in which the CC started making public the prices of individual producers of ready-mixed concrete there is strong indication that the main result of this was an increase in prices, cf. Albæk, Møllgaard and Overgaard (1997).

5.2.5 Measures against Harmful Effects of Anticompetitive Practices

This chapter of the DCA covers Sections 11-15. Recall that among these, only Section 15 pertains to publicly owned or regulated undertakings.

DCA Section 11 empowers the CC to initiate negotiations with those exerting anti-competitive practices, in order to 'terminate the harmful effects.' If negotiation fails, the CC may, according to Section 12, issue an order which may imply total or partial termination of agreements, decisions, stipulations, and business conditions. If the harmful effects cannot be terminated in this way, then the CC may issue an *order to supply* according to subsection 2 of Section 12: It may order one or more of the undertakings to sell to specified purchasers on the same conditions that the undertaking would normally offer in similar sales situations. The undertaking may, however, always request cash payment or adequate security. The use of orders to supply vis-à-vis barriers to entry is discussed further in Section 3.2 below.

Section 13 of the DCA allows the CC to impose a cap on prices or profits *if* existing prices or profits clearly exceed competitive levels, *and if* a reduction towards competitive levels cannot be achieved by other means. Direct price control is thus a last resort.[8]

DCA Section 14 prohibits resale price maintenance, unless approved by the CC. The CC may grant approval only when called for by weighty reasons. This asymmetric treatment of one particular vertical restraint is discussed thoroughly in Albæk, Møllgaard and Overgaard (1995).

Section 15 of the DCA applies in the case of a publicly owned or regulated undertaking and empowers the CC to publicly address the competent public authority and point to the potentially harmful effects on competition. The use of this section in general and towards the removal of entry barriers in particular is discussed in Section 3.3.

5.2.6 Appeal

The Appeals Chapter consists of three sections (16-18). Section 16 stipulates that CC rulings may only be referred to the Competition Appeals Tribunal (CAT) in the first instance. Section 17 sets the rules for the members of the CAT: The Chairman must be eligible as a judge of the Supreme Court and the two other members must have economic and legal expert knowledge. They must be independent of business interests. The exact rules of the activities of the CAT are at the discretion of the Minister of Industry.

Those that may bring cases before the CAT are, according to Section 18, the party to whom the decision is directed or any party who may have significant individual interest in the case. They have to bring a decision before the CAT at the latest four weeks after the decision of the CC has been made known to them. The CAT's decision may in turn be brought before the High Court within eight weeks. The plaintiff could in this case be the CC if the CAT changed the CC's decision.

5.2.7 Penalty Provisions and Other Powers

Chapter 6 of the DCA covers Sections 19-21 and concerns offences that may be fined and the access to search the premises of companies.

[8]Section 13 further specifies the considerations that should be taken into account when the CC fixes prices or margins: The point of reference should be a firm that is managed with technical and commercial efficiency. The price should cover the 'necessary costs as well as a profit reflecting the risk involved in manufacturing and sale of the product or the service etc.'

DCA Section 19 empowers the CC to impose daily or weekly fines as a coercive measure towards a party that neglects to notify the CC according to Sections 5-7 in due time. According to Section 20, various offences are punishable by fine, if intentional or flagrantly negligent. Offences comprise failure to notify the CC; misreporting to the CC or the CAT; resale price maintenance; and disregard of an agreement with, or an order from, the CC. Both persons, companies, municipalities and the state are punishable by fine. Section 21 empowers the CC to, according to a court order, on the spot, acquaint itself with, and make transcripts of, all information that is needed to carry out its supervision, and with the assistance of the police to gain access to the premises and vehicles of an undertaking or a combine.

5.2.8 Commencement

This last chapter of the DCA basically tells that the Act came into force on January 1, 1990, and replaced the Monopolies and Restrictive Practices Act as well as the Prices and Profits Act. In addition, transitional rules were laid out. Finally, Section 23 excludes the Faroe Islands and Greenland from the jurisdiction of the DCA.

5.3 Barriers to Entry

In our reading, the DCA provides three measures that may affect barriers to entry:

1. transparency;

2. orders to supply; and

3. addresses to public authorities.

This section discusses these measures in turn – relating the CC's practice to economic theory as well as to the outcome of the effort.

5.3.1 Transparency vis-à-vis a Private Monopoly

The Report defines transparency as 'the easiest and most inexpensive possible access for producers, distributors and consumers to obtain information about prices, business conditions etc.' (p. 175). Increased transparency is expected to make a market more easily contested (Ministry of Industry, 1986, pp. 175-177, our translation):

> Increased transparency will thus by itself be conducive to counteract more durable monopoly gains at certain undertakings, as such gains may be expected to imply that other producers' interest in the market in question be increased. This mechanism assumes, however, that there is free entry to the market...
>
> ...If there is a high degree of transparency about the competitive conditions and at the same time a high degree of occupational and geographical mobility among entrepreneurs and workers, competition will be able to work efficiently, so that extraordinarily large profits in certain industries will not endure, as increased entry will quickly affect prices and margins. This applies in particular if there is the possibility of competition from abroad, too.
>
> ...
>
> The question of increased mobility has needless to say many aspects that go beyond competition policy. Suffice it to mention education and research, labor market organization, housing problems and demographic conditions, in particular inflow of young people. But competition legislation may have an impact on 'entry to the market' by the creation of increased transparency in the market and by removal of restraints of trade that hamper mobility.

The idea seems to be that one just has to make potential competitors aware that there are monopoly profits out there, and they will enter the market. This seems to assume the 'hit-and-run' entry behavior that is, indeed, a prerequisite for the contestable market hypothesis to work well, see Baumol, Panzar and Willig (1982) and, for a critique, Martin (1993, ch. 11). If, however, there are sunk costs and/or large economies of scale, such behavior is not to be expected: Entrants will take the incumbent's reaction into account before deciding whether or not to enter. However, entry may occur in different ways: In addition to setting up shop (i.e. greenfield investment), in a small open economy there is, as the quote indicates, also the possibility of importing the goods which may facilitate hit-and-run competition.

Geroski (1995) indicates that, in general, there is reason to doubt both that entry will come quickly following high profits, and that it will reduce mark-ups. Among a series of stylized empirical results regarding entry, he emphasized the following: 'Entry seems to be slow to react to high profits' (p. 427); 'Entry seems to have only modest effects on average industry price-cost margins' (p. 430); 'The response by incumbents to entry is selective' (p. 431); and 'Prices are not usually used by incumbents to block entry' (p. 433). Thus, Geroski concludes that 'entry is generally a poor substitute for active rivalry amongst incumbent firms in a market. Entry can be (but is not always) too slow, too small scale and too erratic to matter much in many circumstances. Although the current anti-trust emphasis on entry barriers is welcome (and long overdue), it is nevertheless the case that the pro-competitive effects of entry seem to be easy to exaggerate.' (p. 437).

Although one might contest the conclusion of Geroski, a case that illustrates the limitations of the transparency principle to promote entry, as well as the non-price response to entry of one of the few significant, private monopolies in Denmark, is the case of Aalborg Portland (AP in the following). Since 1975 AP has been the sole Danish producer of cement. In the 70's and 80's, AP's prices were directly regulated by a series of agreements between AP and the Monopolies Control Authority (MCA), the predecessor of the CC, according to the Act on Supervision of Monopolies and Restraint of Trade. When the new DCA came into force, AP was immediately requested, by reference to DCA Section 7, to report price lists, business and delivery conditions, general conditions for discounts and bonuses, organizational links, and mergers and acquisitions in which AP takes part. This request has since been renewed in continuation. The CC advances the following motivation for the request (CC, 1996, p. 44; our translation):

> The purpose of the obligation to report is partly to create increased transparency on the market for grey and white cement in which competition cannot be regarded as sufficiently active, partly to allow the Council to follow the development of the market.
>
> The Council did not find reasons to accept a request from the company that information included in the reports be kept secret.
>
> The Council has in this decision attached importance to the fact that Aalborg Portland is the only Danish producer of cement,

> and that it may still have dominating influence on the Danish market.

Further to this, the CC has gone through AP's accounts for the period covering 1990-1993, in order to assess its price setting and earnings, see CC (1995, pp. 39-40). It found that the price of grey cement in exports was much below the one charged to the domestic market and argued that this would only be acceptable in the short run. To this end, the CC requested AP to share the costs of production between the domestic market and export markets. It argued that AP's earnings on the domestic market were clearly above what may be achieved on a market with active competition, while its earnings on the export markets were negative. The buyers of the Danish cement exports are themselves producers of cement, and indeed one of them is Blue Circle, the largest UK producer who owns AP in part (50%).[9]

AP disagrees with the proposed reallocation of production costs towards the export market and argues that its capital equipment has been acquired with the purpose of serving the Danish market, while the export markets are marginal. The CC counters that exports of grey cement amounts to 54 percent of production in 1993, and that exports of white cement amounts to 93 percent of production, implying that exports are not marginal to AP. However, the CC does not want to intervene directly in the market as yet (CC, 1995, p. 40, our translation):

> Notwithstanding the high earnings, the Council, however, did not find reason to request a lowering of the prices of the company, as intervention according to Section 13 of the Competition Act requires excessive earnings of a certain duration.

This seems to indicate that this 'certain duration' is at least five or six years as no steps to intervene have been taken so far. All in all, the position of the CC seems to be that transparency might induce entry, that there is not sufficient competition but that this situation may last for more than five years before direct intervention is to be considered.

Entry to the Danish cement market is unlikely to happen as a green-field investment: Minimum efficient scale (MES) is large compared to the domestic

[9]Low export prices may thus reduce earnings in the Danish company and increase earnings in the UK company, thus amounting to a transfer to the latter. For tax reasons, this may be privately optimal for the two companies seen as a whole.

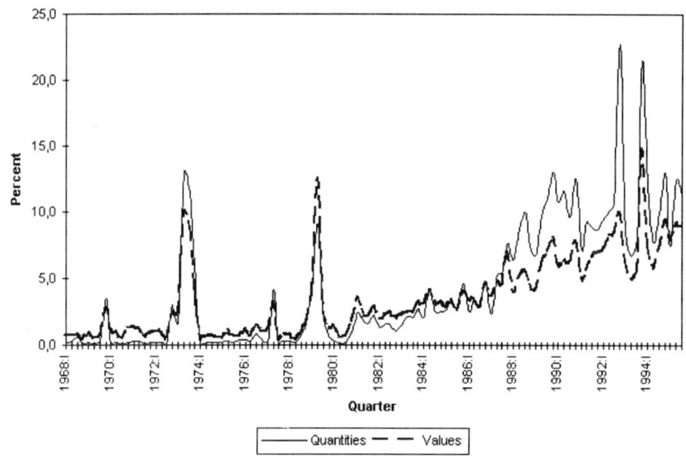

Figure 5.1: Imports relative to domestic production of cement, 1968–1995

market. According to Johansen (1989, p. 112), the newest and largest kiln inaugurated on December 6, 1988, can serve the entire domestic market for grey cement. Other kilns have remained in operation. Thus, capacity is in excess compared to the size of the Danish market. Furthermore, cement production exhibits large economies of scale in capital and labor according to McBride (1983). This makes entry by new producers unlikely due to excess capacity and the fact that MES is large compared to domestic market. In other words, the domestic market is not contestable in this way.

However since the mid-80s there has been entry in the form of imports. Until then, imports were relatively unimportant as may be seen from Figure 5.1, showing imports relative to total domestic production both in volume and in value terms.

Until 1980 imports were insignificant compared to domestic production. Except for two peaks coinciding with the energy crises of 1973 and 1979, and, thus, with domestic supply disruptions, imports were only about 1-2 percent of production. After 1980, and in particular after 1985, imports have increased to between five and ten percent of domestic production. Since 1985, imports have had a higher share in volume than in value terms, reflecting a lower unit value in imports than in domestic production. This is predominantly caused by a larger fraction of high-valued white cement in domestic production than in imports.

In the 1980s, the importers got their cement in East Germany and in Poland. Main importers of East German cement were Stub Trading (ST) and Mørch & Son (MS), while cement from Poland was imported by BC Industri Cement Aps. (BC).

One of the non-price responses of AP was the development of an anti-chromate-eczema process. The content of chromate in cement causes allergic reactions that may develop into a chronic disease. By adding a compound to the cement this effect may, however, be neutralized. The compound was added to the entire production of AP. In 1983 a Government order prohibited sale after 1st April 1984 of cement that was not neutralized in this way. AP now holds a patent on the anti-chromate-eczema process in a number of countries and has managed twice to prohibit sale of East German cement by an injunction granted according to the patent.

The largest importer of East German cement, MS, contended that AP had approved the quality of East German cement in AP's own laboratory in 1986 and that the patent was invalid, as the anti-chromate-eczema process was described in a journal already in 1977. However, AP has sued MS for damages amounting to DKK 100 million and approached MS' customers telling them that they might be liable to pay damages, too. Although running until 1994, MS's contract with the East German cement producer was abruptly discontinued in 1990 when the East German producer was acquired by a French cement group. Now, MS has a joint venture with the Bouri group, a cement trading company and continues to import cement to Denmark.

The importer of Polish cement (BC) entered a settlement with AP in 1988 implying that AP took over the yearly import of 60,000 tons of Polish cement in five years, mixing it with its own cement production.

It would thus seem that AP has countered attempts to enter fairly effectively, if not completely. One may then wonder, why other European producers did not enter the market. The answer has a clear EU dimension: In November 1994, the Commission decided to impose fines on the European Cement Association (Cembureau), eight national cement associations and thirty-three European cement producers – AP being one of them – for infringement of Article 85 of the Treaty of Rome.[10] Their offences were a general market-sharing agreement, transnational restrictive practices and re-

[10]The source of this and the following is EU Commission (1994).

strictive practices relating to exports (market sharing and information sharing). The infringement had gone on since 1983, a fact which caused the total fine (ECU 248 million) to exceed any level previously imposed under EU competition law. AP received a fine of ECU 4 million.

The prime infringement was the 'Cembureau agreement of not transhipping to internal European markets.' The Commission first found evidence of this agreement – which may never have been written down – when it made an investigation of Blue Circle. As an example, an internal document entitled 'Import Threat' contained the following paragraphs (EU Commission, 1994, p. 28):

> Assuming that the Cembureau policy of non-transhipment holds and our assumption that West German imports are not going to prove profitable, there would appear to be only three major residual threats.
>
> 1. Bags, of bulk in 5,000 tonne pneumatic vessels from East Germany
> 2. Bags, including big bags, from Poland
> 3. A large entrepreneur with a mother ship using 25,000 tonne vessels from South European Comecon ports.
>
> There is a small residual threat of the small independent North Spaniards importing here but their tonnage, quality and organization are limited.

This indicates that the Cembureau agreement was a rather comprehensive market-sharing agreement. When the French group acquired the East German producer, and when AP made an agreement with the Polish producer, the Danish market may not have been contested by imports to any significant degree. It would thus seem that AP has been sheltered from most competition from abroad by entry barriers connected with 1) economies of scale; 2) market-sharing agreements on a European level; and 3) non-price responses to entry, such as patenting.

All in all, it seems that the DCA does not provide significant measures against such a private monopoly: It was the CC's intention to promote competition in the market for cement by means of transparency, but this proved largely insufficient. In particular, the transparency principle allows what the

CC perceives as monopoly gains to persist for more than five years. The measure of last resort – direct intervention in the price setting behavior – has not been applied yet. In case it were, for Aalborg Portland this would represent a return to the situation it faced under the 1955 Monopolies Act.

5.3.2 Orders to Supply and Refusals to Deal[11]

A large part of Danish competition practice regarding barriers to entry has been concerned with taking steps to counter refusals to deal. So, whereas the economics literature seems to concentrate on *horizontal* aspects of barriers to entry (economies of scale and scope, limit pricing, advertising requirements, etc.), Danish legal literature mainly treats issues involving *vertical* restrictions which limit access to markets.

One reason for this is probably that it is hard for antitrust authorities to know when and what to do against horizontal barriers to entry, while it is rather more easy to tell a manufacturer that he cannot refuse to deal with a certain applicant. Another reason is that decisions made by the CC under the abuse-control principle of the present Danish competition law does not create the same strong kind of precedent as do decisions made under a prohibition principle such as, for instance, that of the European Union. Hence, the CC ends up dealing with a lot of what appears to be economically relatively insignificant cases in which retailers complain about the behavior of their manufacturers.

The starting point for the discussion is the recognition that in general a firm is free to choose for itself to whom it wants to sell its product. There are, however, situations in which dealing obligations are needed to secure a well-functioning market economy. These can usefully be divided into two groups, general exclusivity clauses, and individual refusals to deal.

By general exclusivity clauses are meant those types of agreements in which, for instance, a manufacturer agrees to deliver only to members of a certain trade association. By restricting the membership of the trade association, competition can be effectively restricted. The anticompetitive effects of these clauses are fairly obvious, and these agreements are now rare, as they have been combatted by the competition authorities for decades.

It is obviously harder to decide on what to do about individual refusals to deal. The legal basis for intervention is given in Section 12 (2) of the

[11] This section draws in large part on Koktvedgaard (1994, ch. 6).

DCA which gives the CC the power to order a manufacturer to sell to a particular applicant on 'normal conditions for similar sales.' Koktvedgaard (1994) writes that the area is characterized by individual decisions but that the situation can loosely be summarized as follows: A manufacturer must deliver to an applicant if

1. the supplies are of fundamental importance for the applicant; this is not the case if there is reasonable access to substitute products;

2. the manufacturer has considerable strength in the market;

3. there are no important reasons for a refusal to deal; refusals furthermore have to be administered according to objective and reasonable criteria used in a consistent manner.

The last condition is, of course, particularly apt to invite discussion. Although the starting point is, as mentioned above, in principle the opposite, that a manufacturer is free to choose with whom it will deal, in practice, important manufacturers are generally assumed to have an obligation to deal, and they will have to present 'important reasons' in order to be allowed not to deal with certain applicants.

Koktvedgaard (1994) lists five possible such reasons. One is the cost structure of the manufacturer. Manufacturers are usually allowed to make 'reasonable' rules about minimum deliveries, transportation cost payments, and the physical form of the delivery. In case of capacity limits there are examples of the competition authority ordering existing capacity to be divided to accommodate new clients. The CC cannot, however, order the manufacturer to increase production. Another reason which has been accepted previously, but is now losing importance, is the need to require adequate training on the part of the applicant. Third, manufacturers may require that their product be sold in a way that does not, for instance, erode its image. This argument is normally accepted by the CC, if the requirements are universal and consistent, and if everybody fulfilling the requirements is granted delivery. Fourth, a manufacturer is normally *not* required to deliver to a competing manufacturer. Finally, a manufacturer can refuse to deliver to an applicant acting disloyally towards the manufacturer or his product, if the 'offence' is clear.

While the CC has a reasonably established policy of using Section 12 to open access to existing markets in cases of refusal to deal, there has recently been a case in which the CC, without success, tried to open up a *new* market. A newly founded Danish electricity intermediary wanted access to the monopolized electricity distribution system on the island of Sealand, in order to sell electricity produced in Sweden to large industrial clients. The intermediary wanted the CC to use Section 12 (2) to order Elkraft, the company owning the distribution system, to allow the intermediary access to its system. The CC decided in favor of the intermediary, but was subsequently overruled by the CAT who argued that 12 (2) could not be used in this case, since Elkraft had never sold access to its system, hence, could not be said to be in the business of selling access to its system, and, therefore, could not be ordered to sell on 'normal conditions for similar sales'. One could add that no 'normal conditions' can exist if access never has been sold before.

This decision by the CAT suggests that the CC can never use 12 (2) to intervene in a situation in which a firm has not sold a product or a service on market terms before. In the present situation concerning electricity markets where EU-regulation and further Danish legislation are awaited, the outcome of the decision may be entirely reasonable, since the question of access to the Danish electricity distribution systems will then be answered by the political system. There are at the moment intense political debates over similar 'bottleneck access' problems in other heavily regulated industries such as the railway system and the telecommunications industries. These issues are relatively new in Denmark and should arguably be decided in the political system, including the EU, and not by the CC using a law not designed for these issues.

The decision by the CAT does, however, lead one to question whether the present formulation of 12 (2) is adequate. Could one not imagine a situation in a less politicized industry in which a new product creates a new market which is then completely monopolized by a vertically integrated firm taking advantage of a strong first mover advantage? The present formulation of 12 (2) and the decision of the CAT seem to strip the CC of any power of opening up such a market for new competitors in the downstream market. Hence, if there are problems in this market, the CC has to revert to controlling the behavior of the monopolist using e.g. Section 13, instead of trying to support structural changes leading to more competition, something which would seem to be more in the spirit of the law.

5.3.3 Public Undertakings and Regulation

As a final case we study how entry opportunities in various sectors are affected by public intervention in the free enterprise economy. It is clear that the state and government agencies, more generally, interfere with the normal working of competition and, particularly, with the possibility of entry. This interference manifests itself at several levels: First, and most obviously, legislative and executive acts affect competition in all sectors of the economy. Secondly, the public sector is directly involved in the provision of goods and services, be this through nationalized industries or public undertakings of various kinds. Thirdly, and perhaps less obviously, yet, very importantly, the government interferes through rules and guidelines pertaining to quasi-public and private undertakings that have been granted special or exclusive rights.

As outlined in Section 2, the DCA applies, at least in principle, to all kinds of undertakings, irrespective of ownership patterns, etc. However, the sanctions and instruments available to the CC (set out in Sections 11-14 of the act) do *not* apply to public undertakings, nor to the business activities of quasi-public and private undertakings that are more explicitly regulated through either legislation or executive acts. For such undertakings, the only means of enforcement available to the CC is to formally address the relevant government agency, through a so-called Section 15 Address. In such a formal address, which is made public, the CC can call attention to the possible harmful effects on competition of the regulation in question and recommend that the regulation be changed. However, the government agency in question is not obliged to follow the recommendations of the CC, nor even to answer the formal address.

Beyond the DCA, public interference with the normal working of competition is subject to Article 90 of the Treaty of Rome, in so far as the subject matter has a *community dimension* (see e.g. Goyder (1988) or Fejø (1993)). Article 90, which is aimed explicitly at the member states, makes clear that public as well as quasi-public and private undertakings who have been granted special or exclusive rights are generally covered by the rules of competition (Articles 85-94). The article makes exemptions possible, but the scope for this has been dramatically narrowed in recent years, with the Commission showing great vigor in combatting anti-competitive effects of government intervention throughout the Community.

In Denmark, and, quite possibly, Europe in general, there is little doubt, empirically, that a large proportion of the economically significant barriers to entry and competition stem directly from government intervention in the economy. Some of these barriers may obviously be well motivated by concerns that are unrelated to competition (such as public health, national security, regional demographics, national heritage, etc.), but the fact remains that many barriers seem to have outlived their historical motivation. Below, we shall detail a couple of cases that illustrate the difficulties of the CC in the dealing with entry barriers that arise as a result of government intervention in the economy.

Before turning to these cases let us briefly comment on the general experience under the regime outlined above. It should be obvious that the CC will have great difficulties in upholding the purpose of the DCA vis-à-vis public firms and regulated firms, if the case before it has no obvious Community dimension, and it is confronted by an intransigent government agency. In such a case, the best the CC can hope for is that the weight of the evidence presented in a Section 15 Address will compel the Danish Parliament or senior ministers to change either the specific legislation or guidelines under which the agency is operating. The evidence, however, seems to suggest that on many occasions the recommendations of the CC have not been followed (see e.g. CC (1994, 1995, 1996) and Hylleberg (1995)), at least not in the short term. Whether the recommendations of the CC turn out to have a positive long term effect remains to be seen. Examples of Section 15 Addresses in cases with little community dimension, and where the recommendations have had little effect on entry opportunities so far, include the statutory monopoly granted to pharmacies on the sale of drugs, non-advertising clauses in regulation of doctors, dentists, etc., regulation of establishment of general medical practices, exclusivity clauses in the legal profession, and exclusivity granted to firms controlling and certifying lifts (elevators).

From the above list it is evident that many key cases are related to the (liberal) professions. Over the last few years the CC has taken a keen interest in the lack of competition in these professions (see e.g. Hylleberg (1995)). From a Danish perspective this sector is particularly interesting since the widespread barriers to entry and competition stem from a (historical) combination of tendencies to form very strong trade associations (*guilds*) that provide detailed rules on conduct together with tight public regulation of the persons or firms that can supply particular services. This immediately implies that the trade associations in these professions have had reliable and powerful allies in the regulating government agencies when complaints have come before the CC, or when the CC has initiated its own proceedings. An interesting case, reported by the CC (1994, 1995, 1996), concerns pharmacies. The CC has tried to intervene against various trade association rules and guidelines on price and mark-up calculations which have dulled price competition almost completely in this industry. In addition, the CC has tried to contest the statutory monopoly granted to pharmacies on the sale of drugs.[12] In particular, the CC has disputed the arguments for the monopoly on non-prescription drugs. Even though much of this is disguised as a case against the restrictive behavior of private firms, in reality this should be seen as an attack on the widespread public regulation of the industry. As a result, the difficulty of the CC in upholding the purpose of the DCA in this sector of the economy is related to the lack of instruments available to promote competition. The upshot, so far, of these various lines of attack is that nothing much has happened in this sector, since the Ministry of Health has proved to be a mighty opponent unwilling to roll-over and lie down. Since the Danish market for (over-the-counter) drugs has a rather limited, immediate community dimension, there are very few signs that the Commission might, at some point, intervene, and this is of course common knowledge to the CC, the Ministry of Health, and the pharmacy trade association when they play the national regulation game.

If a case of barriers to competition or entry related to public or publicly regulated undertakings has a potential community dimension, the picture may be somewhat different as a couple of recent cases will illustrate. In such cases Article 90 of the Treaty of Rome applies, and it would appear that the recommendations of the CC in a Section 15 Address under the DCA would be more difficult to ignore. However, as we show, this does not imply that the mere threat of intervention by the Commission at a later stage makes life easy for the CC. We focus on the operation and access to ports and entry into the (passenger and goods) ferry industry.

To set the scene, we note that the Danish National Railway Company (DSB in the following), in addition to its primary activity, is heavily involved in the operation of ports and ferries. DSB is fully owned by the Danish Government (through the Minister of Transportation)[13], and owner-

[12] According to the Ministry of Business and Industry (1996, pp. 299-300), cost prices of Danish pharmacies exceed the average EU level by twenty-two percent. Deregulation may thus lead to large gains to consumers.

[13] Some significant changes to the structure and status of the DSB have been made since the cases referred to took their beginning. However, none of these seem particularly

ship and operation of some public ports have been delegated to DSB by the government. In particular, the DSB owns and operates the ferry ports of Rødby (in the southern part of the country) and Elsinore (north of Copenhagen). Major ferry links to Germany and Sweden, resp., originate in these ports. Through the ownership of DSB, the Minister of Transportation controls access to these ports by other ferry operators. Until recently, sole access to the ports have been granted to DSB ferries (in collaboration with ferries operated by the German National Railway Company and the Swedish National Railway Company, resp., fixing prices and schedules). Hence, the DSB and its partners have had a statutory monopoly, hence, dominant position, which might be abused to form a violation of the general purpose of competition policies. However, it is equally clear that the CC is impotent under the DCA in this case.

In 1990, Euro-Port A/S (a subsidiary of the Swedish shipping company Stena Rederi AB) filed two applications with the Danish Government: One for access to the existing port facilities in Rødby, and one for access to build new port facilities adjacent to existing facilities. Presumably, access to the existing facilities was given priority by Euro-Port. Both applications were turned down by the Minister of Transportation over the summer of 1990. This decision was brought before the Commission by Stena Rederi AB, and on December 21, 1993, the Commission ruled, with reference to Article 90 (3), that the decision by the Danish Government was in violation of Article 90 (1) together with Article 86 (abuse of dominant position). Basically the argument of the Commission was that the denial of access was an extension of dominant position way beyond that which might be exemptable under Article 90 (2). The Danish Government was given two months to take steps to comply, by *either* giving access to existing facilities *or* access to build new facilities (a new harbor!), and subsequently the Minister of Transportation allowed Euro-Port access to build new facilities. One can imagine that Stena Rederi, who intended to operate ferries between Denmark and Germany, was somewhat unhappy with this turn of events. On the very same day, December 21, 1993, the Commission ordered, in a closely related case, that Sea Containers Ltd. should be granted access to the *existing port facilities* of Holyhead, UK. It so happens that the port of Holyhead is controlled (through a majority stake) by Stena Sealink Line, another subsidiary of Stena Rederi AB! The arguments of the Commission in the two cases are almost identical,

---

important for our discussion.

i.e. the denial of access on *non-discriminatory* terms is an abuse of dominant position, in the sense of Article 86. Yet, the implications for the incumbents in the two cases seem potentially rather different.

Even though the above cases did not involve the CC directly, they set the scene for a subsequent and almost identical case in which the CC was involved. From the argument presented by the Commission in the two cases above, one would think that administration of access to ports by the Danish Ministry of Transportation has changed significantly, at least since the beginning of 1994. In early 1992, a Danish company, Mercandia, simultaneously filed complaints with the Commission and the CC over a refusal of access to the port facilities of Elsinore. The Commission initially found that this was a case best handled by the national authorities and decided to await the results of this. In May of 1993 the CC made a formal Section 15 Address to the Ministry of Transportation, in which it was recommended that DSB concede access to the existing facilities by alternative operators. This was strongly rejected by the ministry, on the grounds that this would be in violation of DSB's obligations towards its Swedish partner. Towards the end of 1993, anticipating the ruling of the Commission in the cases above, it was revealed that the ministry was soliciting projects for new port facilities (see CC (1994)). Hence, the Ministry of Transportation was clearly intending not to let the CC be a major player in the determination of port access in Denmark. As the possibility of (eventually) being able to operate out of new facilities was clearly unsatisfactory to the plaintiff, the case was referred back to the Commission in 1994 as it became clear that the Ministry of Transportation was not going to comply with the recommendations of the CC (see CC (1996)). Subsequently, the Commission (armed with a sizable stick) entered informal negotiations with the Danish government, and in February 1996 secured access of an independent operator. Mercandia eventually prevailed after winning a bidding contest, and is now operating out of Elsinore with substantial price reductions compared to the previous monopoly prices. In the course of events, the Commission in a statement issued May 30, 1996, made clear its stance on access to 'essential facilities' (also when owned by the public): An undertaking, which owns or operates a port facility, is in violation of Article 86, if the dominant position in this area is used to protect or strengthen its position in the separate, but related, market for transportation services. The Commission emphasized that this is particularly so, if access by competitors to the infrastructure is denied or is granted only on unfavorable terms (CC (1996)). Naively, one might suggest that, with respect to port access, a fairly strong precedent has now been set.[14]

The upshot of these cases would seem to be that, in the absence of a section in the DCA akin to Article 90 in the Treaty of Rome, the Danish competition authorities will continue to have a hard time in dealing with sectors of the economy that have historically been regulated tightly by other government agencies. Concerning the upcoming revision of the DCA, our suggestion on these matters would therefore be to include a section drafted on Article 90 and to provide the CC with stronger means of intervention.

5.4 Conclusion

Based on the cases discussed above, the CC seems to be somewhat impotent with respect to at least certain types of barriers to entry. This impotence is in no small measure related to regulation and interference in the economy by other government agencies. We summarize and conclude with the following remarks:

Transparency: There is no doubt that increased market transparency makes it easier for customers and potential competitors to spot profitable opportunities. Hence, if entry barriers are low and incumbent firms act slowly and in uncoordinated fashion, then increased transparency would tend to promote entry of the hit-and-run type as suggested by proponents of the contestable markets hypothesis. It is equally clear, however, that increased transparency may help incumbent oligopolists coordinate on a speedy response to entry, which would generally tend to delay entry. More generally, it should be reemphasized (recalling the remarks of Geroski (1995)) that the speed with which opportunities are spotted and converted into actual entry is not always high. Finally, the case of large MES compared to the domestic market discussed in Section 3.1 strongly indicates that increased transparency is far from sufficient to guarantee entry. In this case the effective entry barriers seem to have very little to do with (lack of) market transparency. To conclude, we would argue that the creation of transparency is not a very fine-tuned and effective instrument with which to counter barriers to entry.

Restrictive practices and orders to supply: An order to supply is quite obviously a more direct means of intervention than the somewhat "slippery"

[14]However, in an ongoing case, which to us seems fairly similar, DSB is again trying to deny access to an international harbor.

concept of transparency. For this reason alone, it is not surprising that the CC has relied on such orders to reinvigorate its general attack on entry barriers in the Danish economy. We have already noted that there are some natural limitations to the force of precedent set by the case history under an *abuse-control* regime. This obviously raises the general question of whether entry barriers erected through vertical restraints can be more successfully fought in a regime based on *prohibition*. The EU and US experience does not provide a clear answer. Given the success of the Chicago School in explaining the underlying efficiency motive of vertical restraints, there would seem to be a rather limited scope for *per se* illegality, and it follows that the regulation of vertical restraints is not likely to be much easier under a prohibition regime. However, in so far as the horizontal problems underlying various anticompetitive and entry deterring vertical restraints can be classified, then certain prohibitions with a narrow and focused scope might prove effective in dismantling certain entry barriers.

Public and regulated undertakings: In cases involving undertakings under public ownership or explicit public regulation, the current Danish legislation on competition leaves the CC virtually powerless. On this point a revision of the DCA is urgently needed, significantly narrowing the scope for "defences" based on flimsy, yet, often imaginative, interpretations of *the common weal*.[15] Drafting a section on Article 90 in the Treaty of Rome, making explicit that undertakings of the above-mentioned kind are subject to the full extent of the law, would basically reverse the "burden of proof". Hence, legislators would have to argue their case explicitly before instituting restraints on trade and entry.

Access to essential facilities: The two cases on access to essential facilities (electricity distribution networks and ports) discussed in the text quite clearly share some of the same features.[16] The main difference lies in the ownership of the bottle-neck facility; one is owned by the government, another by a private company. Recall that in the case of port access and *public ownership*, the recommendations of the CC eventually prevailed (but only after

---

[15] Recall the opening quote from the Danish Constitution.

[16] One might also imagine a similar problem arising in relation to an attempt to break the cement monopoly discussed. The incumbent monopolist controls the known limestone resources of Denmark. Access to limestone might be construed as a bottle-neck, and a prospective local entrant might be denied access, and we might have a case before the CC. Whether this is a likely scenario is unclear to us, but it is certainly logically possible.

intervention by the Commission), whereas in the case of access to the electricity distribution network and *private ownership*, the CC did not prevail. Two similar cases with the "opposite" outcome might easily be imagined. Take a purely domestic case with no Community dimension. Consider two pairs of ferry ports; one pair is owned by a private company, with one ferry company operating, and the other is owned by the state, which may also happen to be a ferry operator. Assume further that the ports in question are true bottle-necks. Now, an entrant to the ferry industry applies for access to these ports and is denied by both the private and the public port owner. The potential entrant brings its complaint before the CC. The CC will rule (and this is almost certain to be upheld by the CAT) that the private port owner should grant access, and, further, the CC will make a Section 15 Address to the public port owner, recommending that access be granted (which is almost certain not to be followed). Hence, access to the private bottle-neck is granted, whereas access to the public bottle-neck is not granted. This strongly suggests to us that, with the current legislation, exempting publicly owned or regulated undertakings from the provisions against harmful effects of restraints of trade, it will prove impossible to establish a consistent and symmetric regime on access to essential facilities. For this reason alone it is of paramount importance that new legislation makes clear that both public and regulated entities are subject to the full extent of the law.[17]

5.5 References

Albæk, S, H.P. Møllgaard and P.B. Overgaard "Dansk konkurrenceret og vertikal kontrol," *Nationaløkonomisk Tidsskrift* 133, 1995, pp. 268-283.

— "Law-Assisted Collusion? The Transparency Principle of the Danish Competition Act," *European Competition Law Review* 17(6), 1996, pp. 339-343.

— "Government-Assisted Collusion? A Concrete Case," Discussion Paper 97-03, Centre for Industrial Economics, University of Copenhagen, 1997.

[17] Here we shall resist the temptation to further argue that, on theoretical grounds, public bottle-necks may, in fact, be more of a problem than private bottle-necks.

Baumol, W.J.; J.C. Panzar; and R.D. Willig *Contestable Markets and the Theory of Industry Structure.* New York: Harcourt Brace Jovanovich, 1982.

Competition Council *Konkurrencerådets henvendelser til offentlige myndigheder — anvendelse af konkurrencelovens §15 i praksis.* Copenhagen: Competition Council, 1994.

— *Dokumentation 1995.* Copenhagen: Competition Council, 1995.

— *Dokumentation 1996.* Copenhagen: Competition Council, 1996.

EU Commission "Decision of 30 November 1994 regarding a procedure according to Article 85 of the EC-Treaty (Case IV/33.126 and 33.322 – Cement)" *De Europæiske Fællesskabers Tidende* 37(L343), 30 December 1994.

Fejø, J. *EF-konkurrenceret.* Copenhagen: Jurist- og Økonomforbundets Forlag, 1993.

Geroski, P.A. "What do we know about entry?," *International Journal of Industrial Organization* 13(4), 1995, pp. 421-441.

Goyder, D.G. *EEC Competition Law.* Oxford: Clarendon Press, 1988.

Hylleberg, S. *Konkurrencen i dansk erhvervsliv (draft)*, Department of Economics, University of Aarhus, 1995.

Johansen, H.C. *Gennem Forandring til Fremskridt*, Aalborg: Anton M. Jensen, 1989.

Koktvedgaard, M. *Lærebog i konkurrenceret.* Copenhagen: Jurist- og Økonomforbundets Forlag, 1994.

Martin, S. *Advanced Industrial Economics.* Oxford: Blackwell, 1993.

McBride, M. E. "The Nature and Source of Economics of Scale in Cement Production," *Southern Economic Journal*, 1983, pp. 105-115.

Ministry of Business and Industry, 1996, *Erhvervsredegørelse 1996*, Copenhagen: Ministry of Business and Industry.

Ministry of Industry, 1986, *Fra monopollov til konkurrencelov*, Copenhagen: Ministry of Industry.

Trust Commission *Foreløbig betænkning vedrørende en lov om konkurrencebegrænsning og monopollov.* Copenhagen, 1953.

Competition Policies in Europe - S. Martin (Editor)

Chapter 6

Competition Policy: Publicity vs. Prohibition & Punishment

Stephen Martin

6.1 Introduction

The competition policies of the European Union and the United States are based on the principle of prohibition and punishment. Certain types of strategic business behavior are outlawed and firms (in some circumstances, individuals) found to have engaged in such conduct are subject to penalties. Exceptions may be possible,[1] and the enthusiasm with which the rules are enforced is subject to cycles, but the underlying approach is clear.

Well-developed lines of decisions in both jurisdictions limit the exchange of information among competitors. Trade associations are typically permitted to collect information from single firms and report it in aggregate form, but any practice that allows the identification of prices and quantities of particular firms or for particular transactions is viewed with suspicion. Oligopoly theory suggests that uncertainty about what rivals are doing may induce a firm to behave more competitively, and may prevent rivals from retaliat-

[1]Many European Commission block exemptions permit firms with market shares that do not exceed specified levels to engage in various types of behavior that is denied to larger firms. The Commission may set aside the Article 92 prohibition of state aid if such aid is found to serve other EU purposes. In the United States, an early 1950s antitrust challenge to the conduct of major oil companies floundered on the shoals of the foreign relations.

ing against such behavior. Exchanges of detailed information about specific transactions are thought to facilitate tacit collusion by allowing rivals to react rapidly to selective price cuts or to other behavior that might destabilize a cozy oligopolistic equilibrium.[2]

The competition policy of Denmark, in contrast, is based on the principle of abuse control. Interfirm agreements are not prohibited. Specified types of interfirm agreements must, however, be notified to the Competition Council, which has the power and responsibility to investigate arrangements that are thought to have anticompetitive potential. One of the primary policy instruments available to the Competition Council to deal with such arrangements is publicity, the public reporting of the results of investigations into market conditions. The goal is to promote transparency of information about market conditions, and this can involve official circulation of precisely the sort of information that EU and US competition policy forbids firms to make arrangements to distribute.

The genesis of this policy is not entirely clear. One motivation may be that complete and perfect information is part of the classroom model of perfect competition. It does seem to reflect a hostility toward price discrimination, and the expectation that consumers would press for the best prices available if they were made aware of price differences.[3]

To formally analyze the effectiveness of a transparency policy, however, one needs to specify the means by which a transparency policy is expected to affect firm conduct. Hypotheses about such mechanisms were advanced in US debates during the early years after the passage of the Sherman Act, when for a time publicity was part of US antitrust policy.

Early Supreme Court decisions interpreting the Sherman Act raised the fear that it would be ineffective, and in any event early enforcement efforts were not vigorous.[4] A long debate over the strengthening of antitrust policy

---

[2]Experimental evidence suggests that the ability of rivals to identify and punish an individual defector is an important element in maintaining tacit collusion (Holt, 1995, p. 407). Transparency would contribute to making such targeted reactions possible.

[3]There may also be elements of industry capture behind the transparency approach; representatives of the business communicty are traditionally involved in the development of Danish competition policy. For further discussion, see Albæk, Møllgaard, and Overgaard (1996a, 1996b). At this writing, there are proposals to amend the Danish Competition Act by introducing some elements of prohibition and punishment and moving Denmark toward the EU approach. This is discussed OECD (1996) and at the Competition Council's world wide web site, http://www.ks.dk/.

[4]See, for example, Letwin(1965), Chapter 5.

ensued, and this led to the establishment (in 1903) of the Bureau of Corporations, which was charged with gathering information about industrial practices and publicizing abuses.

Publicity was expected to serve several purposes. A major target was corrupt financial practices, which would not now be regarded as falling within the sphere of competition policy (Jenks, 1900, p. 222)[5]

> Publicity regarding the organization of a business, which should compel promoters to show clearly to investors the basis on which a large corporation or a combination of corporations is organized, would certainly put careful investors in a position to protect themselves.

But publicity also aimed to improve market performance by raising the threat of entry or inducing actual entry (Jenks, 1900, pp. 223-4):[6]

> publicity ...which should show with a reasonable degree of detail the profits of the larger combinations would, in case of the abuse of their power, so stimulate competition against them, either actually or potentially, that consumers would to a great degree be protected against excessive increase in prices.

---

[5] Most references to publicity in the influential *Preliminary Report of the Industrial Commission on Trusts and Industrial Combinations* (1900) occur with respect to financial abuse.

[6] An additional element was prominent in a somewhat later British debate on publicity as an element of competition policy — that publicity given to monopolistic practices would so shame the businessmen concerned that such behavior be abandoned (Hilton, 1918, p. 30, quoted in Dennison, 1980, p. 230):

> by ensuring that extortion should be publicly pilloried, [publicity] would do much to prevent it being practised. In quite respectable business conduct, as in other human affairs, many things are done which would not be done if there were a greater probability of their being made public.

Marshall (1923, p. 442) makes a similar argument:

> upright men are often half-way converted towards removing such just grounds as there may be for complaint against their conduct, by reading a well-informed and well-balanced statement of those grounds; and knowing that an impartial public is forming its judgment on them. In this and many other ways a careful authoritative inquiry, with publication of the evidence taken, goes a long way towards removing sources of social harm...

Publicity was endorsed by Governor Theodore Roosevelt in a message to the New York state legislature. Roosevelt thought of publicity as a possible first step toward eventual adoption of a more severe policy (January 1900; emphasis added; quoted by Thorelli, 1954, p. 415):

> Where a trust becomes a monopoly the State has an immediate right to interfere. Care should be taken not to stifle enterprise or disclose any facts of a business that are essentially private; but the State for the protection of the public should exercise the right to inspect, to examine thoroughly all the workings of great corporations just as is now done with banks; and wherever the interests of the public demand it, it should publish the results of its examination. Then, **if there are inordinate profits, competition or public sentiment will give the public the benefit in lowered prices**; and if not, the power of taxation remains. **It is therefore evident that publicity is the one sure and adequate remedy which we can now invoke. There may be other remedies, but what these others are we can only find out by publicity, as the result of investigation.** The first requisite is knowledge, full and complete.

After several years experience with the information-disseminating activities of the Bureau of Corporations, the Sherman Act was reinforced by passage of the Federal Trade Commission Act and the Clayton Act. These laws committed US antitrust to the prohibition and punishment approach, but information-gathering was by no means abandoned. The need for such activity had been highlighted by President Wilson in a 1914 speech to Congress (Baker and Dodd, 1925, pp. 85-6)

> And the business men of the country desire something more than that the menace of legal process ...be made explicit and intelligible. They desire the advice, the definite guidance, and information which can be supplied by an administrative body, an interstate trade commission.
>
> [The opinion of the country] demands such a commission only as an indispensable instrument of information and publicity, as a clearing house for the facts by which both the public mind and the managers of the great business undertakings should be guided....

Information gathering was part of the mandate of the Federal Trade Commission, along with its prohibition and punishment responsibilities (Scherer, 1990).

I develop here a model of firm behavior under alternative competition policies, prohibition and punishment (henceforth, P^2) and publicity, where publicity affects firm conduct because of its impact on the possibility of entry. This permits a comparison of the impacts of the two types of policy on market performance.

For simplicity, I examine an industry that is supplied by a single firm. I begin with the case of a monopolist that does not face the threat of entry but must deal with a P^2 competition policy. Then I turn to the contrasting case of a monopolist that faces the threat of entry without any competition policy at all. Then two cases are then combined compare the impact of a P^2 policy with the threat of entry and a publicity policy on market performance.

6.2 Monopoly with a P^2 competition policy

6.2.1 Enforcement

If publicity is to affect firm behavior, information about the market must in some way be imperfect. I assume that inverse demand curve has a random intercept,

$$p = a + \varepsilon - q \tag{6.1}$$

where the random term ε is uniformly distributed over the interval $(-\alpha, \alpha)$:[7]

$$-\alpha \leq \varepsilon \leq \alpha. \tag{6.2}$$

Marginal cost is a constant c per unit. I will also assume that there is an entry cost K, although this becomes a factor only in the following section.

Three parameters describe the P^2 policy: the threshold price p_G, the probability γ of prosecution and conviction if a price greater than p_G is observed, and the fine F that is imposed if conviction takes place.

The threshold price is a device to model the decision-making process of the enforcement agency: if a price greater than or equal to p_G is observed,

[7] Assume also that $a - \alpha \geq 0$, so that a sufficiently small quantity will always bring a positive price.

the government investigates the activities of the firm.[8]

Competition policy typically does not prohibit monopoly as such: what it prohibits are certain types of conduct by firms with some degree of market power that are thought to be against the public interest. "Against the public interest" may mean that some measure of welfare (such as consumers' surplus or consumers' plus producers' surplus) is reduced, or that the conduct raises the cost of actual or potential rivals. It may refer to some noneconomic objective function. If investigation leads competition authorities to conclude that such misbehavior has occurred, they must decide whether or not to initiate an enforcement proceeding, the exact nature of which will vary across legal regimes If there is such a proceeding, competition authorities may or may not succeed in obtaining a finding that the firm has violated competition policy. I use a single parameter to describe the ambiguity, from the firm's point of view, concerning the possibilities of prosecution and conviction: γ is the probability that a firm is found to have violated competition policy, if a price greater than p_G is observed.

Third, if there is a finding that an antitrust violation has taken place, let F be the resulting fine.[9] γF, the expected fine if an investigation takes place, is an indcx of the severity of competition policy.

6.2.2 The incumbent's payoff function

The probability that the government observes a price at or above the threshold level is

$$\tau_G \equiv \Pr(p \geq p_G) = \Pr(a - q + \varepsilon \geq p_G)$$

[8]In practice, competition authorities receive a variety of signals, including complaints from rivals and customers. By extending the model developed here to include two industries and a budget constraint that limits the investigative possibilities of the enforcement agency, one could explicitly model resource allocation by the enforcement agency. While the economist's natural starting point in such a study would be to suppose that decisions are made to maximize expected consumers' surplus or expected net social welfare, other objective functions have been ascribed to enforcement agencies. See Posner (1976, pp. 230-1); Dorman (1980, p. 1115); Schwartz (1980, p. 1093); Shughart (1996).

[9]It is possible to allow for structural remedies—nationalization or the breakup of the firm—along the lines developed in the section on entry deterrence. Although provision for such penalties is a part of competition policy in many jurisdictions, they are rarely applied. I owe to John Baldwin the observation that the threat of nationalization may have appeared quite tangible at certain times and in certain countries.

Output range	τ_G	**Expected payoff function**
$0 \leq q \leq a - \alpha - p_G$	1	$(a - c - q)q - \gamma F$
$a - \alpha - p_G \leq q \leq a + \alpha - p_G$	$\frac{a+\alpha-p_G-q}{2\alpha}$	$(a - c - q)q - \frac{a+\alpha-p_G-q}{2\alpha}\gamma F$
$a + \alpha - p_G \leq q$	0	$(a - c - q)q$

Table 6.1: P^2 Competition Policy and Monopolist's Single Period Payoff Function

$$= \Pr[\varepsilon \geq p_G - (a - q)] = \frac{\alpha - [p_G - (a - q)]}{2\alpha} = \frac{a + \alpha - p_G - q}{2\alpha}, \tag{6.3}$$

provided this lies between 0 and 1. This is illustrated in Figure 6.1.

If $q \geq a+\alpha-p_G$, realized price is certainly less than p_G and the probability of investigation for competition policy violations is zero ($\tau_G = 0$). If $q \leq a - \alpha - p_G$, realized price is certainly greater than p_G, and investigation is certain ($\tau_G = 1$).

Table 1 describes the three segments of the monopolist's payoff function.

6.2.3 Market performance with a P^2 policy

Extreme values of p_G

In the absence of a competition policy, the incumbent's profit-maximizing output would be

$$q_0 = \frac{1}{2}(a - c), \tag{6.4}$$

sold at expected price[10]

$$p_0 = c + q_0 \tag{6.5}$$

and yielding expected payoff

$$\pi_0 = (q_0)^2 \tag{6.6}$$

The output q_0 would yield the range of possible prices

$$p_0 - \alpha \leq p \leq p_0 + \alpha. \tag{6.7}$$

If $p_G > p_0+\alpha$, then the unconstrained monopoly output could not lead to a realized price high enough to trigger a government investigation. As shown

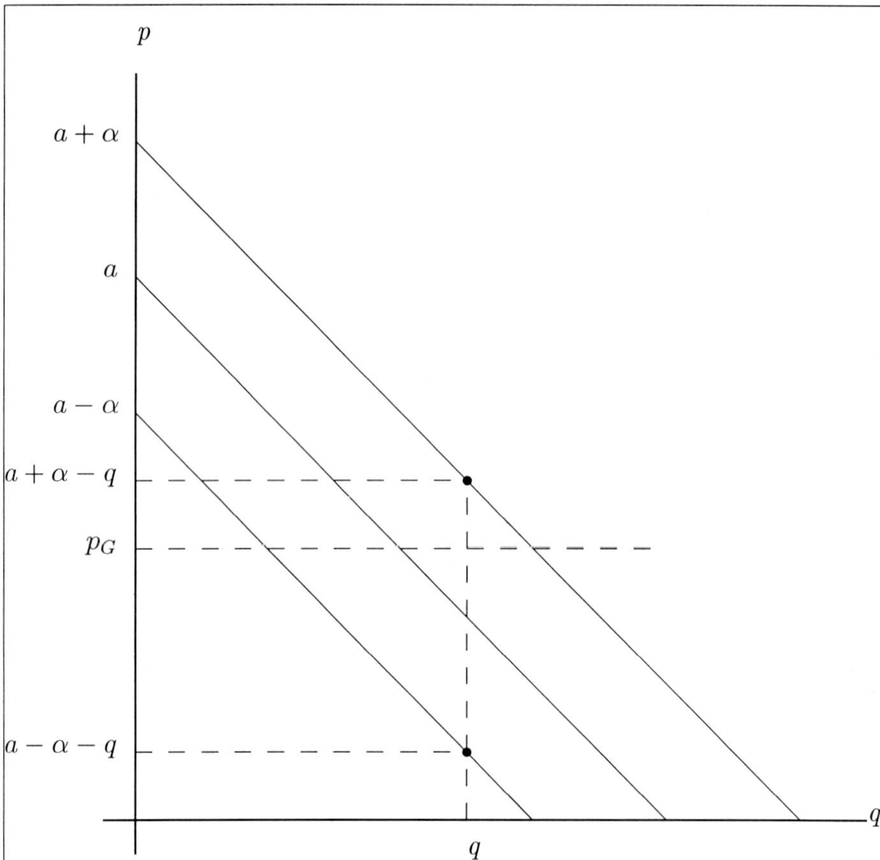

$$\tau_G = \Pr(p \geq p_G) = \Pr(a + \varepsilon - q \geq p_G) = \frac{a + \alpha - q - p_G}{2\alpha}$$

$$(\text{for } 0 \leq \tau_G \leq 1)$$

Figure 6.1: Demand, threshold price p_G

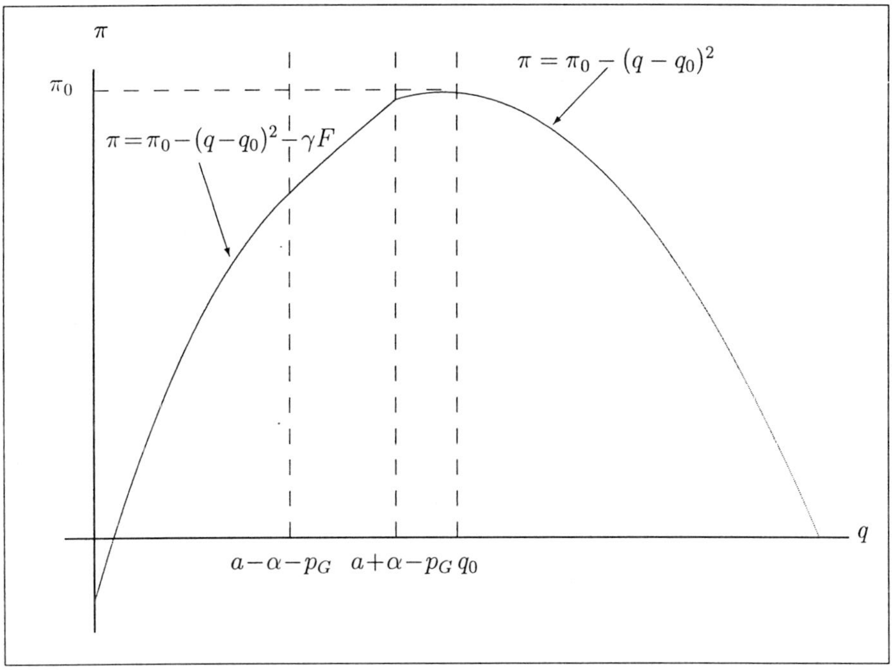

Figure 6.2: Payoff function, $a + \alpha - p_G \leq q_0$

in Figure 6.2, the incumbent's profit-maximizing output for such a threshold price is simply q_0.

At the other extreme, if p_G is very large, the P^2 policy has no impact on the firm's output decision because the output expansion required to avoid or reduce the probability of investigation is so great that the firm prefers simply to produce output q_0 and face the certainty of investigation. The typical payoff function in such cases, shown in Figure 6.3, has a global maximum at $q = q_0$. The threshold price p_G is so low relative to the expected penalty γF that the firm maximizes its expected payoff by producing monopoly output q_0 and accepting the inevitability of investigation. If the threat of punishment is to alter behavior, it must be possible for the firm to avoid punishment at a reasonable opportunity cost.

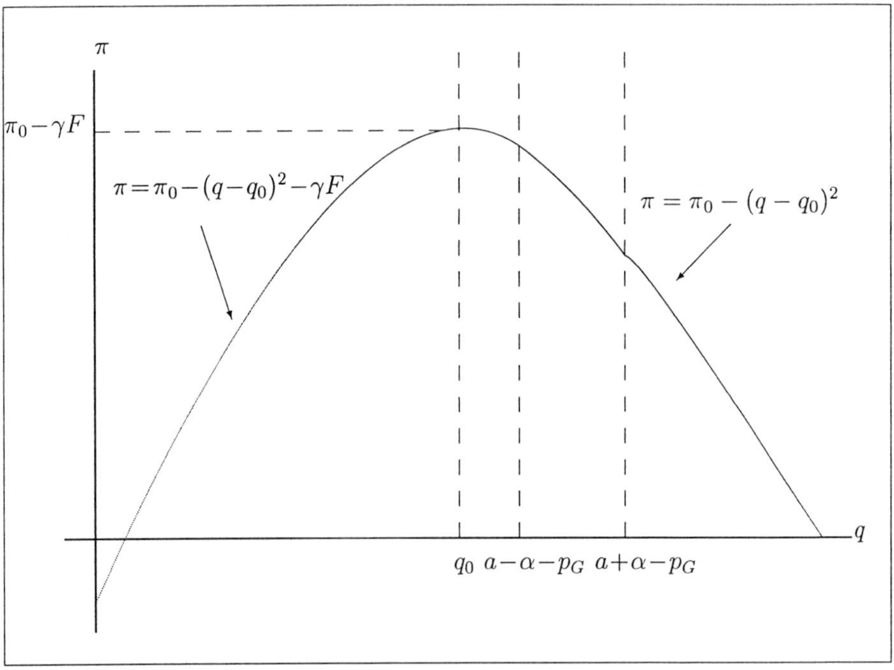

Figure 6.3: Payoff function, $a + \alpha - p_G \geq q_0$

[10]For notational simplicity I omit the expectations operator.

Intermediate values of p_G

Intermediate values of p_G raise the possibility that the firm's profit-maximizing output choice will be in the range $a - \alpha - p_G \leq q \leq a + \alpha - p_G$, where $0 \leq \tau_G \leq 1$ and the payoff function is

$$\pi = (a - c - q)q - (q_G - q)\frac{\gamma F}{2\alpha}. \tag{6.8}$$

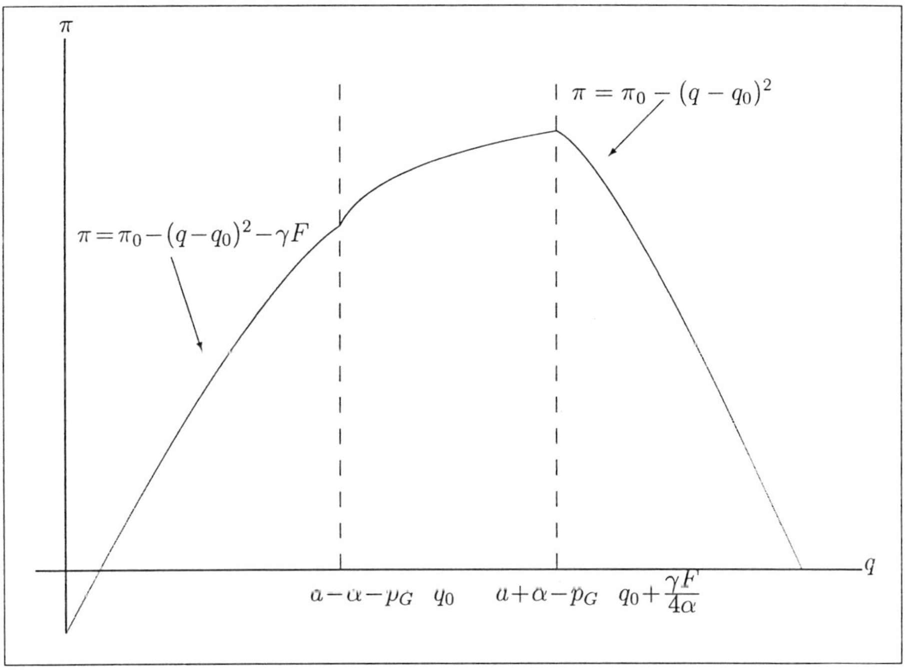

Figure 6.4: Payoff function, $q_0 \leq a + \alpha - p_G \leq q_0 + \dfrac{\gamma F}{4\alpha}$

The payoff function may have three configurations. If p_G is only slightly below $p_0 + \alpha$, the incumbent maximizes its expected payoff by expanding output from q_0 to $a + \alpha - p_G$ and driving τ_G to zero (Figure 6.4). If p_G is somewhat lower, the firm will expand output beyond q_0, but not enough to make $\tau_G = 0$. As p_G falls, the payoff function develops two local maxima (as in Figure 6.5). If p_G is sufficiently small, the local maximum that yields the greatest payoff is at $q = q_0$.

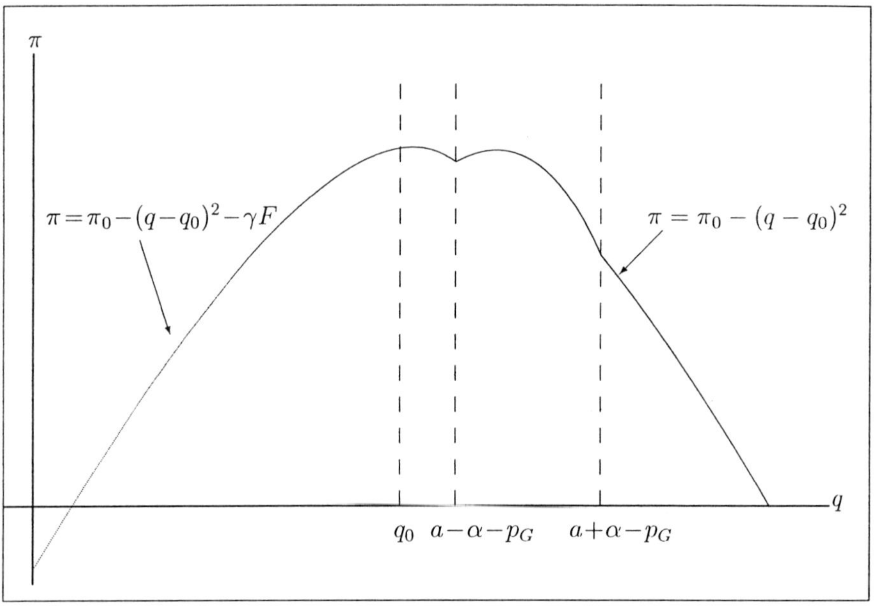

Figure 6.5: Payoff function, $q_0 + 2\alpha \leq a + \alpha - p_G \leq q_0 + 2\alpha + \frac{\gamma F}{4\alpha}$

Theorem 1 (proven in the Appendix) gives the relationship between the threshold price p_G and the incumbent's equilibrium output level. There are two cases, depending on the relationship between the expected fine γF and the demand uncertainty parameter α. In both cases, the threat of antitrust investigation induces output expansion and therefore improved market performance, provided the threshold price that triggers investigation is not too low relative to the expected antitrust penalty. If the incumbent must expand output too much to avoid investigation, it will simply take the greatest short-run profit it can and risk a fine.

Theorem 1 *The relationship between p_G and expected-profit maximizing output q_1 is*

(a) $0 \leq \gamma F \leq 16\alpha^2$

(a1) for $a + \alpha \geq p_G \geq p_0 + \alpha$, $q_1 = q_0$;
(a2) for $p_0 + \alpha \geq p_G \geq p_0 + \alpha - (\gamma F/4\alpha)$, $q_1 = q_0 + (p_0 + \alpha - p_G)$;
(a3) for $p_0 + \alpha - (\gamma F/4\alpha) \geq p_G \geq p_0 - \alpha - (\gamma F/8\alpha)$, $q_1 = q_0 + (\gamma F/4\alpha)$;
(a4) for $p_0 - \alpha - (\gamma F/8\alpha) \geq p_G$, $q_1 = q_0$;

(b) $16\alpha^2 \leq \gamma F$
(b1) for $p_G \geq p_0 + \alpha$, $q_1 = q_0$;
(b2) $p_0 + \alpha \geq p_G \geq p_0 + \alpha - \sqrt{\gamma F}$, $q_1 = q_0 + (p_0 + \alpha - p_G)$;
(b3) for $p_0 + \alpha - \sqrt{\gamma F} \geq p_G$, $q_1 = q_0$.

Theorem 1 is illustrated in Figure 6.6. In case a, $0 \leq \gamma F \leq 16\alpha^2$. As p_G falls below $p_0 + \alpha$, q_1 expands along a downward-sloping 45° line to a maximum of $q_0 + (\gamma F/4\alpha)$. If γF takes its maximum value, $16\alpha^2$, this is $q_0 + 2\alpha$.[11] For lower values of p_G, $q_1 = q_0$.

In Case b, $\gamma F \geq 16\alpha^2$. As p_G falls below $p_0 + \alpha$, q_1 expands along a downward-sloping 45° line to a maximum of $q_0 + \sqrt{\gamma F}$. If F is chosen so that $\gamma F = \pi_0$, the equilibrium choice for the monopolist is to produce the competitive output. If the expected penalty for exercising market power is sufficiently large, the exercise of market power can be completely deterred.

6.3 Entry deterrence without competition policy

6.3.1 Probabilistic evaluation of the threat of entry

Entry games often explicitly model the interaction between one or more incumbents and one or more known potential entrants (see, for example, Martin, 1995). This approach to modelling entry can be traced to Friedman's (1979) influential criticism of naive limit price models.[12] Considering a situation in which (Friedman, 1979, p. 237) "there are no stochastic elements

[11] If α is is sufficiently large, $q_0 + 2\alpha$ will equal the competitive output level $a - c$. The incumbent would shut down rather than produce above this output level.

[12] It is usual to associate the limit price model with the work of Joe S. Bain, although it appears as well in Kaldor (1935) and Clark (1940). Bain (1949, pp. 452-3) makes essentially the same criticism of the naive limit price model as Friedman, which is most accurately thought of as targeting the Sylos-Labini postulate (for discussion of which, see Modigliani, 1958).

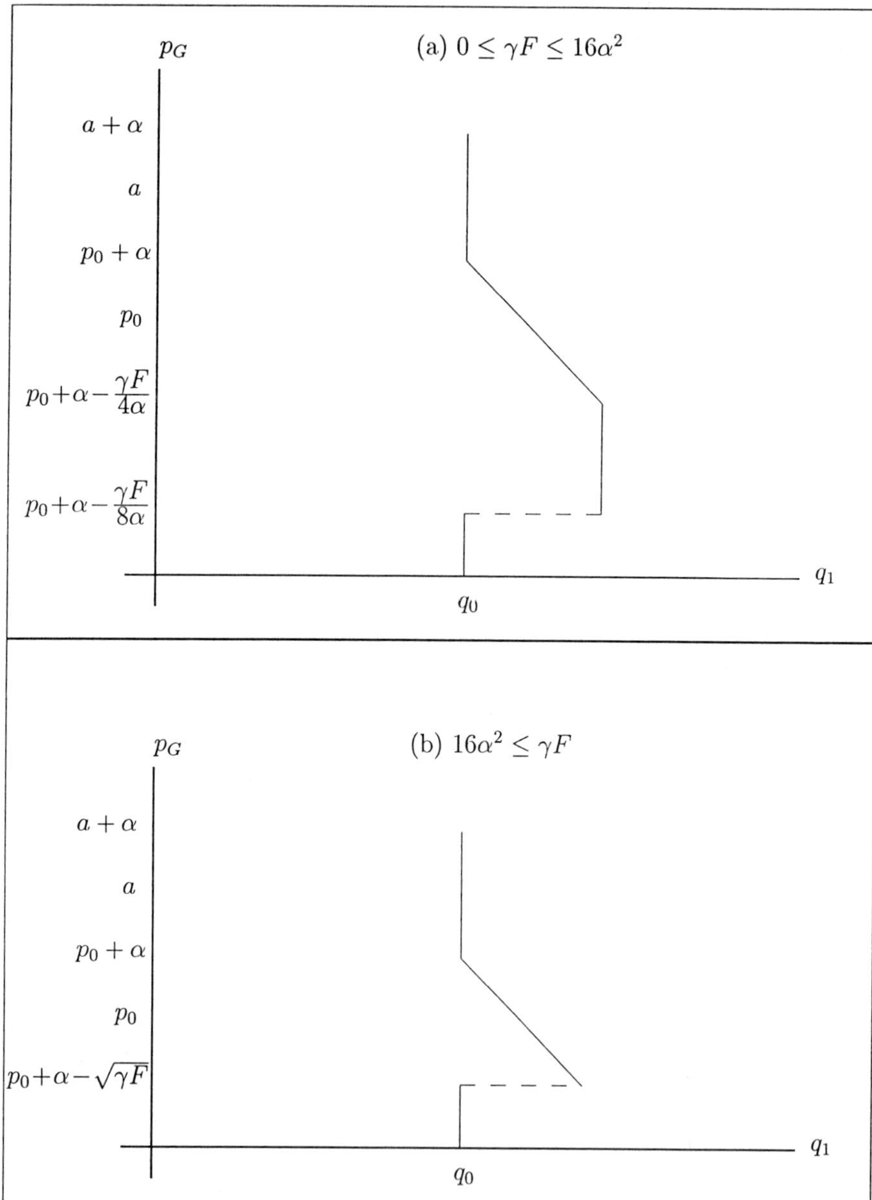

Figure 6.6: Theorem 2.1

... and both the established firm and the entrant know the demand and cost functions which prevail before and after entry," Friedman observes that the notion of limit price is simply out of place (1979, p. 237):

> in the models examined below an entrant has no direct interest in an established firm's pre-entry price policy. What matters to him is the price pattern which would emerge after he were to come in. That is, he wants to know what equilibrium behavior in the market would be if he were in, and he wants to know what profits he would have under such an equilibrium.

Friedman's arguments are cited by Milgrom and Roberts (1982, p. 44) in their own seminal work; they note that his conclusions depend on the assumption of complete information. They relax this assumption by examining a situation in which there is one incumbent and one potential entrant, each uncertain about the other's costs.

Here I relax the assumption of complete and perfect information in another direction, modelling a situation in which an incumbent anticipates the possibility of entry without being able to specifically identify all potential entrants or fully model their actions. I suppose that the incumbent regards entry as a two-stage process. If realized price reaches or exceeds a threshold level p_E, the incumbent expects that potential entrants will actively investigate the possibility of coming into the market.[13] If investigation takes place, no attempt at entry may result. If entry is attempted, it may fail. Let η be the probability that successful entry occurs, given that $p \geq p_E$.

The assumption that entry is investigated only if price exceeds some threshold level may be motivated with reference to recent empirical findings on entry. Although it is common in models of entry games to assume that entry will occur if expected post-entry profitability is positive, Geroski (1995, p. 427) notes that actual entry "seems to be slow to react to high profits." A theoretical rationale for this empirical regularity may be found in the work of Dixit and Pindyck (1994), which suggests that entrants, expecting positive post-entry profit, would nonetheless defer entry until it is sufficiently unlikely that no greater profit opportunity will emerge elsewhere.

[13] For a case study, see the account of decisions about entry that appears in the decision *U.S.* v. *Penn-Olin Chemical Co.* 378 U.S. 158 (1964). For analyses of entrants' post-entry experiences, see Geroski (1991), Geroski and Schwalbach (1991).

For an incumbent that operates in many geographic markets (as in the chain store game), the probability η may be thought of as reflecting the accumulated experience of the firm. Alternatively, one may think of "investigation" as a process by which a potential entrant learns its value of K, with η the entry probability implied by the distribution of entry costs across potential entrants. The assumption that incumbents expect successful entry to occur with only a certain probability, if price is high enough to induce investigation, may also be thought of describing the behavior of incumbents who believe they face (possibly unknown) potential entrants playing mixed strategies.

Let τ_E denote the probability that a potential entrant investigates the possibility of coming into the market. If τ_E lies between zero and one, it is given by

$$\tau_E \equiv \Pr(p \geq p_E) = \frac{\alpha - [p_E - (a-q)]}{2\alpha} = \frac{a + \alpha - q - p_E}{2\alpha}, \tag{6.9}$$

provided this lies between zero and one.

The present discounted value of an incumbent that produces output q is

$$V_M = \frac{(a-c-q)q + (1-\eta\tau_E)V_M + \eta\tau_E V_2}{1+r}, \tag{6.10}$$

where

$$V_2 = \frac{1}{r}\left(\frac{a-c}{3}\right)^2 \tag{6.11}$$

is the expected present-discounted value of a Cournot duopolist in the market.[14]

The first term on the right in (6.10) is the income received by the monopolist at the end of the period, appropriately discounted. At the start of the next period, one of two events occurs. With probability $(1 - \tau_E\eta)$, entry does not occur, and the incumbent's value from that point forward is V_M. This explains the second term in the numerator on the right. With probability $\tau_E\eta$, entry does occur, and from that point forward the incumbent earns Cournot duopoly profit in each period, yielding present value V_2. This explains the third term in the numerator on the right.

[14] Assume also that entry cost K is greater than the noncooperative equilibrium value of a Cournot triopolist, so that at most one episode of entry would take place.

Combining terms, the incumbent's present discounted value is

$$V_m = V_2 + \frac{(a-c-q)q - \pi_2}{r + \eta\tau_E} \tag{6.12}$$

$$= V_2 + \frac{\pi_0 - \pi_2 - (q-q_0)^2}{r + \eta\tau_E} \tag{6.13}$$

$$= V_2 + \frac{\Delta - (q-q_0)^2}{r + \eta\tau_E}, \tag{6.14}$$

writing

$$\Delta = \pi_0 - \pi_2 \tag{6.15}$$

for the difference between monopoly and duopoly profit.

The expected present discounted value of the incumbent exceeds the expected present discounted value of a duopolist by a term that is proportional to the excess of the monopolist's single period payoff over the single period payoff of a duopolist. The modified discount factor that appears in the final term on the right includes the endogenous probability that entry occurs.

Let

$$p_B = p_0 + \alpha - \left[\sqrt{\Delta + \left(\frac{2\alpha r}{\eta}\right)^2} - \frac{2\alpha r}{\eta}\right] \tag{6.16}$$

$$p_C = p_0 + \alpha - \left[\sqrt{\Delta + \left(2\alpha + \frac{2\alpha r}{\eta}\right)^2} - \frac{2\alpha r}{\eta}\right] \tag{6.17}$$

(6.16) and (6.17) are the end-points of the range of threshold values p_E where the first-order condition to maximize (6.14) results in a value of τ_E that lies between 0 and 1. It is shown in the Appendix that

Theorem 2 *the relationship between threshold price p_E and the incumbent's expected-profit maximizing output q_2 is*

(a) for $a + \alpha \geq p_E \geq p_0 + \alpha$, $q_2 = q_0$;

(b1) for $p_0 + \alpha \geq p_E \geq \max(p_B, p_0 - \alpha), q_2 = q_0 + p_0 + \alpha - p_E$;

(b2) $p_0 - \alpha \geq p_E \geq p_B$, if such a range exists,

$$q_2 = \begin{cases} q_0 + p_0 + \alpha - p_E & \text{if } \; p_0 - \alpha \geq p_E \geq p_0 - \sqrt{\frac{\eta}{r+\eta}\Delta} \\ q_0 & \text{if } \; p_0 - \sqrt{\frac{\eta}{r+\eta}\Delta} \geq p_E \geq p_B \end{cases};$$

(c) for $p_B \geq p_E \geq p_C$

$$q_2 = q_0 + p_0 + \alpha + \frac{2\alpha r}{\eta} - p_E - \sqrt{\left(p_0 + \alpha + \frac{2\alpha r}{\eta} - p_E\right)^2 - \Delta}; \qquad (6.18)$$

(d) for $p_C \geq p_E$, $q_2 = q_0$.

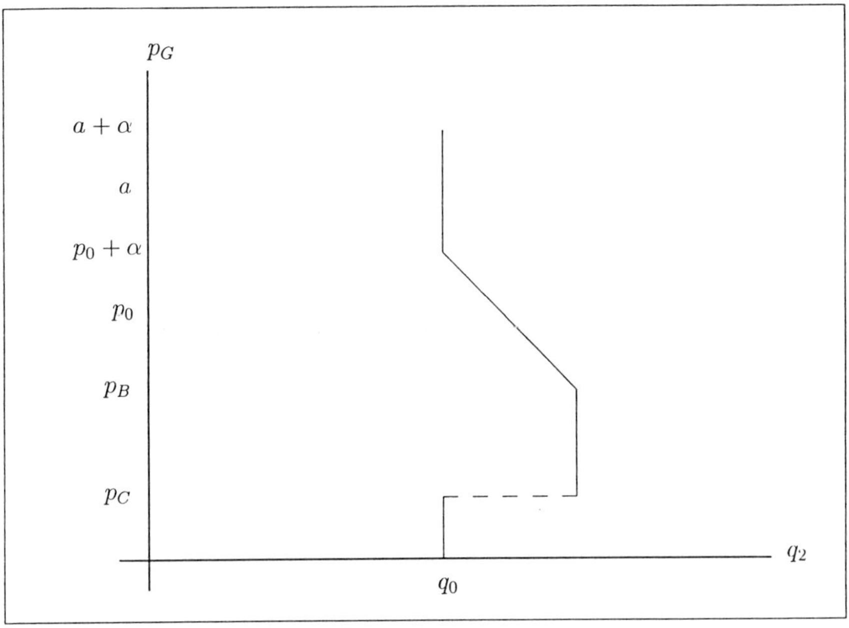

Figure 6.7: Theorem 3.1

Theorem 2 is illustrated in Figure 6.7. The threat of entry, and the resulting loss of value, induce some expansion of output above the unconstrained monopoly level. But output expansion itself implies a loss of value. If the threat of entry is to induce output expansion, the price reduction required to eliminate or reduce the probability of investigation by potential entrants cannot be too great. Otherwise, the profit-maximizing incumbent will simply produce the unconstrained monopoly output.

6.4 Competition policy with the threat of entry

6.4.1 Monopoly entry deterrence with P^2 competition policy

If an incumbent monopolist faces both the possibility of entry and the threat of antitrust enforcement, its expected present discounted value is

$$V_m = \frac{\pi_0 - (q - q_0)^2 - \tau_G \gamma F + (1 - \eta \tau_E) V_m + \eta \tau_E V_2}{1 + r}. \tag{6.19}$$

The interpretation of (6.19) is similar to that of (6.10). Current income now includes an expected antitrust fine. Future expected value is a weighted average of values if entry does not and does occur. Collecting terms, (6.19) can be rewritten

$$V_m = V_2 + \frac{\Delta - (q - q_0)^2 - \tau_G \gamma F}{r + \eta \tau_E}. \tag{6.20}$$

6.4.2 Monopoly entry deterrence with a publicity-based competition policy

The interpretation of τ_E and the entry probability η are unchanged. Now, however, let τ_G, defined as before with regard to a threshold price p_G denote the probability that the government investigates the industry, and ϕ the probability that the government issues a report detailing industry circumstances. Entry now takes place, if at all, either after the firm investigates the industry or after the government issues a report, bringing the industry to the attention of potential entrants. I assume that government and private investigation are independent events, in a probabilistic sense.

The probability of states of the world in which potential entrants make a decision about entry is[15]

$$A = \tau_E + (1 - \tau_E)\phi \tau_G. \tag{6.21}$$

[15] Equivalently, one may write

$$A = \phi \tau_G + \tau_E (1 - \phi \tau_G).$$

This is the probability that there is a government report plus the probability that there is not a government report times the probability that entrants investigate the industry.

The first term on the right is the probability that the entrant investigates the industry. The second term on the right is the probability that the entrant does not investigate the industry, the government does, and the government issues a report about the industry.

The expected value of the incumbent is

$$V_m = \frac{\pi_0 - (q - q_0)^2 + (1 - \eta A)V_m + \eta A V_2}{1 + r}$$
$$= V_2 + \frac{\Delta - (q - q_0)^2}{r + \eta A} \qquad (6.22)$$

6.4.3 Comparative market performance

To compare the impact of the $P^2$and publicity policies on market performance, I present a series of numerical examples.[16] Some parameter values are common to all the examples:

- $a = 101$, $c = 1$;
- $\alpha = 15$;
- $\pi_0 = 2500$, $\pi_2 = 1111\frac{1}{9}$;
- $r = 1/10$;
- $\phi = 1/2$;
- $\gamma F = \Delta$.

The final parameter choice is made in the interest of comparability: the expected lost profit after investigation, under a P^2 policy, equals the lost profit if entry occurs.

For these parameter values, the unconstrained monopoly output is $q_0 = 50$ and the unconstrained monopoly price is $p_0 = 1 + 50 = 51$. Duopoly output and price would be $66\frac{2}{3}$ and $34\frac{1}{3}$ respectively.

[16]Four basic cases must be considered to derive results like those of Theorems 2.1 and 3.1. One is where $q_G \leq q_E - 2\alpha$ and another is where $q_E \leq q_G - 2\alpha$. In these cases, the intervals over which $0 \leq \tau_G \leq 1$ and $0 \leq \tau_E \leq 1$ do not overlap. The remaining cases are $q_E - 2\alpha \leq q_G \leq q_E$ and $q_G - 2\alpha \leq q_E \leq q_G$, for which the intervals over which $0 \leq \tau_G \leq 1$ and $0 \leq \tau_E \leq 1$ do overlap. In each of these four cases, the incumbent's payoff function is defined differently over five segments of output space. Derivation of analytic results requires analysis of the shape of the incumbent's payoff function. Each of the four basic cases has numerous subcases, depending on values of γF, η, ϕ, and $a - c$.

Case 1: High threshold prices

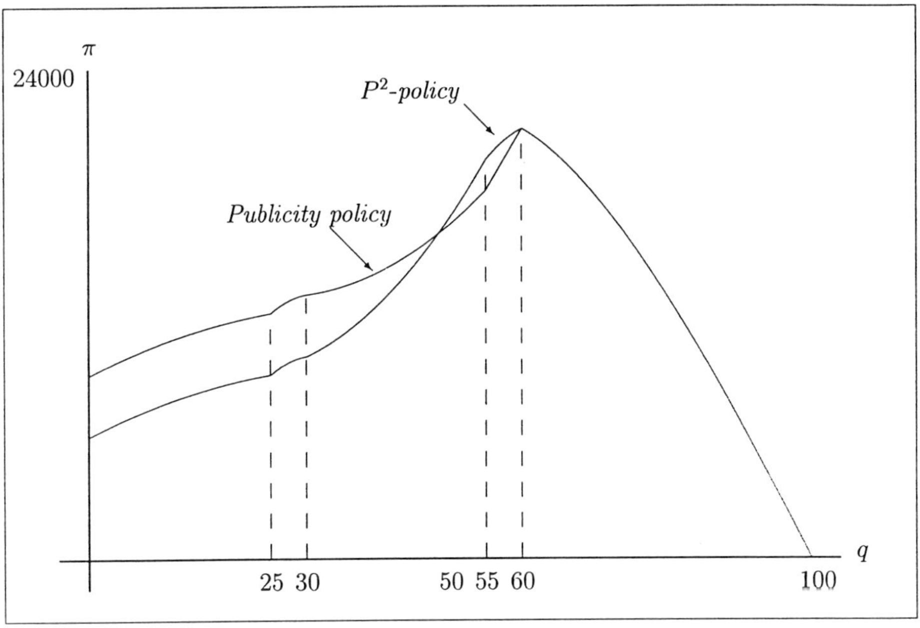

Notes: $a = 101$; $c = 1$; $\alpha = 15$; $\pi_0 = 2500$; $\gamma F = \Delta = 1388\frac{8}{9}$; $\phi = 1/2$.

Figure 6.8: $\eta = 1/2$; $p_G = 56$; $p_E = 61$.

First suppose $p_E = 61$, $p_G = 56$. Threshold prices are relatively close to the unconstrained monopoly level.

The incumbent's payoff functions under the alternative competition regimes are shown in Figure 6.8, for $\eta = 1/2$. The incumbent's value-maximizing output under either competition policy is $q = 60$, implying $p = 41$. By expanding output only slightly above the unconstrained monopoly level, the incumbent makes the probability of entry and the probability of antitrust investigation equal to zero. This output expansion improves market performance, compared with the unconstrained monopoly case.

The classic policy conundrum posed by limit pricing appears: while market performance is improved compared with the unconstrained monopoly case, market performance remains worse than in the noncooperative duopoly equilibrium of a one-shot game.

Case 2: Low threshold prices

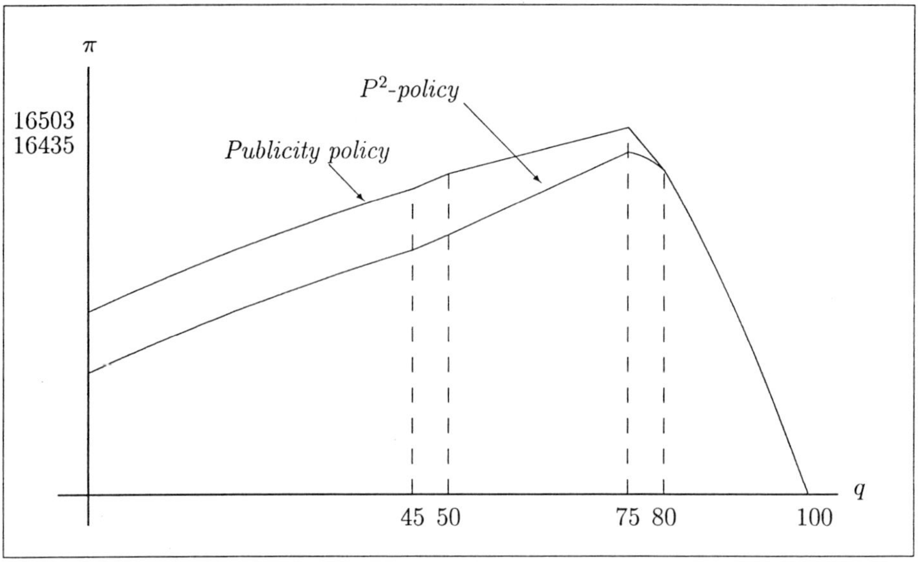

Notes: $a = 101$; $c = 1$; $\alpha = 15$; $\pi_0 = 2500$; $\gamma F = \Delta = 1388\frac{8}{9}$; $\phi = 1/2$.

Figure 6.9: $\eta = 1/2$; $p_G = 36$; $p_E = 41$.

Now keep all parameters from the previous example except the threshold prices unchanged, and let $p_E = 41$, $p_G = 36$. Both policies result in improved market performance, as shown in Figure 6.9: $q_1 = 75$ under either policy. Here $\tau_E = 0$, while $\tau_G = 1/6$, so the possibility of government intervention is not completely foreclosed. Under the publicity policy, $A = 0 + (1/2)(1/6) = 1/12$. ηA, the probability of states of the world in which entry occurs, is $1/24 = 0.042$.

Case 3: Low entry probability

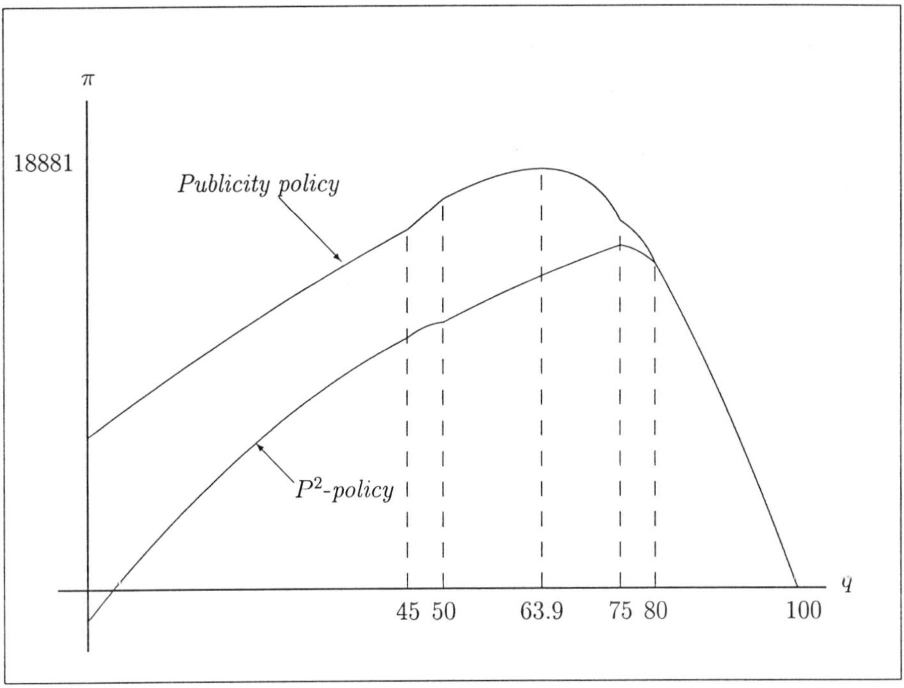

Notes: $a = 101$; $c = 1$; $\alpha = 15$; $\pi_0 = 2500$; $\gamma F = \Delta = 1388\frac{8}{9}$; $\phi = 1/2$.

Figure 6.10: $\eta = 1/10$; $p_G = 36$; $p_E = 41$.

What the first two examples do not bring out is the sensitivity of publicity policy to the probability of entry. Keep all parameters of the previous case fixed, but let $\eta = 1/10$. The resulting value functions are shown in Figure 6.10. The P^2 policy remains almost as effective as before: $q_1 = 75$, $p_1 = 26$; the probability of entry is driven to zero, and the probability of antitrust investigation is 1/6. Under a publicity policy, $q_1 = 63.9$, $p_1 = 37.1$. In this case, $\tau_E = 0.37$, $\tau_G = 0.536$, and $A = 0.539$. ηA equals 0.054. When the probability of entry is very low, a publicity policy is ineffective.

6.5 Conclusion

The relative efficiency of punishment-based and publicity-based policies depends on the relative impact of actual and potential competition on market performance. For a publicity-based competition policy to be effective, incumbents must believe that entry is a genuine possibility. In terms of the model developed here, neither η nor market size $(a - c)$ can be too small, and entry cost K cannot be too large.

If the market will support only a limited number of firms in noncooperative equilibrium, then a publicity policy is unlikely to be effective. Paradoxically, it is small economies like Denmark that should rely on a punishment-based policy, while continent-wide economies like the EU and the US might in principle find a publicity policy effective. This point is not without importance from the point of view of an eventual World Competition Agency, any manifestation of which is unlikely to be endowed with punishment powers in its initial form.

At the same time, for a punishment-based policy to be effective, incumbents must believe that there is a realistic possibility of a fine. If the political establishment lacks the will to support a credible prohibition-and-punishment policy, then a publicity policy may be better than nothing.

Considering the relative impact of P^2 and publicity policies on market performance, publicity should be expected to chill rivalry among actual competitors, while increasing the impact of potential competition. If there are a relatively large number of actual competitors, publicity will be a less effective competition policy than prohibition and punishment. But if there is only a small number of actual competitors, the threat of publicity will increase the power of potential competition, and the reality of publicity may induce entry.

Finally, one should not lose sight of the fact that P^2 and publicity policies are not mutually exclusive. Publicity could be the first stage of a policy that included the possibility of punishment in a second stage if publicity did not result in improved market performance. Further, enforcement proceedings initiated under a P^2 policy would as a practical matter generate publicity that would come to the attention of potential entrants. In this sense, a P^2 policy is also a publicity policy, while the converse is not the case.[17]

[17] Allowing for this in the formal model, (6.19) becomes

$$V_m = \frac{\pi_0 - (q - q_0)^2 - \tau_G \gamma F + (1 - \eta A) V_m + \eta A V_2}{1 + r}.$$

6.6 Appendix

6.6.1 Proof of Theorem 2.1

The payoff function

For notational convenience, define

$$q_G = a + \alpha - p_G. \tag{6.23}$$

The payoff function has three regions.
For

$$0 \leq q \leq q_G - 2\alpha, \tag{6.24}$$

antitrust investigation is certain. The payoff function is

$$\pi = (a - c - q)q - \gamma F = \pi_0 - (q - q_0)^2 - \gamma F. \tag{6.25}$$

For

$$q_G - 2\alpha \leq q \leq q_G, \tag{6.26}$$

τ_G lies between zero and one. The payoff function is

$$\pi = (a - c - q)q - \frac{q_G - q}{2\alpha}\gamma F$$

$$= \pi_0 - \left(q_G - q_0 - \frac{\gamma F}{8\alpha}\right)\frac{\gamma F}{2\alpha} - \left(q - q_0 - \frac{\gamma F}{4\alpha}\right)^2 \tag{6.27}$$

For

$$q_G \leq q, \tag{6.28}$$

$\tau_G = 0$ and the payoff function is

$$\pi = (a - c - q)q = \pi_0 - (q - q_0)^2 \tag{6.29}$$

For purposes of the proof, one must consider three ranges for the expected penalty:

$$= \frac{\pi_0 - (q - q_0)^2 - \tau_G \gamma F + \eta A V_2}{r + \eta A}.$$

(A) $0 \leq \gamma F \leq 8\alpha^2$;

(B) $8\alpha^2 \leq \gamma F \leq 16\alpha^2$;

(C) $16\alpha^2 \leq \gamma F$.

Cases (A) and (B) correspond to case (a) in the statement of the theorem. The results for cases (A) and (B) are the same, although details of the proof differ. Case (C) corresponds to case (b) of the theorem.

(A) $0 \leq \gamma F \leq 8\alpha^2$

Note that in case (A)

$$\frac{\gamma F}{4\alpha} \leq 2\alpha \tag{6.30}$$

(A1) $q_G \leq q_0$.

q_0 is the global maximum of the unconstrained payoff function, and in case (A1) the payoff function and the unconstrained payoff function coincide. Greater outputs mean lower profit; higher outputs mean lower profit and may involve the possibility of antitrust fines. $q_1 = q_0$ is the global maximum in case (A1).

(A2) $q_0 \leq q_G \leq q_0 + (\gamma F/4\alpha)$.

(6.30) and $q_G \leq q_0 + (\gamma F/4\alpha)$ imply $q_G \leq q_0 + 2\alpha$, so $q_G - 2\alpha \leq q_0$.

Over the output range $0 \leq q \leq q_G - 2\alpha$, the payoff function (6.25) is a parabola that slopes upward to the right, with local maximum at $q = q_G - 2\alpha$. Since $q_G \leq q_0 + (\gamma F/4\alpha)$, the payoff function (6.27) is a parabola that slopes upward to the right, with local maximum on $q_G - 2\alpha \leq q \leq q_G$ at $q = q_G$. For $q_G \leq q$, the payoff function (6.29) is a parabola that slopes downward to the right,with local maximum $q = q_G$. The global maximum of the payoff function in case (A2) is at $q = q_G$.

(A3) $q_0 + (\gamma F/4\alpha) \leq q_G \leq q_0 + 2\alpha$.

By inequality (6.30), such a region exists.

By subtraction, $q_G - 2\alpha \leq q_0$, so $q_G - 2\alpha \leq q_0 \leq q_0 + (\gamma F/4\alpha) \leq q_G$, and $q_0 + (\gamma F/4\alpha)$ lies within the range $(q_G - 2\alpha, q_G)$. Over the output range $0 \leq q \leq q_G - 2\alpha$, the payoff function (6.25) is an upward sloping parabola, with local maximum at $q = q_G - 2\alpha$. Over the output range $q_G - 2\alpha \leq q \leq q_G$, the payoff function is (6.27), which has a local maximum at $q = q_0 + (\gamma F/4\alpha)$. Over the output range $q_G \leq q$, the payoff function (6.29) is a downward sloping parabola, with local maximum at $q = q_G$. The global maximum in case (A3) is $q = q_0 + (\gamma F/4\alpha)$.

(A4) $q_0 + 2\alpha \leq q_G \leq q_0 + (\gamma F/4\alpha) + 2\alpha$.

By subtraction, $q_0 \leq q_G - 2\alpha \leq q_0 + (\gamma F/4\alpha)$. Over the output range $0 \leq q \leq q_G - 2\alpha$, the payoff function (6.25) is a parabola with local maximum at $q = q_0$. The firm's payoff at $q = q_0$ is

$$\pi(q_0) = \pi_0 - \gamma F. \tag{6.31}$$

Over the output range $q_G - 2\alpha \leq q \leq q_G$, the payoff function is (6.27), which has a local maximum within this range at output level $q_0 + (\gamma F/4\alpha)$. The firm's payoff at this output level is

$$\pi\left(q_0 + \frac{\gamma F}{4\alpha}\right) = \pi_0 - \left(q_G - q_0 - \frac{\gamma F}{8\alpha}\right)\frac{\gamma F}{2\alpha} \tag{6.32}$$

Comparing (6.31) and (6.32), the global maximum is at output level $q_0 + (\gamma F/4\alpha)$ if

$$q_G \leq q_0 + \frac{\gamma F}{8\alpha} + 2\alpha; \tag{6.33}$$

otherwise, the global maximum is at $q = q_0$.

(A5) $q_0 + (\gamma F/4\alpha) + 2\alpha \leq q_G$.

By subtraction, $q_0 + (\gamma F/4\alpha) \leq q_G - 2\alpha$. Over the output range $0 \leq q \leq q_G - 2\alpha$, the payoff function (6.25) is a parabola with local maximum at $q = q_0$. Over the output range $q_G - 2\alpha \leq q \leq q_G$ the payoff function (6.27) is a downward sloping parabola with local maximum at $q = q_G - 2\alpha$. Over the output range $q_G \leq q$ the payoff function (6.29) is a downward sloping parabola with local maximum at $q = q_G$. The global maximum in case (A5) is at $q = q_0$.

Results for case (A) may be summarized as

(a1) for $q_G \leq q_0$, $q_1 = q_0$;

(a2) for $q_0 \leq q_G \leq q_0 + (\gamma F/4\alpha)$, $q_1 = q_G$;

(a3) for $q_0 + (\gamma F/4\alpha) \leq q_G \leq q_0 + (\gamma F/8\alpha) + 2\alpha$, $q_1 = q_0 + (\gamma F/4\alpha)$;

(a4) for $q_0 + (\gamma F/8\alpha) + 2\alpha \leq q_G$, $q_1 = q_0$.

If these results are rewritten in terms of p_G and p_0, one obtains the statement of case (a) given in the text.

(B) $8\alpha^2 \leq \gamma F \leq 16\alpha^2$

In case (B)

$$2\alpha \leq \frac{\gamma F}{4\alpha} \leq 4\alpha \tag{6.34}$$

(B1) $q_G \leq q_0$. The arguments given for case (A1) establish that the global maximum is at $q = q_0$.

(B2) For $q_0 \leq q_G \leq q_0 + 2\alpha$.

By subtraction, $q_G - 2\alpha \leq q_0$. This and (6.34) establish that in case (B2)

$$q_G - 2\alpha \leq q_0 \leq q_G \leq q_0 + 2\alpha \leq q_0 + \frac{\gamma F}{4\alpha} \leq q_0 + 4\alpha. \tag{6.35}$$

Over the output range $0 \leq q \leq q_G - 2\alpha$, the payoff function (6.25) is a parabola that slopes upward to the right, with local maximum at $q = q_G - 2\alpha$. Since $q_G \leq q_0 + (\gamma F/4\alpha)$, the payoff function (6.27) is a parabola that slopes upward to the right, with local maximum on $q_G - 2\alpha \leq q \leq q_G$ at $q = q_G$. For $q_G \leq q$, the payoff function (6.29) is a parabola that slopes downward to the right,with local maximum $q = q_G$. The global maximum of the payoff function in case (B2) is at $q = q_G$.

(B3) $q_0 + 2\alpha \leq q_G \leq q_0 + (\gamma F/4\alpha)$.

By subtraction, $q_0 \leq q_G - 2\alpha$; there is one local maximum at $q = q_0$, with payoff (6.31), and another at $q = q_G$, with payoff

$$\pi(q_G) = \pi_0 - (q_G - q_0)^2. \tag{6.36}$$

Comparing payoffs, the global maximum is at q_G if

$$q_G \leq q_0 + \sqrt{\gamma F}. \tag{6.37}$$

This condition is met if

$$q_0 + \frac{\gamma F}{4\alpha} \leq q_0 + \sqrt{\gamma F} \tag{6.38}$$

or

$$\gamma F \leq 16\alpha^2 \tag{6.39}$$

This condition is always met in case (B3), so the global maximum value in case (B3) is at $q = q_G$.

(B4) $q_0 + (\gamma F/4\alpha) \leq q_G \leq q_0 + (\gamma F/4\alpha) + 2\alpha$.

By subtraction, $q_0 \leq q_0 + (\gamma F/4\alpha) - 2\alpha \leq q_0 + (\gamma F/4\alpha) \leq q_G$. The arguments of case (A4) apply, with the same result.

(B5) $q_0 + (\gamma F/4\alpha) + 2\alpha \leq q_G$.

The arguments of case (A5) apply, with the same result.

The results for case (B) are the same as those for case (A).

(C) $16\alpha^2 \leq \gamma F$

In case (C),

$$4\alpha \leq \frac{\gamma F}{4\alpha} \tag{6.40}$$

and

$$4\alpha \leq \sqrt{\gamma F}. \tag{6.41}$$

(C1) For $q_G \leq q_0$, $q_1 = q_0$. See discussion of case (A1).

(C2) $q_0 \leq q_G \leq q_0 + 2\alpha$.

By subtraction, $q_G - 2\alpha \leq q_0$; hence $q_G - 2\alpha \leq q_0 \leq q_G \leq q_0 + 2\alpha \leq q_0 + 4\alpha \leq q_0 + (\gamma F/2\alpha)$. The payoff function is an upward sloping parabola over output range $0 \leq q \leq q_G - 2\alpha$, with local maximum at $q = q_G - 2\alpha$. The payoff function over output range $q_G - 2\alpha \leq q \leq q_G$ is also an upward sloping parabola, with local maximum at $q = q_G$. The payoff function is a downward sloping parabola over the range $q = q_G$, with local maximum at $q = q_G$. The global maximum of the payoff function in case (C2) is at $q = q_G$.

(C3) $q_0 + 2\alpha \leq q_G \leq q_0 + (\gamma F/4\alpha)$.

By subtraction, $q_0 \leq q_G - 2\alpha$. Hence $q_0 \leq q_G - 2\alpha \leq q_G \leq q_0 + (\gamma F/4\alpha)$. There is one local maximum at q_0, with payoff (6.31), and another at q_G, with payoff (6.36). (6.37) is the condition for the global maximum to be at q_G.

(C4) $q_0 + (\gamma F/4\alpha) \leq q_G \leq q_0 + (\gamma F/4\alpha) + 2\alpha$.

Here $q_0 \leq q_0 + (\gamma F/4\alpha) - 2\alpha \leq q_G - 2\alpha \leq q_0 + (\gamma F/4\alpha) \leq q_G$. There is one local maximum at q_0, with payoff (6.31), and another at $q_0 + (\gamma F/4\alpha)$, with payoff (6.32). The condition for the global maximum to be at $q_0 + (\gamma F/4\alpha)$ is (6.33), but this condition is never met in case (C). The global maximum of the payoff function in case (C4) is $q = q_G$.

(C5) $q_0 + (\gamma F/4\alpha) + 2\alpha \leq q_G$.

The arguments of case (A5) apply, with the same result.

The results for case (C) may be summarized as

(c1) for $0 \leq q_G \leq q_0$, $q_1 = q_0$;

(c2) for $q_0 \leq q_G \leq q_0 + \sqrt{\gamma F}$, $q_1 = q_G$;
(c3) $q_0 + \sqrt{\gamma F} \leq q_G$, $q_1 = q_G$.
If these results are rewritten in terms of p_G and p_0, one obtains the statement of case (b) given in the text.

□

6.6.2 Proof of Theorem 3.1

Let

$$q_E = a + \alpha - p_E. \tag{6.42}$$

Written in terms of q_E, the root (6.18) is

$$q_2 = q_E + \frac{2\alpha r}{\eta} - \sqrt{\left(\frac{2\alpha r}{\eta} + q_E - q_0\right)^2 - \Delta}. \tag{6.43}$$

For notational convenience, write

$$q_B = q_0 - \frac{2\alpha r}{\eta} + \sqrt{\Delta + \left(\frac{2\alpha r}{\eta}\right)^2} \tag{6.44}$$

$$q_C = q_0 - \frac{2\alpha r}{\eta} + \sqrt{\Delta + \left(2\alpha + \frac{2\alpha r}{\eta}\right)^2}, \tag{6.45}$$

so that

$$p_B = a + \alpha - q_B \tag{6.46}$$

and

$$p_C = a + \alpha - q_B. \tag{6.47}$$

The value function

The proof involves the following properties of the value function when $0 \leq \tau_E \leq 1$ (for outputs in the range $q_E - 2\alpha \leq q \leq q_E$):
(1) $q_0 \leq q_E \leq q_B$ implies $dV_m/dq \geq 0$ for $q_E - 2\alpha \leq q \leq q_E$;
(2) $q_B \leq q_E \leq q_C$ implies V_m has a local maximum within the range $q_E - 2\alpha \leq q \leq q_E$;
(3) $q_C \leq q_E$ implies $dV_m/dq \leq 0$ for $q_E - 2\alpha \leq q \leq q_E$.

Over the output range $q_E - 2\alpha \leq q \leq q_E$ the value function is

$$V_m = V_2 + \frac{2\alpha}{\eta} \frac{\Delta - (q - q_0)^2}{\frac{2\alpha r}{\eta} + q_E - q}, \tag{6.48}$$

with slope

$$\frac{dV_m}{dq} = \frac{2\alpha}{\eta} \frac{\left(\frac{2\alpha r}{\eta} + q_E - q\right)^2 - \left(\frac{2\alpha r}{\eta} + q_E - q_0\right)^2 + \Delta}{\left(\frac{2\alpha r}{\eta} + q_E - q\right)^2}. \tag{6.49}$$

The proof of (1) falls in two parts.

For the root (6.43) to be valid, two conditions must be met. First the discriminant

$$DISC = \left(\frac{2\alpha r}{\eta} + q_E - q_0\right)^2 - \Delta \tag{6.50}$$

must be nonnegative. This condition is met if[18]

$$q_E \geq q_0 - \frac{2\alpha r}{\eta} + \sqrt{\Delta} = q_A. \tag{6.51}$$

If $q_E < q_A$, then $DISC < 0$ and the slope of the value function is positive:

$$\frac{dV_m}{dq} = \frac{2\alpha}{\eta} \frac{\left(\frac{2\alpha r}{\eta} + q_E - q\right)^2 - DISC}{\left(\frac{2\alpha r}{\eta} + q_E - q\right)^2} > 0. \tag{6.52}$$

The other condition that must be met for the root (6.43) to be valid is that the implied value of τ_E lie between 0 and 1. This condition is met for[19]

$$q_B \leq q_E \leq q_C. \tag{6.53}$$

Consider now q_E in the interval $q_A \leq q_E \leq q_B$, from which

$$q_0 - \frac{2\alpha r}{\eta} + \sqrt{\Delta} \leq q_E \leq q_0 - \frac{2\alpha r}{\eta} + \sqrt{\Delta + \left(\frac{2\alpha r}{\eta}\right)^2}$$

[18] There is another output range over which $DISC$ is nonnegative, but this is ruled out by the assumption that $q_E \geq q_0$.

[19] There is another output range over which τ_E lies between 0 and 1, but this is ruled out by the assumption that $q_E \geq q_0$.

$$\sqrt{\Delta} \leq q_E - q_0 + \frac{2\alpha r}{\eta} \leq \sqrt{\Delta + \left(\frac{2\alpha r}{\eta}\right)^2}$$

$$\Delta \leq \left(q_E - q_0 + \frac{2\alpha r}{\eta}\right)^2 \leq \Delta + \left(\frac{2\alpha r}{\eta}\right)^2$$

$$-\Delta \geq -\left(q_E - q_0 + \frac{2\alpha r}{\eta}\right)^2 \geq -\Delta - \left(\frac{2\alpha r}{\eta}\right)^2$$

$$0 \geq -\left(q_E - q_0 + \frac{2\alpha r}{\eta}\right)^2 + \Delta \geq -\left(\frac{2\alpha r}{\eta}\right)^2 \tag{6.54}$$

Now since $q_E - 2\alpha \leq q \leq q_E$ we have

$$-2\alpha \leq q - q_E \leq 0$$

$$-\left(2\alpha + \frac{2\alpha r}{\eta}\right) \leq q - q_E - \frac{2\alpha r}{\eta} \leq -\frac{2\alpha r}{\eta}$$

$$\left(2\alpha + \frac{2\alpha r}{\eta}\right)^2 \geq \left(\frac{2\alpha r}{\eta} + q_E - q\right)^2 \geq \left(\frac{2\alpha r}{\eta}\right)^2 \tag{6.55}$$

Adding (6.54) and (6.55) gives

$$\left(2\alpha + \frac{2\alpha r}{\eta}\right)^2 \geq \left(\frac{2\alpha r}{\eta} + q_E - q\right)^2 - \left(q_E - q_0 + \frac{2\alpha r}{\eta}\right)^2 + \Delta \geq 0, \tag{6.56}$$

so the slope of the value function is nonnegative. This establishes (1).

(2) This follows by substituting the root (6.43) into

$$0 \leq \frac{q_E - q}{2\alpha} \leq 1. \tag{6.57}$$

(3) $q_C \leq q_E$. From

$$q_0 - \frac{2\alpha r}{\eta} + \sqrt{\Delta + \left(2\alpha + \frac{2\alpha r}{\eta}\right)^2} \leq q_E, \tag{6.58}$$

we obtain

$$\Delta + \left(2\alpha + \frac{2\alpha r}{\eta}\right)^2 \leq \left(q_E + \frac{2\alpha r}{\eta} - q_0\right)^2$$

$$-\left(2\alpha+\frac{2\alpha r}{\eta}\right)^2 \geq -\left(q_E+\frac{2\alpha r}{\eta}-q_0\right)^2+\Delta \tag{6.59}$$

We are interested in the slope of the value function over the interval

$$q_E - 2\alpha \leq q \leq q_E$$

$$-2\alpha \leq q - q_E \leq 0$$

$$-\left(2\alpha+\frac{2\alpha}{\eta}\right) \leq q - q_E - \frac{2\alpha}{\eta} \leq -\frac{2\alpha}{\eta}$$

$$\left(2\alpha+\frac{2\alpha}{\eta}\right)^2 \geq \left(\frac{2\alpha r}{\eta}+q_E-q\right)^2 \geq \left(\frac{2\alpha}{\eta}\right)^2 \tag{6.60}$$

Add (6.59) and (6.60) to obtain

$$0 \geq \left(\frac{2\alpha r}{\eta}+q_E-q\right)^2 - \left(\frac{2\alpha r}{\eta}+q_E-q_0\right)^2+(\Delta), \tag{6.61}$$

so the slope of the value function is negative.

Now return to the proof of the theorem proper.

(A) $0 \leq q_E \leq q_0$.

q_0 is the global maximum of the unconstrained value function, and in case (a) the value function and the unconstrained value function coincide over the region that includes output q_0. Greater outputs mean lower profit; higher outputs mean lower profit and may involve the possibility of entry. $q_2 = q_0$ is the global maximum in case (a).

(B) $q_0 \leq q_E \leq q_B$.

Remark: the condition for

$$q_B \geq q_0 + 2\alpha \tag{6.62}$$

is

$$\left(\frac{a-c}{2\alpha}\right)^2 \geq \frac{6}{5}\left(1+2\frac{r}{\eta}\right) \tag{6.63}$$

This will be satisfied unless α is large relative to $a-c$.

First consider $q_0 \leq q_E \leq \min(q_0+2\alpha, q_B)$.

This implies $q_E - 2\alpha \leq q_0$. Over the output range $0 \leq 1 \leq q_E - 2\alpha$, the value function is a parabola that slopes upward to the right, with local maximum at $q = q_E - 2\alpha$. By property (1) of the value function, it is upward sloping over the intermediate output range $q_E - 2\alpha \leq q \leq q_E$, with local maximum at $q = q_E$. For $q_E \leq q$ the value function is a downward sloping parabola, also with local maximum at $q = q_E$.

Now consider $q_0 + 2\alpha \leq q_E \leq q_B$, if this range exists. Here $q_0 \leq q_E - 2\alpha$; the value function has one local maximum at $q = q_0$ in the output range $q_0 \leq q_E - 2\alpha$, yielding value

$$V_m(q_0) = V_2 + \frac{\Delta}{r+\eta}, \tag{6.64}$$

and another (by the arguments given for case (b)) at $q = q_E$, yielding value

$$V_m(q_E) = V_2 + \frac{\Delta - (q_E - q_0)^2}{r}. \tag{6.65}$$

Comparing (6.64) and (6.65), the condition for the global maximum to be at q_E is

$$q_E \leq q_0 + \sqrt{\frac{\eta}{r+\eta}\Delta} \tag{6.66}$$

Analysis shows that q_B may be greater or less than the right-hand side of inequality (6.66). Hence if the range $q_0 + 2\alpha \leq q_E \leq q_B$ exists,

$$q_2 = \begin{cases} q_E & q_E \leq q_0 + \sqrt{\frac{\eta}{r+\eta}\Delta} \\ q_0 & q_E \geq q_0 + \sqrt{\frac{\eta}{r+\eta}\Delta} \end{cases} \tag{6.67}$$

(C) $q_B \leq q_E \leq q_C$

The global maximum is found by setting (6.49) equal to zero, yielding the root (6.43).

(D) $q_C \leq q_E$, $q_2 = q_0$

There is a local maximum at $q = q_0$ over the output range $q_0 \leq q \leq q_E - 2\alpha$. By property (3) the value function is downward sloping over the intermediate output range $q_E - 2\alpha \leq q \leq q_E$, and the value function is a downward-sloping parabola over the right-hand output range $q_E \leq q$. Hence the global maximum is at $q = q_0$.

Rewriting these results in terms of p_E and p_0 gives Theorem 3.1.

6.7 References

Albæk, Svend, Møllgaard, Peter, and Overgaard P. B. "Law-assisted collusion? The transparency principle of the Danish Competition Act," *European Competition Law Review* Volume 17, Number 6, 1996a, pp. 339-343.

— "The Danish Competition Act and barriers to entry," October 1996b.

Bain, Joe S. "A Note on Pricing in Monopoly and Oligopoly," *American Economic Review* Volume 39, Number 1, March 1949b, pp. 448-469.

Clark, J. M. "Toward a Concept of Workable Competition," *American Economic Review* Volume 30, 1940, pp. 241-56.

Dennison, Jeannie Anne Godfrey *The reaction to the growth of trusts and industrial combinations in Britain, 1988–1921.* Ph. D. dissertation, Birkbeck College, University of London, 1980.

Dixit, Avinash K. and Pindyck, Robert S. *Investment Under Uncertainty.* Princeton: Princeton University Press, 1994.

Dorman, Roderick G. "The case for compensation: why compensatory components are required for efficient antitrust enforcement," *Georgetown Law Journal* Volume 66, Number 5, June 1980, pp. 1113–20.

Friedman, James W. "On entry preventing behavior and limit price models of entry," in S. J. Brams and Schwodiauer, G., editors, *Applied Game Theory.* Wurzburg-Wien: Physica-Verlag, 1979, pp. 236-53.

Geroski, Paul A. *Market dynamics and entry.* Oxford: Basil Blackwell Ltd., 1991.

— "What do we know about entry," *International Journal of Industrial Organization* Volume 13, Number 4, 1995, pp. 421-44.

Geroski, Paul A. and Schwalbach, Joachim *Market dynamics and entry: an international comparison.* Oxford: Basil Blackwell Ltd., 1991.

Hilton, John "A study of trade organisations and combinations in the U.K.," appended to The Ministry of Reconstruction, *Final Report on Industrial Policy after the War*, 1918.

Holt, Charles A. "Industrial organization: a survey of laboratory research," in Kagel, John H. and Roth, Alvin E., editors, *The handbook of experimental economics.* Princeton: Princeton University Press, 1995, pp. 349-443.

Industrial Commission. *Preliminary Report of the Industrial Commission on Trusts and Industrial Combinations.* Washington: Government Printing Office, 1900.

Jenks, Jeremiah W. *The Trust Problem.* New York: McClure, Philips, 1900.

Kaldor, Nicolas "Market Imperfection and Excess Capacity," *Economica* Volume 2, 1935, pp. 33-50.

Letwin, William *Law and Economic Policy in America.* Westwood, Connecticut: Greenwood Press, Publishers, 1965.

Marshall, Alfred *Industry and Trade.* London: Macmillan and Co. Limited, Fourth edition, 1923.

Martin, Stephen "Oligopoly limit pricing: strategic substitutes, strategic complements," *International Journal of Industrial Organization*, Volume 13, Number 1, March 1995, pp. 41-65.

Milgrom, Paul and Roberts, John "Limit pricing and entry under incomplete information," *Econometrica* Volume 50, Number 2, March 1982, pp. 443-66.

Modigliani, Franco "New Developments on the Oligopoly Front," *Journal of Political Economy* Volume 66, Number 3, June 1958, pp. 215-32.

OECD *Competition Policy in OECD Countries.* 1996.

Posner, Richard A. *Antitrust Law: An Economic Perspective.* Chicago: The University of Chicago Press, 1976.

Scherer, F. M. "Sunlight and sunset at the Federal Trade Commission," *Administrative Law Review* Volume 42, Fall 1990, pp. 461–87, reprinted in Scherer, F. M., editor, *Monopoly and Competition Policy.* Aldershot: Edward Elgar Publishing Limited, 1993.

Schwartz, Warren F. "An overview of the economics of law enforcement," *Georgetown Law Journal* Volume 66, Number 5, June 1980, pp. 1075–102.

Shughart, William F. II "Monopoly and the Problem of the Economists," *Managerial and Decision Economics* Volume 17, Number 2, March-April 1996, pages 217-30.

Thorelli, Hans B. *The Federal Antitrust Policy.* Stockholm: Akademisk Avhandling, 1954.

Wilson, Woodrow "Trusts and monopolies," special address to Congress, January 20, 1914, in *The Public Papers of Woodrow Wilson.* Baker, Ray S. and Dodd, William E., editors. 4 volumes. New York: Harper Brothers, 1925, 1926, Volume 1, pp. 81-88.

Competition Policies in Europe - S. Martin (Editor)

Chapter 7

Vertical Restraints in German Antitrust Law

Ulrich Kamecke

7.1 Introduction

It is not easy to date the beginning of modern antitrust policy in Europe. Some national antitrust laws were enacted immediately after World War II, but the only serious enforcement effort at this time was the reorganization of German industry. So one may consider it as a new beginning when in 1956 and 1957 within two years three major antitrust laws, the British *Restrictive Trade Practices Act*, the German *Gesetz gegen Wettbewerbsbeschränkungen (GWB)*, and the European *Treaty of Rome*, were not only enacted but also enforced by new active antitrust bureaucracies. Since then Europe has experienced a rapid change of antitrust policy on the Community level as well as in the member states. Most national laws have been modified several times and the European Community has established a large number of regulations to adapt the interpretation of the Articles 85–90 to the needs of the antitrust jurisdiction.

Today the European antitrust law has three instruments: a relatively new merger control, a well-established control of an abusive exercise of market power, and a prohibition of agreements which restrict competition (with a large and sometimes complicated system of exceptions). These rules have evolved as a compromise between the opinions governing antitrust policy in the member states. At the same time the different national approaches have (at least formally) been converging to the European standard over the last 40 years. Most member states introduced or amended their antitrust laws so that they harmonize with the European rules. In some countries such as Italy the legislature went as far as to introduce antitrust laws which are almost identical with the corresponding European articles. Others such as Germany have so far been satisfied with minor modifications of their law when it became apparent that the European and the national rules were contradictory. A third group including The Netherlands turned to a more active enforcement of existing antitrust rules. And in many member states including Germany and Great Britain there is an ongoing debate on the necessity to further harmonize national and European rules.

In the German law we find instruments similar to those of the EC, with some important differences. The German merger control and the control of an abusive exercise of market power are in principle very similar to those of the EC even though they can differ considerably in practice . For merger control the similarity is readily explained by the German influence on the debate about the features of the European merger control. For the definition of an abusive exercise of market power there was no direct influence, because the Treaty of Rome and the GWB were discussed and enacted simultaneously. But since the views on this instrument were never very controversial it is not surprising that both the German and the European approach developed very similarly.

For the third instrument, the prohibition of agreements which restrict competition, the German and the European approaches differ considerably. The distinctive features are easily explained by the different intentions of the European and the German legislators. In Europe the first Member States wanted to eliminate national barriers to trade and they were afraid that firms would try to replace the lost legal protection of their governments by private agreements. It is clear that such protection can be implemented with the help of the market sharing or home market rules practiced by the chemical industry[1] as well as the exclusive territories rules or the prohibition of reimports[2] practiced by some durable goods industries. It is therefore natural that the Treaty of Rome did not distinguish between horizontal and

[1] e.g. Soda-ash/Solvay or Polypropylen, see Bellamy and Child [1993], 4-064 or 4-007 ff.

[2] e.g. Consten/Grundig, see Bellamy and Child [1993], p.7-017.

vertical restrictive agreements, but implemented a general prohibition with the possibility to grant exemptions for both.

In Germany, on the other hand, the major objective after World War II was to eliminate formal cartel agreements, because such long term arrangements had been used by the Nazis to implement their war time production. The GWB therefore originally prohibited only formal horizontal agreements in §1 and it allowed only a few well-defined exceptions. A prohibition of concerted practices was not introduced until the dyestuff verdicts of the EuGH[3] and the BGH[4] made clear that the prohibition of restrictive contracts alone was contradictory to the European rules.

Vertical agreements were considered as much less problematic by the German legislature. When the law was created these contracts were seen as a potential source for unwanted market power, but this danger was thought to be comparable to the problems of an abusive exercise of monopoly power rather than to the danger of a formal cartel agreement. As a consequence the legislature imposed a weak abuse control for such contracts which gave the cartel authority the right to prohibit restrictive vertical restraints after the careful application of a rule of reason. To complicate matters the German legislature decided in 1973 that resale price maintenance was no longer acceptable and introduced a strict prohibition of all restraints which regulate the content of a contract with third parties. Moreover, in the latest attempt to harmonize the German and the European antitrust rules in 1989 it authorized the German cartel authorities to enforce the European antitrust rules, which are in some cases contradictory to the German approach, in Germany.

If one wants to compare the national and the EC antitrust policies an introduction to the German policy towards vertical restraints is therefore both a complicated and an important task. It is important not because it is a "hot topic" for the German cartel authority — I will rather demonstrate below that the Bundeskartellamt spends only a minor fraction of its resources on such matters — but because it is the part of antitrust law where the German and the European approaches diverge most, and where both systems are considered to be unsatisfactory by the politicians. And it is complicated because we have to present several ill-structured parts of the German antitrust law, before it is possible to get a rough idea on how this policy works.

The paper is organized as follows. In section 2 I will begin with the pro-

[3]WuW/E EWG/MUV pp. 273 ff.
[4]WuW/E BGH pp.1147 ff.

hibition of resale price maintenance (RPM) and other restraints on resale conditions in §15 GWB, because it is closest to the treatment of cartel agreements both in Germany and in Europe. After this example of the well-known German rigor in antitrust questions, I will introduce in section 3 the German abuse control of exclusive dealing, requirements, and tying agreements, demonstrating that the Germans sometimes (and not only if their banks or public utilities are concerned) deviate in the opposite direction from the European standard. In this section the major differences from the European antitrust rules will be clarified when I point out the consequences of an application of both the German and the European rules to the same case. In section 4 I will finally give a short introduction into the German control of an abusive exercise of market power, because it is not possible to understand the rules against an abuse of vertical restraints without some background information about this related topic.

Even though this short introduction to German antitrust policy towards vertical restraints concentrates on the legal perspective of the problem it is written by an economist for economists. Nevertheless, I hope that my paper summarizes the German law correctly so that a lawyer would only object to the selection and not to the content of my arguments.

7.2 Resale Price Maintenance

7.2.1 History

Before the 1973 amendment of the GWB, resale price maintenance was legal and widely used in Germany. Firms were obliged to register RPM restraints and nonbinding recommended prices with the Bundeskartellamt and so the practice is well-documented. Even Scherer[5] found it apparently quite impressive that 810 undertakings fixed the prices of 174,000 products.

A close look at Table 7.1 reveals that this crude figure exaggerates the anti-competitive impact of RPM, because almost half of the contracts were signed by 19 car producers for various repair parts. Given the complicated incentive and information problems which have to be solved in the market for car repairs these contracts are much easier to justify than RPM agreements for food or for chemical products which include mostly soap, perfumes, aftershaves and the like. But no matter how each particular figure is to be

[5] Scherer and Ross[1990], p. 550.

Industry	Number of Firms	Number of Products
All	810	174,283
Auto Repair Parts	19	84,642
Food	166	4,493
Toys, Jewelry, etc.	92	10,845
Electronics	78	2,300
Chemical Products	142	8,705

Source: Bundeskartellamt (1973).

Table 7.1: RPM in Germany

interpreted, it is quite clear that before 1973 RPM was omnipresent for German consumers.

However, it was not the effect of these contracts on competition which eventually lead to the prohibition of RPM. As in the US 30 years earlier,[6] RPM was welcomed by German politicians because it protected small shop owners against their growing competitors. In the late 1960s powerful chain stores refused to obey to the pricing rules prescribed by medium-sized manufacturers. Since the manufacturers in turn were not willing to risk their business relations over the matter, the small shops ended up being tied to high prices which were systematically undercut by the strongest competitors. This reversal of the consequences of RPM convinced politicians to introduce a prohibition of RPM.

7.2.2 The Legal Rule

The 1973 amendment of the GWB brought a major change in the attitude towards RPM, or, more precisely, towards all agreements which restrict the content of a contract with a third party. In §15 the law declares such restraints null and void, and according to §17 the cartel authorities[7] are authorized to

[6] Scherer and Ross [1990], p. 548–58.

[7] For cases of national importance this is the Federal Cartel Office (Bundeskartellamt) in Berlin, and I will write Bundeskartellamt instead of cartel authorities in the following. For cases of local importance every state has an own State Cartel Office (Landeskartellamt) which is usually a part of the state ministry of economic affairs. The decisions of these authorities are controlled by the Higher Regional Court (Oberlandesgericht), which in the case of Berlin is called Kammergericht (KG). A revision of the decision is possible at the Federal High Court (Bundesgerichtshof (BGH)).

forbid and to fine violations. This *per se* rule does not affect nonbinding recommended prices. Of course the GWB has a paragraph (§25(2)) which forbids all threats and promises meant to induce a behavior which must not be a part of a contract. There even was a case where a store selling watches at relatively low prices, Uhren-Krämer in Berlin, successfully sued the producer Seiko, which had threatened not to deliver unless Uhren-Krämer kept the nonbinding recommended prices for its watches. But usually it is difficult to prove such an allegation so that some voluntary coordination of resale prices remains possible.

7.2.3 Exceptions

There are three important exceptions to §15. In §16 the publishers of books and other printed products are allowed to use RPM in their contracts. This special treatment was an admirable lobbying success of the industry, but for an economist it is difficult to understand why the resale of books calls for a special treatment. The standard political justification for this exception claims that RPM protects small, specialized bookstores which guarantee a desired variety of the supply, but I think it is difficult to establish a logical connection between more variety and less efficient distribution channels. Telser's argument in favor of RPM[8] requires some unusual presale effort which provides a public service to the industry, and again I have difficulties to imagine a special effort necessary to sell a book which qualifies as a justification for this exception. Of course, the Bundeskartellamt has to respect this paragraph, but it has an active policy to keep the number of products falling under §16 as small as possible. It initiated several cases against publishing companies trying to impose RPM on related products like CD-Roms or computer manuals sold together with the software in question. The courts decided that the decisive criterion for this exception is the major use of the product: RPM is allowed according to §16 only if a product is made predominantly for reading. Thus it is allowed if an encyclopedia is sold on CD-Rom while it is not if a handbook is sold together with the software.

The second exception was established by the courts to protect legal agency contracts against the GWB. It is well known that there are firms that employ sales representatives and of course these firms are allowed to determine the prices of their products. But the BGH's interpretation of a commercial agent

[8]Scherer and Ross [1990], p. 551.

goes considerably beyond that of a door-to-door salesman. When the Bundeskartellamt tried to forbid Telefunken's distribution system which imposed RPM on shop owners also selling competing products for other manufacturers, the BGH[9] decided that retailers are true commercial agents if the producer bears an essential part of the resale risk — in this case the risk connected with disposition and storage of the products. But even though this ruling is considerably broader than the standard requirements imposed by the European Court of Justice[10] the requirements on the essential part of the risk turned out to be so restrictive that this form of contract remained rare.

The third exception allows RPM in certain industries, either because price setting in these industries is regulated by law such as the pharmaceutical industry or the transportation sector, or because they are exempt from §15 in the GWB such as the agricultural sector, the banking and insurance industry, exploitation corporations, and public utilities. This protection of key industries against the 'chaos and waste caused by competition' has a long tradition in Germany. So even though this third group of exceptions has little economic impact, it stands as an instructive example for a problematic feature of the whole German antitrust policy.

7.2.4 Conclusion

With §15 the German law has an unusually strict rule against RPM and other clauses which fix resale conditions in a vertical contract. Looking at the established theory of industrial organization,[11] the dichotomy between a strict prohibition of RPM on the one hand and a weak abuse control of the remaining vertical restraints on the other must seem artificial. Just like every other vertical restraint RPM may also serve as an instrument to internalize externalities between the trading partners so that the natural second best cost-benefit analysis would call for a rule of reason approach.

This contract-theoretic point of view neglects the enormous costs of enforcing a rule of reason. The German cartel authority can handle a few hundred cases a year and it has the resources for far fewer thorough case studies. This would make it impossible to eliminate thousands of the RPM agreements which existed in 1973 if the law required an analysis of every

[9] WUW/E BGH 2238 ff.

[10] Bellamy and Child [1993], p. 388–92.

[11] As presented in Tirole (1988, ch.4).

single contract. And faced with the choice between prohibiting or allowing thousands such contracts it was sensible from an antitrust point of view that the German legislature decided to eliminate RPM altogether.

7.3 Other Vertical Restraints

7.3.1 The Legal Rule

In §18 the GWB distinguishes four types of vertical agreements. Here contracts are controlled against abuse if they

(i) restrict the usage of the traded good or service;

(ii) establish an exclusive dealing obligation on either side of the market;

(iii) restrict the resale of the traded goods or services;

(iv) tie the delivery of some good or service to the sale of other unrelated goods or services.

Such contracts are not only wide-spread, they form an essential part of the distribution process in a market economy. Simple sales contracts are often not sufficient to solve the complicated incentive and information problems involved in the marketing of a product. Thus a (1) requirements or tying contract may be necessary to allocate the responsibility for a failure of a durable product efficiently, (2) exclusive dealing can internalize horizontal externalities between competing producers or retailers, and (3) selective distribution can avoid the well-known free-riding on presale efforts of discount stores. On the other hand, it is widely accepted that these types of contracts have some anticompetitive potential. In particular (4) tying practices are often difficult to defend, but an exclusive dealing obligation can constitute a serious barrier to entry into a market, particularly if a large share of the market is bound by similar agreements.

It is therefore natural to allow these vertical restraints unless they seriously restrict the competition in a market. This approach is taken by the German antitrust law which authorizes the cartel authority to control the contracts (1)-(4) against abuse. The Bundeskartellamt can take action against a vertical restraint according to §18 if one of the following three elements is satisfied:

(a) a considerable number of competitors are bound by similar agreements and restricted unfairly in their freedom to compete;

(b) entry into the market is unfairly restricted;

(c) competition in the market is hindered substantially.

The first two of these requirements formulate an explicit rule of reason. The Bundeskartellamt can prohibit a restriction only if the harm which it does to the competitors outweighs the benefit of the legitimate goals pursued by the contracting parties. This rule of reason is applied very cautiously by the German courts.[12] A contract is very likely to be legal if the contracting parties can argue convincingly that they have used the agreement systematically for a legitimate purpose in the past.[13] Only in cases where there is no legitimate goal or where the firms have not pursued the goal in question in the past does the Bundeskartellamt have a good chance to win in court. In 1987, for instance, the Bundeskartellamt prohibited a contract between the German Sport Federation (DSB) on one side and the two public television companies ARD and ZDF on the other[14] in which the DSB granted exclusive broadcasting rights for all its sports events to ARD and ZDF. This contract covered a significant part of the broadcasting rights needed to produce a sports magazine, and it therefore restricted the entry of the new private television companies which were founded in the mid-eighties in Germany. And since ARD and ZDF could not justify the exclusive dealing obligation with a legitimate goal it was possible to prohibit the contract without applying the rule of reason of §18(2)(b).

The third element (c) in §18 protects competition as an institution and not the right of individual market participants. Instead of applying a rule of reason the Bundeskartellamt has to prove that a substantial share of the market is affected by the restraint and it has to argue convincingly that the contracts hinder competition. These two conditions turned out to be interpreted as restrictively as the rule of reason by the BGH. When the Bundeskartellamt tried to forbid a contract in which the largest German travel organizer TUI required that their authorized, independent travel agencies not offer the products of the two largest nationwide competitors NUR and

---

[12] The following is valid also for the rule of reason in the German control of an abusive exercise of market power in §26 discussed in section 3.3 below.

[13] See for instance the discussion of the VW-case below.

[14] WuW/E Bundeskartellamt p.2273 ff., OLG p.4267 ff., BGH p.2627 ff.

ITS,[15] the BGH decided that the contract had a significant impact, but that nevertheless, the Bundeskartellamt had not given sufficient evidence for a substantial restraint of competition, because the competitors had alternative distribution channels and because the Bundeskartellamt could not argue convincingly why the agencies bound by TUI are needed to keep up competition in the market. This restrictive policy made it very difficult for the Bundeskartellamt to prohibit vertical restraints with §18.

7.3.2 A New European Perspective

The 1989 amendment of the GWB offered a new perspective for the control of vertical restraints. According to §47 of the GWB the Bundeskartellamt is now authorized to enforce not only the German antitrust rules but also Articles 85 and 86 of the Treaty of Rome in Germany. Since Article 85 applies whenever a contract has a significant impact on the common market it is possible to apply Article 85 to cases where §18 would not have a chance in front of a German court.

So far the Bundeskartellamt used this new possibility for two types of cases. First it applied Article 85 to the 'demarcation contracts' used by German public utilities, which are exempt from §18.[16] And then it took up this new possibility when it became clear that the exclusive dealing contracts of the large travel agencies TUI and NUR would be declared legal by the BGH in the case presented above. The Bundeskartellamt reopened the case against TUI and NUR and prohibited the contracts as a violation of Article 85(1). TUI and NUR did not challenge this decision in court and so the Bundeskartellamt was successful this time.[17] Moreover, probably encouraged by this easy success, the Bundeskartellamt used Article 85(1) to forbid new exclusive dealing contracts which both TUI and NUR impose on Spanish hotels to hinder the access of the travel agency Alltours in this area. This measure was upheld by the KG in 1995 and is now on appeal to the BGH.[18]

[15]WUW/E Bundeskartellamt p.2283 ff., OLG p.4333 ff., BGH p.2668 ff. and 2869 ff.

[16]European Commission [1995], pp.297f.

[17]In their 1993/94 report the Bundeskartellamt [1995], p.23–24, WUW/E Bundeskartellamt, p. 2761 ff., proudly reports that their measure already shows a substantial effect on the market, because NUR's products are now offered at 3600 travel agencies which were formerly bound exclusively to TUI, while TUI offers their products at 2500 former exclusive NUR agencies.

[18]Commission [1995], p. 298.

It will be interesting to see how the application of European competition rules will change the German antitrust practice in the next years.

7.3.3 Practical Importance

I want to conclude this section with a short look at the number of cases taken up in Germany in the last 10 years listed in Table 7.2. It is not surprising that there were on average only 3 cases per year under §15. RPM is easy to detect and to verify, and the fact that such contracts are null and void in front of German courts makes them useless. The few remaining cases are therefore mainly attempts to test the applicability of §15 to other vertical restraints or to challenge contractual relations which are meant to fall under one of the exceptions to §15.

	§15	§18	§22	§26
Bundeskartellämt	3.1	2.4	8.6	19.6
Landeskartellämter	6.2	8.5	60.8	131.2

Source: Bundeskartellamt (1984)–(1995).

Table 7.2: Average Number of New Cases Per Year, 1985–94

For the enforcement of §18, however, the low number of cases has a very different meaning. Here every contractual agreement is valid unless it is prohibited by the Bundeskartellamt so that the only influence which this paragraph can possibly have is to discipline the behavior of the firms whilst designing their contractual arrangements. But since it is almost impossible to accurately predict which practice will eventually be ruled illegal, it is difficult to imagine that a firm changes its contracts because of §18. Thus the abuse control of vertical constraints in §18 is at best an emergency brake for the most serious violations of fair trade. This may seem disappointing to those who think that vertical restraints are a major source of anticompetitive behavior and who would therefore favor a more rigorous antitrust policy. But if one looks at economic reality, where complicated vertical agreements are a necessary part of a market economy, and if one counts the expensive working hours which the European legislature needed to create a system of block exemptions which is only slightly more restrictive than the German system, even non-Chicagoans may conclude that the German 'emergency brake' is a better approach. It is not surprising that the German cartel authorities did not welcome the strong requirements which have to be satisfied before §18 can be applied. The Bundeskartellamt stopped the prosecution of violators of §18 almost entirely: while it took up between 20 and 40 cases per year before 1975, the average dropped to 10 cases between 1976 and 1984, and it has been down to 2 cases per year since then. However, this decline of enforcement of §18 by the Bundeskartellamt was only partly caused by the strict requirements which the German legislation imposed on the rule of reason. Just like the EC treaty, the German law has rules which allow the control of a dominant position against an abusive exercise of market power. And when the German legislator facilitated the proof of a dominant position in 1973 the Bundeskartellamt tried to subsume as many cases as possible under these rules. Vertical restraints like tying, exclusive dealing, selective distribution, and discriminatory conditions have been successfully challenged as an abusive exercise of market power. An introduction to the German policy towards vertical restraints would therefore be incomplete without a short introduction into this related part of the German law.

7.4 Abuse of a Dominant Position

7.4.1 Introduction

The principles governing the control of vertical restraints in §18 GWB have nothing in common with the prohibition of cartel agreements in §1. Instead they are closely related to the control of an abusive exercise of market power which is regulated in §22 and §26. There is not only a considerable overlap in the applicability of the rules, they also implement a similar rule of reason so that a part of the precedents for §18 were decisions taken under §22 or §26. A good example for this relationship is the case in which the Bundeskartellamt tried to forbid an exclusive dealing arrangement between VW and its authorized VAG repair shops in which the VAG shops agreed to use only original VW spare parts. This contract foreclosed more than 50% of the relevant market to manufacturers of identical parts and so the Bundeskartellamt decided that it was both an illegal vertical restraint according to §18 and an abusive exercise of market power according to §26. The BGH[19] confirmed that the contract restricts the right of VW's competitors and that it therefore falls within the range of both these paragraphs. Nevertheless, it

[19] WuW/E BGH p. 1829.

ruled that the contract is legal, because it judged the right of VW to protect its brand name by controlling the quality of spare parts to be more important than the market foreclosure no matter which rule of reason is applied.

7.4.2 Dominance

The policy to take up more cases as an abusive exercise of market power was encouraged by the change of definition of a dominant position over the last 25 years. Originally the Bundeskartellamt had to prove that there was no competition or no serious competitor in the market before it could fine a firm for an abusive exercise of market power. When it became apparent that this criterion was very difficult to apply the German legislature in 1973 introduced the notion of a dominant position which is defined with the help of the market share and several other criteria in §22(1). Table 7.4 below indicates that §18 lost most of its impact on the control of an abusive exercise of market power after this modification. The threshold market share in German law has always been remarkably low. It is already considered strong evidence of a dominant position if the largest firm in the market has a market share of 33%, and to prove the existence of a dominant position it is then enough to show that the second largest competitor is significantly weaker. For this requirement the German law considers several 'other factors' such as financial power, access to input and output markets, or formal ties with other firms. The importance of these other factors was systematically increased by the courts and the legislature. Today for a finding of dominance it is usually sufficient if the largest firm is the only large firm in the market, if it has a dominant brand name, or if it is more vertically integrated than competitors. If these conditions are met, it is not even necessary to have the critical market share of 33%. In a merger case the other criteria were sufficient to prove a dominant position of Lufthansa in the market for vacation passenger flights in which it held a share of less than 25% with an advantage of not even 10% over the next two competitors.[20] The main argument for this decision was that these two competitors, Hapag Lloyd and LTU, did not have the integrated business structure needed to stand up against Lufthansa.

[20] WuW/E OLG 2849 ff.

7.4.3 Further Requirements

The GWB distinguishes two goals of the antitrust law: the protection of competition as an institution and the protection of the individual rights of the competitors. This distinction justifies, for instance, the different requirements in §18(a) and (b) on the one hand and §18(c) on the other: §18(a) and (b) concentrate on the individual rights of the market participants as they protect mobility in and free access to the market and so they require an explicit comparison of the benefits for the contracting parties with the disadvantages for competitors; §18(c), on the other hand, protects competition as an institution, and so the Bundeskartellamt has to quantify the impact of the contract on market performance. The distinction of the two goals is even more explicit in the construction of the control of an abusive exercise of market power, where §22 protects competition as an institution in a market economy while §26 emphasizes the freedom and the individual rights of the market participants. At least theoretically this distinction has four important consequences.

First we find once again two different versions of a rule of reason in the two paragraphs. In §22 the Bundeskartellamt has to judge the impact of a measure by a dominant firm in the market and so it tries to judge the nature and the significance of such a measure. It investigates whether the strategy in question could be expected under competitive conditions and whether it significantly affects the competition left in the market. In §26, on the other hand, the rule of reason again requires an explicit comparison of the benefits for the dominant firm with the harm done to the affected parties.

Second, the protection of competition as an institution in §22 is more performance-oriented than is the protection of the individual rights. While there is a large overlap in cases where a firm is hindered by a dominant market participant, only §22 can protect the market participants against undue exploitation such as excessive pricing or price discrimination. The requirements to prove such an allegation are, however, again very demanding and so the Bundeskartellamt stopped prosecuting such violations almost entirely after losing more than 300 cases in the three years 1973–75.

The third implication of the distinction concerns the concept of dominance used in the two paragraphs. In §22 competition itself is to be protected and so dominance is naturally defined relative to the market in question. The individual protection in §26(2) goes one step further by admitting that a firm can be powerful relative to another market participant even if it does not have

§§	Type	Practice
22(4) 2 No. 2	Exploitation	Excessive Prices
22(4) 2 No. 3		Price Discrimination
22(4) 2 No. 1	Obstruction	Abusive Rebates
26(2) 1 1.Hs		Tying
26(2)		Predatory Pricing
26 II 2. Hs	Discrimination	Price Discrimination
		Denial of Delivery
26(1)		Boycott

Table 7.3: German Control of an Abuse of a Dominant Position

an overall dominant position in the market. Such a strong position is also possible if there are particular dependencies of a small or medium sized firm which can be caused by long-term relations, by the role of the traded product for the business of the weak partner, or by other special market conditions. This possibility has been used several times to force the delivery of products which the dependent firms needed to stay in business.

The fourth consequence of the distinction concerns the right to initiate a lawsuit. While the protection of competition as an institution is left in the sole responsibility of the cartel authorities, every firm has the right to protect its own interests. Consequently only the cartel authorities can initiate a case according to §22(4), while every affected firm can sue for damages if §26(2) has been violated. Even though Germany has no treble damage clause or similar punishment devices this additional possibility has lead to a considerable number of cases initiated by private companies.

7.4.4 Practice

The law forbids three types of behavior: undue exploitation of market power, undue obstruction of competitors or trading partners, and undue discrimination between trading partners. Table 7.3 indicates that there is a large overlap in practice between §22 and §26 and indeed in most cases it is not entirely clear which of the rules must be applied. This makes the careful legal distinction sketched in the previous section artificial from a practical point of view.

The impact of these paragraphs has been significantly more important than that of §18. Table 7.4 shows that after the modification of the definition

	§18	§22	§26
Bundeskartellamt 1960–1973	26.7	39.3	53.8
Bundeskartellamt 1975–1984	8.6	32.8	58.1
Bundeskartellamt 1985–1994	2.4	8.6	19.6

Source: Bundeskartellamt (1984)-(1995).

Table 7.4: Average Number of New Cases 1960–94

of a dominant position in 1973 the Bundeskartellamt initiated more than 10 times as many abuse cases as cases under §18, and for the regional cartel authorities this ratio is even larger. Of course, not all these cases dealt with vertical restraints in a narrow sense. There was, for instance, a series of lawsuits against firms that refused to deliver their products. But tying practices as in the VW-case mentioned above were ruled illegal according to §22 or §26. These and other similar cases also fall within the range of §18.

Much more striking than this trend, however, is the dramatic decrease of the number of abuse cases taken up altogether by the Bundeskartellamt. There are two possible explanations for this development. Either the powerful firms changed their attitude towards an abusive exercise of market power so that there are almost no cases left which can be prosecuted or the Bundeskartellamt decided to drastically reduce its enforcement efforts. Given that the cartel authorities do not investigate violations of §§18, 22, and 26 actively the first explanation seems unlikely. It is much more reasonable that a consistently low success rate between 20 and 40 percent convinced the lawyers in the Bundeskartellamt that their efforts would better be spent on more promising merger control or cartel cases. This interpretation promises a much more active abuse control for the future: as the right to control mergers of large firms shifts more and more from the Bundeskartellamt to the European Commission, the civil servants in Berlin will look for alternative activities which justify their existence and their budgets. So even though an efficient use of the instruments in the German law apparently calls for a very cautious application of the abuse control, the positive theory of political economy predicts that this abuse control will experience a revival. The future activities of the Bundeskartellamt may therefore serve as a natural experiment to test whether normative or positive theories are more successful in describing the reality of antitrust policy.

7.5 References

Bellamy, Christopher and Child, Graham D. *Common Market Law of Competition,* 4th edition. London 1994.

Bundeskartellamt *Tätigkeitberichte für die Jahre 1972-1994,* Bundestagsdrucksachen 7/986, 7/2250, 7/3791, 7/5390, 8/704, 8/1925, 8/2980, 9/565, 10/243, 10/3350, 11/554.

European Commission *Competition Report 1995.*

Scherer, F.M. and David Ross *Industrial Market Structure and Economic Performance,* 3rd edition. Boston: Houghton Mifflin, 1990.

Tirole, Jean *The Theory of Industrial Organization.* Cambridge Massachusetts: MIT Press, 1988.

Wirtschaft und Wettbewerb/Entscheidungssammlung (WUW/E), Serien B-KartA, OLG und BGH *Ausgewählte Entscheidungen der Kartellbehörden,* Verlagsgruppe Handelsblatt.

Competition Policies in Europe - S. Martin (Editor)

Chapter 8

Competition Policy Towards Vertical Restraints: Implementable Rules for Competition Authorities

Paul Seabright[1]

8.1 Introduction

Public policy towards vertical restraints has been subject to severe swings in intellectual and political fashion in recent decades, and even now remains one of the areas of competition policy where there is least clarity in the public debate, and where it is hardest to see what are the issues dividing those with different points of view. Vertical restraints are, loosely speaking, contracts between firms at different stages in a production chain that specify more detailed commitments by the parties than simply to exchange a given quantity of goods or services at a given price per unit. In the early days of

[1] This chapter draws substantially from material forthcoming in Chapter 2 of Neven, Papandropoulos and Seabrighte (1997). I am grateful to my co-authors for much help and discussion, and also to Mathias Dewatripont, Alberto Heimler, Kai-Uwe Kühn, Patrick Rey and Ralph Winter for valuable comments, and to Stephen Martin for advice well beyond the call of editorship. This work forms part of a project funded through the Centre for Economic Policy Research. None of the above bears any responsibility for the views expressed in this report.

competition policy both in the United States and in Europe, "free" market transactions were often seen as consisting intrinsically of no more than an exchange of goods or services for money at a single unit price. Therefore any contracts specifying more than this were to be seen certainly as restrictive, and presumptively therefore as anti-competitive (the very word "restraints" captures the flavor of this approach directly).

Subsequently, however (and to a considerable extent prompted by the writings of the Chicago school in economics and law), both research and policy have accepted that beneficial economic transactions may take much more varied forms that the two stark polar cases of administrative command within a single enterprise and exchange between independent economic agents for a common unit price on anonymous spot markets. Vertical restraints are not a feature purely of 20th century business practice or of the dealings of large firms with small suppliers and distributors: the novelist Honoré de Balzac used in the 1830s to stipulate in contracts with journals publishing his stories that they should subsequently refuse to publish negative criticism of his work (Robb, 1994, p. 203). There may, in short, be many good reasons why all kinds of economic agents should wish to enter into contractual relations that are more detailed than those embodied in spot contracts but fall short of full economic integration into a single firm. There has been an explosion of theoretical and empirical arguments demonstrating that such contractual relations may enhance the efficiency of the production process. The so-called Chicago approach (and its practical embodiment in US anti-trust policy under Presidents Reagan and Bush) has drawn from such arguments the conclusion that vertical restraints as such should not be proscribed; competition policy elsewhere has typically been more cautious, but even in the European Union has accepted that under a variety of circumstances vertical restraints may have significant beneficial economic consequences.

Most recent academic studies of vertical restraints have accepted that there are many circumstances under which they enhance productive efficiency, but most would also accept that there are significant circumstances in which they may indeed be anti-competitive. Unfortunately the implications of such findings for practical policy are quite unclear. One conclusion that might be drawn is that public policy towards vertical restraints must be inherently highly discretionary and sensitive to the circumstances of particular cases. The following statements, each by an influential scholar in the field, are characteristic of such a point of view (Tirole, 1988, p. 186):

> Theoretically, the only defensible position on vertical restraints seems to be the rule of reason. Most vertical restraints can increase or decrease welfare, depending on the environment. Legality or illegality per se thus seems unwarranted.

and (Kay, 1990, pp. 560–1):

> It should be apparent...that few general rules are appropriate in dealing with vertical restraints...since the same restraints may be, in different circumstances, beneficial or adverse in their impact, ad hoc assessment is inescapable...The best conclusion is that we should look principally at the consequences, rather than the form or first order effects of the restraints.

However, Tirole goes on to say that "this conclusion puts far too heavy a burden on the anti-trust authorities," though he argues that before a different conclusion is warranted "it seems important for economic theorists to develop a careful classification and operative criteria to determine in which environments certain vertical restraints are likely to lower social welfare" (ibid.).

Given that assessment of the precise impact of a given vertical contract on competition will often be a delicate matter, the benefits of discretion in implementing competition policy in this field are important. But discretion also has its costs. It makes decisions by the authorities hard for firms to predict, and increases the risk that firms may be breaking the law when they have been trying in good faith to abide by it. Discretion also increases the risk that decisions may be systematically tilted towards those parties with the resources to employ the cleverest lawyers and economists: in the field of vertical restraints good consultants can often devise economic models to support any desired conclusion about the impact of a given vertical restraint on economic welfare. More generally, discretion creates opportunities for regulatory capture and the distortion of policy towards those with the means to exert influence. And the exercise of discretion imposes administrative costs and costs of delay: a large number of agreements between firms with no adverse impact on competition have nevertheless to go through a lengthy vetting procedure, often lasting several years, before the firms concerned know whether the agreements are legally acceptable. Finally, the exercise of discretion increases the risk of inconsistency between decisions and between different branches of competition policy, with consequent distortionary incentives for the way in which firms plan their business strategies. For instance, European Union policy towards vertical restraints is significantly more restrictive than its policy towards vertical mergers (see Neven, Papandropoulos and Seabright, 1997, section 2.5).

These considerations suggest that practical policy towards vertical restraints should seek to balance theoretical rigor with simplicity and predictability. It should attach significant weight to diminishing the extent of discretion exercised by the competition authorities. This chapter will therefore develop an approach to vertical restraints that consists of developing a sequence of rules of thumb that allocate a burden of proof, as well as determining the kinds of argument and evidence that might constitute such proof. It will outline reasons for thinking that vertical restraints should be presumed not to be anti-competitive unless certain conditions hold, and will then seek clear and relatively simple means of identifying in practice whether those conditions are fulfilled.

The structure of the chapter is as follows. Section 2 sets out a formal framework for analysis, describing what vertical restraints are and what are the issues they raise for public policy. It suggests that public policy should principally concern itself with external effects of vertical restraints. Section 3 then examines more systematically what those external effects might be, by looking at three types of third party that might be adversely affected by a vertical restraint. Section 4 concludes by outlining a procedure for competition authorities to use.

The criteria by which vertical restraints are to be evaluated deserve explicit comment. Economic analysis tends to focus on considerations of efficiency, and US anti-trust law has also tended to give the main weight to efficiency over other considerations such as equity. In the European Union, other considerations than efficiency play an important role. In particular there has been an important emphasis on the role of competition policy in promoting market integration. Of course market integration can be and often has been justified in terms of the promotion of long-run efficiency; nevertheless it is clear that it has come to assume a fairly autonomous status as a goal of competition policy in the EU. It is not the purpose of this chapter to comment on the relative merits of these various criteria, but it is desirable to make explicit the terms of the trade-off between them. For instance, it is important to illuminate the circumstances under which the pursuit of market integration may involve a sacrifice of efficiency. The theoretical analysis will therefore evaluate vertical restraints primarily from an efficiency point of view.

Before turning to Section 8.2 let me summarize the argument to come. Although the pure Chicago view that vertical restraints always enhance productive efficiency is not credible, the Chicago approach has yielded one particularly important insight that is sometimes overlooked by authors who call for context-sensitivity in public policy. This insight is that vertical restraints are agreements between producers of complementary goods or services (see Baxter, 1989). Agreements between producers of substitute goods or services are always and rightly suspect from the point of view of public policy, for the simple reason that the exercise of market power by one producer always benefits the producers of substitute products. If two of us produce goods that are substitutes we have an incentive to connive in each other's exercise of market power. However, the exercise of market power by a producer always harms the producers of complementary products, since (by definition of complementarity), anything that raises the price or reduces the output of a good will reduce demand for a complement. In particular, an inefficiency in the production of a good will typically harm the producer of a complement.

To the extent that public policy is rightly concerned to prevent the abuse of market power, this simple insight makes it clear why, from an efficiency point of view, vertical contracts should indeed be presumed innocent unless proven guilty: each party to such a contract has a fundamental interest in preventing rather than facilitating the exercise of market power by the other. Each party to the contract is therefore in some sense an ally rather than an enemy of the public interest, and can shoulder some of the burden of policing the competitive process. From time to time, of course, a firm may sign a contract that is harmful to its own interests, but it is no part of the mandate of a competition policy to tell firms how to manage their own business.[2] It is precisely because firms generally know better than the

[2]It is possible that, in the context of long-term relationships between firms, one or other party may be coerced into accepting contractual terms as a result of making relationship-specific investments that it would not have accepted had it known them in advance. This is sometimes known as the "hold-up problem." More insidiously, the fear of a weak *ex post* bargaining position, and the lack of commitment mechanisms to prevent such a situation, may deter firm from entering into long-term relationships in the first place. Such phenomena might well provide a rationale for ruling illegal certain types of contract. But there is no reason why contracts embodying vertical restraints are any more suspect than those merely embodying unfavourable prices (indeed, arguments of the kind just sketched have been used as a rationale for minimum wage legislation). A theory of vertical restraints as

authorities how to do so that in a modern capitalist economy contracts freely entered into are generally presumed to be acceptable unless they harm third parties. The most obvious mechanism for harming a third party available to producers of substitute products, namely the exercise of market power, is one that producers of complements have ordinarily no incentive to adopt.

This insight does not, however, imply the Chicago conclusion that vertical restraints can always be presumed innocent, period. There are two reasons why not. First, and most fundamentally, a vertical contract may indeed harm third parties: a variety of ways in which this may happen will be described below, as well as some simple ways in which the danger may be diagnosed in practice. Secondly, when one of the parties to a vertical contract possesses market power in its own market, it is no longer true to say that it has in all circumstances an interest in ensuring efficiency in the provision of complementary goods or services. This is because its market power creates a division between the interests of its marginal customers and the interests of its intra-marginal ones — that is, between the interests of those customers who are just on the point of indifference between the firm's products and those of a rival, and the interests of the remaining customers who have a clear preference for the firm's products. Both marginal and intra-marginal customers share an interest in the production of a given good or service at lowest cost, but they may have divergent preferences regarding the combination of characteristics embodied in that good or service (a matter of allocative rather than productive efficiency). There is no reason to expect a vertical contract between profit-maximizing firms with market power to reach an allocatively efficient trade-off between different aspects of a product's characteristics — price and quality of after-sales service, for example. Figure 8.1 illustrates, using an Edgeworth box to represent transaction possibilities between Firm 1, a manufacturer, and Firm 2 a distributor. Unbroken convex curves represent the preferences of marginal consumers as between price of the final product and after-sales service, and broken curves represent the preferences of intra- marginal consumers. Unbroken concave curves are the iso-profit curves of firm 2 (which bears the costs of providing after-sales service and also receives the sales revenue). In this interpretation the indifference curves of marginal consumers are also iso-profit curves for Firm 1, since its profits

such should take as its benchmark case contracts willingly entered into by both parties (this need not imply that they have equal bargaining power, merely that each of them expects to be at least as well off in the presence of the contract as in its absence).

depend solely on the numbers of consumers buying its product. Point P therefore represents the profit-maximizing contract between firms 1 and 2. This is clearly inefficient since a small movement in the direction of the arrow (drawn to be tangent to the unbroken indifference curves) yields a first-order utility gain to intra-marginal consumers while causing only a second-order loss to marginal consumers and to the profits of firm 2. As drawn this shows the outcome where consumers who do not wish to pay for large amounts of after-sales service nevertheless have to do so.[3] In sum, therefore, producers with market power have a group of consumers who are intra-marginal and are therefore disenfranchised (rather like minority shareholders) in matters affecting allocative efficiency. This differs from competitive markets where all consumers are marginal, and from considerations of productive efficiency where marginal and intra-marginal consumers have identical interests.

Nevertheless, this potential conflict between the interests of marginal and intra-marginal customers affects all aspects of production where choices between combinations of product characteristics are concerned, and is as true of integrated firms as well as non- integrated ones linked by contracts. Integrated firms will choose combinations of product characteristics that do not reflect the preferences of intra-marginal consumers, and the fact that they implement these product choices by administrative command rather than by contract does not fundamentally change the character of the problem. Any potentially inefficient properties of the vertical contract are more properly thought of as a symptom than a cause of the market power concerned. Conversely, the imposition of restrictions on allowable contractual forms can be justified, if at all, only as an imperfect intervention made necessary by the inability of the authorities to alleviate the intrinsic problem which is the original market power.

Strictly speaking, the intra-marginal customers of the contracting parties can be thought of as among the possible third parties that may be harmed

---

[3] Discussions of distribution contracts in the cosmetics industry are sometimes thought to be characterized by exactly this inefficiency: everyone has to pay for the glamorous sales ambience that benefits only the marginal customer. But other industries have if anything the opposite tendency: in computer hardware, for example, after sales service is often lamentably poor because of the intensity of price competition for the marginal customer. This contrast illustrates just how difficult it is for competition authorities to use the argument just outlined as a guide to policy: there is no general presumption that the balance between price and non-price factors will be systematically distorted by market power in any particular direction.

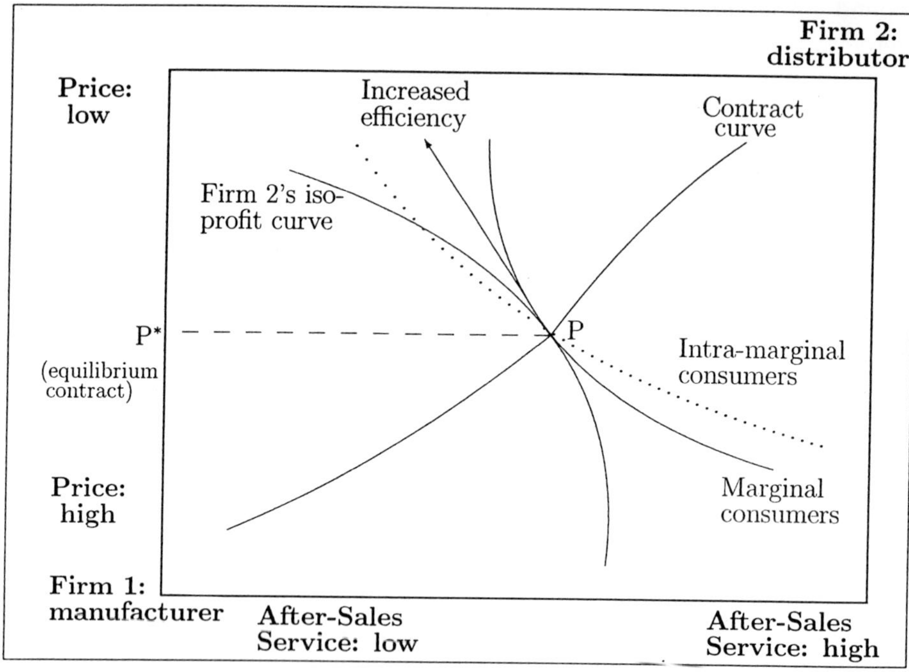

Figure 8.1: Welfare consequences of a vertical contract

by a vertical contract. In the policy rule proposed here, therefore, vertical contracts are presumed acceptable unless there is a substantial adverse net external effect on a third party.[4]

Third parties may be divided into:

1. Customers
2. Competitors
3. Potential entrants to the industry

and Section 8.3 proposes ways of identifying circumstances in which such adverse external effects are likely.

[4]For those who find acronyms helpful as mnemonics, this policy rule, dependent as it is on identifying a Substantial Adverse Negative Externality, can be described as SANE.

In order to understand these circumstances, however, it is important first to see why it is that vertical contracts are important to firms in the first place. This is the first task of Section 8.2.

8.2 A Framework for Analysis

Consider a pair of (possibly multiproduct) firms 1 and 2, each of which may be identified with a collection of human and non-human assets that are jointly controlled by each firm's owner(s). 1 and 2 produce vectors of goods or services (hereafter "goods") $\underline{x}$ and $\underline{y}$. The two firms are said to be vertically related if one of them sells to the other a good which:

a) is complementary to a good produced or owned by the other;

b) is sold on to a third party together with the complementary good, or is transformed or used up with it in the process of producing a composite final good.

Note that it may sometimes be difficult to determine the direction of the vertical relation. Suppose, for example, that a manufacturer of beer distributes its product to a bar or other outlet on a sale-or-return basis. Is the outlet purchasing beer for resale or is the manufacturer purchasing distribution services? The answer would seem to depend on which party could claim ownership of the beer while it is in the custody of the outlet immediately prior to final sale. If, for example, the outlet goes bankrupt, does the stock of beer revert immediately to the manufacturer or does it count among the assets of the outlet to which the manufacturer may claim in order of precedence among other creditors? If the former, it is natural to say that the manufacturer has purchased services from the outlet; if the latter, the purchasing relationship is reversed. Either way, the basic economic characteristics of the relation between the two parties while they continue in business may be the same whichever of them is the "upstream" firm, suggesting that it would be unwise to make prescriptions of importance turn on the direction of the vertical relation.

Note also that two firms may be vertically related even if they are also horizontal competitors. Firm 1 may sell a good x in $\underline{x}$ to Firm 2; x may be complementary to a good y_1 in $\underline{y}$ even if it is also a close substitute of another good y_2 in $\underline{y}$. Thus, for example, Firm 2 may be a car manufacturer that produces its own spark plugs and also purchases spark plugs from Firm 1.

In use of its assets to produce its vector of outputs, each firm has access to a set of strategies. These strategies may or may not be contractible (in the sense that the firm may credibly commit itself in an enforceable contract to choose among them in a certain way). Specifically, Firm 1 chooses a strategy which is a pair (s^C, s^N) from the set $\{S^C, S^N\}$, where S^C is the set of strategy components to which the firm can contractually commit itself, while S^N is the set of strategy components to which it cannot.[5] Likewise, Firm 2 chooses a pair (t^C, t^N) from the set $\{T^C, T^N\}$.

Contractible strategy components include the prices at which each firm sells its output, the total level of output transferred to or from the contracting partner, and (importantly) whether or not the contracting partner has other contracts, either with the same partner or with some third party. *Non-contractible* components may include the level of effort each firm puts in to producing or improving the quality of its goods, and the level of costs it incurs in doing so.[6]

A vertical restraint on Firm 1 by Firm 2 can then be defined as any contractual agreement such that:

1. Firm 1 and Firm 2 are vertically related;

[5] In a fuller model, it might be thought appropriate to make it endogenous which components were contractible and which not, but nothing of importance turns on this point.

[6] It might be thought that, since the firm itself is not a single entity but a hierarchy characterized by agency problems, the firm as such has no more privileged access to or control over its non-contractible strategies than its contracting partners do. Firm 1, it might be argued, cannot contractually control the actions of the employees of Firm 2 — but neither can Firm 2, understood as the legal entity rather than the collection of individuals. However, this overlooks a crucial difference between Firm 1 and Firm 2 with respect to the actions of Firm 2's employees: since Firm 2 owns the assets with which they work, it can institute much more thorough and invasive mechanisms of monitoring than Firm 1 can. The owners of Firm 2 can and do send supervisors into the buildings in which the employees work; Firm 1 can send representatives to the buildings of Firm 2 to inspect the work that is being carried out, but they have the right of admission only if the owners of Firm 2 or their representatives choose to allow them in. To put the matter another way: ownership of a firm's assets allows the owners access to a range of strategies that would not be possible under any other contractual relationship than ownership, because it allows physical access to the place in which those strategies must be implemented, and it carries with it the right to deny such access to any parties who are not owners. Ownership preserves privacy, one might say.

2. Firm 1 undertakes to restrict its choice of strategy components to some strict subset $\{S'^C, S^N\}$ of its strategy set, this subset either fully specified in the agreement or left to the partial discretion of Firm 2.

3. The restriction of Firm 1's strategy affects the quantity or quality produced or sold of one or both of the complementary goods in virtue of which the firms are vertically related.

Condition 3 is intended to distinguish genuine vertical restraints from other agreements (e.g. horizontal cartel agreements) between firms that also happen to have a vertical relationship.

Different kinds of vertical restraint can then be characterized according to the subset of strategies to which they restrict Firm 1's choice:

(i) *Price/quantity restrictions*: In determining the price of the composite good (or the joint price for the two complementary goods), firm 1 may choose only within the subset of strategies characterized by a given price p^* or set of prices P^* (e.g. those below some maximum or above some minimum). The choice of this price set is left to the discretion of Firm 2. Given demand conditions, price restrictions and quantity restrictions are two aspects of the same phenomenon. If there is uncertainty the two will differ in respect of the allocation of risk to which they give rise.

(ii) *Restrictions on dealing in substitutes.* There are two main kinds of restriction:

- The first consists of dealing restrictions: Firm 1 may not choose any strategy that involves purchasing from or selling to a competitor of Firm 2. When Firm 1 distributes the goods manufactured by Firm 2 this is usually known as exclusive dealing. When Firm 2 is the distributor it usually takes the form of territorial exclusivity, since the basis of Firm 2's market power is usually geographical. However, the exclusivity may sometimes refer to types of service or product (such as the mail order component of a certain retail business).

- The second type of restriction on the purchase of substitutes is non-linear pricing: Firm 1 may pay a certain price in a transaction with Firm 2 only if it also purchases specified numbers of other units of the same or a substitute good at a different (actual or implied) price. At its simplest this may consist of a two-part tariff, in which the right to trade at all requires a franchise fee while subsequent units require only a fixed marginal cost.

(iii) Restrictions on dealing in complements. Once again there are two main types:

- First there are input restrictions: Firm 1 undertakes to use specified levels of inputs of certain types (e.g. advertising), or inputs purchased from certain sources (e.g. Firm 2). Such restrictions may take the indirect form of selective distribution, where Firm 2 supplies only through Firm 1 and a limited number of other outlets that it has selected as being likely to provide the appropriate inputs (usually complementary services).
- The second type of restriction on dealing in complements consists of tying (this may also apply to goods that are neither substitutes nor complements). Here Firm 1 undertakes, as a condition of the contract, also to purchase or sell a certain number of units of a complementary good (other than an input into the composite good, which is already covered under input restrictions). Note that this form of tying represents a restriction on one of the two firms; exclusive dealing can also be thought of as a form of tying, but a quite different kind, namely one that imposes tying on the final customer.

These three fundamental categories cover all the main kinds of vertical restraint that are practically relevant. For example, Dobson and Waterson (1995) treat eight main kinds of restraint, which fall into the following categories under our classification:[7]

1. *Price/quantity*: retail price maintenance, quantity forcing;
2. *Substitutes*: non-linear pricing, exclusive distribution, exclusive dealing;
3. *Complements*: service requirements, selective distribution, tie-in sales.

[7] For an excellent analytical survey of vertical restraints, see also OECD (1994).

Having defined this terminology we can now go on to ask the two fundamental questions about vertical restraints. First, why should Firm 1 willingly submit to a contract restricting its freedom as an economic operator? To put it another way, how could the restriction of the strategy set of Firm 1 yield sufficient benefits to Firm 2 to enable Firm 2 to compensate it adequately for the losses that a restriction on economic freedom must entail? Secondly (and more centrally for competition policy) can we identify any general reasons why agreement on such a contract might be damaging to third parties?

To take the first question first, we can distinguish three types of reason why firms might wish to engage in vertical restraints:

1. there may be externalities between them in the exercise of their *contractible* strategy components s^C and t^C which they wish to internalize by agreeing to implement them according to a cooperative solution;

2. there may be externalities between them in the exercise of their noncontractible strategy components s^N and t^N which they are unable to internalize directly, but which they hope to offset by agreeing to choices of s^C and t^C that will give them private incentives to set (second-best) optimal levels of s^N and t^N.

3. the restriction on the strategy set of Firm 1 may enhance the credibility of certain threats or promises it may wish to make to some third party, and thereby benefit Firm 1 directly regardless of any additional beneficial impact on Firm 2.

These three motivations can be summarized as the direct externality motive, the indirect externality motive, and the strategic credibility motive. The following include some common examples of vertical restraints designed with these motivations in mind:

1. *Direct externality*

   — retail price maintenance to avoid "double marginalization," where an externality arises from pricing decisions (a contractible component of the strategy set), and would lead to excessively high prices in the absence of the vertical restraint.

   — agreements on the amount of advertising and promotion expenditure to be undertaken by either manufacturer or distributor.

2. *Indirect externality*:

   — two-part tariffs to avoid double marginalization (here the pricing decision for the final product is treated as non-contractible, either intrinsically or because it depends on information — e.g. about demand — that is itself non-contractible).

   — retail price maintenance to provide incentives for investment by distributors in product quality, where such investments lead to a reputational benefit by both distributor and manufacturer.

   One of the features of the indirect internalization of externalities is that there will often be several forms of vertical restraint that are capable of achieving the same goal. For example, the provision of incentives to a retailer to invest in pre-sale service and information may be possible through retail price maintenance, or through the granting of exclusive territories in a way that guarantees a certain margin to the retailer. When there is no uncertainty in demand or in costs the two may have identical effects, though in conditions of uncertainty they will typically differ (Rey and Tirole, 1986).

3. *Strategic credibility*:

   — refusal to supply as a means of preventing arbitrage between distributor territories between which a manufacturer is practicing price discrimination.

   — retail price maintenance as a way of making price collusion easier to observe and police by members of a cartel.

   — tying purchase of a monopolistically supplied good to the purchase of a more competitively supplied good to discourage entry by rival suppliers of the competitively supplied good (exclusive dealing is a special case of this).

If any of these three motives provides an explanation why a firm might submit itself voluntarily to a restriction on its future commercial freedom, what can be said about the welfare implications of such contracts, and the role of public policy? The fact that the two firms are producers of complements provides a strong prima facie reason to treat agreements between them as benign. The logic behind doing so can be given a simple formal expression.

Taking as a measure of social welfare the sum of profits and consumer surplus in the markets for two goods 1 and 2, the derivative of social welfare with respect to the prices of each of the two goods can be written, using obvious notation, as follows:

$$\frac{\partial SW}{\partial p_1} = \frac{\partial \pi_1}{\partial p_1} + \frac{\partial \pi_2}{\partial p_1} + \frac{\partial CS_1}{\partial p_1} + \frac{\partial CS_2}{\partial p_1} \tag{8.1}$$

and

$$\frac{\partial SW}{\partial p_2} = \frac{\partial \pi_1}{\partial p_2} + \frac{\partial \pi_2}{\partial p_2} + \frac{\partial CS_1}{\partial p_2} + \frac{\partial CS_2}{\partial p_2} \tag{8.2}$$

When the two firms are setting prices non-cooperatively it follows that

$$\frac{\partial \pi_1}{\partial p_1} = \frac{\partial \pi_2}{\partial p_2} = 0 \tag{8.3}$$

The terms $\partial CS_1/\partial p_1$ and $\partial CS_2/p_2$ are always negative. The remaining right-hand side terms in each equation are also negative if and only if the two goods are complements, and therefore the sign of the derivative of social welfare with respect to price is unambiguously negative. This means that, at the non-cooperative outcome, the derivative of firm 1's profit with respect to the price set by firm 2 has always the same sign as the derivative of social welfare with respect to that price (and analogously for firm 2). In other words, at the non-cooperative outcome each firm always has an incentive to influence the price of the other in a direction that unambiguously improves social welfare.[8]

The argument just outlined can be seen as a generalization of the double marginalization argument for vertical restraints, one that may apply even if the firms concerned are not both pricing above marginal cost. What this indicates is that double marginalization is not just one among a range of phenomena with which vertical restraints can deal, but is in some sense typical of a very general problem that may arise between producers of complements: the exercise of market power by one will tend to harm the other, and therefore agreements between the firms are likely, in the absence of externalities, to rein in rather than exacerbate the market power which is at the root of the problem. For the authorities to treat vertical restraints as automatically

[8] If the problem is concave it is straightforward to show also that social welfare is higher at the joint profit-maximizing equilibrium than at the non-cooperative outcome.

suspect is to forgo the advantages of enlisting valuable allies in the task of policing market power.

Of course, as was discussed in section 1, the conclusions of this simplified model will not necessarily carry over to a more sophisticated one. If non-cooperative price setting is determined by some other mechanism than individual profit-maximizing by each firm (say because of collusion), or if consumer surplus depends upon more than one choice variable (say price and quality of after-sales service) between which marginal and intra-marginal consumers may have differing marginal rates of substitution, or if there is some competitor that suffers a negative externality, the unambiguous positive relation between the demands of social welfare and the incentives of each firm with respect to the other's choice will no longer hold. However, all of these cases involve some party other than the two firms that is adversely affected by the contract. It therefore seems appropriate to conclude that vertical restraints should be given the benefit of the doubt unless such adverse effects can reasonably be shown to exist.

To summarize, the important issue for competition policy is whether in engaging in such vertical restraints the parties impose additional negative externalities on any third party. When the motive is strategic this will often be the case (since by definition some third party must be affected, and the effect may be negative), though when the motive is the internalization of externalities it need not be. Third parties for these purposes fall into two main categories: competitors (actual or potential) in the market for the product of either firm, and customers in such a market. The negative externalities of greatest concern will therefore be those inflicted upon actual or potential competitors or upon customers. The former kind of externality will typically be of concern because it subsequently lead to costs imposed upon customers, but it is useful nevertheless to distinguish analytically between externalities inflicted directly upon consumers (e.g. via the facilitation of collusion), and those inflicted indirectly by damaging a competitor whose actions could have been beneficial to customers.

A different question about vertical restraints also suggest itself: why might firms wish to have a contractual relationship rather than full integration? Broadly speaking we can note that non-integration of the two parties may yield advantages due to greater credibility of their commitments. Duopolists may be able via delegation of price-setting behavior to distributors to maintain a more collusive outcome than otherwise possible; an incumbent firm may be able to commit to a more aggressive response to entry if it is not vertically integrated; management may be able to set more credible incentives for distributors if those distributors are separately owned; and so on.

In implementing competition policy the authorities would wish to ask whether vertical restraints impose significant negative externalities compared to a situation of non- integration without vertical restraints, and also compared to a situation of full vertical integration. Only if the answer to both questions is positive, or if the answer to the first is positive and the authorities would be justified in forbidding vertical integration, will there be a prima facie case for intervention. Section 3 now considers how the possible presence of negative externalities might be diagnosed.

8.3 Who Suffers from External Effects?

What, therefore, are the most likely circumstances under which significant adverse net externalities are likely to occur? Let us classify such circumstances according to the identity of the affected party:

8.3.1 Final customers

Two distinct ways can be distinguished in which externalities may be inflicted on final customers. The first, already discussed above, is when a distinct subset of customers (who are intra-marginal) is adversely affected by the terms of contracts designed to meet the preferences of marginal customers alone (see Winter, 1994, for an example). For instance, customers who value pre-sales advice relatively little may be forced by retail price maintenance to consume more such service than they require.

The second way is when the terms of a vertical contract act to weaken competition between different types of final product (or interbrand competition as it is usually known). This may occur for a variety of reasons, of which three can be distinguished in the literature. First, exclusive dealing may raise the costs to consumers of comparing products or obtaining relative price information: there is an established literature documenting the potential adverse consequences of "switching costs" for social welfare (see Klemperer, 1995). Secondly, a vertical contract may allocate profits between manufacturer and dealer in such a way as to weaken the incentive of either link in the chain to steal business from rival brands by cutting prices. Rey and Stiglitz (1988) show that when there is competition between two pairs of manufacturers and distributors, a vertical restraint may lead to higher prices (because of lower marginal profits from price-cutting) than either full vertical integration or vertical disintegration with an ordinary linear contract. Thirdly, measures such as retail price maintenance may make it easier for members of a cartel to police price-cutting behavior by its members, and thus to enforce cartel discipline more effectively (see Jullien, Rey and Vergé, 1997, and Dobson and Waterson, 1996, for developments of this argument).

Specifying these possibilities theoretically does not imply that the relevant externalities are straightforward to diagnose in practice. In the example of the trade-off between price and service quality imposed by retail price maintenance, it would be necessary to establish that those consumers with relatively low willingness to pay for service quality were indeed intra-marginal (the opposite is equally plausible). Even if this were so, it would be necessary to establish further that, in consuming more service than they wished, they were significantly worse off than in the absence of retail price maintenance, when price competition could drive levels of service provision below what all consumers including themselves might wish.[9] Nobody with the experience of shopping around to have their car serviced cheaply can be wholly confident that price competition will lead to optimal outcomes.

The Rey-Stiglitz case is one that is even harder to use to identify externalities in practice. Before the vertical restraint could be diagnosed as harming consumers, it would be necessary to establish either that full vertical integration between manufacturers and distributors would itself harm consumers, or that a vertically integrated structure could not credibly duplicate (by means of an appropriately-structured commission payment system) the incentives to weaken price competition created by the vertical contract.

Like the Rey-Stiglitz case, the fear that retail price maintenance helps to enforce cartel discipline, if it is to inform practical policy, depends upon our having some confidence that we understand cartel behavior and the circumstances that promote collusion. In practice we are far from being able to do so on a systematic basis. Nevertheless, the strength of interbrand competition makes a difference: it is hard to see retail price maintenance in bookselling, for example, as having any potential for enforcing collusion.

The possibility that exclusive dealing weakens price competition by rais-

[9] This argument highlights the importance of establishing that the net externality is negative and not just that there exists a negative externality of some kind.

ing switching costs is probably the most straightforward of the three to identify in practice. It is most likely to lead to significant adverse net externalities when the costs in time and effort of comparing brands between different outlets is high relative to the value of the goods. This is more likely to be true for "impulse" ice-cream than for cars (to take two examples relevant to EU policy). It should also be noted that goods subject to significant repeat purchasing are less likely to be subject to switching costs merely because of exclusive dealing unless some important degree of territorial monopoly is involved: once a consumer has chosen which pub to visit there may be significant costs of switching to another pub, but relative prices may play a part in determining which pub to visit in the first place, provided there are enough pubs within convenient travelling distance (something that drink-drive laws may unintentionally make less likely).

In all of these examples it is clear that the possession of significant market power by each brand is a necessary condition for the vertical restraint to damage consumers. So an important lesson for competition policy is that it is only if inter-brand competition is weak that a negative externality upon consumers is even worth investigating. A second lesson is that weakening inter-brand competition by raising switching costs is the most straightforward of these possibilities to diagnose empirically with any confidence.

8.3.2 Existing competitors

The possibility that negative externalities may be inflicted on existing competitors has been well explored in the literature under the label "raising rivals' costs" (see Salop and Scheffman, 1983; Krattenmaker and Salop, 1986). The most common example is when access to a scarce input is restricted by means of a vertical contract, so that rivals are forced to use more expensive supplies. Their ability to compete is therefore weakened and the market power of the parties to the vertical contract is enhanced.

It is clear that the mere fact that a contract prevents a supplier from dealing with a rival does not inflict a significant externality. It is only if that supplier enjoys sufficient market power for the rival's costs to be raised to an appreciable extent that the fear may be justified. This is something that may not always be easy to establish empirically,[10] but at least it is possible

[10]This is particularly true if the scarcity of the resource varies significantly according to unforeseen events. Bolton and Whinston (1993) develop a model in which the desire for

to see what questions a competition authority needs to ask.

8.3.3 Potential entrants

When vertical restraints have the effect of raising rivals' costs to a level at which the rivals cannot operate profitably at all, they cease to be actual competitors and the result is known as "market foreclosure." This may happen because vertical contracts tie up scarce distribution facilities, such as sole access to licences or the sole prime site in a city. The result is damaging for exactly the same reason as raising the costs of actual competitors is damaging.

A puzzle about such vertical contracts is why one party should willingly submit to restraints that prevent it from seeking out more favorable terms if such are available. Why should the owner of a prime retail site wish to promise not to let it to a higher bidder than the present incumbent, since any such promise will discourage entry by precisely the kind of bidders who would drive up the value of the site? Why should a manufacturer write long-term contracts with suppliers or distributors that discourage the entry of other (presumably more efficient) suppliers or distributors? The literature on foreclosure provides two important answers. The first is due to Aghion and Bolton (1987). Long-term contracts, with liquidation damages, do indeed discourage some entry by more efficient suppliers (which disadvantages the purchasers of their goods). But for those suppliers who nevertheless enter, the damages represent a kind of entry fee that allows the combination of the manufacturer and the existing supplier to claim some of the rent that the entrant would otherwise obtain in virtue of its greater efficiency. The negative externality, in other words, takes the form of a tax on entry; like all taxes its effects consist partly of a transfer and partly of a deadweight loss (the latter being the entry foreclosed). The private benefits to the party imposing the tax consist purely of the transfer, but the social costs include the deadweight loss.

The second reason why a manufacturer might wish to exclude the entry of other suppliers than those currently in the market has been discussed in detail by Rey and Tirole (1996), drawing on earlier arguments of Hart and Tirole (1990) and McAfee and Schwartz (1994). This is that a manufacturer with market power (or, more generally, any owner of a bottleneck facility),

---

security of supply promotes vertical integration which is sometimes socially harmful.

faces in its dealings with distributors a commitment problem that tends to dilute the exercise of its market power. Having signed contracts with its distributor it has an incentive to renegotiate these secretly so as to increase the amount of output sold, the benefits from this increase coming at the expense of a negative externality inflicted on the other distributors. Although the manufacturer is better off doing so given the contracts it has signed with other distributors, the knowledge ex ante that it will be tempted to do so lowers its expected profits and increases the overall output in the market. This temptation is greater the more competitive is the distribution segment. Certain vertical restraints, therefore, by restricting the degree of competition in the distribution segment, act as a commitment device to prevent the manufacturer from conducting such secret agreements. The possibility of excluding a genuinely more efficient distributor is seen as a necessary price to pay for this commitment mechanism — but from the point of view of society as a whole, both the commitment mechanism and the exclusion of more efficient distributors have positive costs. The likelihood of vertical restraints playing this role is clearly increasing in the degree of market power enjoyed by the manufacturer, as well as in the ease with which such a manufacturer would be able, absent the restraints, to engage in secret renegotiation of contracts.[11]

It is often hard for the competition authorities to know whether the costs of potential foreclosure are significant when set against some of the benefits that vertical contracts may bring. Indeed, it is often hard for firms to know whether in writing vertical contracts they may risk damaging their own interests by discouraging entry by more efficient suppliers, or discouraging experimentation in conditions of evolving demand. Martin (1993, p. 350) argues that "case study evidence supports the argument that vertical restraints are likely to outlast the period in which they are socially beneficial," and in fact some of the evidence he cites implies that they are no less likely to outlast the period in which they are privately beneficial. For instance, when a challenge by the FTC forced the Levi Strauss company to abandon its policy of retail price maintenance, "stores specializing in jeans cut price, while Levi Strauss's sales and stock market value *increased* sharply" (p. 349, emphasis added). This poses a dilemma for competition authorities: they may believe

[11]Ironically, efforts by the authorities to prevent discrimination between customers, by making such renegotiation more difficult, may act as a commitment device helping the owner of the bottleneck facility to maintain its market power, as Rey and Tirole point out (*ibid.*, pp.22–4).

that a given vertical restraint is not in the interests of the companies that have agreed to it; they may be right in their belief; but is it appropriate for competition authorities to be offering management consultancy advice to companies under the guise of enforcing the law?

Underlying the argument in this chapter is the view that competition authorities should avoid becoming management consultants in disguise. They should seek to identify significant externalities, and where these can be shown with reasonable confidence to exist, they should be prepared to prohibit the contractual behavior that threatens to inflict them. But in principle, and in the absence of such externalities, the right to contract between parties that are not competitors (producers of substitute products) should be left to the wisdom — or the foolishness — of the parties themselves.

8.4 Policy implications: a practical procedure

The arguments so far reviewed suggest that economic principles recommend a 3-part rule:

First, do the parties to the contract operate in the same product market or in markets for sufficiently close substitutes? If not, there is a prima facie presumption that their contract is legal. If they do, then their contract should be treated as a horizontal restraint with a (rebuttable) presumption of illegality.

Secondly, is inter-brand competition sufficiently weak that, if the parties to the contract were vertically integrated, they would together possess substantial market power in the market for their combined final product? If not, then their contract is legal, unless it can be shown (à la Rey-Stiglitz) that the parties are seriously likely to exert more market power without vertical integration than in an integrated state.

Thirdly, is there any evidence of a substantial adverse net external effect exerted by this contract on any third party (compared with a situation in which the contracting parties simply traded goods or services at a given unit price)? Specifically, are consumers, existing competitors or potential entrants likely to be damaged by the contract in one of the identifiable ways outlined above? If not, the contract can be declared legal.

The investigative work required of such a rule falls into clear categories. The first stage requires market definition similar to that undertaken in merger investigations. The second requires an assessment of dominance. And the third requires an identification of actual parties and a quantification of likely harm. The third stage is more complex than is typically required in a merger enquiry, but not least of the merits of the proposed rule is that the first two stages, which ought to suffice for clearing the great majority of vertical contracts from any competition concerns, can be carried out with a methodology that is entirely consistence, in speed as well as substance, with that employed in investigating mergers.

8.5 References

Aghion, P. and Bolton, P. "Contracts as a Barrier to Entry," *American Economic Review* Volume 77, Number 3, 1987, pp. 388-401.

Baxter, W. "Substitutes, Complements and the Nature of the Firm," in Mathewson, Frank, Trebilcock, Michael and Walker, Michael, editors: *The Law and Economics of Competition Policy.* Vancouver: Fraser Institute, 1990.

Bolton, P. and Whinston, M. "Incomplete Contracts, Vertical Integration and Supply Constraints," *Review of Economic Studies* Volume 60, Issue 1, Number 202, January 1993, pp. 121–48.

Dobson, P. and Waterson, M. "Vertical Restraints and Competition Policy," University of Warwick, mimeo, 1995.

— "The Competition Effects of Resale Price Maintenance," University of Nottingham, mimeo, 1996.

Hart, O. and Tirole, J. "Vertical Integration and Market Foreclosure," *Brookings Papers on Economic Activity* Microeconomics 1990, pp. 205–85.

Jullien, B., Rey, P. and Vergé, T. "Pratique des prix imposés et collusion," IDEI, University of Toulouse, mimeo, 1997.

Kay, J. A. "Vertical Restraints in European Competition Policy," *European Economic Review*, Volume 34, 1990, 551–61.

Klemperer, P. "Competition When Consumers Have Switching Costs: an overview of recent work with applications to industrial organization, macroeconomics and international trade," *Review of Economic Studies* Volume 62, Issue 4, No. 213, October 1995, pp. 515-39.

Krattenmaker, T. and Salop, S. "Anticompetitive Exclusion: Raising Rivals' Costs to Achieve Power over Price," *Yale Law Journal* Volume 96, Number 2, 1986, pp. 209-293.

Martin, S.*Advanced Industrial Economics.* Oxford: Blackwell Publishers, 1993.

McAfee, R.P. and Schwartz, M. "Opportunism in Multilateral Vertical Contracting: Nondiscrimination, Exclusivity and Uniformity," *American Economic Review* Volume 84, Number 1, March 1994, pp. 210–30.

Neven, D., Papandropoulos, P. and Seabright, P. *European Competition Policy and Agreements between Firms: Article 85 in Theory and Practice.* London: CEPR, forthcoming, 1998.

Organization for Economic Cooperation and Development (1994): *Competition policy and vertical restraints: franchising agreements.* 1994.

Rey, Patrick and Stiglitz, Joseph E. "Vertical restraints and producers' competition," *European Economic Review* Volume 32, Number 2/3, March 1988, pp. 561-68.

Rey, Patrick and Tirole, Jean "The logic of vertical restraints," *American Economic Review* Volume 76, Number 5, December 1986, pp. 921-39.

—"A Primer on Foreclosure", IDEI, University of Toulouse, mimeo, 1996.

Robb, G.*Balzac.* London, Picador, 1994.

Salop, Steven C. and Scheffman, David T. "Raising Rivals' Costs," *American Economic Review* Volume 73, Number 2, May 1983, pp. 267-71.

Tirole, J. *The Theory of Industrial Organization.* Cambridge, Mass.: MIT Press, 1988.

Winter, R. "Colluding on Relative Prices," C.R.E.S.T., mimeo, 1994.

Competition Policies in Europe - S. Martin (Editor)

Chapter 9

Competition Policy in Belgium

Leo Sleuwaegen
Patrick Van Cayseele

9.1 Introduction

Competition policy in a small and open economy such as Belgium requires a specific approach, one which searches for rules and instruments that are compatible with those used by the European authorities and at the same time covers those cases that escape the application of EC competition policies or are specific to the Belgian market.

The focus of the newly implemented policy in Belgium is twofold. The first focus on concentrations of firms that structurally segment the market and build up dominant positions on the Belgian market. The second focus is on preventing anticompetitive behavior by firms on the Belgian market. In view of the small size of the market and its open character, many of the cases have extra-territorial implications and call for a Community-wide or coordinated multinational treatment.

We detail the principles and procedures behind the new approach and the relationship of Belgian to EC competition policy in Sections 9.4 and 9.5. Section 9.2 presents some essential elements of Belgian industrial organization, which offer a better perspective within which to understand the design of the new competition policy and why it came to replace the long-used policy of price controls and sector agreements, as explained in Section 9.3.

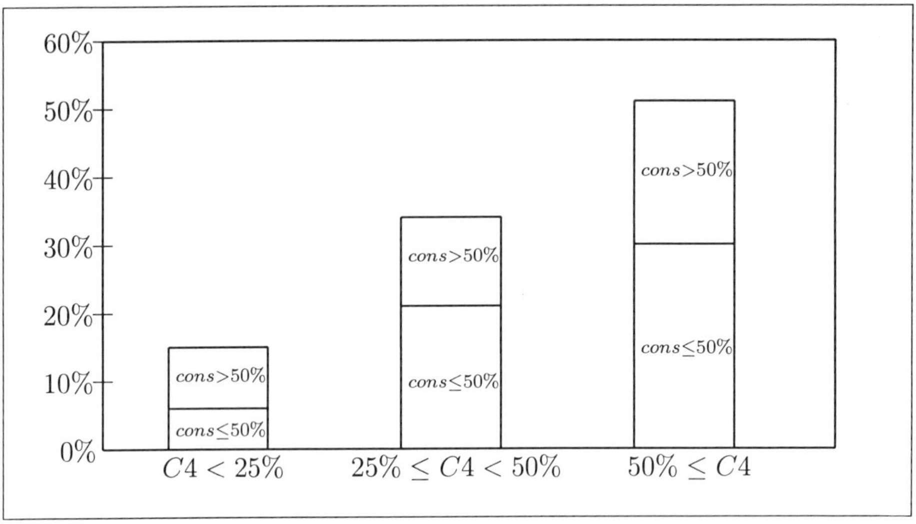

Figure 9.1: Industrial concentration in Belgium, 1990. Share of total manufacturing sales accounted for by concentrated, medium concentration and unconcentrated industries

9.2 Competition Policy in a Small Open Economy

The openness of the Belgian economy is reflected in very high import and export flows, close to 70 per cent of gross domestic product, and in a strong presence of subsidiaries of multinational firms which account for half of all industrial output in Belgium. Both features have a profound impact on the structure and performance of Belgian industries. Figure 9.1 shows the importance of manufacturing industries classified following the level of concentration for the year 1990. A distinction is made between industries with a four-firm concentration ratio ($C4$) of 50 percent or higher, medium-concentrated industries with a concentration ratio between 25 and 50 percent, and unconcentrated industries with a concentration ratio of less than 25 percent. The height of the bar indicates the importance of the industries as a percentage of total manufacturing sales. The upper part ($cons > 50\%$) reflects the share of local industries, i.e. industries for which local producers account for more than 50% of domestic consumption.

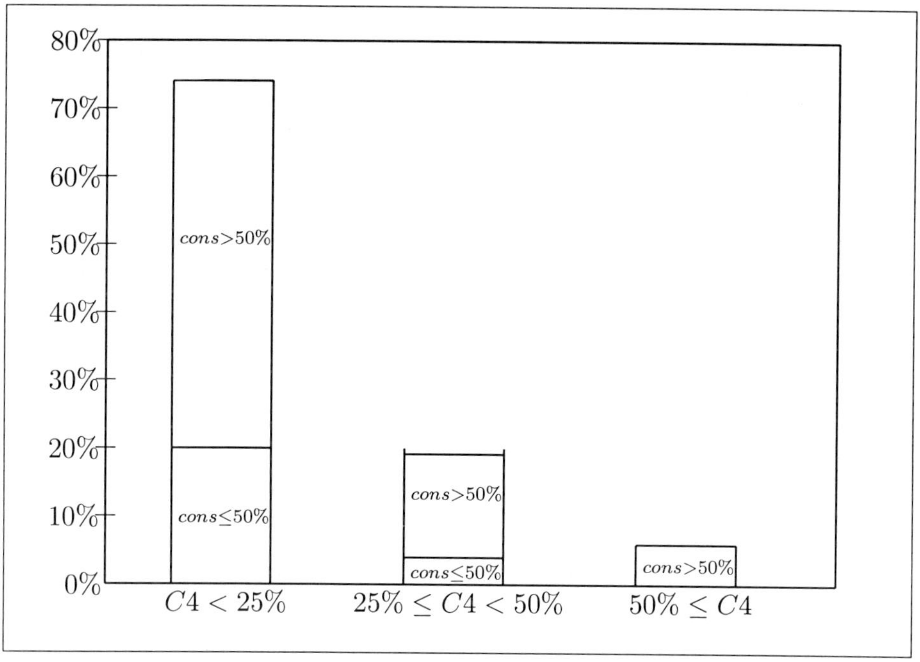

Figure 9.2: Concentration adjusted for international trade. Share of total manufacturing sales accounted accounted for by concentrated, medium concentration and unconcentrated industries

Figure 9.1 shows that concentration is rather high in manufacturing. However, the high concentration figures are largely explained by the sales data used to construct the concentration ratios. The data refer to sales by firms located in Belgium and include export sales to other countries. Imports, in spite of their importance, are not included in the total sales figure used as the denominator of the concentration ratio. In order to come to more meaningful indicators, we examine adjusted concentration ratios, which correct for export sales and include import sales in the denominator.

The adjusted 'domestic' concentration ratio is computed as follows:

$$C4 = \frac{\text{sales of 4 largest firms minus their exports}}{\text{sales of all firms minus their exports plus imports}}. \tag{9.1}$$

The adjusted concentration measures yield an indication of the importance of domestic concentration. Very few industries are characterized by high domestic concentration. Indeed, Figure 9.2 reflects another important characteristic of the Belgian economy, the overwhelming importance of small and medium-sized firms with most of their sales on the domestic market. Small and medium-sized firms accounted for more than 97 percent of the total number of firms and 42 percent of total employment in Belgium in 1990.

The other feature of the openness of the economy, the significant presence of multinational firms, has also an important impact on industry structure. The great majority of the subsidiaries located in Belgium have been attracted to Belgium because of the central location of the country in Europe, and use their subsidiaries to export to other parts of Europe. They typically operate on a larger scale and dominate the highly concentrated industries, characterized by high R&D and advertising intensities. Figure 9.3 shows the scatter diagram of (unadjusted) concentration versus foreign control, i.e. the share of sales accounted for by subsidiaries of multinational firms in the industry. The diagram shows a significant correlation (0.3) with a tendency for concentration to rise with foreign control. The regression line plotted within the scatter diagram suggests that concentration rises by 0.22 of a percentage point for every one percentage point increase in foreign control.

The openness of markets to international trade provides an important source of discipline on market performance. In an early study on the subject Phlips (1979) found no significant correlation of profitability with domestic concentration for a set of Belgian manufacturing industries during the period 1958–1964. Using data referring to the seventies, Jacquemin, de Ghellinck and Huveneers(1980) and Huveneers (1981) find import penetration to have a significant negative impact on price-cost margins across industries, with an additional negative effect for concentrated industries. This finding is echoed in another study of Geroski, de Ghellinck, and Jacquemin (1988) where, using a more flexible approach, it is found that trade has a large, but not an overpowering effect on performance, that the effect is largely dependent upon a range of industry structural variables, beyond concentration, and that the degree of openness itself is endogenous. The same study also found that the presence of multinationals exerts a negative impact on domestic profitability for closed industries shielded from international competition and a positive effect on profitability for open sectors

These findings point to the typically wide scope of operations of these firms, based on the exploitation of scale and scope economies in differentiated industries on a global scale. The negative effect on closed, often public

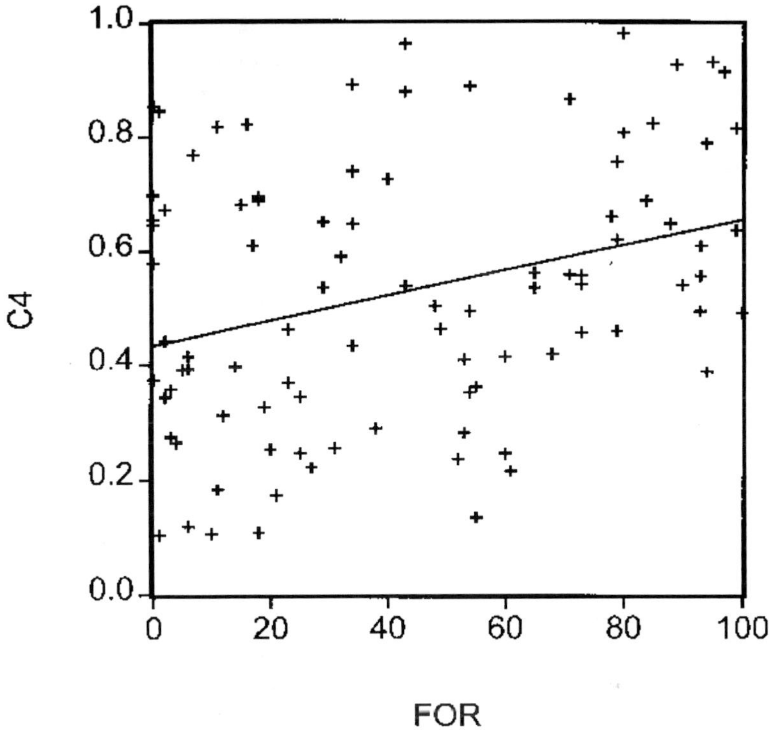

Figure 9.3: Foreign control and industrial concentration in Belgium

procurement, industries reflects the trade-barrier jumping character of direct investments made by multinational firms as the only means to penetrate the Belgian market (Sleuwaegen and Lyons, 1996).

Findings similar to those found for profitability also occur in studies focusing on the pricing behavior of Belgian firms. Kervyn de Lettenhove (1979) observed that Belgian prices followed foreign prices. His study suggested that West German manufacturing industry, taken as an aggregate, acts as price-leader for Belgian manufacturing. The same finding occurred in a cross section study covering 45 manufacturing industries (Yamawaki, Sleuwaegen and Weiss, 1989). In studying pricing over time Huveneers (1981) finds for a set of 31 manufacturing industries that 14 industries behaved as price-takers and 17 behaved as price-setters that were only partially constrained by the prices set by foreign competitors. Performing a similar analysis Frantzen (1986) observes foreign price constraints on domestic as well as export prices for a set of four broadly defined industries. The constraining effect is stronger for export prices than for domestic prices, suggesting that full competitive arbitrage had not removed all price differentials between foreign markets and the Belgian domestic market over the period 1964–1978.

The studies reviewed focused on time periods before the full completion of the single market. Together with the creation of the single market, the strength of trade as a source of discipline on market performance has grown substantially over time. The creation of the single market has stimulated intra-EU trade such that the import propensity rose from 33 percent of GDP in 1957 to 57.3 percent in 1995. The removal of tariff and recently, non-tariff barriers has led to increasing EC-wide competition and a growing harmonization of price levels across the EU (Buigues and Ilzkovitz, 1988). The lifting of all types of barriers implies that national markets are no longer artificially protected and offer fewer possibilities for profitable national market segmentation and price discrimination.

As a result of this trade liberalization, the relevant market widens and pricing and profitability adjust to European-wide concentration and other structural market conditions for trade intensive industries (Sleuwaegen and Yamawaki, 1988). Growing intra-European trade, which provides strong discipline for the competitive conduct of Belgian firms and the need to coordinate competition policies across member states, has stimulated Belgian policymakers to abolish their policy of price controls which, in the mean time, had also proven to be less effective and sometimes appeared to help firms or federations of firms to fix noncompetitive prices. The need to guard competition and to intervene in industries, especially service industries, where the strength of 'trade as a discipline' is rather limited and for which trade and investment liberalization is taking place only gradually, have very much inspired the development of a specific Belgian competition policy which has substituted for the heavily criticized price controls system.

9.3 A Brief History

A description of the history and origin of Belgian competition policy essentially involves explaining the abolition of the policy of generalized price regulation which persisted until the end of the 1980s.

Generalized price controls involved the obligation for firms to notify price increases and obtain approval from the Ministry of Economic Affairs. The regulation of nominal prices by governmental market intervention was often initiated to dampen inflationary pressure and, consequently, the loss of purchasing power. In a small open economy, however, international competition and arbitrage by buyers is important, which explains why the price level is determined in large part by the evolution of the exchange rate on the one hand and the evolution of world prices on the other.

From a micro-economic point of view price regulation is considered to "correct" undesirable market outcomes. Price regulation here is an instrument for the politician/administrator to implement "fair" prices, which divide the surplus between consumers and producers in a "just and equitable" way. Another way of seeing "fairness" in this context is fairness between various consumers of the firm. A classic example is the pharmaceutical industry where the problem arises of consumers in different countries paying a "fair" share of the common development costs of pharmaceuticals.

Analysis of the industrial economic aspects of regulation show, however, that price regulation may not be only in the interest of the government but also in the private interests of politically effective groups such as firms and labor unions. Cooperation between firms producing similar products which results in a common price can increase their revenues, as well as their costs (e.g. costs of arriving at an agreement or the costs of dealing with defection). Without any price regulation this cost/benefit ratio can be too high to arrive at a price agreement between firms. In this context other arguments can explain the existence of regulatory action as a means to foster cooperative behavior in industry. De Bondt (1978) sums up the following arguments:

- the repetitiveness in preparing notification files often at a sectoral level not only stimulates, but requires, interfirm communication on cost and other data-communication that otherwise may be a barrier to industry cooperation receives an official rationalization under price regulation;

- disagreements among industry members on an acceptable common price hardly threatens their cooperation since the responsibility for price decisions ultimately rests with governments;

- price reductions, as acts of intra-industry rivalry, are discouraged by certain 'escalator' contracts, so the likelihood of defection is much smaller than it would be with a private cooperation agreement given the character of the contracts and the implications of non-compliance.

From the same positive analytical point of view, it has also been argued that if the government brings a certain product under its control it gives a signal to the producers to organize so as to try to get a higher price via political pressure. In addition:

- price regulation mechanisms may affect wage bargaining between firms and unions;

- price regulation mechanisms may create an incentive for firms to bias their choice of a production technology (so-called Averch-Johnson effects). Choices will depend on how the firm believes that it can affect output prices through its choice of technology and on the measures taken by administrators to counter these effects;

- price regulation mechanisms also affect other aspects of firm behavior and decision-making, for instance with respect to non-price versus price-competition.

Following these arguments price regulation is likely to be more important and beneficial to industries where tacit collusion is difficult to organize. Such industries are mostly characterized by low concentration, product differentiation and important cost differentials among firms. Brennan (1982) investigated the economic consequences of the prior notification scheme of price regulation at the level of the individual decision-makers involved, and found that

- characteristics of the industry influenced the notification behavior of the firms with respect to the timing and magnitude of a requested price increase;

- sectors responded differently to parallel changes in cost variables;

- exogenous cost elements, including imported intermediate goods in contrast to endogenous ones, were typically considered more favorably by the Minister of Economic Affairs;

- less favorable decisions with respect to authorized price increases were typically associated with longer investigation and decision periods.

The results suggested that price controls distorted the signaling role of prices in the economy, and, hence lead to an inefficient allocation of resources. Price controls also appeared to be ineffective from a macro-economic point of view. De Grauwe and Fremault (1987) showed that Belgian inflation during the periods that price controls existed could almost completely be explained by purchasing power theory and that the role of price regulation was negligible. From their findings one cannot, however, exclude that price controls pushed the level of inflation below the level predicted by purchasing power theory during certain periods. However, those periods were followed by an overtaking movement that pushed the level of inflation above the one predicted by purchasing power theory.

The ineffectiveness of price controls at the macro-economic level, and their inefficiency at the micro-economic level, has finally led to the abolishment of generalized price controls. Prices controls persist in only in a few so-called 'strategic' sectors. These sectors include primarily pharmaceuticals, energy, and public utilities. Regulation in these sectors seems to be characterized by inefficiencies similar to those mentioned in the context of general price controls (Van Cayseele, 1987).

Together with the rising critique of price controls, new initiatives at the European level to further integrate the economies of the Member States and coordinate competition policies were taken. Moreover, the subsidiarity principle that was made explicit in the 1992 Maastricht Treaty made the development of a specific Belgian competition policy necessary.

9.4 The New Competition Law

On August 5, 1991, the Belgian Parliament passed the "Belgian Law regarding the protection of economic competition." The law became effective on April 1, 1993. The law was a substitute for the price control system and replaced the 1960 law on competition which had only a very restrictive application in cases of 'abuse of economic power' and involved a very complex decision procedure.

Except for some important differences, the new law to a large extent copies Treaty of Rome Articles 85 and 86. The Belgian law provides for a 'de minimus' clause and grants extra exemptions for small- and medium-sized firms when the cooperative agreements are considered to strengthen their competitive position. The law also includes a control of concentrations at the national level, very similar to the EC merger control regulation, but requires notification of all concentrations for which the combined sales of the undertakings exceed 1 billion of Belgian Francs and where the undertakings jointly account for more than 25 per cent of the relevant market.

All sectors are covered by the law. For state-owned enterprises the law adopted the principle of Article 90 of the Treaty of Rome that the application of the law may not hinder the specific tasks allocated to state-owned enterprises. The law provides for several institutions, including the 'Service for Competition' (Dienst voor de Mededinging/Service de la Concurrence), a subdivision of the Ministry of Economic Affairs that is responsible for investigation and the application of the decisions taken within the framework of the competition law. The Council for Competition (Raad voor de Mededinging/Conseil de la Concurrence) is an administrative court and acts as an independent authority in deciding on the cases prepared and proposed by the Service. Still another body, the Commission for Competition, which is part of the Central Economic Council, advises on competition policy in general and proposes applications and/or amendments to the law. The law stipulates monetary sanctions up to a maximum of 10 per cent of annual turnover of the companies involved. Decisions can be appealed before the Court of Appeal in Brussels.

The first case treated under the law dates from June 21, 1993 (Morton International and Hoechst AG). Since then, and until the end of September 1995, the Competition Council had met 202 times. In 115 cases, the Competition Council reached a decision.

From an operational viewpoint, four categories of cases can be distinguished Table 9.1 provides an annual breakdown of cases following the four basic categories.

Concentrations refer to the mandatory notification of mergers. Complaints regarding unfair competition are a second category, while requests for exemptions, for instance regarding cooperations, are a third category. A final category groups miscellaneous types of demands, often requests to take provisional measures to safeguard the continuation of businesses which, for instance, face market foreclosure.

Since decisions regarding concentrations have to be taken within one month, the Service for Competition had no time to report to the Council on complaints or exemptions. Instead, all manpower has been constantly allocated to preparing on time the reports on concentrations. This clearly shows from a breakdown of the decisions taken by the Council in Table 9.2.

	1993	1994	1995 (up to October)	Total
Concentrations	30	39	36	105
Complaints	17	20	14	51
Exemptions	3	9	19	31
Other	3	9	3	15
	53	77	72	202

Table 9.1: Number and type of cases introduced under the new competition law

	1993	1994	1995 (up to October)	Total
Concentrations	24	42	35	101
Complaints	1	1	3	5
Exemptions	1	—	—	1
Other	—	—	—	—

Table 9.2: Number of decisions taken by the Council

A comparison of the firsts row of Tables 9.1 and 9.2 clearly shows a near perfect match between the notifications of concentrations and the decisions of the Council on these issues. This near perfect and extremely speedy follow-up of concentrations is achieved entirely at the expense of the other categories. As said, the bottleneck is to be found at the level of the Service for Competition, which has insufficient resources to prepare all the necessary information before cases other than concentrations can be dealt with by the Council.

Several actions have been taken to alleviate this problem. First, the Council has advised the Minister to raise the thresholds for notification of concentrations. This advice has been followed: the thresholds for mandatory notification of a merger now are a market share of 25% (instead of 20% initially) of the relevant product or geographic market and combined sales of up to 3 billion Belgian francs (initially this used to be 1 billion).

9.5 Scope and Application of the Law

At this writing, it is still too early to do an in-depth investigation of the economic effects following the implementation of the new competition law.

What can be provided in a meaningful way is the relationship of the new policy to EC policies. Also the economic principles used in applying the law can be made explicit. The section ends with a discussion of some problems encountered in applying the law. The focus is on control of concentrations as this is practically the sole area in which the law has been applied so far.

9.5.1 Differences from the EC merger regulation

The Belgian law controls mergers if at least one of two criteria are fulfilled. These criteria are formulated as thresholds. Furthermore, there is a one-stop shop principle, that is, either the European Community or the State Law has to take the decision. Hence the division of powers can be summarized by means of the decision tree shown in Figure 9.4.

Concentrations which involve companies with annual sales exceeding ECU 5 billion worldwide, and where at least two of the companies involved in the merger have sales in excess of ECU 250 million, and where at least one of the participating companies realizes more than one third of its sales in another Member State, have a Community dimension and must be notified to the EC authorities. The Belgian law requires a merger to be notified as soon as the aggregate sales exceed some ECU 75 million and the combined market share exceeds 25 per cent for the relevant products.

The current Belgian law shows some remarkable differences with the EC merger regulations. These differences concern institutions and the underlying economic principles guiding merger control. First of all, in the Belgian case there is a sales as well as a market share threshold in the notification rule. Second, as opposed to the European law, the Belgian law explicitly allows for an efficiency defense. That is, should a merger operation prove to be harmful in that it creates too much market power, the merging parties can defend the merger on the ground of one of the following arguments:

— the merger creates cost efficiencies in production or distribution

or

— the merger enables the larger entity to perform better in technology development.

The procedure to verify whether or not a merger creates market power is guided by recent insights from industrial economics. As such, the first step in the actual procedure involves the definition of the relevant antitrust market and the scope of operations of the merging parties within that market. Next, an inventory of possible barriers to entry is made. That is, the potentiality

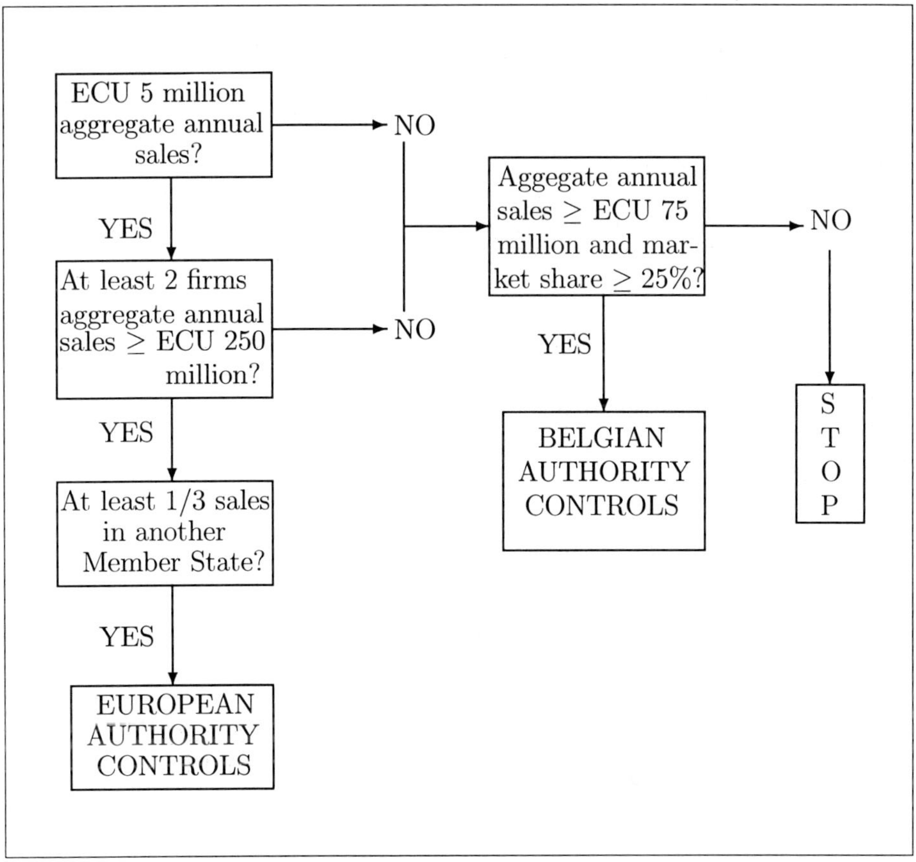

Figure 9.4: Triage of cases between Belgian and European level

of entry is verified so as to check whether or not the market is contestable. Should the merger prove harmful, economic analysis will be used to assess potential improvements in efficiency or innovation following the merger.

Two further differences with respect to European law need to be noticed. The Belgian economy is a small and open economy, with many sectors composed of small and medium sized firm. Taking into account these features, the Belgian law explicitly allows for mergers between smaller firms which may help them to improve their strategic export position. Similarly, the law grants exemption to groups of small firms which engage in certain cooperative practices, if these may help them to improve their international competitive position. While all these elements appear to make Belgian antitrust policy very lenient, it should be noted that, as of this writing, there are no cases in which any trade-off has been made between cost or scale efficiencies, strategic export motives or small business considerations on the one hand, and market power disadvantages on the other.

Finally, the most important difference involves the institutions that have been created under the Belgian law, with the installation of an administrative court, the Council for Competition, which rules independently of political pressure. In reality, however, the Council has no means of its own, and depends for investigation and information on the Service for Competition which is part of the Ministry of Economic Affairs, and hence ultimately responds to politics. The drawback of this organization is that the Council cannot interfere with the investigation (hence has to decide on what is made available by the Service), nor does it have the means to commission specific studies or to call on experts. The Service for Competition itself is understaffed, with a majority of the staff members coming from the price controls administration.

9.5.2 Application of the law

As mentioned before, because of a lack of resources the law has only been effectively applied in the context of concentrations. In addition to the recent raising of the thresholds from a 20 per cent market share to a 25 per cent market share, there is a new proposal to further reduce the workload of the authorities in the area of concentration and to free some resources to deal with complaints about anti-competitive practices. This proposal involves the writing of a brief report and simply taking no decision within 30 days in those concentration cases where it is obvious that the market structure does not change. By default then the merger is accepted. This absence of a change in market structure will be a fact in the so-called O+ case. This situation refers to situations where the target company holds, on its own, a 25% market share, while the acquirer is not active at all in the markets of the target company. Article 11 of the Competition Act refers to a combined market share, so for these cases notification is mandatory although nothing really changes in terms of the market structure.[1]

[1] Although clearly one should verify whether the conduct is likely to be changed by the merger, for instance by the fact that the acquirer has financial ties with another firm in the market, which previously did not exist. For this reason the idea is to check whether or not such relationships exist. Yet in a landmark case (*Incentive AB/Investments AB Cordo*,

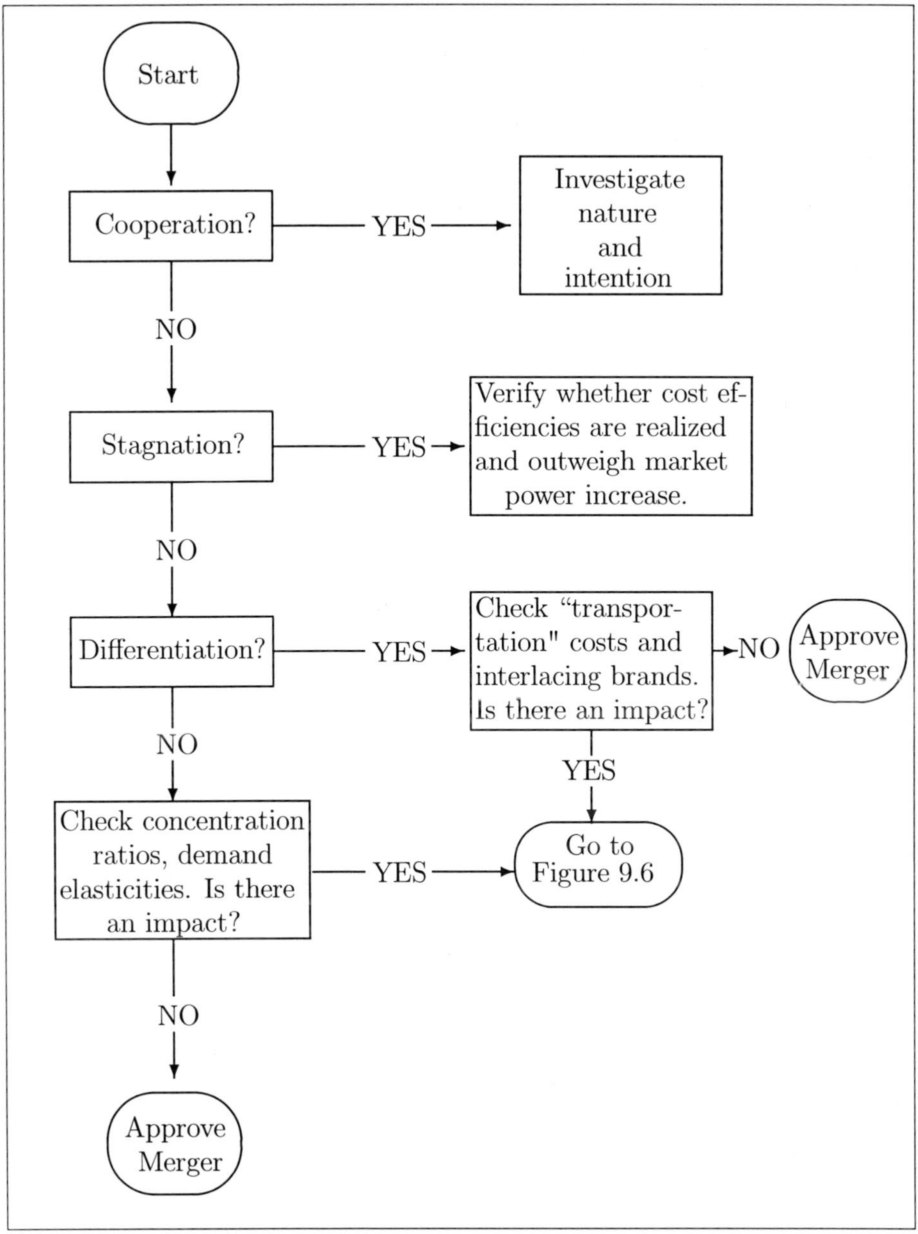

Figure 9.5: The treatment of mergers in Belgium

The treatment of the merger cases itself is guided by recent insights from modern industrial organization theory (Van Cayseele, 1994). The actual procedure can be systematized following the decision trees shown in Figures 9.5 and 9.6. A first step in the investigation consists in finding out whether any form of cooperation exists in the industry, and what the implications of such a cooperation are in terms of the proposed merger. Usually this step involves checking for the existence of joint ventures or other cooperative agreements and verifying that the merger has no intention of limiting future competition in the product market. The next step is to verify the development of the industry, in particular whether the sector is stagnating or in decline, to take into account the elimination of (over)capacity and failing-firm arguments.

A distinction is made between industries composed of firms producing homogenous goods and those producing differentiated products. Here, of course, the interchangeability of the products and hence the delineation of the relevant market is in order. In determining whether the concentration should be notified, it is necessary to verify whether 25% of the relevant market is involved. Clearly then a critique of the law has been that it mixes up the issues: one of the criteria to investigate whether or not market power is increased by the merger is used one stage before, in determining whether the operation should be notified (Sleuwaegen, 1994; Van Cayseele, 1994). It therefore has been proposed to eliminate the market share threshold to determine whether or not notification is necessary.

Next, if it turns out that the merger probably will cause undesirable competitive outcomes within the new market structure, the contestability of the industry is investigated. Figure 9.6 shows how this is done. First, information regarding the nature of the inputs is analyzed. The inputs include intangible assets, such as technological know-how protected by a patent. Next, the issue whether there are economies of scale is investigated in relation to the nature of the inputs to find out whether strategic barriers to entry could be created through the merger. Finally, long-term contracts and the use of severance fees as an equilibrium entry blocking device are taken into account (see Aghion and Bolton, 1987). Belgian laws, however, make it difficult to apply such strategies (Van Cayseele and Wuyts, 1995).

---

case 94-C/C-22) the Competition Council held that no notification is required provided the merger meets simultaneously the following criteria:

a) the acquirer is not active in the same markets as those of the target company, nor in any vertically related market; and

b) the acquirer is not be active in any of these markets outside Belgium.

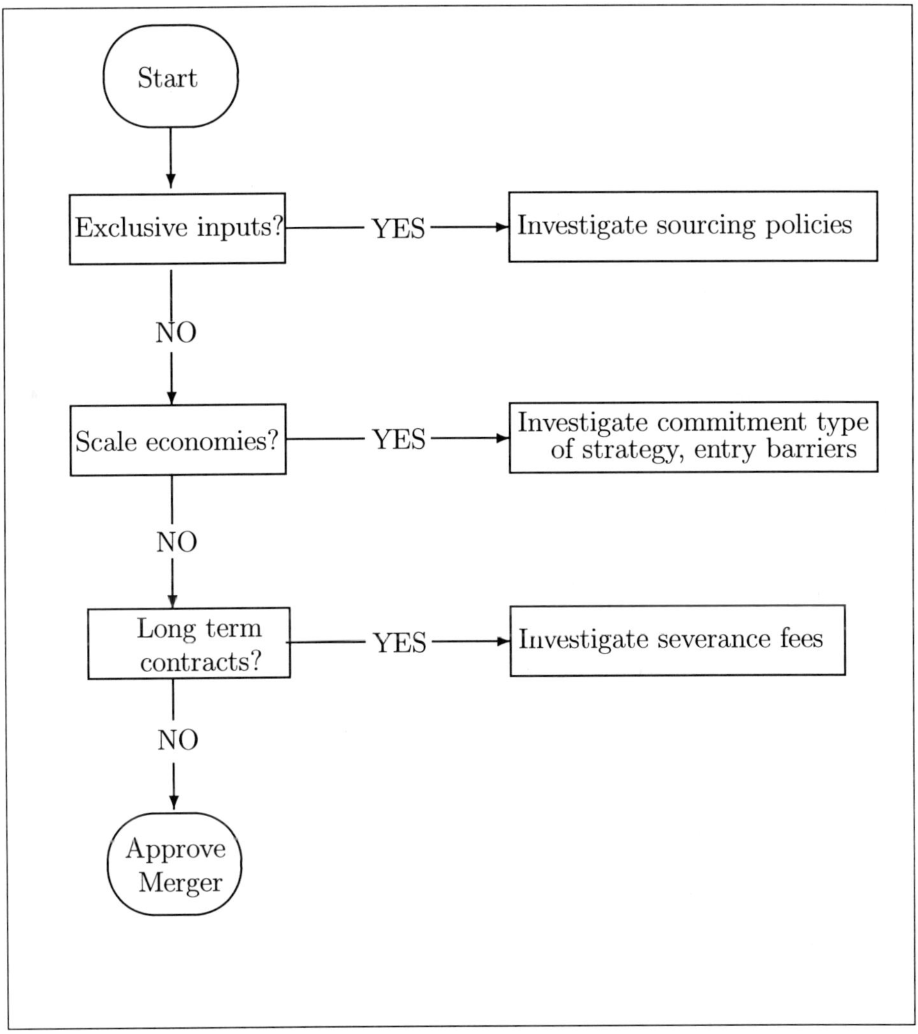

Figure 9.6: Decision tree to investigate barriers to entry

So far, only 2 mergers have been effectively blocked. Both of the proposed mergers were considered to lead to the development of oligopolistic dominance in locally organized industries. The two industries involved a branch of the chocolate industry and a branch of the specialized distribution sector. One proposed merger in the chemical industry was withdrawn by the parties during the investigation. Two other mergers were conditionally approved.

9.6 Conclusions

Competition policy in Belgium is of recent origin. The passing of the Competition law in 1993 resulted in the creation of several new institutions and procedures to safeguard fair competition on the Belgian market. To some extent the new law replicates Articles 85 and 86 of the Treaty of Rome and the Merger Control Regulation of the European Community on a Belgian scale. However the law and the actual procedures used in applying the law allow for the specific open character of the Belgian economy and the overwhelming presence of small and medium sized companies. It provides exemption for cooperative practices and concentrations of small firms if the cooperation or concentration helps them to improve their international competitive position. The law also provides for an explicit efficiency defense.

Another interesting difference from the European system is the establishment of an administrative court, independent from political influences, which is responsible for decision making. However, the dependence of the court on information and services from the Ministry of Economic Affairs for investigation constrains its independence and effectiveness. So far, Competition authorities have exclusively dealt with the control of concentrations, and, because of a lack of resources, have been unable to respond to complaints about the abuse of a dominant position or other anti-competitive practices of firms. Recent proposals to enlarge the staff and restructure the organization of the different administrative services aim at remedying this untenable situation.

9.7 References

Aghion, P.and P. Bolton "Contracts as a Barrier to Entry," *American Economic Review* Volume 77, 1987, pp. 388–401.

Brennan, J.*An Empirical Investigation of Belgian Price Regulation by Prior Notification: 1975-1979.* Doctoral Dissertation, K.U. Leuven, 1982.

Buigues, Pierre and Ilzkovitz, Fabienne "The single market: implications for Belgian industry," internal paper of the Commission of the European Communities, Document II/420/88-EN, 1988.

De Bondt, R. "Industrial Economic Aspects of Belgian Price Regulation," *Tijdschrift voor Economie en Management* Volume 23, 1978, pp. 249–64.

De Grauwe, P. and A. Fremault "Micro- en macro-economische effectiviteit van de Belgische prijsreglementering," *Leuvense Economische Standpunten*, n° 38, 1987.

Frantzen, D. J. "Cost shifting and Price flexibility in the Small Open Economy: a Disaggregated Study for Belgian Manufacturing," *Applied Economics* Volume 17, 1985, pp. 173–89.

— "The Cyclical Behaviour of Manufacturing Prices in a Small Open Economy," *Journal of Industrial Economics* Volume 34, 1986, pp. 389–407.

Geroski, P., de Ghellinck, E. and Jacquemin, A. "Inter-industry Variations in the Effect of Trade on Industry Performance," *Journal of Industrial Economics* Volume 37, 1988, pp. 1–17.

Huveneers, C., 1981, "Price Formation and the Scope for Oligopolistic Conduct in a Small Open Economy," *Recherches Economiques de Louvain*, 47, pp. 209–42.

Jacquemin, A., de Ghellinck, E. and Huveneers, C. "Concentration and Profitability in a Small Open Economy," *Journal of Industrial Economics* Volume 29, 1980, pp. 131–44.

Kervyn de Lettenhove, A. "Taux de change, inflation et compétitivité externe," *Recherches Economiques de Louvain* Volume 45, 1979, pp. 55–94.

Phlips, L. *Effects of Industrial Concentration: a Cross-section Analysis for the Common Market.* North-Holland Publishing Company: 1979.

Sleuwaegen, L. "The Relevant Antitrust Market, in Competition Policy and Integration, Community Merger Control Policy," *European Economy*, n° 57, 1994, pp. 111–27.

Sleuwaegen, Leo and Yamawaki, Hideki "The Formation of the European Common Market and Changes in Market Structure and Performance," *European Economic Review* Volume 32, Number 7, September 1988, pp. 1451–75.

Van Cayseele, P. *Regulation and International Innovative Activities in the Pharmaceutical Industry.* Doctoral Dissertation, K.U. Leuven, 1987.

— *De Belgische wet op de mededinging. Concentraties in een industrieel economisch en internationaal juridisch perspectief.* Antwerpen: Maklu, 1994, 152 p.

Van Cayseele, P. and F. Wuyts "Legally Enforceable Damages and the Use of Contracts as a Barrier to Entry," Financial Economics Research Paper, n° 20, 1995, C.E.S., Leuven.

Yamawaki, Hideki, Sleuwaegen, Leo, and Weiss, Leonard W. "Industry Competition and the Formation of the European Common Market," in Weiss, Leonard W., editor. *Concentration and Price.* Cambridge, Mass. and London: MIT Press, 1989, pages 112-43.

Competition Policies in Europe - S. Martin (Editor)

Chapter 10

French Competition Policy

Saïd Souam[1]

10.1 Historical Background

After the 1789 French Revolution, the legislature rejected the corporate organization of the old regime and in 1791 instituted freedom of trade and industry.[2] The famous Le Chapelier law made *coalition* an offense in the same year. But these legal provisions regarding freedom of competition were related more to the setting up of a new public order, like freedom of thought or of religious thinking, than to the institution of a new basis for market relationships.

Another important step was the enactment of the penal code in 1810. Article 419 of this code condemns coalitions for price-fixing. At the beginning, all coalitions were condemned without distinction. But from the middle of the 19th century, the economic order prevailed over the public order: courts did not condemn those coalitions whose aim was to remedy economic difficulties resulting from tough competition, price decreases or foreign competition.

The coalition offense was abolished in 1864. This permitted the establishment of professional organizations, unions and cartels. The economic penal code constrained some phenomena which happen after shortages, such as

[1] I would like to thank Patricia Charléty-Lepers, David Encaoua, Stephen Martin, Patrick Rey and Bernard Salanié for helpful comments and discussion of an earlier version of this chapter.

[2] Loi des 2-17 Mars 1791.

excessive prices or concerted speculations.

Once again, however, these practices were fought more for the sake of public order rather than for economic purposes. The fact of the matter is that the notion of competition did not prevail at all among the French policy-makers. Until very recently, anything that contributed to strengthening the power of the State was viewed favorably. This so-called "*tradition jacobine*" is also a legacy of the French Revolution. The French tradition of government intervention in the market mechanism increased between WW I and WW II. After the Great Depression, the idea that the economy should be planned prevailed. Strong cartels emerged during this period.

10.2 Reconstruction of the French Economy

Although the first French laws on competition date back to the 18th century, the most important evolution has taken place in recent decades. Immediately after World War II, the need to reconstruct the French economy led to a planning process based on strong public market intervention. The aim of this economic planning was the modernization of French industry. This included nationalization of a significant part of the industrial sector, strict price controls and extensive subsidies policy.

A price control ordinance was adopted in 1945.[3] It gave the government the power to freeze wages, and all prices were under state control. In the same 1945 ordinance all concerted practices, conventions, express or tacit agreements, or coalitions whatever their form or their cause were considered illegal, if their object or their potential effect was to impair the exercise of competition by preventing a decrease in costs or selling prices or by facilitating an artificial increase in prices.

At that time, it was generally believed that anticompetitive practices should be condemned because they led to price increases and therefore contributed to inflation. This reflected a lack of an economic basis in the analysis of the effects of competition. The idea that economic efficiency is better guaranteed by competitive markets had real difficulty achieving acceptance among policy-makers.

[3]Ordonnance N°45 – 1483 du 30 Juin 1945 relative aux prix.

10.3 The first French Competition Law

In 1953, the first French competition statutes were enacted, but without any economic objectives. Their enactment was mainly for the sake of appearances and was not really effective (Dumez and Jeunemaître, 1996). It was in fact in response to external pressure from the United States that France began to implement a competition policy; the same is true for Great Britain and Germany.

These statutes were mainly seen as a complement to the 1945 ordinance on price control (Jenny, 1990). Agreements between firms were prohibited under a rule of reason. Only those agreements which could increase prices were condemned. During this period, competition was not believed to be an appropriate way to increase economic efficiency and production. The French government and most influential business leaders favored a strong industrial policy. The enforcement of the competition statutes was very weak. The *Commission Technique des Ententes*, which was created to give opinions on the cases referred to it, analyzed only some minor cases. The Minister of Economic Affairs was in fact the chief enforcer. Ten years after passage of the original law, an amendment added a provision prohibiting anticompetitive practices by firms holding a dominant position to the law.

10.4 The 1977 Competition Law

The most important changes in French competition law occurred under the impetus of Prime Minister Raymond Barre.[4] Indeed the reform of 1977[5] introduced some important innovations in the law. First of all, the new advisory body in charge of investigating collusive behavior between firms and abuses of dominant position, the *Commission de la Concurrence*, obtained the right to initiate and prosecute some cases.[6] The Commission was also allowed to impose fines on firms engaged in anticompetitive practices. These fines could not exceed 5% of the annual sales of the firms involved. Another important innovation was that for the first time, professional and consumer organizations were allowed to initiate a complaint by referring it to the Com-

[4] Former chairman of the European Commission and Professor of Economics.

[5] Loi N°77 – 806 du 19 Juillet 1977.

[6] This possibility was rarely used at first since the Commission did not have enough resources.

mission. But the Minister still had the final decision power.

A procedure for selective merger control was also introduced in the 1977 reform. This decision was largely motivated by discussions during the 1972 European Summit in Paris regarding the establishment of a control of mergers at the European level. The French administration, engaged in an extensive industrial policy program, was disturbed by the possibility of European merger control, and implementation of merger control at the national level was seen as a way to bypass the European merger control project (Jenny, 1990).

The control was exercised by the government through an agency, which was in fact part of the old price control administration. A merger could be examined if the total market shares of the merging firms exceeded 40% in the case of horizontal mergers, and 25% for non-horizontal mergers. The notification of a merger was not compulsory and the government sometimes used the threat of a control to deter foreign acquisitions of French firms. The underlying opinion was that French firms were too small and the amounts of capital were not important. Therefore, the authorities encouraged mergers as a means of creating firms that would be large enough to compete in international markets.

In the event, concentration increased in many industries and the Minister referred only one merger project per year to the Commission.[7]

Even though the Minister in charge of economic affairs still kept the investigative power and made the final decisions, the 1977 reform was seen as the beginning of a new era. The imposition of fines in certain cases and the publicity given to them by the media contributed to promoting the idea that competitive market processes could be better for the French economy and that anticompetitive practices should be severely punished (Brault, 1987).

10.5 Current French Competition Law

10.5.1 The New Competition Rules of 1986

Around 1983, a new consensus emerged among politicians. Many discussions and reports showed the necessity of introducing changes in French competition law. Some amendments to competition law were added during 1985 and

[7] Only 8 mergers were examined by the *Commission de la Concurrence* during the period 1977–1986.

1986, before the most important change happened. Indeed, despite the resistance of the administration, which tried to reappropriate all investigative powers and control of the *Commission de la Concurrence*, a new ordinance was enacted. As Brault (1987) explains, the 1986 ordinance was the expression of a cautious liberalism and could be seen as a basis for building a free market economy. The new ordinance enacted in 1986 established the free market economy as the model to be used in France. This is why the 1945 ordinance on price control was abolished. The 1986 ordinance states in its first article that prices are freely determined through competitive processes. Only the prices of some products and services remain under the control of the government.

10.5.2 The 1986 ordinance

The implementation of the competition law in France is the concern of both the *Conseil de la Concurrence* and Courts of common law.

The 1986 ordinance[8] contains 7 titles and 63 articles. Article 2 of Title II creates the *Conseil de la Concurrence* which replaces the *Commission de la Concurrence*. The Conseil is considered a quasi-judicial body, independent of the Ministry in charge of economic affairs. The 1986 ordinance named it as the chief enforcer of French competition law, in charge of prosecuting anticompetitive agreements and abuses of market power. It also gave the Conseil the power to impose fines or issue injunctions to the firms which violate the law.

Under 1987 amendments,[9] appeals against decisions of the Conseil are to the *Cour d'appel de Paris* (rather than the *Conseil d'Etat*). The amendment thus separated the administration from the interpretation and the enforcement of competition law; the Minister is no longer involved. This decision was taken after an intense debate. These changes are fundamental since they substitute judicial oversight over interpretation and enforcement for political discretion.

[8] The 1986 ordinance was modified by several amendments: loi n°87–499 du 6 Juillet 1987, loi n°92–1282 du 11 Décembre 1992, loi n°92–1336 du 16 Décembre 1992, loi n°92–1442 du 31 Décembre 1992, loi n°93-122 du 29 Janvier 1993, loi n°94-89 du 1 Février 1994, loi n°95-95 du 1 Février 1995 and finally by loi n°96-588 du 1 Juillet 1996.

[9] Loi N°87 – 499 du 6 Juillet 1987 et Décret N°87 – 849 du 19 Octobre 1987 relatif aux recours exercés devant la Cour d'appel de Paris contre les décisions du Conseil de la Concurrence.

The decisions of the *Cour d'appel de Paris* can be appealed to the *Cour de Cassation* which is the highest French judicial body.

The core of the 1986 ordinance is Title III, which is completely devoted to anticompetitive practices. Two articles are at the heart of this Title: Articles 7 and 8.

Article 7 prohibits all concerted actions, conventions, explicit or tacit agreements, or coalitions which have as an object or which tend to create the following restrictions:

— limiting access to the market or the free exercise of competition by other firms

— lessening competition by artificially favoring a change of prices

— limiting or controlling production, investment or technical progress

— market or resources sharing between the firms.

Article 8 prohibits, under the same conditions, the abuse by a firm or a group of firms of:

— a dominant position within the internal market or a substantial part of it,

— a state of economic dependency of a client without an equivalent alternative supplier or distributor.

Examples of these abuses include refusal to deal, tied sales, bundling and discriminatory prices.

Article 10 explicitly introduced the possibility for firms to use an efficiency defence. Firms can justify the practices they use on the ground that they increase efficiency or bring economic progress and that the consumers will take advantage of it. But these practices must not impose restrictions unless they are necessary to reach the efficiency goal.

In French competition law, unlike that at the European level, there is no obligation of notification.

Title IV is devoted to transparency rules and restrictive practices. The behavioral rules enunciated in this title are very different from the ones in Title III. Indeed, the practices to which the title is devoted are prohibited *per se*, independently of their impact on the market. These dispositions play a complementary role to Title III dispositions. They are supposed to strengthen the judicial system necessary to good market functioning.

The control of concentrations is defined in Title V. The other titles deal with the investigative powers and other organizational details.

10.5.3 The Origins of Submissions to the Conseil

The following institutions can refer a case to the *Conseil de la Concurrence*:[10] the Ministry in charge of economic affairs, firms, local communities, professional organizations, unions, consumer organizations, Chambers of Commerce, Guild Chambers, Chambers of Agriculture and the *Conseil de la Concurrence* itself.

The Ministry in charge of economic affairs initiates nearly half of the cases. These cases originate in the DGCCRF (*Direction Générale de la Concurrence, de la Consommation et de la Répression des Fraudes*) which is an administrative agency depending on the Ministry. The civil servants of this agency may investigate practices denounced by persons or firms. These investigations can lead to a case being referred to the *Conseil de la Concurrence.*

The Conseil can also give its advice on some consultative cases referred by the government, the Ministry in charge of economic affairs, the Courts and other institutions.

The government must consult the Conseil on every proposal to regulate prices in monopolized sectors,[11] every amendment of law which can lead to a restriction of the exercise of a profession, or reduce the access to a market, or impose uniform practices in terms of pricing or sale conditions.[12] The Conseil must also give its advice on every proposed exemption of agreements between firms that take an anticompetitive character according to Article 10 of the 1986 ordinance.[13] Except for the cases involving exemption of certain types of agreements, the final decisions are taken by the Minister. The Ministry in charge of economic affairs may also optionally refer to the Conseil mergers or proposed mergers which can lessen competition according to Article 38 of the 1986 ordinance. But a merger prohibition by the Conseil takes effect only if accepted by the Minister, who has the sole ability to take the final decision.

[10] Articles 5 and 11 of the 1986 ordinance give an exhaustive list of who can refer a contentious matter to the *Conseil de la Concurrence.*

[11] Cf. Article 1 of the 1986 ordinance.

[12] Cf. Article 6 of the 1986 ordinance.

[13] This is an exemption procedure inspired by the Article 85-3 of the Treaty of Rome.

10.6 The Enforcement of Competition Law in France

I now turn to the contents of French competition law and the way it has been enforced. Ten years after the 1986 ordinance, one can observe that the *Conseil de la Concurrence* has intervened in a broad and large number of cases. The jurisprudence offers a global idea, although not complete, of the approach used by the French authorities to enforce competition law.

The ambiguity of certain notions gives authorities discretionary power, as shown in the range of decisions taken by the *Conseil de la Concurrence*. In fact, there is a trade-off between rigid rules and discretion. Rigid rules favor transparency and thus enhance the judicial security of firms. Conversely, discretion favors flexibility and a case-by-case approach depending on the industry in question.

The rule of reason is widely used in French competition law. However, some practices (price discrimination, selective distribution and refusal to deal) were prohibited *per se* even though this prohibition may not be justified from an economic point of view. Jurisprudence has moved from *per se* prohibitions of these practices to a rule of reason approach and to their legalization under certain restrictive conditions.

10.6.1 Anticompetitive Agreements

Article 7 forbids all anticompetitive agreements which can lessen or restrain competition. From the point of view of the *Conseil de la Concurrence*, the existence of an agreement is considered to be established when there is proof of an unambiguous arrangement of wills between different parties.

For example, the fact that in a meeting the question of prices has been discussed is not sufficient evidence to establish an agreement, from the Conseil's point of view. In practice, evidence for an agreement is obtained by two means. The first is a material proof which consists in all the documents regularly obtained, or findings of the investigators. The second consists in a body of evidence which if taken separately is not a proof of collusion but which can be one if taken as a whole.

The latter approach is controversial, but usually used in French competition law. This approach is accepted by the *Cour de Cassation*. It is particularly used in public and private procurement, where the bidders rarely generate material evidence of collusion. Indirect proof of collusion (for example, very similar bids[14]) is then used.

French jurisprudence allows us to give a typology of anticompetitive agreements: horizontal agreements, cooperative firms and agreements between firms of the same group. Vertical agreements are treated separately.

Horizontal agreements can be of different kinds: agreements on price, settling and diffusion of price lists, recommendations and directives by professional organizations on prices and discounts. In its 1992 report, the *Conseil de la Concurrence* emphasized that these organizations are highly involved in such anticompetitive arrangements. It is worth noting that between 1987 and 1992, 140 professional organizations have been sued for anticompetitive practices condemned by Title III of the 1986 ordinance. There are still many cases involving these organizations. French authorities treat explicit agreements among firms to fix prices, price increases or market sharing, as illegal *per se*. Other practices are essentially treated under a rule of reason.

10.6.2 Dominant Position, Economic Dependency and Anticompetitive Abuses

The concept of abuse of a dominant position was introduced for the first time by an amendment to the 1945 ordinance for the sake of harmonization with the European competition law.[15] Article 8 of the 1986 ordinance prohibits the abuse of a dominant position or of a state of economic dependency when its objective or its effect is to restrict competition within a market.

Even if the Conseil in theory has the power to define the relevant market, in practice this is obtained after an adversarial debate between the parties before the *Conseil de la Concurrence*. This makes it the most controversial part of the analysis. In many cases, the definition used by the *Conseil de la Concurrence* and the *Cour d'appel de Paris* has been rejected by the *Cour de Cassation* as too narrow. When delimiting the relevant market, the *Conseil de la Concurrence* uses several criteria dealing with the substitutability between products, characteristics of the products or services, technical conditions of use, prices, strategies of the producers and sometimes methods of sale.

[14] Décision 90-D-37 concerning a public procurement for the construction of an old people's home.

[15] Loi N°63 – 628 du 2 Juillet 1963.

Definition of a Dominant Position

The *Conseil de la Concurrence* defines a dominant position as a situation where a firm can go beyond the competition within the relevant market. This means that a dominant firm is largely independent of the strategy of its competitors. It is directly inspired by the definition used by the European Community Court of Justice in the United Brands Company case,[16] to which French authorities explicitly refer in some decisions.

To establish the existence of a dominant position on a relevant market, the *Conseil de la Concurrence* takes different elements into consideration. These elements can be connected to the structure of the industry, the behavior of the firms, or to their profits.

The structural element is related to market structure and to the firm's environment. Market share is an important criterion. Even if this criterion is not completely determinant, French jurisprudence allows us to give some general indications of how it is used. A large market share (typically 70% or 80%) is usually viewed as sufficient to establish the existence of a dominant position. Conversely, if a firm has a small market share (under 30%), it is supposed not to be in a dominant position. In between, the Conseil takes into account the relative market shares of the competitors of the firm in the relevant market.

A second important criterion deals with barriers to entry. Moreover, the authorities ask the question whether the position of the firm on other related markets should be taken into consideration. *A priori*, only the relevant market should be taken into consideration, but sometimes a firm can use its position on another market to impair its competitors within the market under examination.

Concerning the structure of the firm, other criteria are taken into consideration

. The authorities consider the degree of vertical integration of the firm, the scope of its production and also its financial power. These elements can establish the existence of a dominant position. Vertical integration can, for example, give the firm a better source of supply compared to its competitors. Similarly, if a firm is financially powerful, or if it belongs to a powerful group, it is assumed to be likely to use predatory pricing to prevent future entry of competitors. This is why the profit performance of firms is used cautiously by

[16] *United Brands* v. *Commission* [1978] ECR 207.

authorities as an index of dominance. Current losses may actually indicate predation by a firm holding a dominant position.

Behavioral criteria are used as a final complement to the structural elements to establish the existence of a dominant position.

Abuses of a Dominant Position

A dominant position in itself is not condemned *a priori*.[17] Only the anticompetitive practices of firms holding such a dominant position are condemned. The most important abusive practices which are condemned are refusal to deal, tied sales, discriminatory sale conditions and the breach of trade relationships if a firm does not accept unjustified trade conditions.

Abuses of a State of Economic Dependency

Until recently, the notion of economic dependency did not exist in French competition law. It developed because of the important change which occurred in producer-retailer bargaining power. France has seen a great wave of concentration in the retail sector. This resulted in the creation of *"super-centrales d'achat:"* large retailers grouped their purchases within the same central buying operation in order to obtain better sale conditions from their suppliers. There also exist the so-called *"centrales de référencement,"* participants in which group their orders to have better conditions of sale. Manufacturers pay premiums just to be included in the lists of products the distributors use for their orders.[18]

In 1985, the *Commission de la Concurrence* suggested that some practices, such as ending a deal with a supplier for the sole reason that he refused to give unjustified trade advantages, the discriminatory deterrence of entry of new retailers or new suppliers in a market, should be condemned. But the legislation then prohibited these practices only if a firm held a dominant position. The Commission suggested that the law be changed to prohibit these practices whatever the position held by the firms within the market. This suggestion was not accepted, and Article 8 of the ordinance established the offense only in the presence of a dominant position.

[17] As in the case of monopolisation of an industry by merger of several firms.

[18] They are called referencing premiums and the products are then referenced on the central buying lists.

To condemn a firm according to Article 8-2, the authorities first have to prove economic dependency and secondly that the dependent firm is subject to anticompetitive practices. Moreover, these practices should have, as an object or as an effect, impedance or restriction of competition, or the altering of competition within a market. Originally, the legislature wanted to prohibit abuses of economic dependency against producers. But the majority of the decisions taken by the Conseil concerned the converse situation, where retailers claimed to be in a state of economic dependency.

The criteria used by the authorities to establish the existence of economic dependency differ slightly depending on whether a retailer or a producer is in a state of economic dependency.

First of all, the Conseil uses the value of the brand to establish the existence of economic dependency of a retailer. The second criterion is the market share of the supplier during the period. The Conseil analyses its fluctuations in order to assess the position of the supplier within the relevant market. The third criterion is the share of the supplier in the retailer's turn-over. The last criterion used is the absence of equivalent conditions offered to the retailer in the market. This stresses the importance of delimitation of the relevant market since three of the criteria are related to it.

Concerning the economic dependency of a supplier, the Conseil uses two important criteria. The first is the proportion of the supplier's turn-over realized through the retailer. The second deals with the importance of the retailer in the trade of the concerned products. If these two criteria are not directly observable, the Conseil looks at the supplier's financial resources, the value of the brand, the duration and the nature of the relationship between the two parties and also the level of the mark-up of the other suppliers in the market.[19]

The authorities try then to give an answer to two important questions in order to completely define the economic dependency:

1. Does the concentration of the supplier's sales result from a strategic choice or from a technical necessity?

2. Is there any equivalent solution offered to the supplier in the market?

Once existence of a state of economic dependency has been proved, the authorities have to prove whether a firm has abused this situation by using

[19]Décision 93-D-21 relative à des pratiques mises en oeuvre lors de l'acquisition de la Société européenne des supermarchés par la société Grands Magasins B du groupe Cora.

anticompetitive practices. This analysis is made under the same conditions as under Article 7. These practices should have as an object or as result the impairing or restriction of competition. This emphasizes the rule of reason used by the French authorities.

The first decision taken by the *Conseil de la Concurrence* concerning an abuse of an economic dependency of a supplier by a client was related to some practices used by *Grands Magasins B*, a subsidiary of the group Cora, when acquiring the *Société européenne des supermarchés*. The Ministry of economic affairs argued that Cora group had abused its purchasing power over some of its food suppliers to compel them to participate financially in the acquisition. The *Conseil de la Concurrence* and the *Cour d'appel de Paris* rejected the arguments of the Ministry.[20] The Conseil considered that evidence of absence of reputation, small size of the suppliers, long term relationships with the retailer and the fact that an important part of their business was done with group Cora, were not sufficient to establish the existence of a situation of economic dependency. The investigation in fact showed that some of these suppliers were not compelled to participate, and that some others on which a pressure had been exercised did not accept.

At this writing, no firm rule can be derived from the French jurisprudence. The notion of economic dependency is relative and subject to diverse interpretations. In fact, even the concept of abuse of a dominant position can be subject to diverse interpretations. This situation is illustrated for example in the case TV Mondes vs. Compagnie Générale de Vidéocommunications, where the *Conseil de la Concurrence* qualified the discriminatory practices as abusive[21] but the *Cour d'appel de Paris* adopted the opposite position.[22]

10.6.3 Transparency Rules and Restrictive Practices

The concept of pricing transparency is well known. Title IV of 1986 ordinance is completely devoted to those practices. The characteristics of the dispositions are quite different from those of Title III, which deals with anticompetitive practices. The practices in question are prohibited *per se*. Some dispositions have a complementary role to those regarding anticompetitive practices. They reinforce the judicial device necessary for good market per-

[20] Décision 93-D-21 du Conseil de la Concurrence et arrêt du 25 Mai 1994 de la Cour d'appel de Paris.

[21] Décision 91-D-51 du 19 Novembre 1991.

[22] Arrêt du 17 Juin 1992 de la Cour d'appel de Paris.

formance by enhancing the transparency in favor of the buyers. This is particularly the case for dispositions concerning the communication of price lists, general conditions of sale or of services and also those relative to invoicing.

Other dispositions, which are not justified from an economic point of view, prohibit some practices which are seen to be unfair. Another important difference between the two titles deals with sanctions. Indeed, unless these practices are examined under Title III, the sanctions do not fall within the competence of the *Conseil de la Concurrence.* They only fall within the competence of the civil or commercial Courts. Title IV offers a wide range of intervention to the economic administration (Boutarde Labarde and Canivet, 1994). According to the civil liability introduced by Article 36 of the ordinance, the administration can ask on behalf of the victims that certain practices (price discrimination, refusal to deal, tied sales and bundling) be stopped.[23]

We will see that legislation has moved on, and that a recent law has radically changed some stipulations of the 1986 ordinance. Many detailed dispositions are in fact cited in the 1986 ordinance. Refusal to deal is condemned under a rule of reason.[24] Moreover, every purchase should be carried out with a detailed bill mentioning among other things the names of the parties, their addresses, the date of the purchase, the quantity and the price. A later amendment extended this to include discounts.[25] The law punishes every infringement of this disposition by a fine (between 5000 and 100000 FF in the 1986 ordinance, now 500000 FF[26]).

Concerning typically vertical relationships (more particularly producer-retailer ones), retail price maintenance is illegal *per se*.[27] But French jurisprudence makes a distinction between RPM and recommended prices. Indeed, recommended prices are not forbidden if they are not binding. But a producer can be fined if he uses breach of relationship as a threat if the retailer does not use the recommended prices. Certain practices are penalized and others are treated under a civil liability regime. Every infringement of the general dispositions of competition law concerning invoicing, resale at a loss,

[23]These practices were penalised before the 1986 ordinance.

[24]Article 30 forbids refusal to deal with a buyer without a legitimate motive and also forbids tied sales.

[25]Loi N°92–1442 du 31 Décembre 1992.

[26]Loi N°93–122 du 29 Janvier 1993.

[27]There are some exceptions. The retailers of books can make, for example, a maximum rebate of 5% relatively to the editors' prices.

general conditions of trade, RPM, and payment delays is penalized.

Three behavioral practices (discriminatory practices, refusal to deal and tied sales) were depenalized in 1986. They involved the civil liability of their author, who could be obliged to make up for the caused harm.

It is worth noting that the question of prohibition of RPM, refusal to deal, price discrimination and reselling at a loss, was completely unrelated to any economic purpose. In the 50s France saw the development of large retailers. There then followed a great conflict between large retailers, small retailers, and also producers. The administration believed that the existence of large retailers could be an effective tool to fight inflation. It prohibited RPM and refusal to deal. After that, small retailers lobbied the administration, arguing that the producers discriminated against them and that the large retailers were reselling some attractive products at a loss. Such lobbying was successful and discrimination among retailers and reselling at a loss were declared unlawful.

The late 70s have seen a great concentration in the retail industry, and the balance of bargaining power has been completely reversed. The early 80s have seen extensive lobbying of the producers against the prohibition of refusal to deal. They argued that they can be dependent on the large retailers who asked for more and more unjustified discounts by threatening them with refusal to buy if they did not offer them those rebates. Moreover, the disequilibrium appeared not only between distributors and producers but also between the large distributors and the traditional ones. Price discriminations and more favorable buying conditions offered to the large distributors were seen by the traditional distributors as unfair and as leading to a tougher price competition that was against their own interests. The 1986 reform also took the evolution of the bargaining power between producers and retailers into consideration. The introduction of Article 8-2 concerning the abuse of a state of economic dependency was made to somewhat reduce the great influence the retailers kept.

The prohibition of refusal to deal created some specific judicial regimes, the objective of which was to permit selection of some retailers (when it is viewed to be useful) while protecting the retailers from the possible arbitrary decisions of the producers. Selective distribution and exclusive territories are also considered under Article 7. Their treatment is under a rule of reason. They are considered legal if the criteria used by the producers are objective, for example for an adequate distribution of the products. Moreover, they should not limit the trade freedom of the retailers and should be applied without discrimination.

10.6.4 The 1996 Changes

A new law[28] was voted in 1996. As we have already seen, the 1986 ordinance explicitly took into account the great power obtained by retailers through the abuse of a state of economic dependency. Enforcement was weak and concentration increased during the last decade. This is why the underlying opinion was that the 1986 ordinance should be changed in order to take effectively into account the disequilibrium between producers and retailers. It explicitly seeks for more fairness and balance in commercial relationships.

Some points were considered not to be sufficient for a fair competition in the markets: treatment of some predatory behavior, treatment of the abuse of economic dependency and also reselling at a loss. The law abolishes the *per se* prohibition of the refusal to deal and of tied sales. It also regulates some practices of large retail industry such as the payment of referral premiums and abusive refusal of deal.

Reselling at a loss

In the 1986 ordinance, the legislature introduced an explicit prohibition of reselling at a loss. Article 32 of the ordinance stated that every retailer who sells products at a price less than its purchase price would pay a fine lying between 5000 FF and 100000 FF. The price below which the retailers were prohibited from reselling was supposed to be the invoice price plus taxes and possible transport costs. The aim was to prevent the "fidelity rebates" producers gave to the large retailers through conditional discounts paid at the end of the year and depending on the total volume of sales.

The difficulty with the enforcement of this article was that the distributors were allowed to prove that in fact they paid less for the products than the invoiced amount. This created endless discussions in the Courts about what should be considered a discount.

Fighting reselling at a loss seems to be one of the most important objectives of the new law. The aim is to preserve the small trade and to avoid price wars among some large distributors. The new Article 32 of the ordinance refers explicitly to a unit invoice price plus taxes and possible transport

[28] Loi N°96–588 du 1er Juillet 1996 sur la loyauté et l'équilibre des relations commerciales.

costs. Other discounts should not be taken into account in computing the reference price at which the products are resold. This means that if a rebate is not certain at the invoicing time, it should not be considered when checking the price below which it is forbidden to resell. The sanctions are substantially reinforced. Indeed, infringement of the prohibition is subject now to a fine of 500000 FF. Moreover, publicity for reselling at a loss is also prohibited and the retailers can be fined at a level equal to half the publicity expenses. A new provision on penal liability is explicitly provided in the new law.

Refusal to deal

The abolition of the *per se* prohibition of refusal to deal is made for the sake of restoring an equilibrium between producers and large distributors. The possibility of refusal to deal is considered as a means to counteract the ending of a relationship by distributors, which can leave producers at their mercy. But even if refusal to deal is not prohibited *per se*, it can be prohibited if it results from an arrangement under Article 7 of the ordinance, or if done by a firm holding a dominant position under Article 8 or if it is considered as a discrimination (Article 36). Tied sales, as well, are no longer prohibited *per se*.

Restrictive practices

Enforcement of the abuses of a state of economic dependency was seen to be inefficient under Article 8-2. The new law creates three new cases of economic dependency, the aim of which is to counteract the market power of large retailers.

Article 36-3 prohibits trying to obtain advantages from a producer without a written commitment to a volume level. The objective is the ending of referral premiums without a sufficient counterpart. Manufacturers in fact pay a premium in order to be in the lists of products of the "*super-centrales.*" Without an explicit and written commitment to a certain volume level, these premiums are prohibited whatever the trade conditions given to the manufacturers.

Article 36-4 prohibits obtaining or trying to obtain rebates, delays of payment, or better trade conditions under the threat of ending trade relationships. Finally, Article 36-5 prohibits ending of trade relationships without a written notice according to the usage of the profession. The *per se* prohibition of these practices will probably make the fight against abuses of a state of economic dependency more effective. Moreover, these practices only fall under the competence of the judge. One can think that judges may be more prone to restore a certain equilibrium to the commercial relationships than was the Conseil (Vogel, 1996).

Predatory Practices

Another important motive for which French competition law was amended, is fighting predatory practices the large distributors use to the detriment of traditional retailers. A new offense was introduced into the current law. Article 10-1 prohibits every sale to consumers at abusive low prices with respect to costs of production, transformation and marketing, if the object or the result of these practices is to eliminate a rival from a market or to impede its entrance in it. It is worth noting that the final version of the law is very different from the initial propositions which were considered as a return to a general price control banned by the 1986 ordinance. Even if the final version limits the conditions under which certain price practices would be considered as abusive in terms of predatory pricing, the general terms used will probably create many difficulties in its interpretation by the Conseil.

Retail Networks

As we have seen before, the organization of retail networks is considered under Article 7. It can also benefit from an exemption under Article 10 of the 1986 ordinance. The underlying opinion is that the legislation did not sufficiently protect the adherents of these retail networks against free riding, which is seen to be unfair competition and was always fought by the authorities. The aim of the new dispositions taken is to reinforce this fight.

The law now prohibits *per se* every participation (whatever direct or indirect) in a violation of a selective distribution of some product exempted under Article 10. A violation can engage the author's liability. Even if the law restricts the prohibition only to the exempted retail networks, the networks legalized under a rule of reason may also benefit from these new dispositions (Vogel, 1996).

10.6.5 Merger Control

The object of merger control is to follow the evolution of market structures and to intervene to prevent mergers which can harm competition, or which can restrain it significantly.

As we have seen above, this control was introduced very late in France.[29] The control procedure is different from what we can see at the European level or in the United States. Indeed, in France there is no compulsory notification of mergers. The initiation of the control procedure, which is *ex post*, can only be done by the Minister in charge of economic affairs. But until very recently, concentration control has not been an important aspect of enforcement of competition law in France. On average, only one concentration project has been sent for an advice to the *Conseil de la Concurrence* by the Minister.

The activity of the *Conseil* concerning concentration control has increased over these last years. In 1992 for example, the Conseil had to give its advice in only 3 cases. This number increased to 9 cases in 1993 and 15 cases in 1994. But there were only 5 projects of concentration transmitted to the *Conseil de la Concurrence* in 1995.

The 1986 ordinance gives an inclusive definition of a concentration in order to take into account all forms of external growth of the firms. Article 39 of Title V gives the following definition: *"Concentration results from every act, whatever its form, which consists in a transfer of property of the whole or a part of the goods, ownership, or obligations from a firm to another, or which has as an object or as an effect, to allow a firm or a group of firms to exert directly or indirectly its influence over other firms ."*

The jurisprudence, afterwards, shaped the administrative approach. For example, one important aspect of the jurisprudence was given by the *Commission de la Concurrence* in an opinion, the 14th March 1985, on the situation of the central buying offices and their groupings. The Commission argued that if these central buying offices organize financial solidarity, or sharing of logistic resources between their members, then they can be considered as concentrations. This also would be the case if they use the same commercial sign, or respect a same common purchase and sale policy.

Some guidelines were diffused after lawyers asked for more transparency

[29] There still exist some specific regimes. For example, there exist specific regulation rules for the finance and banking sector (Loi N°84–46 du 24 Janvier 1984). This is also the case for the press and audiovisual communication which were explicitly excluded from the field of application of the 1986 ordinance (Loi N°25 du 17 Janvier 1989).

from the French authorities concerning practice in this domain (DGCCRF, 1992). But these guidelines are not as detailed as the American Merger Guidelines.

The analysis, described hereafter, takes three steps. The first step consists in examining whether the operation is a concentration in the sense of Title V of the 1986 ordinance. It begins with the definition of a relevant market after an adversarial debate. Given this definition, the second step deals with the thresholds defined in the ordinance. The third step is the most important one from an economic point of view and consists in evaluating the effect of the operation on competition in the market.

Indeed, the authorities have to evaluate the effects of the concentration on competition and balance those effects with the possible efficiencies brought upon by the merger. The Conseil also takes into account the competitiveness of the firms in an international context.[30] If the direct effect of the concentration is not balanced by the benefits, the Conseil can specify some corrective measures to be taken in order to maintain or establish sufficient competition in the market in question. For example, when the Gillette Company notified its decision to buy the Parker Pen Holdings Limited, the Conseil accepted the concentration on the condition that the two parties engaged to take sufficient actions to develop Waterman S.A., a subsidiary of The Gillette Company.[31]

The 1986 ordinance gives the conditions under which an operation is considered as a concentration and can be controlled by the Ministry in charge of economic affairs. The first condition deals with market share. If the total market share of the firms directly involved or those tied to them is greater than 25% of the market or of a substantial part of it, the operation can be controlled. If this is the case, the ministry in charge of economic affairs can refer the matter to the *Conseil de la Concurrence*. It can then accept or reject the opinion given by the Conseil.

If this criterion is not satisfied, the Conseil can use the total annual sales criteria. If the annual total sales exceed 7 billions of francs, and under the condition that at least two of the firms involved have a turn-over of more than 2 billions of francs, then the operation can be controlled. Every project or concentration which satisfies one or both of these two conditions can be submitted to the opinion of the *Conseil de la Concurrence* by the Minister in charge of economic affairs. These conditions are only seen as

[30] Cf. Article 41 of the 1986 ordinance.

[31] Avis N°92–A–11 du Conseil de la Concurrence.

necessary conditions to trigger control from the authorities, but the control is not systematic.

There are in fact only a few examples where the Conseil has advised against the completion of concentration. Even in such cases, the Minister in charge of economic affairs did not always follow the opinion given by the Conseil.[32]

In some cases, the Conseil asked for some corrective measures in order to make competition more effective or to introduce it in the industry. We can cite the example of reciprocal buyout of some cinemas in Paris between Pathé Cinéma and Gaumont. The operation did not verify the market-share criteria defined in the ordinance, but the Conseil found that it was met in the Parisian market, which is a substantial part of the French market. The corrective measures taken were that Gaumont sell some cinemas within Paris.[33] In some cases the Minister rejected the corrective measures given by the Conseil.[34]

In many cases the Conseil took into account the competitiveness of firms facing international competition. A concentration can be accepted if it enhances international competitiveness although it lessens competition inside the French market.[35] This is a version of the efficiency defense.

Finally unlike the European approach, French competition law does not make any distinction between concentrative and cooperative joint-ventures. All these operations are covered by Title V of the 1986 ordinance.

10.7 Conclusion

The changes French competition law has seen during the last fifty years can be considered as an important step toward promoting competition on French markets. The fact that enforcement of a part of competition law is done by the courts or the Conseil can be considered as a revolution relative to the underlying opinion concerning market organization. As we have seen

[32] Cf. also Avis N°94–A–22 concerning a buyout of Codes Rousseau by Média Communication in the sector of the services and products for teaching driving.

[33] Cf. Avis N°93–A–1 concerning a reciprocal cession of cinemas between Gaumont and Pathé Cinéma and also Avis N°93–A–12 concerning buyout of certain cinemas in Paris by U.G.C.

[34] Cf. Avis N°94–A–26 concerning the buyout of two radio stations Fun Radio and M 40 by the CLT.

[35] This is also the case in industries in decline.

before, the first decisions taken for that purpose were preceded by an intense debate. But even if economic analysis has been widely used in recent years, economists are not really involved in the enforcement process. Policy-makers still want to control the economic running of French markets. This was the case for example in 1995 with the first propositions to the Parliament for changing French competition law concerning some individual practices. The project was criticized as being simply a return to general price controls which were abolished by the 1986 ordinance. This brought some new dispositions to the law which can be seen as motivated more for political than for economic purposes.

This leads to the discussion of the objectives assigned to French competition policy. On the one hand, through the Conseil's enforcement the promotion of economic efficiency seems to be one of its most important objectives. But on the other hand, concerning individual practices and merger control the objectives do not seem to be very clear and can change with economic and political situations. Indeed, as we have seen before the law moved from *per se* prohibition of certain practices to their legalization through a process which was completely disconnected from economic questions like efficient allocation of resources. As the most recent changes show, fairness of competition is considered as an important objective assigned now to the French competition law.[36]

Merger control remains under political control in France. Indeed, the Minister in charge of economic affairs still has the power to refer mergers to the Conseil. The Conseil only advises the Minister who holds the power to take final decisions. With merger control, the authorities have a powerful tool to monitor markets. Moreover, mergers are referred to the Conseil on the basis of several factors, often motivated by what is supposed to be of public interest. The great discretion authorities have weakens the enforcement of French merger control.

Despite the dichotomic enforcement by the civil courts and the Conseil on the one hand and Ministry in charge of economic affairs on the other, French competition law is considered as a modern law similar to the European competition law and also to some extent to the American antitrust law. The similarity to the other modern competition laws comes essentially from the enforcement by a quasi-judicial body the *Conseil de la Concurrence*. The 1986 ordinance was seen as an attempt to harmonize with the European

[36]The 1996 law is entitled: on fairness and equilibrium of trade relationships.

competition policy. Indeed, Articles 7 and 8 are to a large extent similar with Articles 85 and 86 of the Treaty of Rome.

Finally, an important characteristic of French competition policy is the extensive use of a rule of reason. Only some practices like RPM and anti-competitive agreements like agreements on charged prices or market-sharing remain illegal *per se*.

10.8 References

Boutard Labarde, M.-C. and Canivet, G. *Droit français de la concurrence.* Librairie Générale de Droit et de Jurisprudence, Paris 1994.

Brault, D. *L'Etat et l'esprit de concurrence en France.* Economica, 1987.

Direction Générale de la Concurrence, de la Consommation et de la Répression des Fraudes *Méthode d'analyse pour le contrôle des concentrations.* Etudes DGCCRF, Juillet 1992.

Dumez, H. and Jeunemaître, A. , "The Convergence of Competition Policies in Europe: Internal Dynamics and External Imposition," in S. Berger and R. Dore editors, *National Diversity and Global Capitalism.* Cornell University Press, 1996.

Jenny, F. "French Competition Policy in Perspective," in W. S. Comanor et al., editors, *Competition Policy in Europe and North America: Economic Issues and Institutions.* London: Harwood Academic Publishers, 1990.

Vogel, L., in *Contrats-Concurrence-Consommation.* Editions du Juris-Classeur, Août-Septembre 1996.

Competition Policies in Europe - S. Martin (Editor)

Chapter 11

Irish Competition Policy and the Macroeconomy

Frank Barry
Francis O'Toole

11.1 Introduction

The failure to recognize the importance of competition policy and the non-traded sector in economic development has contributed to a situation in Ireland in which the implementation of an activist competition policy has proceeded at a much slower pace than is required. Economic policy in Ireland appears to be based on the mercantilist notion that the internationally trading sectors of the economy are the engines of growth. For example, a recent report to the government, which dealt with the largely non-internationally-traded service sector, argued that "Non-traded activities are in effect dependent on the internationally traded sector. ... Those activities that are internationally traded determine the rates at which the economy can grow" (Department of Employment and Enterprise, 1993).

The non-traded sector continues to be economically discriminated against vis-à-vis the traded sector. One of the cornerstones of Irish industrial policy, once the economy adopted an outward-oriented strategy in the early 1960s, was Export Profits Tax Relief. As a result of representations from Brussels this was replaced by a special low rate of corporation tax (10 per cent) for the manufacturing sector in 1981. In comparison, the services sector continues to pay the standard rate of corporation tax (36 per cent).[1] In addition, the vast bulk of grant aid to business goes to the manufacturing sector. The agricultural sector continues to be subsidized by the Common Agricultural Policy while the construction sector is bolstered by mortgage interest tax relief, urban renewal schemes and the non-existence of an effective residential property tax. The net result is economic discrimination against the services/non-traded sector. This is reflected in the fact that the share of market services in Ireland's GDP is the lowest among EU member states (1993 figures).[2]

Competition policy in a small open economy is particularly relevant for this services/non-traded sector since the traded sector operates in an environment of international competition. However, the Competition Authority has a staff of less than twenty persons while the staff of the three industrial policy authorities comprises over one thousand persons.[3] Adoption of a more activist competition policy would be welfare-enhancing not only in terms of increased output and reduced prices within the non-traded sector itself but also because of knock-on effects in the traded sectors; the prices of non-traded goods are important determinants of the success or failure of the traded sector, both through their impact as intermediate inputs and through their effect on wage demands and hence on the factor costs payable by the traded sector.

The mercantilist perspective has been bolstered by the implicit acceptance of the proposal that the adoption of an activist industrial policy creates employment while the adoption of an activist competition policy destroys employment. This paper attempts to go some way towards correcting this misconception. Following an overview of competition policy in Ireland, it is argued that the adoption of an activist competition policy in the non-traded sector would increase, rather than decrease, total employment.

---

[1]The 1996 Budget introduced a lower rate of corporation tax (currently 28 per cent) which applies to the first £50,000 of a firm's profits.

[2]To some extent these numbers are distorted by the practice of transfer pricing in the manufacturing sector. Nevertheless, Ireland's poor employment creation record in the 1980s is ascribable to poor performance in the services sector relative to the EU average.

[3]However, the recent appointment of a Director of Enforcement to the Competition Authority, the imminent appointment of a number of economists and solicitors to the staff of the Competition Authority and the proposed setting up of a Telecommunications regulatory agency is suggestive of a change in approach.

11.2 Competition Policy in Ireland Prior to 1991

Legislation to prohibit restrictive business practices in Ireland was first enacted in 1953 with the Restrictive Trade Practices Act which established the Fair Trade Commission. Legislation was based on the "control of abuse" principle with restrictive practices considered on a case-by-case basis. Services, apart from distribution, were excluded from the domain of the legislation. The 1972 Restrictive Practices Act extended the legislation to include professional services, but other sectors such as banking, the supply of electricity, the provision of public transport and the services of local authorities continued to be excluded. The Minister (Industry and Commerce), on the advice of the Commission, could issue a Restrictive Practice Order to cover a particular trade. The 1987 Restrictive Practices (Amendment) Act brought the previously-excluded service sectors, apart from local authorities, within the domain of the legislation. Restrictive Practices Orders covered markets which accounted for about 35 per cent of consumer expenditure by 1991 (OECD, 1993a, p. 71).

A failing of competition policy in Ireland over past decades was that it had been Order-led; for sectors of the economy not covered by an Order, it remained legal to engage in price-fixing and market-sharing and no Order existed in respect of any professional service. Repeated enquiries were carried out into the behavior of several trades as new practices emerged requiring new enquiries culminating in new Orders. The compliance of Irish businesses with respect to these Orders is also questionable, as evidenced by 1988 data revealing that a majority of petrol stations, restaurants and pubs outside the Dublin region failed to comply with price display orders.[4]

Policy towards mergers and monopolies was (and, to a large extent, is) dictated by a separate piece of legislation — the Mergers, Take-overs and Monopolies (Control) Act 1978. The Minister for Enterprise and Employment (previously known as Industry and Commerce) had (and, to a large extent, has) sole jurisdiction over acquisitions and mergers. All proposed acquisitions and mergers involving two parties with gross assets above £10m and/or gross turnover above £20m had to be notified to the Minister for ap-

[4]The Groceries Order which prohibits below-cost selling in the groceries market remains in force. Cost is, however, defined as "net-invoice" cost which may differ from actual cost. See Walsh and Whelan (1996) for an interesting welfare analysis of the Groceries Order.

proval. Although this Act could also have been used to impose severe sanctions on monopolies no such sanctions were imposed (Massey and O'Hare, 1996, p.105).

11.3 The Competition Act 1991

The Competition Act, which came into force on October 1, 1991, introduced a prohibition-based system of competition law to Ireland. Articles 85 and 86 of the Treaty of Rome are reflected in Sections 4 and 5 of the Competition Act. Section 4 of the Act refers to anti-competitive agreements between undertakings and restrictive trade practices are prohibited under Section 4(1). Exemptions, through the issuing of licences, can however be granted under Section 4(2) if the restrictions promote economic progress, consumers receive a fair share of the resulting benefits, the restrictions do not eliminate too much competition and no unnecessary restrictions are included in the agreement. Section 5 of the Act refers to the abuse of a dominant position. The Competition Authority was established under the Act to play a supportive and advisory role; it had no enforcement powers. It had no power to investigate agreements either on its own initiative or as a result of complaints by third parties. The onus was placed on injured third parties to take an action in the High Court for an injunction or damages; there have been very few court actions claiming breaches of the Act.

Agreements between undertakings must be notified to the Authority in order to obtain a certificate (where, in the opinion of the Authority, the notified agreement does not offend) or a licence. A large number of commercial agreements have been notified to, and considered by, the Authority. As of the end of 1994, the Authority had dealt with 805 of 1,270 notified agreements.[5] Although there have been very few outright refusals by the Authority, some have been very significant; licences have been refused for minimum resale price maintenance agreements in the case of books and for stock exchange rules on fixed minimum commissions on gilts. One quarter of notified agreements were either withdrawn or found "offensive" although less than 4 per cent of agreements were ultimately refused a certificate or licence. Almost 51 per cent of notifications decided upon were certified although some of these agreements had to be amended before certification.[6] One-third of the agree-

[5] This section draws from Massey and O'Hare (1995).

[6] Almost 55 per cent of the 407 agreements certified by the Authority involved shop

ments were covered by one of the following category licences subsequently issued by the Authority: exclusive purchase agreements between suppliers and individual filling stations for motor fuels, exclusive distribution agreements and franchise agreements; these (vertical) agreements involve firms engaged at different levels of the production and distribution process. These category licences mirror block exemptions issued by the European Commission. The Authority's view, which is in line with the European Commission's view, is that non-price vertically restrictive agreements offend against Section 4(1) but if "constructed properly" satisfy the requirements for the issuing of a licence. Vertically restrictive agreements containing price restraints do not appear capable of meeting the Competition Authority's requirements for the issuing of a licence.

Much discussion has focused on whether the EU block exemptions should have been incorporated into the legislation. Their inclusion would have eliminated the need for a significant number of agreements to be notified and would have reduced the Authority's workload.[7] A more fundamental weakness was the absence of an active state enforcement mechanism. Although Section 6 allows the Minister to take action to obtain an injunction for breaches of the Act, no such actions have been brought (even though in 1995 the Authority advised the Minister that an action should be brought in a case involving the newspaper industry).

The Minister (Enterprise and Employment) may request the Competition Authority to give its views on a proposed acquisition or merger. The Authority, however, is required to consider not only the effects of the proposed acquisition or merger on competition but also the effects of the proposed acquisition or merger on the level of employment, regional development and other economic and social variables. Somewhat controversially the Competition Authority has also asserted its independent right to examine proposed acquisition and mergers under Section 4(1) and it is conceivable that they could be examined under Section 5.

---

lease agreements, the vast majority in respect of retail outlets in shopping centres; clauses restricting the types of retail business are deemed essential for the successful development of shopping centres.

[7]Examples exist whereby the EU block exemptions have been incorporated into the domestic legislation of EU member states (Massey and O'Hare, 1996, p. 117). It should be noted, however, that some of the exclusive distribution agreements notified to the Authority did not comply with the EU block exemption.

11.4 Enforcement Powers: The Competition (Amendment) Act 1996

The passing into legislation of the Competition (Amendment) Bill 1996 is suggestive of a significant change in emphasis. The primary aim of this legislation is to provide more effective enforcement of competition policy. It is now a criminal offence not to comply with the conditions of a licence granted by the authority. This Act criminalizes anti-competitive behavior and allows for prison sentences of up to two years and fines of up to 10 per cent of a firm's world-wide turnover. New powers of search and greater rights of discovery, including the right to conduct a "dawn raid," have been granted to the holder of the newly-created post of Director of Competition Enforcement and the ability to initiate prosecutions, both civil and criminal, now resides with the Authority. Furthermore, it can now carry out studies without being requested to do so by the Minister.

11.5 Competition Policy & the Traded Sector

At a European level Articles 92 to 94 of the Treaty of Rome refer specifically to state aids. Article 92 appears to forbid state aids although "aid to facilitate the development of certain economic activities or certain economic areas... " may be considered compatible with the common market "where such aid does not adversely affect trading conditions to an extent contrary to the common interest." This suggests that grant aid at a broad level is allowed. Article 93 outlines procedures for introducing or altering state aids and Article 94 outlines the details with respect to qualified majority voting by the Council in the context of state aids.

In the context of industrial policy, limits are placed on state aids with respect to grants for initial investment (e.g. capital grants and loan guarantees) and operating aids (e.g. marketing aids). The lower rate of corporation tax (10 per cent) has been approved by the Commission until 2010. Special tax rates with respect to the Irish Financial Services Centre (IFSC) have been approved until 2005. This 10 per cent tax is seen as a state aid but aid to manufacturing in Ireland is within EU limits for Objective 1 regions.

Overall state aid to industry in Ireland as a percentage of GDP fell from 2.7 per cent in the 1986-88 period to 2.0 per cent in the 1988-90 period (OECD, 1993a, p. 81). These figures can be contrasted with equivalent EU figures of 2.2 per cent and 2.0 per cent, respectively. State aid (inclusive of tax expenditures) to the manufacturing sector, however, is very high in Ireland. The Irish figure, as a percentage of GDP, went from 6.4 per cent for the 1986-88 period to 4.9 per cent in 1988-90, compared to EU averages of 4.0 per cent and 3.5 per cent for equivalent periods (OECD, 1993a, p. 81). Grant aid for fixed investment as a percentage of initial investment was close to the EU average but grant aid for fixed investment in terms of job creation targets was very high by EU standards and very close to allowable limits.

11.6 The Scope for Competition in the Non-Traded Sector

A recent OECD (1993a) Report on competition within the non-traded services sector in Ireland is informative. Allowing for lags in domestic price adjustment to exchange rate fluctuations, and for different indirect tax rates, the aggregate price level for private consumption in 1985 was found to be 8 per cent above that of the UK, and by 1990 it was 10 per cent higher. Three consumer areas in particular stood out. There were (i) food, beverages and tobacco, (ii) transport and communications, and (iii) medical and health care.[8] The Report also notes the existence of entry barriers to the following job categories: engineering, accountancy, architecture, surveying, auctioneering and the estate agency business. The Report comments on the system of fee-determination, the existence of advertising agreements and restrictions on the provision of services in a number of markets. The Report also refers to the high ratio of retail to wholesale outlets — figures for 1988 in Ireland and the United Kingdom were 7.9 and 2.3, respectively — which the Report claims is indicative of an environment supportive of collusion. Certainly wholesale margins are high relative to those at the retail level.

Within the semi-state services sector the Report of the Industrial Policy Review Group (1992) highlighted the need for "... greater competition in air services, telecommunications and energy supply...". The Report noted with disapproval the use of cross subsidies in the cases of Whitegate oil products

[8] Fingleton (1995) contains an illustrative example from the drinks market which appears to show the effect of the single market program as well as the lack of competition in the non-traded services sector — in the period between 1986 and 1994 the real price of draft stout (e.g. Guinness) in public houses increased by 1.6 per cent per annum while the real price of packaged stout (in off-licences) decreased by 1.8 per cent per annum.

and the fertilizer industry and encouraged the use of "... explicit subsidy for social services ...".

Articles 37 and 90 refer to the public sector and semi-state monopolies. According to Article 90 the existence of a state monopoly is not in itself contrary to the Treaty but the manner in which it is exercised could breach the Treaty. Post and electricity services are defined as public services and fall within the remit of Article 90. Article 37 prevents state monopolies from discriminating against nationals of other Member States. The European Union envisages total deregulation of the telecommunications market by 1998 (Ireland has, however, "successfully" lobbied for a two year derogation) and the liberalization of all postal services, except internal letter deliveries. Within the energy area, European Council Directives exist to improve the transparency of gas and electricity prices and to ensure the possibility of the transit of gas and electricity between member states. To some extent, events are overtaking policy in the area of the semi-state bodies as witnessed by the arrival of new technologies in the post and telecommunications area and the *de facto* deregulation of the inter-city bus segment of the public transport market. Open tendering for the construction of a new electricity-generating facility is, however, to be welcomed.

In summary there appears to be a competitive lightly-taxed traded sector supported by activist industrial policy and a non-competitive heavily-taxed market services sector supplemented by an excessively regulated publicly-owned enterprise sector in Ireland.

11.7 The Macroeconomics of Competition Policy

One of the most important questions to be asked of competition policy concerns its welfare effects. While consumers would clearly gain from lower prices, one of the factors inhibiting the introduction of strong pro-competition measures is the fear of substantial job losses in the sectors to be deregulated; in the presence of labor market rigidities these job losses might not be offset by job gains elsewhere in the economy. There is also the fear that opening up these sectors to foreign competition may result in profits being captured by foreign competitors. It is these issue we wish now to address. In the context of inflexible labor markets, we will begin by assuming that real wages are rigid, and then discuss the types of rigidities that arise in conventional modelling of trade union behavior. We will then discuss the profit-shifting argument.

11.7.1 Effects of Competition and Deregulation under Real Wage Rigidity

Competition policy is modelled as being equivalent to trade liberalization; prices are reduced as monopoly positions are eroded and domestic firms that cannot compete at the lower international prices lose market share and shed labor.[9] In this model it is assumed that the real wage (the nominal wage relative to the consumer price index) stays constant. The only macroeconomic effect allowed is that declining prices of deregulated services and utilities translates (through a reduction in the consumer price index) into lower wage demands for the rest of the economy, which therefore expands.

Specifically, consider a small open economy that produces two potentially internationally-tradable goods: one of these is produced under competitive conditions and trades at world prices, while production of the other good is regulated. Regulation, by assumption, raises price above international levels.

Real wage rigidity implies that the wage function,

$$w = F(p_c, p_r) \tag{11.1}$$

is linearly homogenous, where $F()$ is related to the consumer price index; $F_1, F_2 > 0$, and w is the nominal wage. The reduction in p_r, the price of the goods produced in the regulated sectors, therefore gives rise to a less-than-proportionate decrease in w; domestic output and employment in the deregulated sectors is therefore reduced. The wage shock, however, is transmitted to the competitive sectors of the economy, so w/p_c falls, and output (Y_c) and employment (L_c) in this sector are raised.

Policy in the present model therefore reduces employment in the deregulated sectors and raises employment in the rest of the economy. The net effect on aggregate employment, L, is therefore ambiguous at an *a priori*

[9] This is, of course, an overly pessimistic view to begin with, since trade liberalization will typically reduce output in the formerly protected sectors while deregulation will frequently, through the erosion of monopoly positions, lead to an expansion of output and employment in these sectors.

level. The effect can be calculated using equation (11.1) and the definition of L:

$$L = L_c\left(\frac{w}{p_c}\right) + L_r\left(\frac{w}{p_r}\right) \tag{11.2}$$

where both derivatives are, of course, negative. Aggregate employment will fall or rise depending on whether the following condition is met or broken:

$$\left[\frac{e\left(L_r; w/p_r\right)}{e\left(L_c; w/p_c\right)}\right]\left[\frac{e\left(w; p_c\right)}{e\left(w; p_r\right)}\right]\frac{L_r}{L_c} > 1 \tag{11.3}$$

The functions on the left-hand side are the elasticities of sectoral labor demands and of wage demands. Total employment is therefore more likely to fall, the greater is the elasticity of labor demand and the initial level of employment in the sectors being deregulated, and the lower the influence of these prices on wage demands (the latter obviously being related to the share of these goods in private consumption). This is a standard condition in the small-open-economy literature.

On the assumption that the sectors being deregulated are (i) Utilities, (ii) Distribution and (iii) Transport and Communications, we can make use of the following illustrative numbers:

$e\left(L_r; w/p_r\right)$	1.00
$e\left(L_c; w/p_c\right)$	0.82
$e\left(w; p_c\right)$	0.68
$e\left(w; p_r\right)$	0.32
$L_r/(L_r + L_c)$	0.35
$L_c/(L_r + L_c)$	0.65

The competitive sectors we assume consist primarily of manufacturing. The manufacturing-sector labor-demand elasticity is derived from Bradley, FitzGerald and Kearney (1993). This is likely to be an underestimate, as we are ignoring in this calculation the components of services which are not being deregulated, and these, like the sectors to be deregulated, are likely to have higher labor-demand elasticities than manufacturing. This assumption therefore generates overly pessimistic conclusions in the present case.

Bradley, FitzGerald and Kearney (1991) find that the labor-demand elasticities for service sectors are "generally higher than those observed for the manufacturing sector." We set the elasticity of labor demand in the sectors being deregulated at a value of unity. This value of unity is derived from

Bradley, FitzGerald and Kearney (1991) and Denny, Hannan and O'Rourke (1995). As Distribution is by far the largest of the sectors to be deregulated, its relatively high elasticity brings the average elasticity up to unity. The higher this elasticity is, the greater the job losses predicted as a result of deregulation, and the higher therefore is the imputed initial level of featherbedding. The present exercise will generate these imputed numbers.

To calculate the impact of prices on wage demands, we want the share of the sectors being deregulated in the Consumer Price Index. The impact of p_r on wages we guess to be around .32, and the impact of p_c to be around .68. Finally we need sectoral employment shares in total Industrial plus Market Services employment. Utilities comprise around 2% of this aggregate; Distribution around 23.5%, and Transport and Communications around 9.4%. The share of L_r is therefore 0.35 and the share of L_c is 0.65.

This yields a value of around 1.4 for the elasticities condition in equation (11.3) above, indicating that deregulation of the economy would reduce employment if the mechanism focused upon in the present model were the only one in operation. If, for example, electricity prices played an insignificant role in consumer spending then manufacturing wage demands would hardly be affected by electricity deregulation; if this were the only effect of deregulation then the (assumed) loss in electricity-sector jobs would dominate any gain in manufacturing employment.

We can also tell from this simple model the imputed levels of overmanning if prices fell by 10 per cent as a result of the opening up of these sectors to foreign competition. The above equations imply that the elasticity of total employment with respect to p_r is:

$$\frac{dL/L}{dpr/pr} = e\left(L_r; w/p_r\right) e\left(w; p_c\right) \frac{L_r}{L} - e\left(L_c; w/p_c\right) e\left(w; p_r\right) \frac{L_c}{L} \tag{11.4}$$

Plugging in the estimates discussed above we see that a 10 per cent fall in p_r results in a fall of around 0.7 per cent of (industrial plus market services) employment. In this scenario, around 2.4 per cent of the workforce would be laid off from the R-sector (implying that around 20,000 jobs represent featherbedding), while only 1.7 per cent of the workforce would find jobs in the expanded C-sector (through the reduction in real product wages in that sector). This represents a net loss of around 6,000 jobs.

We must now recognize, though, that the reduction in consumer prices, the sole mechanism taken into account so far, is only one of a number of factors determining the overall outcome. Another crucial one is the role played by the highly regulated sectors as inputs into production processes in other sectors in the economy.[10] Furthermore, the analysis above failed to take into account the fact that demand for the now cheaper output of services and utilities will expand, moderating to some extent the job losses in the newly-liberalized sectors.[11] These factors are, however, taken into account in the recently-constructed Computable General Equilibrium (CGE) model of the Irish economy (Denny, Hannan and O'Rourke, 1995, and O'Rourke, 1994). In other respects the structure of the CGE model is similar to that of the very basic model outlined above. In particular, to take account of unemployment as an enduring characteristic of the Irish labor market, the real wage in the CGE model is very inflexible; the only factor which influences it, and then only to a small extent, is the prevailing rate of unemployment.[12] Since the model is perfectly competitive the "competition policy" is again modelled as the opening up of some of the sheltered sectors to free trade. These sectors (Utilities, Distribution, Transport and Communications) are assumed initially to exhibit prices 10 per cent higher than their foreign counterparts.

As expected, increased imports into one of the newly liberalized sectors reduces domestic output and employment in that sector, but, since these goods serve as intermediate inputs into other sectors, the output of the final goods sectors expands. Particularly large positive effects are found for traded services, traditional manufacturing and high-tech manufacturing, in the case of distribution-sector liberalization. The heartening result is that in each case the net effect on employment is positive, although the typical reduction in the unemployment rate is only around two percentage points (O'Rourke, 1994).[13]

[10] An interesting example of the importance of this mechanism is provided by the boost to tourism arguably given by the 1986 liberalization of Irish-UK airline routes. Air passenger traffic between Ireland and the UK increased by 18.6 per cent per annum between 1986 and 1990, compared to a rise of only 5.5 per cent in transatlantic traffic (OECD, 1993a).

[11] This factor does not appear in the above model because of the assumption there that the regulated sectors become perfectly tradable, and so demand-conditions no longer play a role in output determination. This assumption does not apply in the CGE model, which instead makes the Armington assumption that domestic and foreign tradeables are imperfect substitutes.

[12] The long-run semi-elasticity of the real wage with respect to the unemployment rate in the model is set at -0.035.

[13] The model though has an endogenously determined labor supply, through migration possibilities, so the increase in employment is greater than the reduction in unemployment.

11.7.2 Union Responses to Deregulation

There is a lot of evidence to suggest that the assumption that labor market rigidities are independent of the policy environment in place is far too strong. Making labor-market rigidities endogenous has important implications for the present analysis. To see this, consider the similarity between, on the one hand, the arguments for maintaining the monopoly power of incumbents in a particular sector (because of labor rigidities) and, on the other, the arguments frequently advanced in the declining industries literature for granting temporary subsidization.

A strand of that literature holds that if a sector is struck by an adverse shock that reduces its demand for labor, and if that sector's wage fails to adjust downwards, excessive labor will be released. This labor will then end up either unemployed, or, depending on the degree of wage flexibility in the rest of the economy, will be employed elsewhere at excessively low wages. The policy prescription frequently advanced is that the declining industry should be subsidized to some extent so as to replicate as closely as possible the behavior of an undistorted economy.[14]

Note that this "traditional" view is exactly that which motivates those worried about the employment implications of deregulation. Deregulation, they suggest, in the context of rigid labor markets, would lead to job losses in the liberalized sectors and could raise overall unemployment. When labor-market rigidities are endogenous, however, this policy can do more harm than good. Several results from diverse areas of economics are supportive of this view.

Calmfors and Horn (1986), for example, show that a government commitment to partially offset the unemployment generated by labor-market inflexibilities actually raises overall unemployment. This occurs because unions have an incentive to exploit their knowledge of government policy — "By reducing the opportunity cost of wage increases in terms of lost employment, the policy rule induces the trade union to raise the wage. Since government employment (protection) makes up for only a fraction of the employment loss in the private sector, the result must be a fall in total employment."

Several other papers endogenize labor-market rigidities in the context of sectoral shocks by adopting either the monopoly-union model or the Nash

[14] Variations on this argument can be found for example in Lapan (1976), Hillman (1977), Ray (1979), Neary (1982) and Fields and Grinols (1991).

bargaining approach to union behavior.[15] In the monopoly-union model the wage differential between the unionized (protected) sector and the rest of the economy varies inversely with the elasticity of labor demand in the protected sector. Lawrence and Lawrence (1985) confine themselves to cases where sectoral shocks reduce the elasticity of labor demand; this will arise, for example, if investment in the sector is hit so sharply that the possibility of substituting capital for labor is closed off. Wage demands in the sector will rise in this case, though protection would strengthen the hand of unions still further in seeking higher wages and would not revitalize the industry.

This argument clearly will not go through if the elasticity of labor demand in the sector remains constant or actually increases. Barry (1995b) shows, however, that under these circumstances the cost-to-benefit ratio of protection increases.[16] If intervention to correct the distortions associated with monopoly-union power was not implemented before the shock, due to the high social cost of taxation, protection is even less appropriate after the shock.

This is also the implication drawn in Barry (1995a) who employs the Nash bargaining approach. This paper shows that the union in a regulated sector will release less than the socially efficient amount of labor in the event of a shock (so as to moderate the drop in wages its members must face). Protection of the sector under these circumstances reduces efficiency still further.

This literature, therefore, suggests than when labor-market rigidities are endogenous, the argument for protection or regulation based on labor-market rigidities is invalid. Furthermore, a recent analysis of the behavior of two Irish semi-state companies, TEAM (a business which grew out of the aircraft maintenance function of the state airline) and Irish Steel (a company purchased by the government immediately after the Second World War and finally privatized only in the last few years) revealed many of the dangers recognized in this theoretical literature on public assistance to industry.

In the case of Irish Steel, Barry and Durkan (1996) concluded that "...protection, and the knowledge that it would be continued, increased the power of the workforce and pushed up wage demands, inhibiting further the competitiveness of an industry that was in any case unlikely ever to have been

[15] See Oswald (1985) for an introduction to these models.

[16] The cost of protection in this case is the marginal social cost of raising taxes to finance the protection. Some of Honohan and Irvine's (1987) estimates of this cost for Ireland range to well in excess of £1 per £1 of additional tax revenue.

able to survive unaided." The situation of TEAM Aer Lingus was recognized to be different in that TEAM is a potentially sustainable company. However, recent intervention by the government saw the return of restrictive work practices. The fact that earnings within the company are well above the average for equivalent skill levels is a further indication of "monopoly union" behavior, suggesting in light of the literature described above that intervention would tend to increase rather than decrease the level of distortions. This literature then serves as a warning that it is incorrect to carry out an analysis of competition policy on the assumption of distorted labor markets without taking into account the impact of policy on these distortions.

11.7.3 Foreign Penetration

We now wish to turn to the other argument advanced against deregulation, i.e., the capture of profits by newly-entered foreign competitors. Consider a sector in which positive profits can be made because of barriers to entry. Assume also that in the initial situation government regulation prohibits entry of foreign firms into the domestic market. When these regulations are removed a foreign firm enters the domestic market (either through exporting from abroad or through producing in the home market) but remaining barriers to entry ensure that profits are not bid down to zero. It is possible in this situation that the economy suffers a welfare loss due to rents being shifted from the domestic to the foreign firm (Krugman and Venables, 1990).

In Figure 11.1, this occurs as follows. p_0 is the pre-liberalization price, p_1 the post-liberalization price, and C the constant marginal cost. Q_0 is the initial quantity sold (all by the domestic firm), Q_1 is the post-liberalization quantity, which consists of q_1 sold by the domestic firm and $Q_1 - q_1$ by the foreign firm. In this event the rectangle marked "−" represents welfare loss and the triangle marked "+" shows the welfare gain. It is clear that if price effects are very modest, then the economy can suffer a net loss. The more competition that ensues, however, the more profit levels are driven towards zero, and the greater the likelihood of net gains.[17] This yields the Krugman-

[17] One adverse consequence about which a considerable literature has arisen concerns the increased risk premium that may be charged to small immobile borrowers as indigenous financial services with local knowledge are crowded-out by international companies; see Branson (1990), Honohan (1995). Their situation may deteriorate through more of the systems's overheads being recovered from them, as others can shop around in the newly liberalized market. Again, the less efficient the pre-liberalization system was, the more

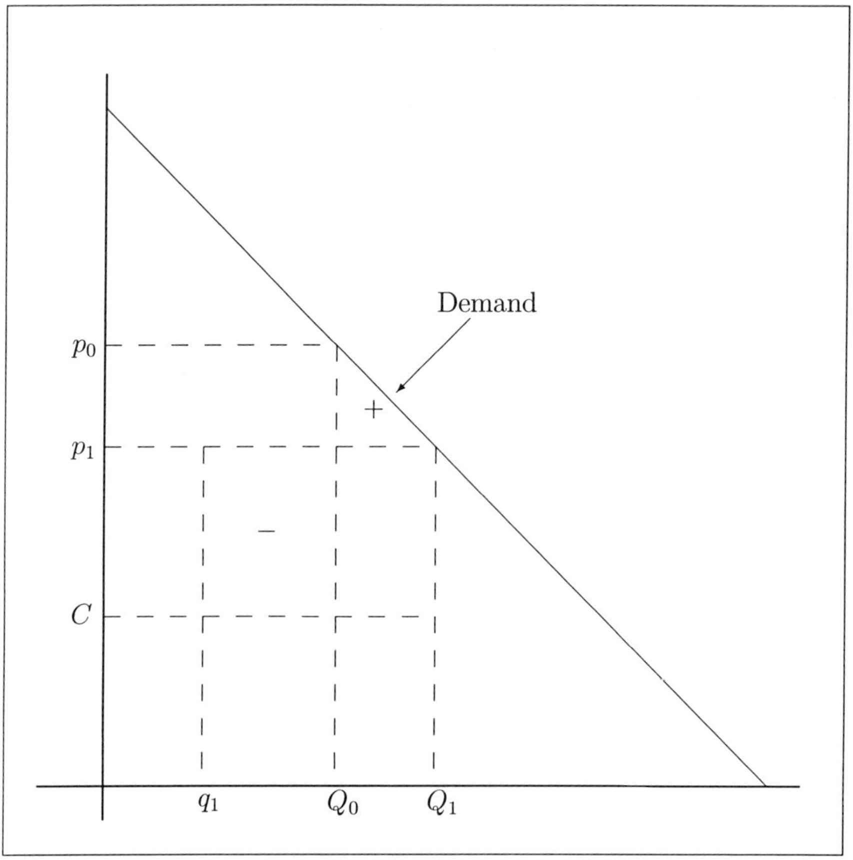

Figure 11.1: Foreign penetrtion and the welfare consequences of deregulation

Venables U-curve: there are net losses associated with very low level foreign entry, but beyond some threshold level net gains expand with further entry.

Another way of generating this U-curve is to note that peripheral economies may lose out from trade liberalization (and, by analogy, from deregulation) if they lose the sectors that are characterized by increasing returns to scale (Krugman and Venables, 1990); as trade costs fall from very high levels this is more likely to occur as the benefits of centralization close to major markets manifest themselves. As trade costs fall from more moderate levels,

likely even this group is to gain (in absolute, though not in relative terms).

however, the labor-cost advantage of a peripheral location comes to dominate, and the periphery is instead likely to gain both in terms of its share of increasing returns to scale industries and in terms of welfare. The U-shaped curve thus depicts the share of high-profit and/or increasing-returns sectors that the periphery captures as deregulation proceeds, and aggregate welfare also follows this pattern.

Are there any general principles which would allow us decide whether liberalization is more likely to raise or reduce welfare? One principle is immediately clear from the diagram: the more foreign competition (foreign entry) is stimulated, the more likely it is that net benefits result. Another principle is also clear from the diagram, as Barry (1996) points out. This is that if domestic producers are inefficient relative to their foreign counterparts, even if only to the extent of being unable to match them in scale, liberalization is more likely to be beneficial (because foreign firms set their prices lower than they otherwise would). In the extreme, domestic producers would be driven out of the market completely if the foreign firm's costs were lower and if prices were driven below the level of domestic costs; in this case benefits to the consumer would outweigh producer losses. The general equilibrium considerations discussed earlier, whereby price reductions in the deregulated sectors reduce wage demands and other input costs elsewhere in the economy, magnify further the gross benefits illustrated in the present diagram.

Two further points, one empirical and one conceptual, tend to further reduce the pessimistic possibilities that show up in the U-curve analysis. Conceptually the Krugman-Venables argument is less potent in the case of functions or sectors which are non-internationally-tradable by nature rather than simply as a consequence of government regulation (these would include retailing and perhaps most transport services, for example). Liberalization of non-tradable sectors will generally lead to increases rather than reductions in domestic output, offsetting further the adverse possibilities identified above. With distorted labor markets, furthermore, the adverse effects that the diagram illustrates as a possibility are less adverse, since foreign penetration occurs through foreign direct investment (FDI), which generates jobs, rather than through imports. The pessimistic results may therefore be taken to be more potent with respect to the location of sectors or functions which are by their nature internationally tradable. It warns that deregulation can lead to the disappearance of these sectors from the periphery, with possible adverse consequences for periphery welfare.

To explore whether this is likely to happen or not, it seems worthwhile to look at the experience of the increasing-returns segments of manufacturing in the EU periphery, as these were liberalized rather earlier than is the case with services. Barry (1996) looks at developments in these sectors in the Irish economy. Rather than taking rents from the home market (as in the pessimistic scenario in the above diagram), he suggests, multinational IRS-sector companies used Ireland as a location from which to capture rents in the European core.[18] That paper also argues that similar developments have been taking place in the other EU periphery economies (Greece, Spain and Portugal).[19]

If the analogy with the manufacturing sector experience is valid, it suggests that the periphery, aided by FDI inflows, is unlikely to do badly in the newly-tradable services sectors, and in those services sectors that remain non-tradable after liberalization, substantial FDI inflows are also likely to be beneficial.[20,21]

11.8 Conclusions

This paper considers a number of arguments about the possible adverse macroeconomic consequences of competition policy. For the most part, it is suggested, these arguments are based on assumed labor-market rigidities that are taken to imply that deregulation will raise unemployment. We presented a series of increasingly complex models designed to analyze this issue.

[18] It is very likely that the wage-bill contribution alone of these foreign firms dominates the whole value-added contribution of the increasing returns to scale sectors in the pre-liberalization period.

[19] These developments furthermore appear to be driven by "absolute" rather than by "comparative" advantage (Barry and Hannan, 1996), so there is little reason to expect that developments in the Market Services sectors should be different.

[20] Buigues and Sapir (1993) have recently shown the crucial role played by FDI in the transformation of the services sector. For the period reported upon in that study (the early 1980s), FDI flows to the service sector accounted for over half of total FDI flows in the EU.

[21] Data for service-sector FDI inflows into Ireland are very poor. For the other three economies, however, the substantial increase in service-sector FDI inflows consequent upon liberalization indicates that optimism may also be warranted in this sphere. Data are from the OECD (1993b). These show FDI flows into the Portuguese tertiary sector rising from 0.2% of GNP in 1982 to 2.49% in 1991; for Spain the equivalent numbers are 0.27 rising to 2.59%. Greece displays an increase from 0.17% of GNP in 1987 to 0.20% in 1991.

The first model assumes, in the context of a rigid economy-wide real wage, that the only positive effect of competition policy lies in the knock-on effects to the tradable sector of a reduced CPI (which reduces wage demands). We saw that if this is the case then deregulation is indeed likely to raise unemployment.

Our second model, however, took into account two extra channels: first, that the price reductions in the liberalized sectors would stimulate demand for their output and so moderate the employment loss in those sectors, and secondly, that these price reductions stimulate the output of other sectors not just through the wage effect but also because the output of the regulated sectors serves as an input into other production processes. We saw that the Irish CGE model, which takes these effects into account, predicts that total employment will rise as a result of deregulation.

Two further points reinforce these more optimistic conclusions. The first is that while deregulation will occasionally cause a reduction in sectoral employment levels through the loss of featherbedding opportunities, as is the case in the first two models, it will also frequently induce increased sectoral output and employment through removing monopoly power. The final model suggests that the previous analyses, carried out on the assumption of exogenous labor-market rigidities, yield far too much ground to those in favor of continued regulation. Recognizing that labor-market rigidities are endogenous (i.e. responsive to policy changes) suggests that continued regulation makes the sectors less and less competitive over time, weakening substantially the whole case for regulation.

Finally, we dealt with a number of issues that arise when the sectors to be liberalized are characterized by excess profits and/or increasing returns to scale, and are opened up to foreign competition either though imports or through FDI. In some models peripheral economies can lose out if these sectors are taken over by foreign companies, whether located at home or abroad. We argued that, even if this is found to happen, the consequences are rather less dire than predicted since the periphery sectors are likely to have been inefficient initially. This has two implications: first, they would not have been earning rents from exporting activity to begin with, and so the rent-shifting argument to justify their protection is weakened, and second, inefficiency on the part of indigenous industry induces foreign firms to enter with prices that are low relative to those of domestic firms. This makes it more likely that foreign entry is welfare enhancing.

We then went on to argue that in fact the peripheral regions of the EU have been experiencing rapidly increasing FDI inflows into services as well as manufacturing (as a consequence of liberalization). If entry into periphery markets is strong enough this guarantees that the gains to consumer welfare dominate the losses to periphery producer welfare.

11.9 References

Barry, F. "Declining High-Wage Industries, Efficient Labour Contracts and Optimal Adjustment Assistance," *Canadian Journal of Economics*, Volume 28, 1995a, pp. 94–107.

— "Declining Industries and Monopoly Unions: A Further Argument Against Protection," Centre for Economic Research Working Paper 95/4, 1995b, University College Dublin.

— "Peripherality in Economic Geography and Modern Growth Theory: Evidence from Ireland's Adjustment to Free Trade," *World Economy*, Volume 19, Number 3, 1996, pp. 345–65.

Barry, F., and J. Durkan "TEAM and Irish Steel: An Application of the Declining High-Wage Industries Literature," *Irish Journal of Business and Administrative Research*, Volume 17, 1996, pp. 58–72.

Barry, F., and A. Hannan "On Comparative and Absolute Advantage: FDI and the Sectoral and Spatial Effects of Market Integration," Centre for Economic Research Working Paper 96/19, 1996, University College Dublin.

Bradley, J., J. FitzGerald and I. Kearney "The Irish Market Services Sector: An Econometric Investigation," *Economic and Social Review*, Volume 22, Number 4, 1991, pp. 287–309.

— "Modelling Supply in an Open Economy using a Restricted Cost Function," *Economic Modelling*, 1993, pp. 11-21.

Branson, W. H. "Financial Market Integration, Macroeconomic Policy and the EMS," in Bliss, Christopher and de Macedo, Jorge Brage (eds.), *Unity with Diversity Within the European Economy: The Community's Southern Frontier*. Cambridge: Cambridge University Press, 1990.

Buigues, P., and A. Sapir "Market Services and European Integration," *European Economy/Social Europe*, No. 3, 1993.

Calmfors, L., and H. Horn "Employment Policies and Centralized Wage Setting," *Economica*, Volume 53, 1986, pp. 281–302.

Denny, K., A. Hannan and K. O'Rourke "A Computable General Equilibrium Model of the Irish Economy: Technical Appendix," Centre for Economic Research Working Paper 95/2, 1995, UCD.

Department of Employment and Enterprise *Employment Through Enterprise*. 1993.

Fields, G., and E. Grinols "Import Competition in the High-Wage Sector and Trade Policy Effects on Labor," *Quarterly Review of Economics and Business*, Volume 31, Number 2, 1991, pp. 31–56.

Fingleton, J. "Competition and Efficiency in the Services Sector," in J. O'Hagan (ed.) *The Economy of Ireland*, Gill and Macmillan, 1995.

Hillman, A. L. "The Case for Terminal Protection for Declining Industries," *Southern Economic Journal*, Volume 44, 1977, pp. 155–60.

Honohan, P., and I. Irvine "The Marginal Social Cost of Taxation in Ireland," *Economic and Social Review*, Volume 19, Number 1, 1987, pp. 15–41.

Honohan, P. "The Single Financial Market in Europe: How far has it got?," ESRI Banking Research Centre, mimeo, 1995.

Krugman, P., and A. Venables "Integration and the Competitiveness of Peripheral Industry," in Bliss, Christopher and de Macedo, Jorge Brage (eds.), *Unity with Diversity Within the European Economy: The Community's Southern Frontier*. Cambridge: Cambridge University Press, 1990.

Lapan, H. E. "International Trade, Factor Market Distortions and the Optimal Dynamic Subsidy," *American Economic Review*, Volume 66, 1976, pp. 335–46.

Lawrence, C. and R. Z. Lawrence "Manufacturing Wage Dispersion: An End Game Interpretation," *Brookings Papers on Economic Activity*, 1985:1, pp. 47–106.

Massey, P. and P. O'Hare "Measuring the Impact of the Competition Act," mimeo, 1995.

— *Competition Law and Policy in Ireland*, Dublin: Oak Tree Press, 1996.

Neary, J. P. "Intersectoral Capital Mobility, Wage Stickiness and Adjustment Assistance," in J. Bhagwati (ed.), *Import Competition and Response*, Chicago and London: University of Chicago Press, 1982, pp. 39–67.

O'Rourke, K. "Industrial Policy, Employment Policy and the Non-Traded Sector," *Journal of the Statistical and Social Inquiry Society of Ireland*, 1994.

Organization for Economic Co-operation and Development *OECD Economic Surveys 1992 - 1993 Ireland*, OECD: Paris, 1993a.

— *International Direct Investment Statistics Yearbook*, OECD, Paris: 1993b.

Oswald, A. J. "The Economic Theory of Trade Unions: An Introductory Survey," *Scandinavian Journal of Economics*, 1985, pp. 160–193.

Ray, E. J. "Factor Market Distortions and Dynamic Optimal Intervention: Comment," *American Economic Review*, Volume 69, 1979, pp. 225–37.

Report of the Industrial Policy Review Group *A Time for Change: Industrial Policy in the 1990s*, Dublin Stationery Office, 1992.

Walsh, P. and C. Whelan "The Optimality of Loss-Leading in Multi-Product Retail Pricing: A Rationale for Repealing the 1987 Groceries Order in Ireland," Technical Paper 96/1, Trinity College Dublin, 1996.

Competition Policies in Europe - S. Martin (Editor)

Chapter 12

The Interaction Between Community and National Competition Policy: the Italian Case

Fabio Gobbo[1]
Massimo Ferrero

12.1 Introduction

Competition policy in Italy began six years ago, even though the original draft legislation dates back to the early Fifties. The essentials have been enacted into law, laying down the economic behavior to be controlled and the procedures for so doing (in particular with the institution of the Autorità Garante della Concorrenza e del Mercato, the antitrust agency). It is therefore a very recent policy, that has come into being against the background of increasing European integration (before the signing of the Maastricht Treaty, but after the Single European Act had given a major boost to the establishment of the Single Market), in an economy that was (and still is) characterized by the presence of a few large multinational groups and the massive presence of State-owned corporations.

[1]The views expressed in this chapter are those of the authors and do not involve the responsibility of the Autorità Garante della Concorrenza e del Mercato.

The purpose of this paper is to highlight several experiences of enforcing competition law in Italy and offer a number of suggestions that might be taken up in similar economic environments. These will be formulated after analyzing the institutional aspects of Italy's competition policy, and holding it up against the Community's competition legislation.

12.2 Institutional aspects of competition law in Italy

Until the Eighties Italy had no antitrust policy (except in the wake of Community action). The economic system was characterized by broadly-based direct government intervention in production and by extremely wide-ranging regulation covering areas which in other countries were left to market forces. One typical example of this was the extremely common use of the government franchise ('concessione'),[2] which is still used to a certain extent. This situation was due to the way Italy perceived the government's role in the economy, as a necessary protagonist on markets, because there was little confidence in their spontaneous operation. The economic goals that were adopted from time to time often needed adjusting or had to be taken over by the public sector.

However, since the beginning of the Nineties the role of the State has changed. It is now commonly held that the main effect of government intervention in the economy was the inefficiency it produced rather than the targets it attains. In other words, direct public intervention (State-owned corporations) coupled with indirect public intervention (regulations) produced negative results, or anyway led to an inefficient overall performance of the markets concerned.

One of the main causes of this — even though there are many different aspects — is the lack of any real stimulus to competition. In Italy, the State-owned corporations failed to perceive the need to pursue greater efficiency, whether they were working in a competitive environment (maximization of profits was by no means a priority for the managers of these firms, whose losses were covered by government grants) or in a monopoly situation; fur-

[2]Under the government franchise system, specific economic activities are the statutory preserve of government which issues operating franchises to private concerns to perform them.

thermore, the presence of the statutory monopolies made it possible to exploit the related market power.

Italy therefore saw the need to deregulate, leaving more leeway to the market; but this by no means did away with all forms of public intervention. Regulation is always possible to prevent failures and the malfunctioning of the market; in Italy's case, then, it was not so much a matter of deregulation as of re-regulation, in other words of redefining the spheres to be regulated. The emergence of a national competition policy was part of this process.

Discussions about introducing competition legislation, and the forms it would take, lasted as long as forty years, from the early Fifties until 1990. A number of bills were tabled unsuccessfully throughout that period, because the role vested in the government, to which reference was made earlier, required operational instruments wholly contradictory to the principles of any kind of antitrust legislation. In particular, such legislation would have clashed with such extremely widespread practices as price control and tax incentives for small and medium enterprises, or for companies set up in Southern Italy, and would have placed State-owned corporations on the same level as private firms (exactly as has occurred under the new antitrust legislation), thereby robbing the State-owned corporation of its role as a tool of economic policy.

Competition policy implements Article 41 of the Constitution, protecting private enterprise. This functional linkage is essential for the purposes of enforcing competition policy and interpreting the competition law, in that it gives competition a paramount role in protecting a right guaranteed by the Italian Constitution. It safeguards the constitutional right in two ways: by providing protection against constraints imposed by the government, and against distortions to the correct operation of market forces caused by companies. Furthermore, the law has filled a huge gap in Italian legislation, because Italy was one of the last of European Union member states to institute an anti-trust authority. In short, the main features of the Italian competition policy are as follows:

1) *Total compliance of the fundamental principles with Community principles.*

Regulation of agreements, abuse of dominant position and mergers and acquisitions are essentially the same as the EU's. In particular, in Italy as at the EU level exceptions for limited periods may be granted to agreements or categories of agreements restricting competition provided that these improve the conditions of supply and result in a substantial benefit to consumers.

With regard to dominant positions, the law prohibits only their abusive exploitation, not their mere existence.

Mergers and acquisitions, lastly, are subject to prior clearance when the parties to them have a turnover exceeding specific thresholds.

Compliance with European competition law is not only guaranteed by the similarity between Italian and Community law but also by the explicit reference that Italian law makes to Community principles for the purposes of interpretation;

2) *Enforcement powers are vested in an independent agency (Autorità Garante).*

The Autorità Garante is not subject to any type of parliamentary or government control: its five members (the Chairman and the four members) are appointed for a period of seven years (which is longer than any one parliament) by the Speakers of both Houses of Parliament (who are generally appointed by a consensus of all the political parties, and play a strictly 'super partes' role), and may not be reappointed for a second term. Like the European Commission, it has total organizational independence which was exercised by the adoption of a set of Staff Regulations and another set of regulations governing the organization of the body and its activities; it also has unfettered freedom to spend the financial resources appropriated to it every year by Parliament when the State budget is adopted. This independence of the Authority is designed to safeguard its impartiality and its independence of judgment, which is particularly important in an economy in which the public sector still plays such a large part.

The independence of the Autorità Garante is peculiar to Italy, at least to the extent to which it operates: there is no equivalent organization in France, Germany, the United Kingdom or even in the United States with the same degree of independence and autonomy as the Autorità Garante. The very few direct constraints on the work of the Autorità Garante are the government's right to lay down general not-binding criteria to which the Autorità Garante refers when specific conditions are met to authorize mergers or acquisitions which would otherwise be prohibited (conversely, laying down criteria for authorizing agreements or categories of agreements that restrict competition but are beneficial to consumers, is the responsibility of the Autorità Garante itself); this means that the government can only influence the work of the Autorità Garante in general terms but not in respect of individual cases.

The only forms of control over it are the possibility of appealing against its decisions to the Administrative Court, the auditing of the use of the resources (including its labor force, set at a maximum of 150 permanent employees and 50 employees under fixed-term contract) by the Court of Auditors, and the requirement to submit an Activities Report to the Prime Minister and Parliament by 30th April each year.

It should also be noted that despite the fact that the government may not directly influence the Autorità Garante, it can lay down indirect constraints through regulations: the more specific and all-embracing the regulations are, the less discretion is left to the Autorità Garante to enforce legislation to protect competition.

3) *"Judicial" activity*

The Autorità Garante is vested with the same investigative powers as the European Union Commission for the enforcement of Community law. At the same time companies under investigation have the same wide-ranging rights of defense against it. The procedures laying down the principle of *audi alteram partem* between the parties and the Autorità Garante and the kind of decisions adopted by the latter — namely ascertaining that certain types of conduct constitute formal infringements of the law rather than taking decisions in the exercise of total discretion — make its activities much more similar to a court of law than an administrative body.

4) *The Autorità Garante's reporting powers*

The Autorità Garante may draw the attention of the Parliament and the government to distortions to competition caused by current legislative provisions or proposed legislation and regulations, and may issue opinions on specific competition-related issues; this is one of the peculiarities of the Italian institutional system which the Parliament deemed necessary to introduce because it feared that Italy's lack of a genuine competition culture at the time might raise obstacles to competition guaranteed by the law. However this is a purely advisory power, because the institutions which receive the reports, namely the policy-makers, are not required to take account of them in their work. Consequently, the effectiveness of any activities by the Autorità Garante in this area depends on the prestige and influence it manages to build up for itself.

5) *The enforcement powers over certain sectors are vested in other institutions* (Banca d'Italia for credit, Garante per la Radiodiffusione e l'Editoria for broadcasting and publishing).

The Autorità Garante can only submit opinions to these entities, but they are not binding; the legislature did not wish to take away the powers over antitrust (to be exercised under the same rules that govern the work of the Autorità Garante) from institutions already responsible for monitoring other aspects: the stability of the whole system and the protection of depositors with regard to credit, and freedom of information with regard to publishing. However, the Autorità Garante has general powers over these sectors to carry out fact-finding surveys of a general nature about competition.

12.3 Comparison with EU competition policy

Italy's competition policy is firmly based on that of the European Union; this is due to the fact that the two have substantially similar competition regulations and enforcement procedures, and the fact that Italian law specifically and explicitly refers to Community principles for the purposes of interpretation. Moreover, very close cooperation exists between the Autorità Garante and the European Commission mainly because the Autorità Garante is the equivalent agency to the European institutions in all matters relating to competition policy; consequently the Autorità Garante personnel sit on the Advisory Committees on restrictive practices and dominant positions and on concentrations, while officials from the Autorità Garante are present when inspections are conducted in Italian companies by the Commission officials. For the past three years an official of the Authority has been seconded to the Merger Task Force of DG IV, and so on.

These basic similarities are inevitable for two reasons: first of all, because of the need to harmonize the domestic legislation of Member States and to harmonize these with Community law in order to ensure that similar economic conducts are not dealt with differently, merely because they have effects on Europe as a whole rather than on more restricted markets; and secondly, and as a result of the former point, because Italian law was enacted much later than the introduction of European competition policy and it was logical to draw on the mass of experience accumulated by the Community.

The greatest difference between the two systems relates to the institutions responsible for enforcement: in Italy the Autorità Garante is independent of government, while at the European level it is the Commission which enforces the Articles of the Treaty regarding competition and the legislation stemming from them. The point is that the Commission is also responsible for developing legislation, acting therefore both as the legislature by laying down the rules (for example the regulations exempting certain categories of agreements), the executive, and the judge in assessing individual cases.

That decisions on individual cases taken by the Commission may be appealed against to the Tribunal of First Instance and the Court of Justice is quite immaterial: the mixing of roles is aggravated by the fact that the Commission is responsible for implementing many other policies, and its individual decisions can therefore be affected by considerations that have absolutely nothing to do with competition policy.

12.4 The enforcement of competition policy in Italy

12.4.1 General considerations

The enforcement of competition policy in Italy over these first six years, also thanks to the recent boost given to the work of the Autorità Garante after the inevitable starting phase, has been both wide-ranging and extremely influential. When the Act came into force, Italy's economy had no kind of competition culture whatsoever, government was massively involved not only in regulating the economy but also directly in production, and there was a concentration of large companies in the hands of family "dynasties." Today, now that the starting period is over, the Autorità Garante is gradually broadening its influence and becoming increasingly active, carving out a role for itself that everyone acknowledges and which is in accordance with the purposes for which the Act was originally intended.

The Autorità Garante has played an active part in the current process of transformation of the Italian economy, characterized by the gradual liberalization and the opening up to competition of many areas of the economy, and by the — albeit slow — withdrawal of government from production activities. Telecommunications, airport services and harbor operations are the sectors on which the Authority's activity has had the greatest impact so far.

Despite this process of liberalization, for essential public services the government must continue to play an active regulatory role to ensure that all the citizens are provided with uniform services on an equitable basis. Free competition must not be seen as the ultimate goal to be pursued for its own sake, because under certain circumstances there are other goals that should perhaps prevail over the maximization of general welfare that competition can bring. Competition must therefore be seen as an instrument, to be used only when it is useful in the pursuit of whatever goals are laid down from time to time.

In these cases a clear distinction must be drawn between the scope of activity of the various regulatory institutions and of the antitrust agency; each one must be able to play its respective role without jeopardizing the goals of or encroaching on the powers and responsibilities of the others.

Regulation and antitrust are in reality quite distinct: both are directed towards the same goal, namely the maximization of social welfare by guaranteeing greater market efficiency. But the similarities end there. A first difference is in the concept of welfare that they pursue: whereas antitrust is concerned with the greatest prosperity of the whole system, which may be achieved even at the expense of individual situations (some individuals may not consume some specific commodity), the purpose of regulation is to ensure access by everyone to the regulated commodity or service, under guaranteed equitable and non-discriminatory access conditions.

This latter consideration introduces yet another difference: regulation requires value (equity) judgments, antitrust enforcement does not. Antitrust legislation is concerned with ensuring the correct functioning of market forces, while regulation "makes" the market; in other words, it replaces the market by artificially fixing its structure, dimension, and the prices practiced on it.

However, in some circumstances regulation can be a policy for promoting competition when the goals set for it make it necessary to open the market, or to set prices that are closer to a competitive price than those spontaneously fixed by the market operators themselves.

Ultimately, regulation can play a role in improving the competitive conditions of the markets, but only by limiting its task to introducing new "rules of the game." The control of the compliance with these rules must be entrusted exclusively to the institution that performs this task also in unregulated industries.

The need for this clear separation of tasks is due to the conflicts that might arise between antitrust considerations and the purposes of regulation if both activities were to be entrusted to the regulatory agencies. The advocates of this approach emphasize that the regulator has far more information available over the regulated industry than an antitrust agency has; one might nevertheless retort that when the regulator is "captured" the effects extend to the antitrust activity, while this "capture" is less probable in the case of an antitrust institution which has relations with representatives of every area of the economy.

Italy's situation with regard to the allocation of responsibilities is as follows: the Banca d'Italia and the Garante per la Radiodiffusione e l'Editoria are wholly responsible for enforcing competition policy in the areas they regulate. The Act instituting the regulator for electricity and gas provides that competition policy shall be enforced by the Autorità Garante while the regulator will be required to report any alleged violations of the Competition Law to the Autorità Garante. Moreover, with regard to competition aspects, the Autorità Garante will be required to issue opinions regarding the grant of franchises, service contracts and other regulatory instruments.

12.4.2 Specific areas

Mergers and acquisitions

Despite the immense amount of work in this area (they accounted for 2,517 of the 3,157 cases concluded at 31 December 1996, but 926 of them related to infra-group operations which since March 1995 are no longer dealt with) the Autorità Garante has only taken action in very few cases, *prohibiting the operation in only four cases, and imposing certain conditions in eight other cases (in three cases the conditions were negotiated with the companies involved) before granting clearance*. The reason for this very low level of intervention is the fact that large operations creating dominant positions on Italian markets often fall within Community jurisdiction, while operations creating positions of (quasi) monopoly on niche markets involve companies whose turnover is not high enough to make it compulsory for them to give prior notice.

The industries which mostly are subject to investigation by the Autorità Garante are chemicals, traditionally characterized by high concentration degrees for technical/economic reasons, and the food industry where mergers and acquisitions have long been a typical feature due to the industry's need to face the increasing strength of the distribution system.

Agreements

The law provides that companies may notify agreements to request prior authorization from the Autorità Garante. However, this right has not been used widely for two reasons. Until a short time ago (until 1 July 1996) no official form existed for submitting such notices, and no statutory provision exists in Italy (of the kind that exists in EU law) exempting from penalties on companies that notify an agreement and implement it, within the terms communicated, before the Autorità Garante takes a decision.

The Autorità Garante has dealt with 202 cases of agreements. The areas where it has most frequently found competition distortions (67 in all, but in 22 of these cases the agreements were authorized after the parties amended them) were in the cement and concrete industry, where typically standardized products are sold within limited geographical markets, and in the insurance business, where the uncertainty of operating conditions facing insurance companies naturally leads them to reduce the uncertainties caused by corporate rivalry.

The 5 exemptions granted for agreements distorting competition out of the 21 applications received, were in the industries of insurance against natural disasters, industrial gases and distribution of insurance policies by banks (a type of linkage for which a number of cases were examined, most of which did not give rise to any anti-competitive problems).

The Autorità Garante's assessment of agreements proved to be particularly suitable for the *application of principles of economic theory*, due to the need to evaluate the effects of the agreements on competition.

Abuse of dominant position

The Autorità Garante has done a great deal of important work in this area (31 abuses have been ascertained out of a total of 156 cases examined), particularly in areas in which monopolies and dominant positions are guaranteed by Italian law. In the telecommunications industry, where the Autorità Garante was forced to take the Italian legislature's place in the liberalization process (in one case in the telecommunications industry, where it declared a European Union Directive, which after the deadline had not yet been received into Italian law, to be all the same enforceable), and in the airports sector, where it dissolved the monopoly enjoyed by the airport management companies over the supply of handling services to the airlines, so that the airlines can now provide their own. In future, this trend should not change, because the Autorità Garante will deal above all with network services sectors for which it will be necessary to coordinate with the new regulatory institutions that are now coming into existence.

Because of the particular features of the firms involved in these cases, abuse of dominant position is mainly judged on the basis of juridical considerations.

Reporting to the Parliament and the government

This is an activity which has increased considerably over the past 20 months (46 reports out of a total of 82 cases), but the reactions to it have been varied. The opinions of the Autorità Garante were mainly accepted when they related to Bills, for which it is technically easier to remove the anticompetitive provisions. But even in these cases its opinion was not always taken up.

The most important reports related to telecommunications, where Autorità Garante have played a very important part in encouraging the GSM mobile telephone service to be opened up to competition, and to the electricity industry where the Autorità Garante has long advocated the need to separate generation, transmission and distribution, which are currently held by Enel, the statutory monopolist, in view of the full liberalization when Enel will be privatized.

State-owned corporations

The Autorità Garante has adopted a narrow interpretation of the provision exempting from competition law those companies which are entrusted with the operation of services of general economic interest or operate on the market as statutory monopolists, only in so far as the anticompetitive conducts are indispensable to perform the specific tasks assigned to them. It has therefore found these companies in breach of the law when performing activities not falling within the scope of the exclusive activities for which they have a statutory monopoly, and also when their conduct had not been strictly necessary for the purposes of performing the activities over which they had a statutory monopoly.

The industries most involved were, as indicated earlier, telecommunications, where the Autorità Garante prohibited two proposed concentrations, and airport services.

Self-production

The activity here refers to the case mentioned earlier, namely, establishing the right of companies to produce by themselves those services which are supplied on the market by statutory monopolists.

Relations with other institutions responsible for enforcing the competition policy

The Autorità Garante has adopted a narrow interpretation of the legal provision entrusting other institutions with the task of enforcing competition law in specific industries, restricting as far as possible the areas to which this provision applies. As stated earlier, in these cases the Autorità Garante offers opinions to the agency responsible for the final decision.

These cases totaled 282. In some instances there have been discrepancies between the opinion submitted and the final decision, not only on marginal issues but also on aspects relating to the infringement or non-infringement of the law (for example, the Autorità Garante was of the opinion that one particular merger would create such a dominant position that it would reduce competition on the Sardinian bank markets, and should therefore be prohibited; yet the Banca d'Italia authorized the operation, albeit subject to certain conditions). The provisions applying to these sectors nevertheless create uncertainty regarding the identity of the institution responsible for appraising individual cases (in this respect the Autorità Garante and the Banca d'Italia have cooperated to identify which markets fall within their respective jurisdictions) and the criteria they should adopt for their assessments, which may be in conflict. This is presumably due also to the difficulties that arise when the assessment is not based purely on competition criteria, but it also relates to the other areas of supervision entrusted to these institutions.

12.5 Significant cases examined

12.5.1 Airports

The Autorità Garante took action against the companies responsible for managing the facilities and supplying handling services in Italy's two main airports at Rome and Milan. The cases examined related to the right of airlines to provide their own handling services, and the tariffs charged for handling services by the companies.

With regard to the first aspect, the service providers only permitted certain airlines to provide some of their own handling services, refusing authorization to other airlines on the grounds that the airport facilities were inadequate. The authorized airlines, however, were charged not only a rental fee for the facilities they actually used but also a royalty related to the level of the traffic which they handled themselves; even so, the royalties charged discriminated in favor of the Italian national airline. The overall system was nevertheless designed to discourage airlines from providing their own handling services, because of the onerous conditions imposed by the airport management companies.

Tariffs comprised two components: one for the standard services supplied to all aircraft, and one for services supplied on request. In the case of large aircraft a lump-sum tariff was charged that included all the standard services, including those not actually provided (because some of the standard services were provided by the airlines themselves, or they used more modern services in lieu of them, included in the services on request).

The Autorità Garante ruled that the competition law also applied to airport management companies, because they operated only the activity, considered to be of general economic interest, of managing airport infrastructure under a statutory monopoly. This monopoly therefore did not include the supply of handling services. This being so, the Autorità Garante found an abuse of dominant position by the airport management companies in their conduct designed to:

— impose unjustifiably onerous conditions and tariffs, in the case of the lump- sum tariffs for services not actually supplied, and regarding to the royalties charged in addition to the rental for the facilities on which airlines performed their own handling services;

— hamper market entry by the airlines wishing to produce their own services, explicitly refusing authorization or imposing excessively onerous conditions on them;

— apply discriminatory conditions against airlines wishing to produce their own services;

— subordinate the supply of particular services to payment for other services not actually supplied (tie-in), in the case of the lump-sum tariff.

This was one of the most important cases dealt with in the short life of the Autorità Garante, because it was one of the first decisions taken against companies responsible for managing services of general economic interest. It has established the principle that exceptions and waivers to competition law must be extremely restrictively and rigorously applied to statutory monopoly-holders. The Autorità Garante's action here has also opened up the market, because in Italy's airports a growing number of airlines are now providing their own handling services.

12.5.2 The GSM cellular telephony system

Action was taken in this sector by the Autorità Garante even before the market was opened up to competition in the spring of 1994, when the government appointed a second operator to join the public carrier, SIP (now Telecom Italia Mobile, TIM).

In the wake of a general fact-finding survey of the industry, the Autorità Garante pointed out that there was no economic justification for the monopoly enjoyed by SIP, because average production costs at the level of an individual plant, switching exchange and network were not falling (in other words, it was not a natural monopoly). Proof of this was to be found in the fact that in other countries where analogue cellular telephony was provided on a competitive market, the companies had acquired such efficient dimensions that they were able to earn adequate profits; they also charged lower tariffs, which had led them to offer a more highly developed service than the one provided by monopoly-holders (including Italy).

Having ascertained the viability and the appropriateness of opening up GSM telephony to competition, the Autorità Garante analyzed the difficulties that this would probably create. The position of SIP as the basic telephony and analogue cellular telephony monopoly carrier gave the company a number of advantages: the possibility to partly use its analogue network, which already existed (while the competitor would need to set up a new network of its own), and the fact that SIP had a well-established commercial network and a well-known brand name. Coupled with the fact that SIP was already working experimentally on the GSM market, this made it necessary to introduce competition into the market without further delay.

However, the Autorità Garante felt that it was also necessary to ascertain whether SIP was exploiting these advantages to behave in such a way as to constitute abuse of dominant position, by *de facto* impeding market entry to other competitors once the GSM market had been liberalized. The aggressive commercial policy being implemented by SIP, particularly by spreading the image of a company that was already operating on a firmly established basis in the market, and not only experimentally as was in fact the case, could raise insurmountable entry barriers, and as such suggested that a dominant position was being abused.

Partly as a result of these actions, the government awarded a franchise to a second operator. Fears regarding barriers to entry in this market proved well-founded. Once again, the Autorità Garante had to take steps to support competition, submitting reports to the government and Parliament to remove the statutory provisions that created objectively different operating conditions between the two firms, and once again finding the public service company responsible for anticompetitive behavior (in the meantime SIP had become TIM). In its contracts with distributors of subscriptions to its GSM services, TIM had included an exclusive clause, preventing the distributors from selling the services of the other operator. TIM was entitled to terminate the contract with distributors failing to comply with this obligation, which caused them to forfeit part of the commissions paid to them for earlier contracts concluded with subscribers, as well as to lose the right to sell subscriptions both to the GSM service and the analogue service. Since the TIM network included most of the leading and largest distributors, and TIM's strategy to retain the distributors' loyalty was proving particularly effective, a major obstacle had been placed in the way of developing the service offered by the second operator just when it was entering the market.

Despite all the difficulties, however, the liberalization process that actually began in December 1995 when the second operator began marketing its services, seems to have produced its first results. Both companies have been competing fiercely throughout 1996 with a string of promotional offerings[3] differentiating their supply of services; in only three months (up to the end of March 1996) the second operator had managed to acquire a 20% share.

12.5.3 Liberalized telecommunications services

The Autorità Garante has taken an approach aimed to promote competition in this sector, rather than defending competition as such. One small company, Telsystem, that wanted to provide services to closed user groups, had asked the public telecommunications carrier, Telecom, to lease it a number of lines to link the members of these closed groups in exchange for a rental fee. Telecom, however, repeatedly refused to lease these lines on the grounds

[3]This strategy, based on offering special conditions for the connection charge for individual subscribers rather than by reducing call charges, could in fact prove to be anticompetitive, if the operators used it to "capture" customers, and it were not easy to move from one system to the other if the operators increased tariffs.

that Telsystem's activities did not fall within the scope of those that had been liberalized by Directive 90/388 which, at all events, had not yet been received into Italian law.

The Autorità Garante ruled that even though these services were not expressly dealt with in the Directive, they nevertheless fell within the scope of the Directive which only expressly excluded voice telephony. Moreover, the Directive was enforceable in Italy because the deadline for its reception into Italian law had already expired and it contained unconditional and sufficiently specific provisions for it to be applied (conditions which EU case-law considers sufficient for a directive to be enforceable in any Member State even if it has not yet been incorporated into domestic law). Telecom was therefore under an obligation to lease the lines to the company requesting them and its refusal to do so excluded a competitor from an open market, and therefore constituted an abuse of dominant position.

Directive 90/388 was received into Italian law only two months after the Autorità Garante's decision (after it had reported to the government and Parliament a number of points included in the various draft decrees to enact it on the grounds that they contained provisions that were not fully in accordance with the spirit and the letter of the Directive), so the innovative effect of Autorità Garante's decision cannot be appraised.

However, in this case it reiterated the principle that any exemptions or waivers to competition law must be considered exceptional, and the statutory provisions guaranteeing these exemptions must be interpreted very narrowly.

12.5.4 The insurance sector

The three cases described above were in sectors in which companies operated under a statutory monopoly. We will now examine an area in which many companies compete, namely, the insurance business, where the Autorità Garante has had to intervene on a number of occasions. Three anti-competitive agreements were detected.

In the first case, 16 of the Italian leading insurance companies were found to have held regular meetings over three years to exchange information on their activities, to agree upon common policy conditions, including premiums, in a number of areas in insurance against loss and damage with regard to major hazards, and to ensure compliance with these agreements, and with a non-competition agreement with regard to contract renewals. In view of the seriousness of these conducts, the Autorità Garante fined the companies;

the fines are still the highest it has ever imposed.

Another case related to crop hail insurance. There were two consortia operating on this market; the same companies were members of both of them. One was a statutory consortium (by law all the companies operating in this sector had to be members of consortia) while the other one was a voluntary consortium that managed the assets of the former. These consortia had a 97% market share. Through the voluntary consortium, the members shared out the market between them, mutually controlling their activities and restricting the dissemination of new types of policies. The Autorità Garante therefore ruled that this consortium was restricting competition, and therefore prohibited this activity. With regard to the statutory consortium, although it was linked to the former one, it was given temporary authorization as an exception to the ban on agreements restricting competition, because the law was at that time in a state of flux in view of the imminent reception into Italian law of Directive 92/49, such that if the consortium were to wind up its activities the whole market could be paralyzed.

When this authorization expired, the consortium unsuccessfully requested the Autorità Garante to extend the exemption period. The Autorità Garante refused it on the grounds that the Directive had been incorporated into Italian law, while another law was about to be enacted that not only lifted the requirement for insurance companies to belong to consortia, but also limited the size of any voluntary consortia that might be created to a maximum market share of 10% in the case of insurance consortia and 15% for re-insurance consortia.

The third agreement related to small aeronautical risks, for which a consortium operated including virtually all the insurance companies on the market. It circulated a tariff list to its members, to enable them to coordinate premiums and other policy conditions. For risks and hazards not included in this tariff list, the consortium suggested identical conditions to the companies competing for a particular contract. It was also standard practice for companies to offer substantial discounts provided that the insured took out all its policies covering the various aeronautical risks from companies which were members of the consortium. By coordinating the activities of its members the consortium was able to eliminate competition throughout virtually the whole market.

The Autorità Garante did not merely impose fines for anticompetitive behavior in the insurance industry. It also examined various agreements between insurance companies and banks for the distribution of policies through the bank branches. This is a distribution system that has grown enormously in recent years in Italy for life assurance policies, increasing three-fold between 1992 and 1995 to reach 18% of all the premiums paid through all the distribution channels. The advantage of such agreements is evident, reducing distribution costs thanks to the possibility of selling banking and insurance products jointly through the same channels. However they could potentially restrict competition if exclusive clauses were imposed and if they covered a long period. In these cases, when the parties are leaders on their respective markets, the entry by new firms into the local markets is extremely difficult. Any potential market entrant finds it difficult to find outlets through banking channels, when banks with large market shares are tied for long periods by exclusive agreements with competitors that are already working on the market, and they find it difficult to find alternative channels (most of the policies are still distributed through agents working on an exclusive basis for particular companies). This being so, the Autorità Garante only authorized agreements that did not include exclusive clauses. In only one case did it grant a temporary exemption, because the exclusive clause was deemed necessary to benefit consumers by providing them with specific policies for the banking outlets on more favorable terms and conditions than those offered for the same products sold through different channels.

The Autorità Garante therefore applied competition law to the insurance industry in accordance with the EU principles which take account of the specific features of the business in question, characterized by the great unpredictability of the conditions under which the companies operate, but without making it possible to do away with competition by establishing common premium conditions or by sharing the market. At the same time, it judged positively the current developments in the distribution system, considering that they had to be supported under certain circumstances even if this involved introducing some restrictions on competition.

12.6 Suggestions in the light of the Italian experience

In the light of past experience, there are various suggestions that may be made in relation both to European competition policy and domestic policies.

As far as the former are concerned, increasing market globalization and the gradual creation of the Single European Market make it necessary to consider a new approach to intervention policies and for controlling the operation of Europe's markets. Now that markets range over national borders, corporate behavior has repercussions on these same areas, and it is on them that the overall performance of the market must be evaluated in terms of the goals which the market sets. In the supranational ambit, these objectives must therefore be defined at the supranational level jointly with the instruments for pursuing them and the vesting of powers to enforce them. It is therefore at the European level that regulation and competition policies must coexist and primarily operate.

Whereas competition policy has been in force since the creation of the European Community, regulation is implemented only at the level of general principles laid down in the process for the gradual creation of the European market. This final goal determines both the regulation and the competition policy for the European Union, giving them a feature that is additional to the purposes which both of them normally pursue.

Nowadays, as stated above, all these activities are the responsibility of the Commission. In view of the establishment of the Single Market by the end of the century as scheduled, one might envisage a model under which tasks are differently distributed. In particular, the approach to which Italy is working could be established at the European level:

— government lays down goals to be attained in certain sectors and decides on the degree of competition (competition promotion policy) and the level of regulation, laying down the fundamental principles to be applied; today, this role is mainly performed by the Commission, and we see examples in the telecommunications where in addition to liberalization the Commission lays down constraints on companies, such as the need to provide a universal service. The Commission and the Council, as the expression of the political will of the Union and the member states, can continue to play this role;

— the application of regulatory principles laid down by the policy-makers can be entrusted to independent supranational (European) regulators. By 'independent' we mean independence from the Commission. The regulators should deal with laying down rules enforceable in the whole market with a European dimension;

— European antitrust could be applied by a special European agency independent of the Commission, in accordance with the German proposal which has been supported by the Italian Autorità Garante. This would therefore mean separating promotional activities from the protection of competition because of their intrinsically different natures. Whereas promotional policy is characterized by a high level of discretion, forming part of a political environment in which it has to be reconciled with other goals that could clash with it, the latter is more judicial in character, because the agency having responsibility "certifies" the compliance of specific conducts with the law, and can impose fines in cases where this is not so. Decisions involving some discretion, such as exemptions for certain restrictive agreements, might perhaps be excluded from the powers of this agency.

It has been objected that this approach to competition protection activity is also an indirect form of promotion and it is therefore illogical to divide up the promotional activities as a whole between two different institutions. But keeping responsibility for both these activities in the hands of the Commission would lead to a dangerous mixture between lawmaking and "judicial" functions.

Just as today there exist European anti-trust activities and similar activities within each Member State, it might be possible to replicate this with regard to regulatory activities, using Community-level organizations dealing with aspects of pan-European relevance, and national institutions responsible for managing the "domestic" aspects, obviously in application of the principles laid down at the European level. The sharing of powers between the European and domestic levels should be based in both types of policy on the principle of subsidiarity. This is the approach of the draft note of the Commission on its cooperation with national agencies for the application of Arts 85 and 86 of the Treaty, and of the exceptions to the powers generally vested in one of the two levels when a particular case could be better dealt with at the other level (Art 9 of the Concentrations Control Regulation).

As far as national competition policies are concerned, there is a case for the agency responsible for enforcing antitrust policy having maximum independence of government, in order to guarantee that its decisions are independent of political considerations.

As far as individual areas of intervention are concerned:

Mergers and acquisitions: In order to prevent the proliferation of cases which the system of compulsory prior notification based on turnover thresholds might cause, one approach could be to introduce a system based on the right of companies to apply for prior authorization where the administrative costs of the assessment procedure are charged to the companies themselves. For operations without prior authorization it would be possible for action to be taken *a posteriori* if anticompetitive conducts are performed.

Agreements: A system of notification similar to the one used for mergers and acquisitions could be adopted in the case of agreements. Both concentrations and agreements would therefore be subject to a system of partial prior appraisal and subsequent action, if necessary monitoring, with action taken subsequently, if necessary.

Abuse of dominant position: In this area, as has already occurred in Italy, particular care should be paid to prevent dominant positions guaranteed by law from being exploited abusively in order to extend domination over different markets. This conduct must also be considered carefully in small economies where it is likely that dominant positions are more frequent.

Reporting: This is an important activity where there is a poorly developed competition culture and where legislation prevents it from developing. In order to be effective, however, the institutions receiving the reports should not be completely free to decide whether or not to accept them. If they are declined, there must at least be an obligation on government to provide a reasoned reply justifying its refusal to adopt the recommendations.

Public corporations and self-production of services: What was said regarding the abuse of dominant position also applies here. The reporting activities can highlight privileges which are not justified by the general public interest to the benefit of State owned corporations.

Relations with other institutions responsible for enforcing the competition policy: There is a case for the powers of enforcing antitrust policy being vested in one single body in order to prevent duplication of powers and conflicts between antitrust considerations and other criteria related to different tasks.

An exception to this might be in the publishing industry, where the need to protect the fundamental right to freedom of opinion, and the particular delicacy of this task and the difficulty of implementing it, necessarily influence the assessment of competition. Entrusting this last type of assessment to an institution other than the one generally responsible for enforcing competition law could be restricted to the most important aspects relating to freedom of opinion, by laying down objective rules to be applied *per se* (for example restrictions on the market shares of daily newspaper publishers).

Competition Policies in Europe - S. Martin (Editor)

Chapter 13

Competition Policy in Portugal

Pedro P. Barros[1]
José Mata

13.1 Introduction

Modern economies rely predominantly on the working of markets. To ensure that restrictive firm practices do not prevent markets from working properly, competition policies are usually part of the legal framework that regulates economic activities. Currently, Portugal is no exception to this rule. This has not always been the case, however. The first Competition Law was approved only in 1983, and since then enforcement of the law has not been very active. The reasons for the slight attention that competition policy has received in Portugal are twofold. On the one hand, for a long time competition was regarded very suspiciously. Concern was directed to the fear of "excessive competition," which was presumed to generate pernicious outcomes, rather than to the lack of competition. On the other hand, in more recent times the emphasis of economic policy towards business has been centered on improving competitiveness rather than on enforcing competition. The rationale for that emphasis is the presumption that most firms in Portugal are too small to be competitive by international standards. Because of their modest scale, there would be little scope for the exercise of market power.

[1] We are grateful to Luís Miguel Pais Antunes, Alberto Heimler, Maria Manuel Marques, Mário Marques Mendes and workshop participants for useful comments and discussions. All deficiencies are our own responsibility.

In this paper, we review the legal aspects of the Portuguese competition policy and its economic implications and give a brief account of past experience. We start by providing some background on the legal and political framework prevailing prior to 1983 and on changes occurring thereafter. We then proceed with an overview of the firm size distribution and levels of concentration in Portugal . Section 13.3 broadly describes the legal framework. Section 13.4 surveys the procedures related to enforcement of competition policy and summarizes the past experience on restrictive practices and merger cases. The conclusion is that only a few (and relatively unimportant) cases were analyzed. Implementation of national competition policy potentially conflicts with other policies. In particular, it may conflict with industrial and trade policy and with competition policy at the European Union level. Section 13.5 reviews these conflicts. Finally, Section 13.6 offers some thoughts on desirable changes in competition policy. It is suggested that, at the level of principles, the current legal framework is satisfactory overall and that most changes should probably occur at the implementation level. Especially important are changes related to the legal procedures to be followed whenever courts are brought in by appeals of Competition Authority decisions.

13.2 Competition Policy in Portugal: some background

13.2.1 Legal background

For a period of 48 years (1926–74) Portugal was run under a right-wing non-democratic political regime, known as the 'New State' or the 'Corporative State.' Despite its right-wing inspiration, the regime adopted a rather interventionist stand with respect to the organization of the economy. Industries were organized around the Guilds (*Corporações*), associations of agents with interests in the market (industrialists, workers). The key word in the political discourse was cooperation rather than competition, as expressed in the Constitution of 1933 (Article 34):

> The State promotes the development and formation of the Corporative Economy. The Corporative Economy seeks to avoid that its members engage in undisciplined competition, which is con-

> trary to the society's and their own objectives. Instead, it aims that they cooperate as members of the same community.

Market forces, in general, were not thought to have a clearly beneficial role. It was thought that prices should not be determined by supply and demand, but instead by the conscious pursuit of the public interest. Accordingly, the Guilds should play a decisive role in fixing prices.[2]

Industrial Policy was also inspired by the same goal of collective cooperation. The best known example is the law under which investment was regulated (Law 2052, *Lei do Condicionamento Industrial*). The purpose of the law was to reduce social waste through investment regulation. Under this law, entry and capacity expansion required approval by the regulatory institution, the issue being whether or not such investment was beneficial to society (whether or not the market could accommodate new capacity). It is worth noting that only the interests of firms were explicitly taken into account although, presumably, the State would consider consumers' interests.[3] Incumbent firms had the legal right to oppose entry (expansion), arguing that existing capacity was already enough to serve the market. This argument could be challenged by the prospective entrant (expanding incumbent), but the intervention of competitors was, at least, highly dilatory and in many cases incumbents were able to foreclose markets.[4] These dispositions also led to the expectation of a 'paternalistic state,' in the sense of protection of domestic firms, among business people.

In 1974 a Revolution replaced the right-wing regime by a left-wing government, the lack of concern with the presence of market power being replaced by a strong view in favor of State ownership. The Constitution approved in 1976 stated that[5]

> It is the State responsibility to eliminate and prevent the formation of private monopolies *through nationalization and other*

[2] Contemporaneous legal thought states: "Excess of competition generates pernicious outcomes. The Corporative State seeks to discipline these outcomes through legal regulation. (...) The spirit of competition must be destroyed and replaced by the spirit of cooperation, personified by the Guild."

[3] However, there is no evidence that this concern has had any role on policy decisions.

[4] Incumbents could argue based on installed capacity in the industry, or based on previously granted (even if unused) investment permissions and there were episodes of preemption with permissions rather than with capacity.

[5] Article 81; italicized portion deleted in the constitutional revision of 1989.

> *means,* as well as to repress the abuses of economic power and all practices which are detrimental to the public interest.

Accordingly, a wave of nationalizations took place and a considerable fraction of production was controlled by the State.[6] The most extensive nationalizations were performed in the financial sector (banking and insurance) and in heavy industry. However, due to the ownership structure of the economy, State ownership spread over a considerable number of businesses.

The lack of sympathy towards market forces remained or was even exacerbated in the first years following the Revolution. The Constitution explicitly stated that "the State intervenes in the formation and control of prices, in order to rationalize the distribution system and to eliminate the unnecessary stages" (Article 109) and, in an article which was subsequently deleted in 1989, it was established that "the State disciplines and controls the quality and price of imported and exported goods" (Article 110). Many prices came entirely under State control during the revolutionary period.

After several years, this tendency was reversed. Price regulations were progressively relaxed and the privatization of nationalized companies began. Meanwhile, and although the Constitution had established since 1976 the principle that "the State should guarantee fair competition between firms," (Article 81) the first Competition Law was passed in 1983. Portugal was then about to join the European Union (which occurred in 1986), and the law was directly inspired by Community Law. This legislation created the competition authorities, the Directorate General of Competition and Prices (*Direcção Geral de Concorrência e Preços*, Decree of Law 293/82) and the Competition Council (*Conselho da Concorrência*, Decree of Law 422/88), and the basic legal framework, inspired by the Community's system (Decree of Law 422/83 and Decree of Law 136/84).. The system was completed in 1988 with a law on merger control (Decree of Law 428/88).

The legal body remained fairly unchanged until 1993, in spite of the enactment of smaller pieces of legislation. At the end of this year, a new legal framework was put forward (Decree of Law 371/93, effective from the beginning of 1994). The main novelties of this reformulation of the legal background were a more universal application of competition rules, prohibition, in principle, of state aids, the introduction of the concept of abuse of economic dependence, and changes in thresholds for merger control.

---

[6] According to Neves (1994), the gross value added of State-owned firms stood at about 2% of GNP in 1973 and 15% in 1976.

x	100	500	1000
Firms	98.2	99.8	99.9
Employment	57.2	78.9	85.1

Source: Ministry of Employment and own calculations

Table 13.1: Share of firms with fewer than x employees in 1992 (%)

	515 five digit industries				327 industries[(a)]			
	H	C4	C8	C20	H	C4	C8	C20
Mean	0.20	0.52	0.62	0.72	0.09	0.39	0.48	0.60
1st Quartile	0.02	0.19	0.29	0.45	0.01	0.14	0.21	0.32
Median	0.07	0.48	0.61	0.85	0.03	0.30	0.43	0.63
3st Quartile	0.27	0.88	0.99	1.00	0.09	0.57	0.75	0.91
9th Decile	0.59	1.00	1.00	1.00	0.30	0.93	0.99	1.00

[(a)]Note: Excluding industries employing fewer than 500 persons.

Source: Ministry of Employment and own calculations

Table 13.2: Concentration in 1992

13.2.2 Economic background

The tradition above is probably one of the main reasons for the relative lack of importance of competition policy which survives even to this day. A second reason for this neglect is that concern with competition policy is normally dictated by the perception that the exercise of market power may produce socially negative effects, and market power is typically associated with large firms. Unlike the situation in other small European countries, large firms are almost non-existent in Portugal.[7]

Almost 80% of total employment is employed by firms of fewer than 500 people, the largest firm employing 20,000 persons. The turnover of the largest non-financial company in the country is less than 4 billion ECU.[8] These are relatively small numbers by European standards. In fact, only two Portuguese firms are amongst the European market leaders in 100 NACE manufacturing industries (Davies and Lyons, 1996).

Concentration levels are relatively high, due mostly to the small size of

[7]Portugal is one of the smallest and least developed countries within the EU. Its population is about 10 million, and GDP per capita in 1994 was USD 8960.

[8]*Exame 500*, October/November 1995.

markets. When industries employing fewer than 500 people are excluded, concentration levels decrease substantially (Table 13.2). Moreover, Portugal is a relatively open country which naturally limits the scope for the exercise of market power (in 1994 exports and imports were, respectively, 28% and 35% of GDP).[9]

Increased exposure to international competition, due to European Union membership in 1986, contributed to the creation of the notion that the main priority for economic policy towards business would be the improvement of international competitiveness of firms by increasing the scale of domestic firms and by contributing toward the creation of 'national champions.' Although competition policy is no longer viewed with suspicion at the level of principles, it has remained a secondary goal, in practice.

13.3 Competition Policy — the Law

13.3.1 Purposes

The goals of Portuguese competition policy are spelled out in a statement of purpose in the preamble of the competition law (Decree of Law 371/93). Competition policy is intended to support the effective working of the market mechanism and to guarantee equal opportunities for market players. This defense of the competitive working of markets is based on the prevention and punishment of restrictive practices.

This view differs from standard economic analysis, which typically specifies some welfare criterion for evaluation of firms' practices that may restrict competition. In the legislation, there is no specific aim in terms of welfare or consumers' surplus for the competition authorities to pursue. This option results, on the one hand, from the difficulty in specifying in detail a welfare measure with sufficient generality to fit every situation that may occur and, on the other hand, from the notion that a well-functioning competitive market system yields a Pareto optimum. The problems associated with providing a general and workable definition of social welfare justify the view of competition policy in looking at those activities that increase the scope for collusive agreements, either explicit or tacit. Nonetheless, protection against so-called restrictive practices of rivals may be a quite different goal than protection of competition for the benefit of consumers or for efficiency improvements.

---

[9] Banco de Portugal, Annual Report 1994.

There is, of course, room for the competition authority to define the welfare objective in each particular case. For example, in merger evaluation the role of consumers is made more explicit. On the other hand, restrictive practices may be allowed if they generate a positive 'economic balance.' For a positive economic balance to exist, it is required that (Article 5): (i) consumers receive a 'fair share' of any gains resulting from anticompetitive conduct; (ii) the gains cannot be achieved by other means compatible with competitive conduct; and (iii) the practice does not eliminate competition in the market (or a sizable fraction of it). The notion of economic balance is quite vague, without a precise economic content and leaves the Competition Authority with considerable discretion with regard to its evaluations.

From a theoretical point of view, competition policy has the objective of monitoring the growth of firms, either external (mergers) or internal. The control of growth of firms can be either *ex-ante*, based on potential misconduct of firms, or *ex-post*, where the competition authority looks only at effective anti-competitive behavior. Portuguese law combines into a mixed system both elements and follows closely the Community's legislation.[10]

13.3.2 The concept of dominant position

A central concept in Portuguese competition policy, as in other countries and in the European Union, is that of dominant position. A dominant position is defined as the absence of significant competition. This applies to the control of firms' internal growth — abuse of dominant position; and to control of external growth of firms — merger control. The Competition Authority has the task of preventing, or at least monitoring, the existence of dominant positions.

The above definition of a dominant position is a general one and the law presents a very clear and precise definition of what is meant by dominant position for competition assessment purposes, based on market share distribution.[11] A firm is presumed to hold a dominant position in the market if it has a more than 30% market share. There are, however, two qualifications. First, it is allowed that other considerations may outweigh the conditions in this definition — namely entry may change the assessment of dominance in a

[10] The basic references of Community Law on competition policy matters are Articles 85 and 86 of the Treaty of Rome and Regulation 4064/89 for mergers.

[11] The presentation of a market-share definition of (presumed) dominance in Portuguese law constitutes a difference between it and EU law.

significant way. Second, besides defining a dominant position of a single firm, the law also acknowledges that a small group of firms may hold a dominant position. This explicitly recognizes that a small group of firms may act in a coordinated way, as if they were a single dominant firm. Specifically, it is presumed that a dominant group of firms exists if a group of two or three firms possesses a combined market share which is greater than 50%; or four or five firms hold a joint market share of 65% or more.[12] The clear specification of what is considered to be a dominant position in terms of market share makes transparent the conditions under which the intervention from the Competition Authority is likely to occur.

Dominant positions are not illegal *per se*; it is the abuse of these positions that constitute the reason for policy intervention. Abuse of dominant position is defined as a series of practices believed to restrict competition in the market. Based on this concept, competition authorities enjoy a great deal of latitude as there is no automatic trigger mechanism for intervention. Hence, in addition to defining what constitutes a dominant position, the law provides examples of what types of practices may be construed as abusive.

These practices include price fixing schemes, collusive practices and vertical restraints, i.e., contractual dispositions that go beyond the simple statement of the quantity-price pair in the transaction (tied-sales, exclusive territories, etc.). It should also be stated that the same practices are not allowed in general to individual firms, even if a dominant position does not exist (Article 2 of Decree of Law 371/93), if they restrict or undermine competition in the marketplace.

It is however debatable, in economic terms, the real difference between the two legal dispositions. A restrictive practice by an individual firm can, in principle, be legally challenged under Article 2 of Decree of Law 371/93 whatever the market significance of the firm. However, the economic effects of the restrictive practice depend crucially on the firm's market position. In this sense, the more serious problems (the ones to be challenged in terms of adverse economic effects) are most likely to coincide with abuse of dominant position or to fall under the heading of collusive agreements. Thus, although Article 2 and Article 3 of Competition Law are different in legal terms in concerning restrictive practices (the latter article requiring proof of dominant position), its economic effects seem to be essentially the same.

[12]The cut-off point for the number of firms is close to the value pointed out in Selten (1973).

The Portuguese legal dispositions on collusive practices (Article 2) closely follow Article 85 of the Treaty of Rome (the examples of 'unfair' practices are essentially the same).. There is, however, a difference as Portuguese law explicitly forbids refusal to sell as being anticompetitive. Although this idea is not present in the main act of competition policy, another piece of legislation on individual trade practices (Decree of Law 370/93) does explicitly forbid (unjustifiable) refusal to sell in retailing relations. Nevertheless, the enumeration of practices is not exhaustive and enforcement of competition policy at the Community level may well also cover refusal to sell. Thus, the importance of this difference is probably limited.

The Portuguese legislation also introduces another concept of dominance — economic dependence — defined as the absence of alternatives for an economic agent, which implies a strong bargaining position of the other side. This notion may lead to intervention even if a dominant position in the sense defined above does not exist. The economic meaning of this notion is open to discussion. The concept is mainly aimed at producer-retailer relations (especially distribution chains and their suppliers). The typical case involves a strong bargaining position of distribution chains *vis-à-vis* suppliers. From an economic point of view this does not necessarily raise efficiency concerns, especially if retailing activities are highly competitive. The argument for intervention usually mentions that a 'fair' share of the gains from the relation should accrue to the supplier, which is not an efficiency argument but a distributive consideration. As such, it is not clear whether competition policy should pursue it.

13.3.3 Collusive agreements

Cartelization of industry, either explicit or tacit, is forbidden (Article 2 of Competition Law). This principle is a common element to competition policies. There are, however, some other features of the legal framework that curtail, to a certain extent, full use of competition policy to breakup cartels.

Co-movements of prices and information exchange between firms are typically seen as evidence of collusive agreements. It should be noted that firms may ask for clearance of an agreement by the Competition Authority, and this clearance may be given provided that some conditions are met (essentially, a positive economic balance, discussed in subsection 13.3.1). However, interpretation of price lists as evidence of collusion is made difficult by the requirement in commercial law that prices and discounts should be made publicly available (Decree of Law 370/93, Article 2). Competition between firms may take the form of secret price discounts and, if this legal disposition is strictly followed, competition in the market may be hindered to a considerable extent. It is, of course, unrealistic to think that such a disposition can be enforced in a systematic way. More important is the fact that public announcements of discounts may have the role of facilitating collusion and cannot be taken as legal evidence of it. Nevertheless, they can be seen as a first sign of collusive agreements.

In terms of economic effects, agreements and concerted practices are similar. From an economist's point of view, agreements between firms correspond to the notion of explicit collusion, while concerted practices fall under the heading of tacit collusion. Finding evidence of tacit collusion is very hard and the European Commission intervention has emphasized information exchange as evidence of tacit collusion. So far in Portugal, co-movements of prices and information sharing have been the main indicators of collusive anti-competitive behavior. Of course, not all information sharing can be taken as evidence of collusion. The welfare effects of information sharing between firms can be positive or negative, making it difficult to establish general rules. There are, however, some principles that hold in general. The main reason why information sharing may help to sustain collusion is that it facilitates monitoring of rivals (and their deviations to agreements). To this effect, the nature of the information revealed is important. Sharing detailed information on individual prices and quantities is more damaging to competition than sharing general information on market conditions, like overall demand prospects. More frequent information also facilitates collusion (weekly lists of prices are more worrisome than the year's average price). The finer the information is, the easier it is to sustain collusive agreements. Thus, it seems sensible for competition policy to act on certain types of information exchanges among firms.[13]

One must recognize that simple non-cooperative market outcomes may exhibit to the outside observer the same qualitative features as do collusive agreements. For example, in a Nash equilibrium, a demand shock may lead to a common change in prices, even if each firm takes decisions independently of the others.[14] Distinction between tacit collusion and non-cooperative be-

[13]For a more detailed discussion and a suggestion of implementation of guidelines in EU competition policy, see Kühn and Vives (1995).

[14]For a more detailed discussion and a worked-out example, see Phlips (1995).

havior may require sound economic analysis to be performed in order to build a convincing case. This is especially true for tacit collusion, where there is no explicit agreement between firms. For example, Portuguese commercial banks typically had high price-cost margins, namely in the deposits market. However, (local) market power due to geographical segmentation seems to have been the underlying factor rather than collusive behavior among banks (Barros, 1995). This does not imply that banks do not collude on other occasions as in the *Multibanco* case.

The *MULTIBANCO* case. One recent example of an explicit collusive agreement, with imposition of common prices by a set of banks, is the *Multibanco* case. *Multibanco* is the name of the Portuguese ATM network, shared by all banks in the system, and includes also POS ("point-of-sales") terminals in shops. The use of POS terminals is ruled by a direct agreement between the shop and a bank. POS terminals can process payments with debit and credit cards. They compete directly with checks and cash as means of payment.

Payment through POS was, in general, free of charge. In the Spring of 1994, the Portuguese Banks Association (APB) announced the imposition of a proportional fee on the monetary amount of transactions on all POS terminals (about 1%). The reason presented for this fee was that the POS transactions are a service provided by the banking system and, like any other service, it should be paid for by users. The current situation had an implicit cross-subsidization of the service by the other banking services. This fee would be paid by firms and shops, which protested and threatened to pass it on to consumers.

Since the measure was publicly announced by APB and was to be implemented in an equal manner by all banks, the suspicion of a cartel decision arose (in fact, accusations of cartel behavior were widespread in the newspapers). The debate over the issue reached the Parliament, an investigation was performed, and Government intervention took place (enactment of *Portaria* 1150/94, of 27 December 1994).

The decision prohibited the 1% fee and imposed a proportional fee up to a small fixed amount for a six month period. During that period, banks and shops were supposed to sign bilateral contracts. The banks had to notify such contracts to *Direcção Geral de Concorrência e Preços* for supervision purposes. Notifications revealed a considerable diversity in contractual clauses across banks in the value of the fee, requirements of average balance in bank accounts, term of contract, other charges, etc. On the basis of this evidence of cartel disruption the case was not pursued further. This turned out to be a successful, even if unorthodox, intervention by the Government against cartel behavior.

We now want to look at the economic fundamentals of the case. The argument presented by APB for the fee (pricing a previously free-of-charge service) seems to be sound economics, as there are no free lunches. However, a more careful analysis of the case, taking into account the economic incidence of the fee, assuming shops to pass it on consumers, reveals some interesting features. Firstly, since the cost of the service is independent of the amount of the transaction, a fixed fee seems more appropriate than the proportional fee. It is desirable to restrain more 'small' transactions than large ones.[15] In this respect, under a proportional fee, a small transaction has a small fee and the deterrent effect on usage is also small. Secondly, due to the effect on balances of bank accounts, banks should provide the service at below marginal cost in a non-cooperative equilibrium (and for free, if high interest rate spreads characterize the market, which was the case when the service was introduced). These characteristics of the market and of the intended fee seem to corroborate the view of cartel behavior in the banking sector, with the Portuguese Banks Association performing a coordination role.

13.3.4 Predatory pricing

Besides collusion, firms may pursue other strategies in attempting to monopolize the market (or increase their market power), namely predatory pricing, mergers and market foreclosure of rivals through vertical restraints. The last two issues are treated in the next sections.

The basic difficulty in economic discussions about predatory pricing stems from the well-known problems in rationalizing the existence of predatory pricing. Moreover, available evidence of predatory pricing is hardly convincing.[16]

There is no explicit mention of predatory pricing in competition law. The only reference one finds in the law is a reference to prices which are "much too low," although it is not completely clear whether these low prices are due to monopsony power or predatory pricing. Nevertheless, the law seems

[15] For example, paying for the newspaper with a debit card is clearly inefficient. The 1% fee is well below the connection cost.

[16] See, for example, Chapters 11 and 12 in Phlips (1995).

to focus on the exercise of monopoly or monopsony power rather than on the adoption of strategies intended to drive rivals out of the market.

In commercial law, however, there is an explicit mention forbidding sales with losses.[17] This is defined as selling below the price at which the good was bought. Such price is the main component of retail cost and, therefore, it is a good proxy to marginal cost. This clearly centers the notion of selling at a loss on retailing activities and brings it close to the economic notion of predatory pricing. It is not clear whether a similar concept exists in the case of manufacturers. Nevertheless, a firm was once convicted in a competition case of the practice of predatory pricing (case 1/87).

Predatory pricing in the sugar market In this case, a leading firm in the sugar market, RAR (*Refinarias de Açúcar Reunidas*), was found guilty of abuse of dominant position through the practice of predatory prices in one particular segment of the sugar market, the market for packed sugar in 8/10 g packs.

The interest of this case is twofold. First, although competition law does not include predatory pricing amongst the practices which are explicitly forbidden, a firm was found guilty of predatory pricing and convicted under the charge of abuse of dominant position. Second, the convicted firm did not have a dominant position (as defined by the 30% market share) in the particular market in which the abuse was committed. Rather, the defendant was a dominant firm in the overall sugar market while the abuse occurred in a particular segment in which the defendant had no dominant position before the predatory practice.[18] In fact, predation, if it existed, was a means of acquiring market share in this particular segment.

Sugar manufacturing is composed of two distinct stages. In the first stage, sugar refining, there were three firms in the market in the mid-1980s. RAR was the largest of these firms with market shares above 40%. Moreover, due to high transport costs and because RAR has its plants located in the North of Portugal while its competitors (SORES and SIDUL) are located in the South, RAR was virtually a monopolist in the North. The output of this stage (refined sugar) is the main input for the second stage of this process,

[17] Sales of perishable goods are not covered by the disposition

[18] The dominant position has been challenged by Mendes (1990) on the basis that the two main competitors in the sugar market have a common dominant shareholder. In our view, this does not preclude predatory pricing by RAR.

	1983	1984	1985
Overall Sugar			
RAR	45.0	43.0	42.1
SORES/SIDUL	55.0	57.0	57.9
8/10 g packs			
RAR	24.2	19.9	34.5
SORES/SIDUL	26.7	27.2	26.7
Northern independent packers	20.1	25.5	16.5
Southern independent packers	29.0	27.4	22.3

Source: Competition Council, *Annual Report* 1988

Table 13.3: Market Shares in the Sugar Market

the packing of sugar in packs of different capacities ranging from 50 Kg to 8/10 g.

Predation allegedly occurred in one particular segment of the packing market, the 8/10 g packs market. All three refineries also operated in this market, although these operations were relatively unimportant in their turnover (this market accounted for less than 6% of RAR turnover in the 1984–86 period). Apart from the refineries, there were two groups of firms in the market. In the first group, firms were quite small and operated almost exclusively in this market. These were firms located in the North and which used RAR as their source of sugar in bulk. Firms in the second group were located in the South, buying mostly from RAR competitors. Unlike their Northern counterparts, sugar packing was a secondary activity. Their main activity was coffee roasting, sugar being sold through the same distribution network as coffee. Each group comprised more than one dozen firms.

Table 13.3 displays market shares in the overall sugar and in the 8/10 g packets markets. It is visible that in the latter market RAR experienced a considerable increase in market share from 1984 to 1985 at the expense of independent packers, in particular the Northern ones.

This seems to be a direct consequence of a new pricing strategy of RAR, which was adopted in April 1985 and was subsequently found to be predatory by the Competition Council. Table 13.4 summarizes the prices charged by RAR for sugar in bulk and in 8/10 g packs. In April 1985 RAR introduced a new price system for the packed sugar. The novelty of this system was that there were different prices depending on the sales volume. At the same

	1984		1985		1986
	May	October	January	April	March
Bulk	60.9	61.4	64.5	64.5	79.1
8/10 g packs	73.80	74.3	76.5	70.0 72.0 75.0	95.0 97.5 101.0
Margins	12.8	12.9	12.1	5.5 7.5 10.5	15.9 18.4 21.9
Margins (%)	21.2	21.0	18.7	8.5 11.6 16.6	20.1 23.2 27.7

Source: Competition Council, *Annual Report* 1988

Table 13.4: Prices in the Sugar Market (PTE/Kg)

time, all prices in this market were cut by a substantial amount, while prices remained constant in the bulk market. This led to a sharp contraction in the packers' margins and as a consequence, some independent packers ceased their production or experienced significant losses in market share. Eleven months after the price cuts, having driven some packers out of the market and increased its market share by 75%, RAR raised its prices in percentages varying from 109 to 189, leading to margins in the packing activity well above those prevailing before the price cuts.

The practice of such low prices followed by a rise in prices was found to be illegal by the Competition Council on the grounds of abuse of dominant position and RAR was fined in the amount of 5 million PTE. The decision was appealed twice to the Court of First Instance and to the Court of Appeal. The outcome of the judicial process was that the decision was maintained, except that the fine was reduced to 10% of its original amount by the Court of First Instance.

The economic evaluation of the case by outside observers is seriously hindered by the parsimony of the information provided by the Competition Council's report. Firstly, it is not clear that the market should be defined as the Northern market, as price cuts were transmitted to the South and Southern independent producers were also affected by them (lost market share). Secondly, there is no information on entry conditions, nor on whether the independent producers re-entered or gained market share after the price increases in 1985. Without such information it is difficult to judge the impact of RAR's policy on welfare. Thirdly, there is no information on costs. It thus becomes difficult to judge RAR's policy in terms of efficiency or welfare. The fact that costs were not considered in the Competition Council's decision suggests that the fact that RAR's competitors were damaged as a result of its pricing was taken as sufficient evidence to convict the firm. The notion of predatory pricing underlying the decision seems to be one of the practice of low prices as a means of forcing the exit of rival firms, subsequently followed by a raise in prices. This is different from the US antitrust tradition, which focuses on predatory prices as prices below own marginal cost of production. Low prices may simply be due to higher efficiency of the firm. In fact, the market mechanism working as a selection device, only the more efficient firms will survive, the others being forced to exit the market. Low prices *per se* cannot be judged to be anticompetitive. However, low prices for a short period of time, followed by exit of rivals and subsequent rise of prices to higher levels than before the lowering of prices, without the corresponding change in cost conditions, comes closer to the notion of struggle for market power.

13.3.5 Merger control

The importance of the structural control of firms' growth, through merger control, stems from the natural problems in an effective behavior control. In particular, it is usually difficult to prove the existence of abuse of dominant position. Thus, intervention may focus on prevention of potentially harmful market structures rather than on its punishment.

The definition of the scope of application of merger control is based on the fulfillment of one of two criteria: a) the merging entities should have a combined market share in the relevant market that exceeds 30% (that is, they should have or create a dominant position); or b) the merging entities should have a turnover above 30 billion PTE (about 150 MECUs).

To get an idea of the relative magnitude of this threshold, note that only 114 firms have turnover above 15 billion PTE and 440 have turnover above 5 billion PTE. This figures include, however, a considerable number of firms that are automatically excluded from merger control, such as financial institutions and public utilities.[19] It is not clear why firms in the process of privatization should be exempted from merger control. However, the recent practice in proposed takeovers of State-owned banks suggests that discretion by the Government will be the rule. If these firms are excluded, the number of firms with turnover in excess of 15 billion PTE is 90, while above 5 billion PTE there are 389 companies. This suggests that in most cases the market share criterion is going to be the binding one in determining the launching of investigations.

A merger is defined as one firm (or set of firms) obtaining the effective control of another firm (or set of firms). For competition policy purposes, mergers are defined on the basis of control rights, namely on the basis of distribution of control rights that enables effective coordination of firms' decisions. The geographic market is, in principle, defined as the national market, although the practice has revealed that more narrow geographic markets have been used. As to product market definition, there is no guideline, providing full discretion to the analysis of the Competition Authority. This is not uncommon, and only the US merger guidelines actually specify very concrete instructions for delineation of the product market. Furthermore, unlike the US merger guidelines or even the EU merger regulation, the rules given for merger evaluation are quite vague.

The result of the evaluation is to either allow or block the merger.[20] A merger is to be blocked if it creates (or reinforces) a dominant position in the market that increases to a substantial extent the risk of diminished competition. The merger may go through if consumers receive a "fair" share of the gains or the international competitiveness of the merging firms is improved. These two exemptions do not have a clear economic content and allow for broad interpretations, which may seriously undermine the effectiveness of competition laws. In particular, it is not made precise what "fair" means or what an acceptable improvement in international competitiveness is.

[19] The justification for excluding public utilities from merger control seems to be debatable. On strict legal terms, public utilities and public-service firms are excluded from control concerning the scope of the contract of public service and during the term of the contract, but not in other economic activities which they may pursue. The obvious difficulty lies in the definition of the exact boundaries of public service.

[20] A third option besides approval and outright rejection is available: approval under certain conditions, but this has not been much explored (as of 1995). Recent decisions seem to show a desire to further explore this possibility in future assessments of concentration proposals.

The first exemption may be reasonable in some cases. Suppose that scale economies from a merger to monopoly are great enough such that the price after the merger is lower than the pre-merger price. Then, the merger should clearly be approved, even if it creates a monopoly. Of course, the proof of these gains is difficult to make *ex-ante*. *Ex-post*, divestiture is probably quite difficult to enforce, if no such gains emerge. On economic grounds, it makes sense to require an improvement in consumers' welfare, which may not coincide with the legal notion of "fair" share of gains. The exemption is prone to undue use by firms as a defense for the merger. Moreover, the proof that the gains from the merger cannot be obtained by other means (say, by an appropriate contractual relationship) is not required.[21]

The second exemption, reinforcement of international competitiveness of domestic firms, can be rationalized by strategic trade policy arguments. To give an extreme example, if a merger creates a monopoly by national firms in external markets, and domestic consumption is low, the profits gained at the expense of foreign consumers may more than compensate losses to domestic consumers. This, of course, raises issues of international coordination, which will be discussed in a latter section. The main point is that economic justifications for this exemption occur only under very limited circumstances.[22]

Besides these two provisions, for a merger to be blocked, there must be a significant reduction in competition resulting from the merger. There are two important cases in which such a reduction may be quite small: when entry is easy, and when the acquired firm is bankrupt and would otherwise leave the market. The assessment of dominance by the entity resulting from the merger (firm or set of firms under the same shareholders' control) is made, in principle, by computation of joint market share, although it is possible to argue on the basis of the overall market share distribution.

The practice of merger evaluation has focused mostly on the market share threshold, with market shares being computed relative to pre-merger outputs, which may introduce some bias, as the industry equilibrium will change in reaction to the merger. For example, if Cournot competition is a good de-

[21]For example, suppose there are gains from joint exploration of a common resource (say, a distribution network). Then, a contract may be a substitute for a merger.

[22]It is worth mentioning that in other national laws, the international competitiveness standard is introduced for the evaluation of dominance, not as an exemption criterion. In EU law, international competitiveness plays no role in merger assessments.

scription of the market, there is an overstatement of joint market shares.[23] This problem of merger evaluation is not specific to Portuguese law. There is little guidance from economic theory on optimal (second-best) rules of thumb to follow in practice. In this respect, Farrell and Shapiro (1990) proposed a "safe harbor" rule.[24] The rule is based on the concept of effect external to the merger, that is, on the effects on economic agents not participating in the merger. The starting assumption is that if firms propose a merger, their gains are positive. Then, if the external effect is positive the merger should be approved. This type of workable rule is a sufficient criterion for merger approval, as it disregards mergers in which the negative external effect is smaller than the positive gains internal to the merger. It has the advantage of avoiding the need to assess the internal gains to a merger (usually a difficult task for Competition Authorities), at least for some cases.

Development of such simple, theory-rooted, rules, even on an informal basis, may help to build a clear first window in merger review. Their inclusion in the review procedure would be beneficial on two grounds: it would provide a more significant economic content to the analysis and ensure a more uniform and clear review process across cases.

13.3.6 Vertical restraints

Vertical restraints are dealt with in two legal documents: the competition law (Decree of Law 371/93) and a law on individual trade practices (Decree of Law 370/93). Both laws have important aspects related to vertical restraints.

Exclusive dealing and refusal to sell are, in principle, not allowed. Important exemptions are however made: firstly, and most obviously, when there is the suspicion that the buyer will not pay or that the sale is not profitable to the seller; secondly, when the buyer does not guarantee the desired quality in retailing and compliance with the producer's standards. The legislature seemed to have in mind the forbidding of conditions designed to foreclose the market to competitors, through limitation of distribution channels to competitors or their supply sources, but no clear statement is made. Prohibition of refusal to sell seems to incorporate the impossibility for firms to impose resale prices as well, although there is no explicit mention as to what we term in economic jargon Resale Price Maintenance. A firm cannot refuse to

[23]For a more detailed discussion of the point, see Farrell and Shapiro (1990).

[24]This rule has been extended to open economies in Barros and Cabral (1994).

sell with the argument that the buyer does not accept to commit to a resale price.

The economics literature does not provide a straight answer on the conditions under which some practices should or should not be allowed. Under certain circumstances vertical restraints may improve economic efficiency, although they may also have important anticompetitive effects.[25] Thus, no clear guidance can be provided and discretion is needed. The basic economic problem is the existence of an externality from the vertical relationship. The imposition of further contractual clauses on the relationship may mitigate or increase this distortion.

A useful distinction in vertical restraints is between those intended to affect interbrand competition and those that affect intrabrand competition. Usually, the former is seen as having negative welfare effects while the latter may promote efficiency within operations of one manufacturer. Such a distinction is not made in the law and the evaluation of the practice is left to the discretion of the Competition Authority. The need for discretion by the Competition Authority seems to have clear advantages in this case. However, it also has some dangers. The greatest risk lies in the burden of economic analysis it puts on the Competition Authority and the possible inconsistencies across decisions that may occur, which may undermine the credibility of the Competition Authority. It also makes less transparent to firms which forms of behavior the Competition Authority allows.[26]

13.3.7 Exemptions from Competition Law

The general merger control is to be applied to all economic activities other than banking and insurance (financial institutions, in general), the justification being the specific nature of financial activities.

Nonetheless, control for abuse of a dominant position in banking and insurance can be exerted by the Competition authority (as the *Multibanco* case shows).[27]

[25] See Tirole (1988), for example.

[26] For a more detailed discussion, see Seabright (1998).

[27] Nonetheless, the Competition Authority is required to have an opinion of the relevant supervision body of financial institutions (the central bank, the Stock Exchange Commission or the Portuguese Insurance Institute, according to the nature of the financial institution under review).

Also excluded are the public-service activities, such as water concessions, telecommunications, electricity, basic postal services and so on, as long as some public-service contract exists. The exemption is granted only for the period and within the scope of the concession. Other economic activities are, in principle, subject to the general control of anticompetitive behavior. The obvious issue is the definition of what is included in the contract and what is not. Typically those services have been provided by State-owned firms or governmental departments. With the current deregulation and privatization trend there is the possibility that new specialized regulatory bodies appear (this has been the case of telecoms, for example). Whether overlapping jurisdictions will emerge or not, and the way they are to be dealt with is not clear. It will be necessary to form a clear definition of the objectives and instruments of each supervising body and of the hierarchy of decisions. This trend of privatization of the public utilities, and the associated problems in terms of conflict with competition policy, is not specific to the Portuguese legal framework.

The other noticeable exemptions are R&D activities and state aids (provided some conditions are met). The exemption of R&D activities is based on well-known arguments of externalities and it is present in most competition policies. State aids are forbidden if a competition distortion arises, unless granted under a special law from parliament or designed to compensate firms for public service (such as TV broadcasts or special flights to the Portuguese islands of Azores and Madeira). One major problem with this exemption is the possibility of cross-subsidization, as defining what is a public service is usually a difficult task. Of course, on the top of this exemption in national law, and it must be ascertained that state aids do not go against the provisions of the Treaty of Rome.[28]

[28] The case of negotiation with the European Commission of state aids to the Portuguese airline, TAP-AIR PORTUGAL, is a clear example of this. These negotiations are not specific to Portugal. (See the recent case of IBERIA, the Spanish flag carrier.)

13.4 Institutions - the practice of Competition Policy

13.4.1 The institutions

The implementation of competition policy rests on two authorities, the *Direcção Geral de Concorrência e Preços* (Directorate General of Competition and Prices, hereafter DGCP) and the *Conselho da Concorrência* (Competition Council).

The DGCP, a Governmental department, is the first instance in the process of investigations of restrictive practices and mergers. It investigates markets when there is a claim or the presumption that unlawful practices have occurred.

The Competition Council acts as the instance of first decision regarding violations of Competition Law with the power of imposing pecuniary sanctions. Moreover, it may give advice to the Government on merger cases. Although Government-linked, the Council is not part of Government bureaucracy. Its seven members are appointed by the Government. They are recruited amongst experts on the field, and serve in the Council on a part-time basis. The Council is chaired by a justice of law, which is intended to give it some independence.

There is no hierarchical relationship between the Council and the DGCP, and so the instance in which decisions are made is independent of the instance which conducts investigations. On the other hand, the Council does not possess independent investigation resources, and the investigations required by the Council are conducted, upon request, by the DGCP.

The Council's decisions can be appealed to courts of law. Typically, there are two instances (Court of First Instance and Court of Appeal) in which the process can be judged. Decisions handed down by the Court of First Instance are final with respect to facts. Appeals can be made to the court of appeal, which decides only on the application of the Law. This means that factual matters, such as market definition, can be changed from the Council's to the Court's judgment. In fact, appeal from Competition Council decisions leads to full re-evaluation of proof and decisions can easily be overturned.

13.4.2 The legal process

Restrictive practices

The legal process is initiated when an alleged infraction of the competition law becomes known to the DGCP. The facts can be communicated to the DGCP by a number of agents, including private parties who feel injured by the alleged unlawful behavior. The DGCP may also launch an investigation if available evidence raises concerns of anticompetitive conduct. The DGCP then conducts preliminary investigations, which may lead to the opening of a formal procedure. If a formal procedure is initiated, the DGCP brings the case to the Competition Council, which makes a decision. Defendants which are found to be guilty can be asked to cease the offending practice and directed to pay a fine of up to 200 million PTE (1 million ECU).

Both the defendants and the private plaintiffs have the right to appeal to the courts (the State cannot appeal). At this stage, the process follows the normal path in the courts, with a regular trial. Within the court system there are different levels at which the decisions are taken. The Court of First Instance establishes the facts and produces a decision, which takes into account the facts and the relevant law. From this decision, an appeal to the Court of Appeal can be made which, however, will only regard the application of the law. After a decision from the Court of Appeal, an appeal can exceptionally be made to the Supreme Court which, once again, decides only on the application of the law.

It must be said that legal litigation in Portugal usually proceeds very slowly and unlike the situation found in other countries, there is no court expertise on economic matters. Moreover, proof of unlawful practices must be made again and according to general standards. This procedure is prone to two types of problems. Firstly, there is the duplication of efforts, as the work initially done by DGCP may have to be done again by the Court. Secondly, the general legal procedures for establishing proof of facts may not be appropriate for economic issues. For example, by definition, it is not possible to witness tacit collusion, although it may well be present in the market.

This lengthy court process is a strong disincentive for private parties to report cases to the competition authority. It also constitutes a severe blow to the deterrence role of competition law, as punishment of anticompetitive conduct is uncertain and quite surely well off in the future. In fact, it is believed

Cases	Convicted	Acquitted	Other
55	34	18	3

Source: Competition Council, *Annual Report*, various years.

Table 13.5: Decisions by the Competition Council: 1984–1993

Court	Total	Convicted	Acquitted	Barred	Not yet decided
1st instance	21	7	8	2	4
2nd instance	6	2	-	3	1

Source: Competition Council, *Annual Report*, various years.

Table 13.6: Court decisions on cases convicted by the Competition Council: 1984–1993

that adverse publicity effects to a firm from being under scrutiny is a stronger deterrent to misconduct of firms than legally prescribed punishments.

Merger control

For merger control, projected mergers that fall under either of the two criteria are subject to prior notification of the competition authority (DGCP). That is, firms must communicate the intention to merge as well as their assessment of the market. If they do not do so, a fine can be imposed and the merger will be reviewed anyway. The information provided by the merging parties is usually complemented by information collected by DGCP.

The DGCP then evaluates the likely effects of the merger and produces a (non-binding) recommendation. The final decision is made by the Government. If a Government decision is not produced within a given period after notification (about two months), tacit approval results.

13.4.3 The practice of Competition Policy

Restrictive practices

The institutions concerned with the application of Competition Law have not been very busy. From 1984 until 1993, only 55 decisions were made by the Competition Council. The decisions by the Council and by the Courts (when applicable) are summarized in Tables 13.5 and 13.6. Most of the cases brought to the Council were brought under the accusation of collusive behav-

Cases	Cases			Fine (10^3 PTE)		
Convicted	Fined	<500	500	500-5,000	5,000	30,000
34	18	5	6	4	2	1

Source: Competition Council, *Annual Report*, various years.

Table 13.7: Fines: 1984–1993

ior. Refusal to sell and abuse of dominant position are the next most frequent allegations, while pricing practices is the least common accusation. Overall, the Council acquitted the defendants in 30% of the cases and convicted in the rest. Apparently, reversal of the decision was perceived to be likely by the convicted parties. About 70% of those parties convicted by the Council appealed to the Court of First Instance and 2/3 of the convicted cases in this instance appealed to the upper instance.[29] One case was further brought to the Supreme Court, the conviction being upheld.

A more detailed inspection of the competition cases that were brought to the Council reveals that in the vast majority they are of very little importance. For example, of the nine cases decided by the Council in 1993, the defendants were convicted in six cases (one being afterwards acquitted by the Court), but a fine was imposed in only two cases. One of these was a case of collective price fixing, in which an association printed a price list and circulated it to its members. When asked by the DGCP for their own prices, several firms sent the price list printed by the association or submitted a copy of the same list printed on a different letterhead. The association was fined 2000 ECU. In the other case, the offending party was fined a mere 130 ECU, due to the little importance of the offending practice.

Over the whole 1984–1993 period the picture is not much different. Fines were imposed only in half of the convictions, and in 60% of these cases the fine did not exceed 500 thousand PTE (2,5 thousand ECU). The greatest fine ever passed by the Competition Council was in a case of collusive behavior in the market for gases for medical use (case 4/90). Three firms were found to be guilty of collusive behavior and were fined in the amount of 10 million PTE each. The decision was subsequently reversed by the Court.

[29] Acquittal decisions can also be appealed by the private plaintiffs but the rates are somewhat lower. Overall, from a total of 15 cases decided in the first instance, six appeals were made to the court of second instance.

The case of gases for medical use. This case was brought to the attention of the competition authority by a hospital in Lisbon. The market is that of gases (oxygen and nitrogen protoxide) for medical use and the alleged unlawful practice is coordinated price fixing.

Oxygen is used in hospitals in the treatment of respiratory problems and nitrogen protoxide is used as an anesthetic. Both of these products are homogeneous and both of them can be delivered in the liquid or gaseous state.[30] Delivery in the liquid state is cheaper but requires that a deposit and pipeline infrastructure exist in the hospital. In large hospitals, these products are delivered, at least partially, in the liquid state.[31] Since the products are homogeneous, hospitals use a single supplier for each product, which is chosen in an annual auction.[32]

Until 1985 there were only two firms in this market, Ar Líquido, and Sogás. In 1986 a third firm, Gasin, entered the market.[33] In 1987 market shares were 68% for Ar Líquido, 17% for Sogás and 9% for Gasin in the overall gas market. In the oxygen and nitrogen protoxide markets the shares were 52%, 42% and 6% and 53%, 23% and 24%, respectively for the three firms above.

The case (and the facts described here) refers to the auctions for the supply of the two major hospitals in Lisbon. In the 1986 auction, just after the entry of Gasin in the market, the bids submitted by the incumbent firms were lower than the bids they had submitted in the pre-entry year. In that auction Sogás was chosen as the only supplier of all products, with prices which were below the prices set in 1985. In 1987 the bids were once again below the previous year's level. In this year, however, each firm was assigned part of the market supply. Ar Líquido won the gas oxygen contract, Sogás the liquid oxygen and Gasin the nitrogen protoxide.

The case was brought to the Competition Authority because in the 1988

[30] Oxygen for industrial purposes is essentially the same product but, because the product does not need to be so pure, less care is required with the cleaning of containers. This product is cheaper, but it is unsuitable for hospital use. Within oxygen for medical use, there is essentially no variation in quality across suppliers.

[31] There is some substitutability between the different states of the same gas. However, the gaseous state is more convenient in some circumstances, and hospitals also buy the products in this state.

[32] The supplier with the lowest bid is selected. In the case of liquids, the winning firm builds its own deposit on the premises of the hospital and periodically supplies the liquid.

[33] All these firms are owned by multinationals; they all have production facilities in Portugal, but import a significant share of their sales from abroad.

auction this tendency was completely reversed. All bidders increased their bids in percentages varying from 67% to 241%. Moreover, this was done in such a way that no change in their rankings occurred relative to the auctions of the previous year. The result of the auction was that the same suppliers were chosen as in the previous year, but prices were substantially raised (the winning bids being 142%, 187% and 67% higher than in the previous year, respectively for the gas oxygen, liquid oxygen and nitrogen protoxide).

The decision of the Council was to find the three firms guilty of collusive behavior. There was no actual proof that the firms had colluded. However, the Council reasoned that it would have been impossible to achieve such simultaneous large increases in price without changing firms' relative positions without coordination.

The fines applicable to this type of offense may vary from 50 thousand to 50 million PTE.[34] The law establishes that the actual fine should be fixed taking into consideration the seriousness of the offense, the size of the firms involved, the relevance of their market shares and the rents they intended to capture by the unlawful practice. Taking all those aspects into consideration, each firm was fined 10 million PTE. Subsequent to the decision, the firms appealed and the Council's decision was reversed by the Court, for procedural reasons.

Once again, more information than is actually supplied by the Competition Council's reports would be needed for a sound economic discussion of this case. Assuming that the firms had indeed colluded in 1987, one should assess the sustainability of the collusive agreement over time. Punishment of deviations from the tacit agreement under price competition without capacity constraints (which seems to fit market conditions) can be quite harsh, thus helping to sustain tacit collusion more easily. As import prices have not experienced the same price increases, the bids in the 1987 auctions do seem to reflect anticompetitive behavior. Although the case was raised with reference to a particular auction (that for supplying two entities — *Hospitais Civis de Lisboa* and *Hospital de Santa Maria*, both in Lisbon) firms met repeatedly in many different auctions. Multimarket contact also helps to sustain tacit agreements.

Cases	1991	1992	1993	1994	1995	1996[(a)]
pending at the beginning of the year	0	1	3	1	0	1
initiated during the year	15	20	31	24	17	11
concluded during the year	14	18	33	25	16	9
pending at end of the year	1	3	1	0	1	2

[(a)] January–August 1996. Source: Report of DGCP.

Table 13.8: Merger cases reviewed

Merger control

The number of prior notifications of mergers has not been very high (roughly 20 per year since 1991). Several cases were dismissed at once since neither of the two criteria were met (undue notifications). Of those remaining, usually small markets are involved and clearance has been the rule. The merger review process has been relatively fast (Table 13.8), even if one takes into account that no merger has ever been rejected. There is virtually no backlog of decisions.

Table 13.9 shows that most notifications are of horizontal mergers (accounting for 80% of the cases). In terms of nationality of firms involved, it is remarkable that a clear majority of cases has participation of foreign firms (either direct and indirect). Mergers are somewhat dispersed across the board. The only sectors that stand out as having a higher number of mergers are the food and beverages industry and the equipment and machinery industry. Also noticeable are the seven mergers in retail distribution in the period 1994 to the first semester of 1995.

Of the total number of merger notifications (up to the end of the first semester of 1995), only 21 have any economic significance. Of these, roughly half (10) were in compliance with the market share criterion, five notifications were due to the turnover threshold, three notifications met both criteria and the remaining three met none[35] For example, of the 25 notifications to the competition authority in 1994, three did not meet any of the criteria and two were not a merger as legally defined (they were considered to be cooperative

[34] Values at the time of review. Currently, the values have been updated.

[35] They were close, at least, to one of the two criteria and discrepancies in market share assessment by firms and independent computations by the Competition Authority justify these cases.

	1991	1992	193	1994	1995	1996[a]
Concentration						
vertical	1	1	1	2	1	1
horizontal	7	0	28	20	14	10
conglomerate	6	17	4	3	5	–
Nationality of firms						
only national	3	6	14	11	8	6
only foreign	3	4	3	4	3	1
foreign (direct)	5	5	9	6	2	2
foreign (indirect)	5	5	7	4	5	2

[a] January–August 1996. Source: Report of DGCP.

Table 13.9: Nature of mergers

	market share of merging undertakings	Herfindhal index
average	33.66%	2570
standard deviation	16.41%	1586
maximum	75.20%	7083
minimum	5.90%	966

Source: Own computations based on DGCP merger reports.

Table 13.10: Market structure of (selected) mergers

joint ventures). These figures corroborate the view that the market share criterion is the more likely binding condition for merger evaluation.

Table 13.10 presents some information on characteristics of undertakings participating in mergers — those 21 mergers that we consider to be most relevant.[36] Markets involved in concentration cases are fairly concentrated, although substantial dispersion exists.

A recent case has received more attention than others: a merger between the three main manufacturers of milk and dairy products, as a response to the threat posed by the entry of Parmalat, an Italian firm.

[36] A merger may span more than one market. In this case, each market was included. Market definitions as provided by the Competition Authority were used.

The Lactogal case One of the most recent cases of merger review has raised a substantial amount of discussion: the creation of Lactogal, resulting from the merger of three leading milk producers, Proleite, Agros and Lacticoop.[37]

Review procedures were also more publicly known than usual, as part of the discussion took place on political grounds. The merger was viewed as a response of incumbent Portuguese firms (cooperatives of farmers) to the successful entry of an Italian multinational, Parmalat. The proposed merger gives rise to considerable market concentration, with the new firm obtaining about three-quarters of the milk market. The market for milk and dairy products has been fairly isolated from competitive forces. Cooperatives dominated the market and regional territories were clearly in place.

To understand the likely effects of the merger one must consider the relationship between milk manufacturers and farmers.[38] The agricultural structure in Portugal is characterized by the existence of a large number of small farmers. This structure implies high costs to collect the milk from farmers. To save on costs, cooperatives emerged as the main organizational form.[39] In the beginning of the 1990s, the market had a clear regional segmentation. In each region, the corresponding cooperative was close to monopoly (more than 90 % of the sales of each cooperative were made in its region of origin).

Cooperatives had considerable market power over farmers (despite being made up of farmers, cooperatives buy milk from both members and non-members). Milk collection is the main item in costs (about 70 %). The scope for cost reduction is seriously limited by the existence of dispersed raw-milk production. The prevailing market structure had essentially three regional monopolists which were also monopsonists. Margins were relatively high and incentives for efficiency low.

In this environment, it is not surprising that entry was attempted. Parmalat was the first multinational to move into the Portuguese market. The attack on the existing regional (near-)monopolies started in the South, as milk collection costs are lower there. The strategy of entry has included

---

[37] The clearance was given on 11 December 1995. Lactogal was officially created on 1 January 1996.

[38] Hereinafter, 'milk manufacturers' refers to treatment and packaging of milk and milk products, while 'farmers' refers to raw milk producers.

[39] In this respect, Portugal is not atypical in Europe: cooperatives account for roughly 75 % in The Netherlands, around 85 % in Denmark and Belgium, and a little above 52 % in France, for example.

strong investment in advertising, lower prices for consumers and higher prices for farmers (to avoid resorting to imports, which was the initial supply source of milk). Parmalat was willing to pay around 64–68 PTE while average prices at farmers were around 55 PTE. Moreover, the price of Parmalat was stable over the year, unlike the situation found in the cooperatives. Parmalat has also acquired some smaller companies.[40]

Shortly after, the cooperatives had to follow the price strategy of Parmalat, lowering prices to the consumer and raising them for farmers. As a response to the entry of Parmalat, the main cooperatives discussed for nearly a year whether or not they should merge. Finally, the decision to go forward was taken. According to statements to the press by the president of the new company, the merger is intended to achieve some cost savings (estimates from the merging entities are on the order of 25%) but it has the main objective of blocking the growth of Parmalat and of imports. No serious evidence that either of the two claims can be realized (leaving aside whether they should be endorsed or not) was presented. A more convincing, although not explicitly stated, explanation is that reaction to Parmalat's entry into the market destroyed the tacit regional separation of markets. The merger is now necessary to enforce coordination among cooperatives.

The pre and post-merger Herfindahl indexes for relevant submarkets are presented in Table 13.11. The numbers illustrate the potential danger of collusive behavior. The most important submarket, UHT milk, is also one where the increase in concentration is quite high. At the other extreme, the cheese and yoghurt markets are essentially unchanged by the operation.

The threat of imports is expected to be sufficient to exert discipline over market prices. The evaluation process has not proceeded further than to define the relevant market and the market shares of firms. No computation of concentration indexes has been performed, although the assessments seem to have been based, at least partially, on the evaluation of the whole distribution of market shares. Indicators of market power, such as price-cost margins, were not computed either.

Two main issues are the welfare effects of foreign entry and the existence of monopsony power over farmers. On the first issue, the argument against entry of foreign firms looks at profits transferred to the outside. In fact, this profit transfer may exceed the increase in consumers' surplus from lower

[40] Besides Parmalat, the 'white product' (no name brand) of distribution chains have also gained market share in the recent past.

	share of total turnover	market share of merging firms	Herfindahl index		
			pre-merger	post-merger	change
Milk UHT	44.3	75.2	2171	5872	3701
Pasteurized milk	5.20	50.4	3312	5000	1688
Other milk	5.20	96.6	4160	9342	5182
Total Milk	54.7	74.1	2159	5745	3586
Cream	1.80	68.0	2895	5648	2753
Butter	6.40	46.7	3606	4907	1301
Cheese 'Flamengo'		21.1	6255	6530	275
Other cheese		11.0	7463	7509	46
Total Cheese	20.7	18.1	6601	6794	193
Yogurt	16.4	19.3	6682	6885	203

Note: Total turnover is 150,084 Million PTE; Source: DGCP Report.

Table 13.11: Market structure in the milk and dairy products

prices.[41] However, it is not clear how a merger may avoid this. On the other hand, since Parmalat is buying from national farmers at higher prices there are also some rents being transferred from cooperatives to farmers.

The second issue is the enhanced market power of Lactogal over farmers. Negative effects upon farmers are more likely, as manufacturers strengthened their position. Selling to the new firm will be the only option available to some farmers. The magnitude of the effect is probably small, as prior to the merger milk manufacturers already enjoyed considerable market power over farmers. The concern here is mainly a distributive one, as it is largely recognized that very small farmers (sometimes having just a few cows) constitute a very inefficient agricultural structure. Moreover, tacit collusion between manufacturers (domestic and Parmalat) is certainly easier than before the merger.

The threat of imports and of further entry also provides a strong incentive for technical efficiency of the new firm (although no evidence on the minimum efficient scale is available), as monopolies usually have less incentive to promote efficiency within the firm. In this matter, the more competitive environment may prevent what otherwise would be negative effects from the

[41] For a formal model see Barros and Cabral (1992).

merger.

Overall, no precise statement about welfare effects can be made, regardless of the creation of a clear dominant position. The economic analysis of concentration increases in the market suggests that the merger should have been blocked. However, the discipline imposed by the threat of imports may limit the possibility of exercising market power through higher consumer prices. Thus, negative effects upon consumers are probably not too great. Moreover, the exercise of monopsony power over farmers can hardly be much higher than it was before the merger.

The economic considerations were not powerful enough to block the merger but, at least, they justify a close follow-up of prices and contractual dispositions in the market (especially in the relationship between milk manufacturers and farmers).

13.5 Conflicts with other policies

It has been previously argued that the slight emphasis on competition policy in Portugal is due on the one hand to the lack of tradition in that matter and on the other hand to the belief that Portuguese firms are typically too small to be able to exercise market power. This is particularly true since Portugal joined the EU in 1986 and foreign competition increased. In fact, much of Portuguese Industrial Policy has been directed towards increasing the size of Portuguese firms. Moreover, national authorities typically include domestic welfare only in their objective function, and this may conflict with competition policy at the European Union level. We will review here the major areas of conflict between competition policy and other forms of Government intervention, namely industrial policy and trade policy.

13.5.1 Industrial Policy

Currently, Portugal pursues an active industrial policy aimed at reducing the gap between Portugal's industrial competitiveness and other European countries. Industrial policy is highly centered on picking winners and in giving them additional resources for growth. The Decree of Law 177/94 of 27 June, that establishes the legal framework of current industrial policy, proclaims that this policy

> aims to selectively support those Portuguese firms that demonstrate business strategies capable of guaranteeing their sustained development (...), as well as to create business units of a dimension which is compatible with the increasing international competitiveness, namely when achieved through acts of cooperation and concentration.

On the basis of this policy, there is the presumption that Portuguese firms are much too small to compete effectively in international markets. Therefore, within this context, mergers and other forms of concentration of firms are strongly encouraged.[42] Very substantial resources have been expended under industrial policy programs.[43]

Although in the Portuguese Law dominant positions are not illegal *per se* and State aids are not illegal if they originate from specific programs approved in the Parliament or by the Government (Article 11 of Competition Law), there is clearly here a source of potential conflict with competition policy. In fact, whenever enforcement of competition law collides with promotion of 'national champions,' it seems likely, in the face of past decisions, that the Government will decide in favor of the latter.

The emphasis on picking winners seems to neglect the fact that the conditions under which firms became winners in the past are not necessarily the same as those that will prevail in the future, in particular in a context in which innovation is becoming increasingly important. Besides, the conflict between industrial policy/state aids and competition policy may remain over time. Announcement of temporary active industrial policies is typically not time consistent, and the temporary measures tend to become permanent. Protection and subsidies given to support development of "competitive industries" once in place may prove to be difficult to remove.

Moreover, little emphasis has been given to the role of competition in promoting competitiveness and very little scope has been given for market processes to act as a selection mechanism. For example, in order to avoid job losses, the State has frequently allowed firms to continue in their operations without paying their taxes or Social Security contributions. This is implicitly

[42] Other major areas of intervention are related to support to small firms, innovation and adoption of new technologies, promotion of exports and internationalisation of firms and attraction of foreign direct investment.

[43] Over the 1988–1992 period, more than 6 billion ECU were spent as State aids under the PEDIP program, a predecessor of the current industrial policy program.

a State aid to these firms, which is illegal given that it was not approved by the Parliament, and violates the spirit of guaranteeing equal opportunities for all market players. Also, bankruptcy laws have made it very difficult for creditors to demand the payment of their credits through bankruptcy. There have been very few cases of bankruptcy and in many cases they have allegedly served to clear processes of money draining from firms to private accounts.

Finally, conventional textbook analysis of welfare losses due to market power assumes that Governments are indifferent between consumers' and producers' surplus. However, there is no tradition in Portugal of consumer protection and consumers have much less lobbying power than producers. It should not be taken for granted that the revealed preferences of Portuguese authorities have shown indifference between consumers and producers; rather, it is entirely possible that producers' surplus has been given greater weight in the Government's objective function.

13.5.2 Competition Policy and Trade Policy

Another potential area of conflict is between competition policy and trade policy. In general, if Government trade policies aim at protecting domestic firms, they tend to conflict with competition policies. Relevant policies to this conflict can be divided into antidumping measures and strategic trade policy, based on standard instruments such as quotas, tariffs and VERs.

The existence of conflict between the two policies is not always obvious. Conventional wisdom usually thinks of free trade as a substitute for active competition policies. This holds true insofar as international markets are competitive. In this case, opening of domestic markets to international competitive forces will exert a strong discipline on domestic firms. A strict enforcement of competition policy would no longer be necessary. Any abuse of market position creates profit opportunities that would be taken up by rivals. However, under oligopolistic international markets there is still the need for competition policies. And the latter seem to account for a significant share of markets.

Treatment of antidumping complaints is usually dealt with within the context of trade policy.[44] A closer look at the economics fundamentals of

[44] For example, in the European Commission, DG I is responsible for antidumping matters, while competition policy issues are assigned to DG IV.

the problem suggest that a different approach could (should?) be followed. The economic content of antidumping complaints resembles predatory pricing, which is a matter of competition policy. The distinctive feature is the involvement of more than one country, which may raise issues of jurisdiction.

Nonetheless, antidumping measures as defined in legal terms (and application) are a different matter from the economic notion of predatory pricing, as they aim at pure price discrimination across countries. Antidumping analysis typically computes reference prices for the foreign firm and compares them with actual prices charged in the market. This line of procedure disregards the important aspect of market structure in the home market, and *per se* may not be evidence of predatory pricing by the foreign competitor. And, of course, it is well known from the economics literature that price discrimination is not necessarily welfare decreasing.

Antidumping laws typically aim at protecting domestic producers against foreign competitors, and there is no reason why measures designed to achieve this goal would be simultaneously good for domestic consumers (just to focus on effects internal to the country).

It has also been argued that antidumping complaints may act as an anticompetitive device by cartelized industries. This puts the antidumping issue clearly on the side of competition policy. This type of interrelation between the antidumping and competition has been recognized several times, especially in the analysis of the European Commission actions (Messerlin 1990; Vandenbussche 1994). Those authors endorse the view that the threat of filing antidumping complaints can foster collusion between domestic and foreign firms.

The other possible source of conflict is strategic trade policies. The economics literature has produced a vast set of examples where selective intervention of Governments may improve domestic welfare under non-competitive international market structures. The other side of the coin of this research is that informational requirements to implement such policies are quite high and unlikely to be easily met (it is necessary to have knowledge on markets, technologies, firms, etc). Moreover, some recent empirical studies have also found that only marginal gain accrues from such interventions and that associated costs can be considerable.

The information requirements make it quite difficult for a Government to pick the right industries to be supported by trade policy measures. Since trade policy instruments can interfere with competition among firms of different countries (extreme cases being prohibitive tariffs or quotas), defense of competition and of the market mechanism suggests two things. On the one hand, superiority of free trade, and, on the other hand, concerted measures across countries must be taken for trade liberalization to occur and foster competition.

In this view, the conflict between trade policy and competition policy is diminished as trade liberalization acts as a competition enhancement tool.[45] For the Portuguese economy, participation in the European Union means essentially free trade with other member countries, and no significant barriers to trade remain in place. There was a clear competitive effect on the Portuguese economy from joining the European Union. However, due to transport costs and the very nature of some products, there are important markets that remain national or local. In these cases, competition policy still has an important role to play.

The national use of traditional trade policy instruments (tariffs and quotas, for example) is not available since European Union membership. Also, imposition of other barriers to trade, such as technical standards, is being limited to some extent by the efforts of harmonization across countries as part of the Internal Market program.

The most significant 'tool' available to manipulate trade flows seems to be the formation of export cartels, either in an active or a passive role.[46] Export cartels will usually mean dominant positions, even if not monopoly, in the domestic market. Non-intervention by competition authorities can be seen as a passive policy of supporting such collusive agreements. This special type of trade policy may also collide with Community competition policy, as it restricts trade flows between member states. The following case is a good example of the conflict that may arise.

The case of Port wine. Port wine is an interesting case study, because the market is organized as an export cartel, the cartel being managed by the Portuguese State itself.

The main input to produce Port wine is the wine obtained from the grapes grown in a well-defined (demarcated) region around the Oporto area. Port wine is different from the region's common wine in several ways. In order

[45] For a more complete discussion of the relations between trade policy and competition policy, see Motta and Onida (1995).

[46] In the sense that it may correspond to support of 'national champions' the distinction between 'trade' and 'industrial' policies becomes blurred.

to produce Port, the region's wine is fortified with vinic brandy and aged for a number of years. The final product is then obtained by blending in variable proportions wines from different years, in order to obtain a taste which is constant over time.[47] The wine is bottled afterwards. Port wine has a totally distinct flavor from common wine; it is not used as table wine, but as an aperitif or a dessert wine. Being a different product, it targets a distinct market. While most regular wine sells in the domestic market, 80% of Port is sold abroad. Finally, Port wine is subject to a much more stringent regulation than ordinary wine.

The regulatory agency, the *Instituto do Vinho do Porto* (IVP), decides every year on the quantity of regular wine that can be fortified in that year.[48] After having decided on the total amount of wine that shall be fortified, fortification rights are distributed among farmers, based on the area of vineyards registered by each farmer with the registration office. The wine (accompanied by these fortification rights) is then sold to Port wine companies, which take care of the fortification and ageing process.

The total amount of wine that can be fortified in each year has a direct impact on the quantity of Port wine that will be sold in that year, because the amount of Port wine that each company can sell is also regulated and established as a maximum of 30% of the wine bought by the company that year.[49]

These quantity and age requirements create very imposing financial barriers to entry, but there are other types of barriers as well. Until recently, all producers were required to locate their warehouses in one particular location near Oporto. This requirement was relaxed for local farmers, who were allowed to locate their warehouses in a second location in the countryside. These producers are also exempted from minimum stock requirements. On the other hand, however, they are not allowed to buy grapes (or production rights) in the market, if they want to remain exempted from normal business

[47] Exceptionally good years may be declared 'vintage' years. Wines from these years are not blended with wines from other years.

[48] New legislation, dated in April 1995 transferred the power of setting this quantity from IVP to a brand-new association. This association, although chaired by a State representative, is composed of representatives of farmers and trading companies.

[49] This is subject to the restriction that the quantity sold is no more than 1/3 of the total wine stock in the producer's cellars. There are also restrictions on the minimum stock required to be in business as well as the proportions of wines of different ages that producers must keep in the cellars.

regulations. Due to the relaxation of these entry regulations, the number of producers registered with the IVP almost doubled in the 1980s. Because their production is limited by the fortification rights they have, they cannot use all their grapes to produce Port wine and some voices have been raised against the organization of the market.[50]

There seems to be two totally distinct aspects about the organization of the market. The first is a quality enhancement arrangement, the second a quantity cartel. It is not entirely obvious why the first needs the second. One could even argue, as some producers have, that quantity restrictions accompanied by allocation of productions rights based on the area of vineyard leads to the deterioration of quality. The typical vine grower has little incentive to improve the quality of grapes, since the most valuable part of his assets are the production rights and not the grapes.

Current organization of the market seems to be motivated by the fact that most of the market for Port wine is foreign. Higher prices for national consumers are thought to be more than compensated for by the profits accruing to domestic producers.[51] The existing legal procedures, allegedly to certify quality of production, work as devices facilitating collusion. It is probably true that if the market for Port were essentially a domestic one, there would be a different market organization.

A common argument in the industry is that the relevant market should not be defined as the market for Port but rather as the market for spirits, being argued that Port wine competes directly with whisky, cognac, and sherry. It seems reasonable to concede that there is some substitutability between products. At the end of the day, however, the relevant criterion for assessing the existence of market power is the ability to affect prices. Regardless of the way the market is defined, it is clear that the quantity restrictions raise prices well above the competitive level.

---

[50] These new producers are responsible for less than 1% of total production.

[51] Producers cannot be taken to be the Port wine companies only which, moreover, have been largely owned by British interests for a long time. Vine growers from the region, for example, are also getting part of the monopoly rents generated in the market.

13.5.3 Community Competition Policy

EC competition policy has already been reviewed extensively in the literature, and we will not repeat the review here.[52] It is sufficient to say that, in broad terms, Community competition policy has been guided by Articles 85 and 86 of the Treaty of Rome. Neither of the two articles deals explicitly with merger control, which motivated the enactment of Regulation 4064/89. Prior to this, Articles 85 and 86 were interpreted rather broadly as to allow for merger control.

One important aspect in the relations between national competition policies and the Community's competition policy lies in decentralization (or allocation of jurisdictions). From received economic theory, it is not clear what the optimal level of decentralization is. The political concept behind the decentralization of merger decisions to national authorities is "subsidiarity," a principle which has been more explicitly applied to merger policy.[53]

On economic grounds, decentralization of merger policies should be made in those cases where the effects of mergers are felt mostly within the country — that is, when effects external to the country are small. In the extreme case of a merger in a market where there is no international trade, there seems to be no reason for the national authority to take 'wrong' decisions from a Community-wide point-of-view. This is taken into account by looking at mergers in which firms have a high turnover or which have a substantial volume of business done outside the country (more precisely, if 2/3 of business of the parties is done in one country, the merger review is allocated to the national level).

Such a procedure may mean erroneous decisions as some effects external to the country are disregarded, but error-free rules are difficult to define (Barros and Cabral, 1994). For example, suppose a merger in a Cournot oligopoly, where all consumers are in the country, there are foreign firms, and the merger makes a monopoly of domestic firms. In this case, some positive effects of mergers (foreign rivals' response) are ignored in the decision of the domestic authority, and the decision is biased against clearance of the merger. Since 2/3 of the merging firms' turnover is in this country's market, the decision falls under national jurisdiction.

[52] See Neven, Nuttal and Seabright (1993), the special issue of Oxford Review of Economic Policy edited by Hay and Mayer (1993), European Commission (1994), Admiraal (1990) and Comanor *et al.* (1990), among others.

[53] For a discussion, see CEPR (1993).

The rule for allocating merger decisions to national and Community jurisdictions set by the EC regulation makes sense but one should be aware of its limitations. Theoretical predictions of Barros and Cabral (1994) suggest that information on the net trade position of the country to which the decision is delegated should complement the information on whether the external effects to the country are significant or not. It must be recognized that errors associated with decentralization to national authorities' evaluation hinge upon effects external to the country (on consumers and producers of other countries). Thus, internalization of all relevant effects of a merger has to do with net trade position, not only with a firm's share of turnover in foreign markets.

Decentralization of merger policy raises three types of problems. Firstly, undue (de)centralization. That is, the criteria may allocate a merger to the 'inappropriate' merger authority. From an economic perspective, centralization seems to be superior as a centralized authority can, in the absence of market failures, replicate the decentralized outcome if optimal. In the specific case of merger policy, a centralized body would internalize cross-border effects in the decision. However, this argument for centralization may conflict with the political principle of subsidiarity or with the failures that may rationalize it (higher costs of merger analysis for a supranational authority, informational advantages of domestic authorities on firms based in the country, etc).

Secondly, national policies differ, so decentralization to the one country or another is not the same. Thus, equivalent mergers would be treated differently, according to the country in which the concentration takes place. A full-fledged assessment of differences across countries is clearly beyond the scope of the paper. However, a first quantitative indicator to toughness/softness of national merger policies can be obtained from minimum turnover thresholds which the undertakings participating in the merger must achieve in order for that merger to be reviewed by the competition authority.

There are striking differences across European Union countries on the minimum turnover threshold that triggers investigation of mergers.[54] Table 13.12 presents the minimum thresholds (in Million ECUs) for a sample of European Union countries.[55] One should expect larger economies to have

[54]Relative size (market share) thresholds are roughly similar and in the range of 25–30% of market share.

[55]Only one of the criteria (market share or turnover) must be met to trigger a merger review, except in Belgium, where both must be met.

	Turnover threshold[(a)]	Market share threshold
Ireland	25.2	
Portugal	150	30%
Greece	50	25%
Belgium	70	25%
Netherlands	116	
Spain	125	25%
UK	90.9	25%
Italy	300	
France	1060	25%
Germany	1040	

[(a)] Total turnover value. In some countries this is complemented by criteria on the individual turnover of merging firms.
Source: European Commission (1996)

Table 13.12: Criteria for merger review.

higher absolute turnover thresholds and, indeed, this is the case. There are exceptions, however. For example, the UK has a threshold for firms' turnover that halves that of Portugal (which is a much smaller economy). To cope with this size effect, we regress minimum thresholds on (1994) GDP values for nine European Union countries. Figure 13.1 depicts, in a very simple way, the result of this exercise. The vertical axis presents the threshold for merger evaluation and on the horizontal axis we have GDP (values in ECUs and adjusted for purchasing power parity). The straight line stands for the simple regression of the threshold on the GDP values. Statistical results are

$$\begin{array}{ccccc} \text{threshold} & = & \text{-39.724} & + & 0.608\text{GDP} \qquad R^2 = 0.726 \\ \text{(t-statistic)} & & (-0.388) & & (4.605) \end{array}$$

These results illustrate, in a very crude way, two facts. Firstly, the United Kingdom is a clear outlier and has a more rigorous approach to the criteria according to which mergers are to be reviewed by the competition authority. Germany's high threshold seems to be in line with the larger size of the German economy. Toughness of German competition policy is thus mainly due to its enforcement. The two other clear outliers are Portugal and France, which

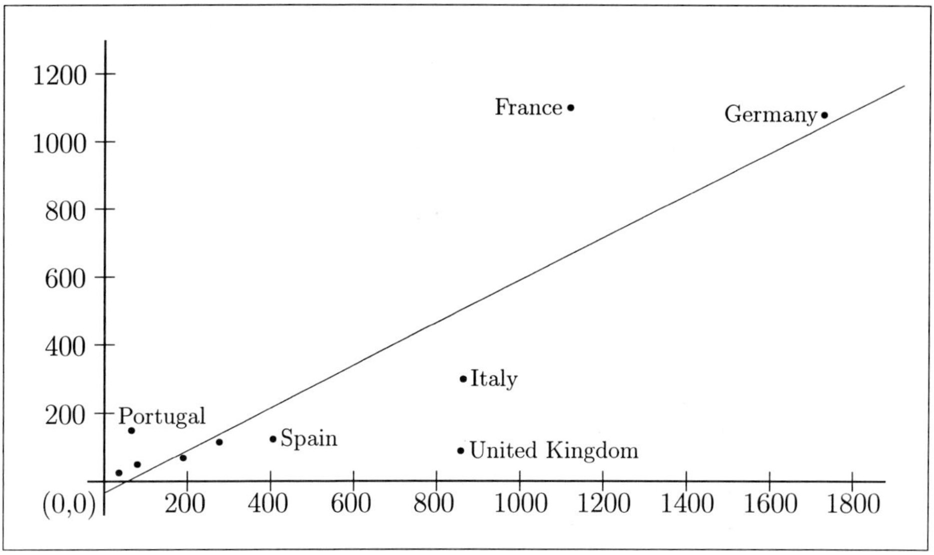

Figure 13.1: Thresholds for merger review vs. Gross Domestic Product

seem to have somewhat more permissive thresholds than other countries. This is particularly clear for Portugal: the turnover threshold is considerably higher than that prevailing in economies of similar size (Greece and Ireland) but also of larger economies (such as Spain and the United Kingdom).

Of course, in reality, differences in the definition of mergers to be investigated are probably not all that significant as market share criteria to be met are more or less similar across countries. Also, no implication emerges as to how strict competition law enforcement is, given that the merger is reviewed. The rough exercise performed, nevertheless, reinforces the point that market share dominance will be the main trigger to merger review under Portuguese law.

Thirdly, as national competition policies may differ from the criteria of the Merger Task Force, firms may try to engage in arbitrage across jurisdictions. This possibility is raised by the different approaches to competition policy enforcement of, for example, Germany and the European Union.

The first problem should stimulate more policy-oriented economic analysis of the optimal rules for decentralization of merger policy. The second and third problems can be mitigated by efforts of harmonization across countries on competition policies.

13.6 Do we need changes in Competition Policy?

Although it is always possible to argue that some fine tuning might be desirable, we submit that, overall, the legal provisions of Portuguese Competition Law are adequate to provide fair protection to the functioning of private markets.[56]

The practice of competition policy is a different story, however. The legacy of a legal and political tradition viewing competition as suspicious (which was prevalent for decades) is still present, despite the fact that the political environment has now changed dramatically. Even today, when protection of competitive conditions is mentioned, it is often meant to protect 'fair trade' in the sense of protecting other business' rights rather than to protect consumers' surplus or improve social welfare. The recycled version of this tradition views competition from Europe as 'potentially harmful,' in the sense that Portuguese firms may not be able to cope with this competition. The suggested remedies for this problem are 'protective measures' or improvement of domestic firms' competitiveness. This sense of priorities has led to secondarization of competition policy *vis-à-vis* policies designed to improve competitiveness, and increasing firms' profits seems to be an objective of economic policy.[57]

This view implicitly assumes that foreign competition will be pressure enough and that there is little need for a strong competition policy. While international competition may exert an important competitive role, this view is wrong, as it is clearly shown in the case of gases for medical use, in which three foreign firms were found guilty of collusive behavior in the domestic market. Even in markets largely exposed to foreign competition, there may be the need for Competition Authority's intervention.

The small number of restrictive practices cases which have been brought before the Competition Council does not seem to be an indication that firms clearly avoid breaking the law. Rather, it seems an indication that the system is not taken very seriously and that there is a widespread lack of confidence in law enforcement. In fact, it is highly disputable that the fines imposed in the

[56] At the level of principles, it might perhaps be desirable to explicitly include consumers' surplus and social welfare as a goal of Competition Policy.

[57] This contrasts with the conventional view in which high business profits are regarded as an indication of the existence of market power, and thus as socially negative.

past have been adequate for compensating the damages or to deter unlawful behavior. In the first place, there does not seem to have been any serious attempt to calculate the harm caused by the anticompetitive practices. The law establishes that the fine should be calculated taking into account the seriousness of the offense and the profits that the offending firms would earn should the offense go unpunished, but gives no clue on how to evaluate the 'seriousness of the offense.'[58] In the second place, given that the probability of detection is lower than one, in order to exert their deterrence role, the fines imposed should be greater than the actual profits obtained from the anti-competitive behavior. There is no information on the profit increase resulting from anti-competitive actions but, judging from the magnitude of the fines, it seems that even expected profits of a minimal nature would provide a sufficient profit incentive for firms to adopt the unlawful behavior, and pay the fine if and when the behavior happens to be detected and punished.

The most important failures of Portuguese competition policy seem to lie at the level of implementation. First of all, decisions on competition issues are not taken by independent entities. For merger cases, the decisions are taken directly by the Government itself. On competition cases, the decisions are taken by the Competition Council, whose members are appointed directly by the Government and serve on a part-time basis. The extent to which the public interest is best defended by such an arrangement is debatable. On the one hand, as the members of the Competition Council do not depend on their positions as members of the Council for their income, they may be less susceptible to outside pressure. On the other hand, as this is a relatively marginal activity for them and their professional prestige is not directly dependent on their performance at the Council, they may have little incentive to take this activity as seriously as they would were it their primary job. On balance, we believe that a stronger Competition Authority would improve the role of competition policy. Decisions would be quicker, policy implementation would be less vulnerable to other considerations and greater consistency in decisions across cases would be achieved.

A different problem to be solved is the relation between the Competition Authority and the various sectoral supervision bodies. The emergence of more sectoral supervision bodies should not curtail the possibility of intervention by the Competition Authority. Any dispute on competition policy

[58] The existence of an explicit goal for the competition authority to pursue (say, social welfare) would make it easier to compute the damages.

matters should be resolved by the latter, not the former. There are two main reasons for ranking the Competition Authority higher. Firstly, to ensure consistency in implementation of a competition policy over all economic activities.[59] Secondly, sectoral supervision bodies are typically more sensitive to firms' interests than to overall effects.[60] Competition policy should be pursued by one institution only. This holds true even under the present state of affairs. Although we think a truly independent competition authority would constitute a better institutional framework, the debate on the hierarchy of supervision bodies versus the competition authority is an independent one.

Another important problem of competition cases is the lengthy judicial process that may follow a decision by the Competition Council. This provides firms holding dominant positions with a very strong bargaining power on competition issues. The threat of legal litigation over many years seems to be sufficient to prevent other firms from bringing more significant cases to the attention of the Competition Authority (informal settling of complaints seems to be common, although no systematic evidence on it is available). Moreover, while the defendants can repeatedly appeal to an upper instance court, the State does not constitute itself as 'the prosecution' and therefore does not appeal.[61] The result is that, if the first decision is to acquit the defendant, that will be the final decision, as well. However, if the first decision is to convict the defendant, then it is highly probable that an appeal will be made and the decision reversed.

Reversal of decisions is made easy because there is no economic expertise in the Courts which will subsequently decide on competition cases. The effectiveness of Competition Law, especially Competition Council decisions, has been seriously challenged by appeals to courts, where rulings have overturned Competition Council decisions in a considerable number of cases. Usually, this overturning is based on absence-of-proof arguments.This seriously questions the usefulness of a competition authority and illustrates that courts are, in general, not prepared to judge on economic offenses to competition. Given the legal system in place, it seems reasonable to ask for this expertise

[59]The argument that these sectors have special characteristics and deserve special status is not sustainable. One can always find a reason for an economic activity to be different from another.

[60]This is true even in the absence of regulatory capture. The hiring of people with the technical expertise for the other tasks committed to these special bodies from firms aligns naturally, at least to some extent, interests of firms and of supervision officials.

[61]Private plaintiffs can (and do) appeal.

by the Courts, which can be achieved either by requiring judges to have some economics studies or by creating an experts office to support case analysis.

A related matter is the evaluation procedure itself. Further use of economic tools and techniques would provide a better assessment of cases and lay down sounder economic foundations for cases (at least, from published reports, there seems to exist room for finer evaluations). Of course, this effort implies extra resources devoted to case analysis and is only worthwhile if decisions can be fully implemented and with a reduced reliance on (uninformed) judge's discretion. This reasoning suggests the (informal) enactment of guidelines for case review, with distinction between merger review and anticompetitive behavior. The development of simple but theory-based rules of thumb should be pursued. At least, a 'screen procedure' for anticompetitive cases — such as the one existing for merger cases (based on market shares and overall turnover) — should be considered. A more detailed description of the procedures to be followed in the evaluation of cases would have two clear advantages. It might improve the consistency of the analysis across cases, and it would make it clearer to firms what type of behavior and mergers are allowed (or disallowed).

The transition from a strong tradition of tight and sometimes direct Government control and intervention to a well-functioning market-oriented economy has proved to be a rocky road. A great many of the shortcomings and deficiencies of competition policy in Portugal may be attributed to its novelty. It is fair to say that some progress has been achieved. Still, further work remains to be done.

13.7 References

Admiraal, P. editor *Merger and Competition Policy in the European Community*, De Vries Lectures in Economics, Basil Blackwell, 1990.

Barros, P. "Multimarket Competition in Banking, With an Application to Portugal," mimeo, Faculdade de Economia, Universidade Nova de Lisboa, 1995.

Barros, P. and L. Cabral "Merger Policy in Open Economies," *European Economic Review* Volume 38, 1994, pp. 1041–55.

CEPR "Making Sense of Subsidiarity: How Much Centralization for Europe?," *Monitoring European Integration* 4, 1993.

Comanor, W.S., K. George, A. Jacquemin, F. Jenny, E. Kantzenbach, J.A. Ordover and L. Waverman, *Competition Policy in Europe and North-America: Economic Issues and Institutions*, Fundamentals of Pure and Applied Economics 43, Harwood, Academic Publishers, 1990.

Davies, S. and B. Lyons, editors *Industrial Organization in the European Union; Structure, Strategy and the Competitive Mechanism*, Oxford: Oxford University Press, 1996.

European Commission "European Economy: Competition and Integration – Community Merger Control Policy," Volume 57, 1994.

— "Green Paper on the Review of the Merger Regulation," Brussels, Belgium, 1996.

Farrell, J. and C. Shapiro "Horizontal Mergers: An Equilibrium Analysis" *American Economic Review* Volume 80, 1990, pp. 107–126.

Hay, D. and C. Mayer, editors "Competition Policy," *Oxford Review of Economic Policy* Volume 9, Summer 1993.

Kühn, K.-U. and Vives, X. "Information Exchanges Among Firms and Their Impact on Competition," mimeo, Institut d'Analisi Económica, 1995.

Messerlin, P. "Antidumping regulations or pro-cartel law? The EC chemical cases" *World Economy* Volume 13, 1990, pp. 465–92.

Motta, M. and Onida, F. "Trade Policy and Competition Policy," mimeo, UPF and U. Bocconi, 1995.

Neven, D., R. Nuttal and P. Seabright *Mergers in the Daylight – The Economics and Politics of European Merger Control.* CEPR, 1993.

Neves, J. *The Portuguese Economy: a Picture in Figures.* Lisboa: Universidade Católica Editora, 1994.

Phlips, L. *Competition Policy: a Game Theoretic Perspective.* Cambridge: Cambridge University Press, 1995.

Seabright, P. "Competition Policy and Vertical Restraints: Implementable Rules for Competition Authorities," this volume, 1998.

Selten, R. "A Simple Model of Imperfect Competition Where Four Are Few and Six Many," *International Journal of Game Theory* Volume 2, 1973, pp. 141–201.

Tirole, J. *The Theory of Industrial Organization.* Cambridge, Mass.: The MIT Press, 1988.

Vandenbussche, H. "Twin cases – cartels and European antidumping policy," Report 94/307, Studiencentrum voor Economisch en sociaal onderzoek, University of Antwerp 1994.

Competition Policies in Europe - S. Martin (Editor)

Chapter 14

Privatization and EU Competition Policy: the case of the Italian Energy Sector

Paola Valbonesi

14.1 Introduction

The relationship between privatization and competition policy is particularly important with respect to public utilities. The services public utilities provide are fundamental inputs for the rest of the economy. It follows that the level of economic efficiency and quality of these services has an effect on competition and on the growth of the economic system as a whole.

The peculiar technical features of production in public utility sectors have long prevented competition; legal monopoly, exclusive rights and regulation have instead been the order of the day. Recent developments in technologies have led to new support for liberalization and a critical reconsideration of the role of the state in these sectors. From the issues of energy conservation and security of supply, on which the debate focused during the 1970s, there has been a move toward a search for technical efficiency in production and surplus redistribution. This has meant, in terms of policy, a new approach to setting tariffs and inclusion of competition in the production of energy.

The aim of the present chapter is twofold: on the one hand, to investigate privatization of public utilities under the EC Treaty and in particular

Directive 96/92/EEC,[1] which regulates the energy sector; on the other hand, to study the privatization, liberalization, and reorganization of the Italian energy sector. These issues are interrelated, given that the new rules would affect privatization itself, and that privatization would introduce new actors in the energy sector.

The chapter is structured as follows. In Section 14.2, I deal with the background of the Commission's latest legislative directive aimed at further liberalization of the energy market. In Section 14.3, I briefly analyze EEC Directive 96/92 on the energy market, focusing on the different phases of production, transmission, and distribution of electricity power and on the issue of access to the network. In Section 14.4, I sketch Italian competition policy in the of public utility sectors and refer to the role of the Antitrust Authority and the newly established Authority for Energy and Gas. In Section 14.5, I present the case of privatization of the Italian energy sector and questions that remain open under Directive 96/92/EEC. In Section 14.6, I draw conclusions.

14.2 EU competition law, public ownership and legal monopoly

The EC Treaty lays down as one of its main objectives the establishment of "an internal market characterized by the abolition, between Member States, of obstacles to the free movement of goods, people, services and capital" (Article 3 c). Moreover, the Treaty requires the Community to establish "a system ensuring that competition in the internal market is not distorted" (Article 3 g). It follows that state-guaranteed monopolies are incompatible with the objectives set out in Article 3. In addition, the specific provisions of the Treaty on the free movement of goods and services, on transport and competition do not contain any general exemption for service sectors.[2] Exceptions to the provisions of Articles 85 and 86 regarding free competition in the EU are to be limited to activities that are necessary to achieve objectives

[1] Approved 19 December 1996.

[2] To the extent that these provisions allow Member States to introduce or maintain restrictions on grounds of public policy, these restrictions must be strictly limited to what can be justified under the principle of proportionality (Articles 36, 56, 66).

of public interest.[3]

Three EC Treaty Articles have long been used to justify the continued existence of monopoly rights conferred on all types of public utilities and in particular in the energy sector. These are Articles 37, 90 and 222.

Article 37 of the EC Treaty explicitly requires Member States to adjust State monopolies so as to exclude discrimination between nationals of Member States regarding the conditions under which goods are procured or marketed. The European Court of Justice has applied Article 37 mainly with regard to trading monopolies, not to production monopolies.

According to Article 90(1) of the Treaty, "Member States may neither enact nor maintain in force, in relation to public enterprises to which they grant special or exclusive rights, any measures contrary to the rules of the Treaty," including the principle of non-discrimination on grounds of nationality (Article 6) and the rules on competition and subsidies (Articles 85–94). It may be interesting to note that, subject to the exception under Article 90(2) of the Treaty, the commercial activities of public enterprises and firms granted special or exclusive rights are thus treated on the same basis as those of private enterprises. Indeed, like Article 222 of the Treaty, Article 90 is neutral as to ownership of business enterprises, and only makes a *functional* distinction in favor of enterprises (public or private) which are required to perform specific tasks in the general economic interest on behalf of all consumers. Moreover, Article 90 gives each Member State the faculty to define which services are actually hindered in their efficiency by a competitive regime. Paragraph 3 of Article 90 allows the Commission to specify, through directives and decisions, the obligations imposed on Member States by paragraphs 1 and 2.[4]

Although Article 222 of the Treaty leaves Member States free to adopt their own systems of property ownership, Member States must refrain from acting in a manner contrary to the Treaty when they engage in commercial activity or influence the conduct of business enterprises. It follows that EU discipline intervenes when the State's presence in the economy limits or cancels out private initiative, jeopardizing the role of competition in the internal market. As a result, EU competition rules can also be used to open up those industrial sectors (such as the markets for energy, telecommunications and

[3]In the Almelo case (c-393/92; 1994, ECR I - 1477), the European Court held that restrictions on imports of electricity were necessary to allow the firm to meet its obligations to provide a public service, as imposed by the Member State.

[4]The Commission has made extensive use of this paragraph in setting out is own action in the telecommunications sector.

postal services) that remain closed despite the establishment of the internal market, because Member States have entrusted management of them to organizations that have been granted with special or exclusive rights.

In the latest *Reports on Competition Policy* the Commission indicated its intention to introduce greater competition by tackling existing monopolies, in particular those related to the distribution of gas and electricity, air transport and financial services. Indeed, the apparent neutrality shown towards public and privileged enterprises in the Rome Treaty establishing the European Community seems to have been replaced in the Maastricht Treaty on the European Union by a policy that clearly favors free markets over state planning. In this perspective, the debate on privatization processes occurring in some Member States focuses on the search for a rational role of the State in the economy. Given the distinction between "formal privatization" — which focuses mainly on changes of ownership — and so-called "functional privatization" — which considers the issue of State participation — the current processes of privatization in the EU come under this latter definition. Functional privatization pursues efficiency not only through redefinition of property rights but also through redefinition of the rules which should implement a better allocation of productive factors. Economic initiatives, whether public or private, should be pursued without those privileges which are typical of State power. If the State decides to act as an entrepreneur, it should submit to market rules like all other enterprises, without using state undertakings as a *longa manus* of its economic policy. The same reasoning applies to private firms which have obtained exclusive rights from the state.

The link between privatization and competition policy appears evident: the privatization process could bring new vitality into the economy if it is carried out through real competition (i.e.: re-organization of monopolistic sectors, abolition of entry-barriers to new competitors). Moreover, it should be stressed here that the relationship between the liberalization process in the European market and privatization processes at the national level has a relevant character and two-way direction. On the one hand, privatization depends on the regulatory context — and then on liberalization in the sector — given that the value of the firm to be privatized is related to the structure of the market.[5] On the other hand, the liberalization process depends on privatization of the sector given that it is usually during this process that

[5] That is to say, the value of a firm is different if the firm has a monopoly of the sector or if it is operating in a competitive market.

functions of the specific sectoral authority as well as those of other regulatory bodies are defined. This trade-off between the two processes converges on a general re-organization of the public utility sector where liberalization and privatization take place.

Referring in particular to the energy sector, at the Community level different steps have been progressively taken in the direction of liberalization. The right of transit on the transport network has been recognized by Directive 90/547/EEC (October, 1990) as well as the recommendation of the marginalist criterion when setting tariffs, application of principles of transparency in final customer prices (Directive 90/377/EEC), and regulation of tender procedures (Directive 90/531/EEC, September 90; 93/38/EEC, June 93).

Moreover, the Commission has aimed to introduce the so-called rule of *Third Party Access* (TPA), for both producers and consumers, to bring about a competitive market through substitution of producers for consumers and vice versa. This rule may be described as creating an obligation for the network operator to transport third parties' electricity and gas through its grid, under terms to be agreed on a commercial basis, provided there is adequate capacity and it is technically possible to do so. This would lead to the creation of an energy market at European level, with a system of interconnected networks giving large consumers the possibility of bargaining directly with producers from different countries. Moreover, in these terms, third-party access implies the organizational and administrative unbundling of three activities — production, high voltage transport and distribution — which were traditionally integrated in one operation connected with suppliers upstream and consumers downstream.

The Commission presented the timing and mode of integration of national markets in a directive proposal on February 1992. The main provisions of this proposal were:

- the activities of electricity production and construction of lines would henceforth be permitted on the basis of a transparent and non-discriminatory licence system which would take into consideration *inter alia* environmental constraints;

- unbundling of management and accountancy in vertically integrated companies as regards their production, transport and distribution activities;

- introduction of third-party access addressed — at least at the initial stage — only to some classes of consumers (i.e.: large industrial consumers and distribution companies exceeding a certain threshold) scheduled by 1996.

However, this directive proposal was rejected by the Council of Ministers in June 1992 and in November 1993 the European Parliament expressed its opinion on the Commission's original proposal, modifying important parts of it. In particular, the fundamental points in the Parliament's position were:

- maintenance of electricity production monopolies, except for new supply needs, which will have to be covered by means of calls for tender open to all Community operators or to newcomers;
- maintenance of the "concession" for the electricity distribution networks;
- a move from the "right for third parties to have access to the network" initially proposed by the Commission to "access freely negotiated between the parties," with arbitration systems in the event of dispute;
- unbundling limited to accountancy aspects only, without separation between production and transport activities;
- to condition any new future liberalization through previous harmonization in several fields (in particular the environment and taxation).

In February 1994 the Commission drew up a new directive proposal which reflected some of these criticisms. In particular, in this new proposal third party access is limited: the previous system of access to the network is no longer generally regulated, but specifically "negotiated" by the parties involved. This means that there is no longer a sort of general or standard contract, as contained in the previous directive proposal, to which parties[6] should conform. Parties are now free to negotiate the conditions of transactions under the constraints determined by the controlling institutions through the agreed procedures.

As shown in Figure 14.1, general third-party access differs in many respects from negotiated TPA. In particular, in the former there is a complete

[6] On the one hand generators and consumers and on the other, owners of the transmission and distribution network.

separation between the financial contract and the physical supply of electricity. This means that under general TPA a supply contract is drawn up between the producer and the consumer (and/or distributor), and this contract does not affect management of the dispatch activity[7] which is regulated between the producer and the network operator. In this way contracts between the producer and final consumers are avoided, as are triangular contracts, thus reducing transaction costs.[8] Given these considerations, the general third-party access system is superior to the negotiated TPA in terms of economic efficiency, and the advantages gained with the general TPA are greater as the number of subjects involved (producers, consumers, and/or distributors) increases.

Moreover, in the Commission's proposal of February 1994:

- unbundling of management has been abolished while unbundling of accounting is strengthened by provision of right of access for the competent national institutions to the sector enterprises' accounts;
- the system of calls for tender for new production capacities has been accepted and included;
- the regulation which defined the conditions of safety in supply and which justified the limits to system access laid down by each member state has been cancelled. The Treaty's general regulation and the usual appeal procedures now apply;
- the elements related to the nature of electricity as a "public service" which can be translated into constraints imposed by national authorities on enterprises involved in distribution and transmission are defined precisely and strengthened.

The decision to unbundle accountancy and management as regards generation, transport and distribution activities of vertically integrated firms directly affects the reformed structure of the electricity market itself and, in particular, the entry of newcomers. In fact, the unbundling of accountancy has far-reaching effects on the relative price structure, reducing the ability

[7] Dispatch activity coordinates the demand and supply of electricity, organizing the transport of high voltage electricity on the transmission network.

[8] This point is developed by De Paoli (1996), p.138, along with an interesting graphical analysis from which the present figures are taken.

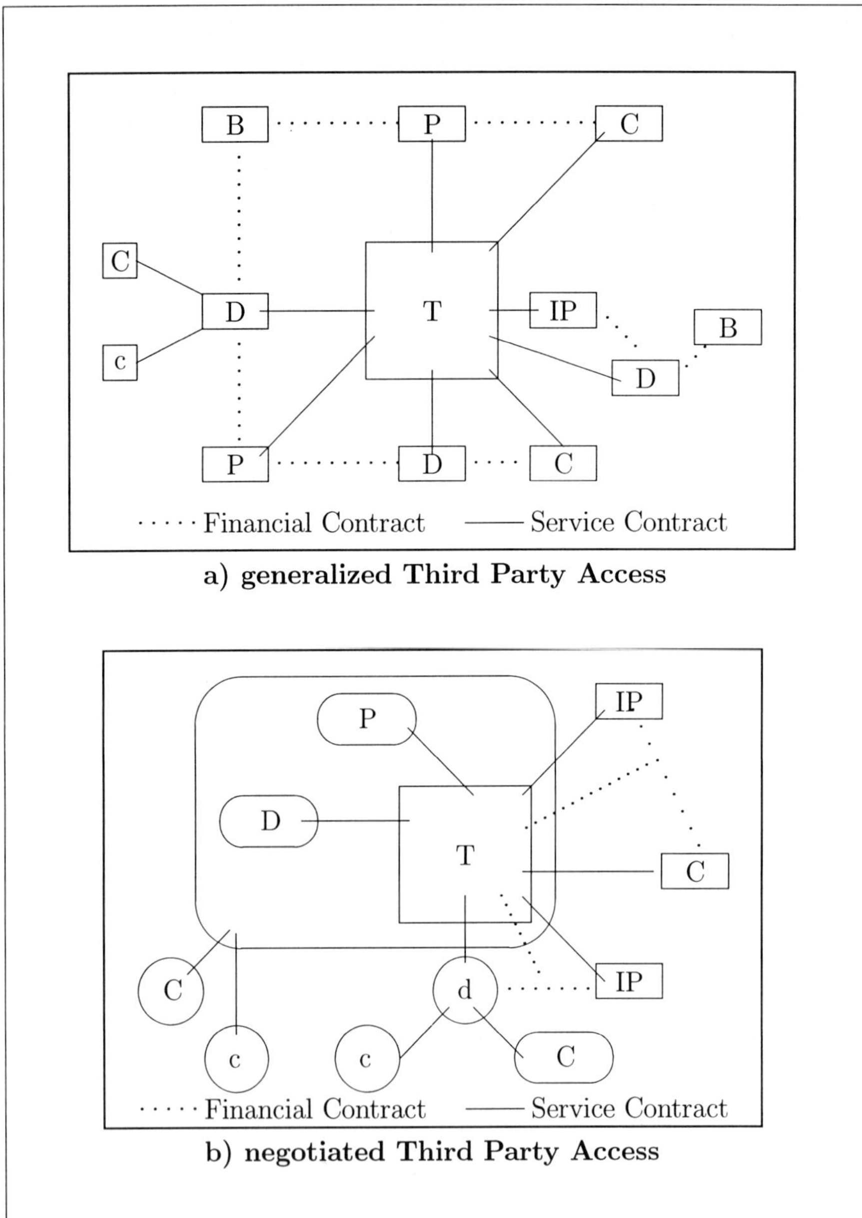

P = producer; IP = independent producer; T = transporter; D = distributor; d = small distributor; C = large consumer; c = small consumer; B = broker.

Figure 14.1: Third Party Access

to cross-subsidize. The unbundling in management would increase transparency, allow the responsibilities of managers to become more focused and provide increased assurances of investor protection, so that necessary expansion would take place. But since management unbundling has been abandoned, these last effects will not be realized, with important consequences for the decision-making process. Moreover, considering the externalities between generation and transmission, access price and access conditions to the grid determine the profitability of each production plant. Given the presence of sunk costs, it follows that the entry conditions facing new operators in electricity supply are significantly affected by unbundling in both accountancy and management.

Major criticisms of this proposed directive have been made. One notes that the limits imposed on the Commission by the "rule of subsidiarity," which states that the Community's competence cannot include areas that may be regulated by national institutions without being prejudicial to the aims of the Treaty, may impact on the introduction of third party access.

Other criticisms emphasize that third-party access would entail risks in terms of safety of supply. There is no reference in the directive proposal to Community responsibility with respect to this issue and the problem is considerable. On the one hand, there is the large geopolitical diversification of external suppliers and the Community's heavy dependence on them (40% in 1992, 60% foreseen by the Commission in 2010). On the other hand there are the objectives of environmental policy laid down by each Member State, objectives which may involve distortions in production costs and jeopardize the functioning of the competition mechanism. Moreover, these risks are not balanced by anticipated efficiency gains. A study of savings from complete integration of the European transmission system compiled for the Commission emphasized that the potential savings in terms of the percentage of total supply costs when existing transport capacity is used to capacity are extremely moderate.

Another line of criticism concerns the timing outlined in this proposed directive. The heterogeneous organizations of the Member States' electricity sectors raises doubts about the efficacy of TPA. In fact, if the electric industry were vertically segmented (as in Denmark, Spain, the Netherlands, and the United Kingdom) it could be easily adapted to the TPA rule, but this is not the case of highly integrated electricity systems (France, Germany, Italy).

In contrast to the directive proposal, which includes TPA, the French "Acheteur Unique" (AU) proposal, originally formulated in the Mandil Re-

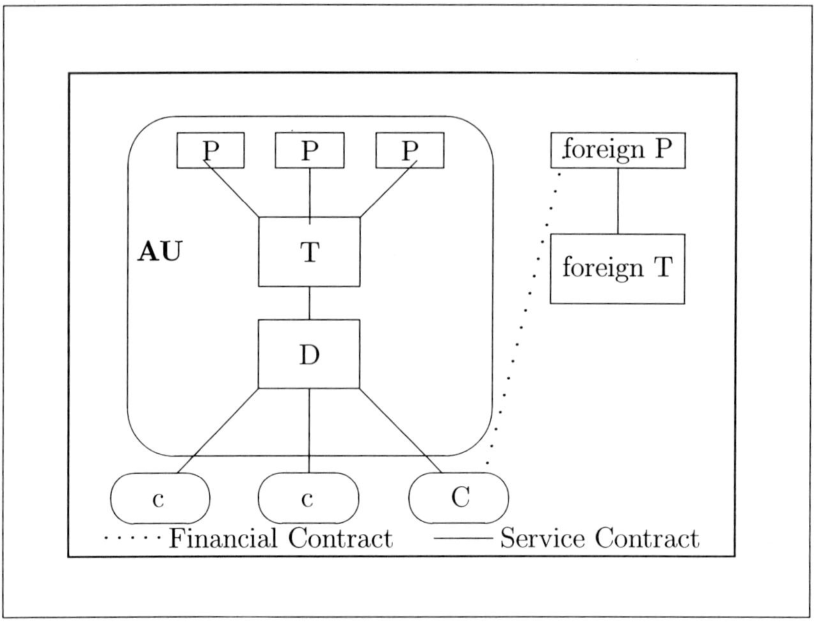

P = producer; T = transporter; D = distributor; c = small consumer; C = large consumer.

Figure 14.2: French Acheteur Unique Model

port (1994), allows for pluralism in supply — that is, competition among producers — along with the preservation of only one general purchaser and seller. According to this model, the AU plans long term contracts, and vertical integration of the sector is protected. In fact, in the original AU model (see Figure 14.2), the transmission-dispatch operator is not separated from the distributor since the former acts for the latter.

This means that the AU is an organizational model with only one subject which in the long and short run buys the power required to satisfy national demand from producers, and sells to the consumers guaranteeing equal treatment (conditions of consumption being equal). Moreover, the AU should fulfill the obligation to supply and the defend the general economic interest through short and long term planning.

The original formulation included of the Mandil Report has been improved by several changes, mainly

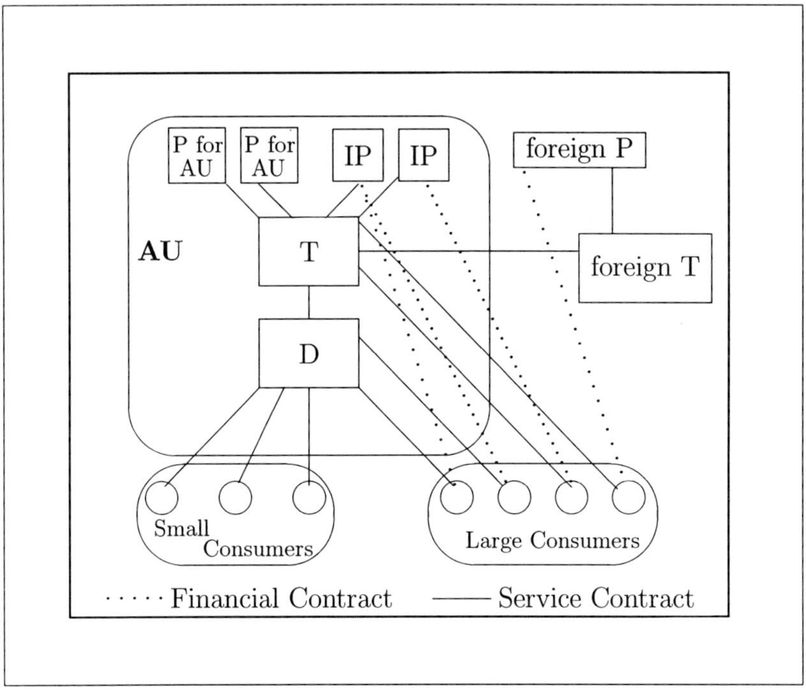

P = producer; IP = independent producer; T = transporter; D = distributor; c = small consumer.

Figure 14.3: Acheteur Unique with small and large consumers

- a distinction between free and constrained consumers, which establishes a double regime of AU; and
- the organization of the sector where multiple distributors are present.

As shown in Figure 14.3, in the AU regime where free and small consumers are distinguished, the supply of real services is separated from the supply of financial contracts: the latter take on greater relevance, making the AU 's coordination of the system more complex.

When the local distribution for small customers in a specific area is allocated to a number of actors, the result is a system with multiple distributors determining the local equilibrium between demand and supply of electricity. This system may include traders if distributors are allowed to draw up bi-

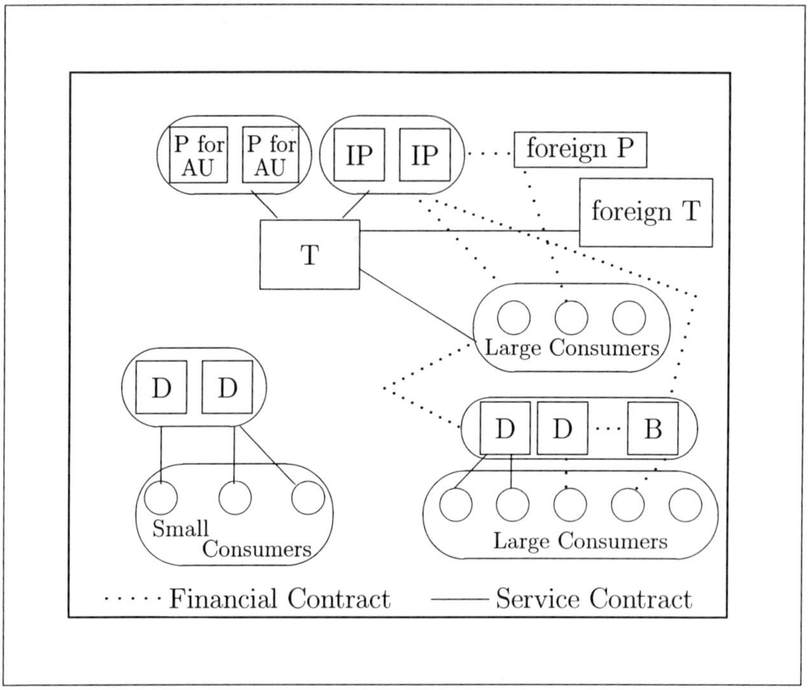

P = producer; IP = independent producer; T = transporter; D = distributor; c = small consumer; C = large consumer.

Figure 14.4: Acheteur Unique with multiple distributors

lateral contracts with free customers. As shown in Figure 14.4, the types of contracts increase and the organization of the system is again more complex.

Given the very different national systems, these models of the organization of the electricity market were the subject of long discussions at the Community level, and in July 1996 the European Council and Parliament worked out a "Common Position" which was submitted to the Plenary Parliament meeting in November and was approved as Directive 96/92/EEC on December 19, 1996.

The analysis of this Directive is the focus of the Section below, but I should refer here to the communication on "Services of general interest in Europe" through which — in early September 1996 — the Commission responded to the worries of Member States with a strong public sector tradition. In this communication the Commission stresses its attachment to the promotion of services of general interest in the European Union. It underlines the freedom of Member States to define and regulate general interest services in conformity with Article 90 of the EC Treaty. Assessing the overall situation with regard to public services, the Commission concludes that the achievements made are encouraging and the legal instruments of the Treaty are satisfactory. In particular, the Commission points out that Article 90 has proven its worth in fully guaranteeing beneficial interaction between liberalization and the general interest and is therefore best left untouched.

However, in the communication the Commission proposes, within the framework of the amendments to the Treaties prepared by the Intergovernmental Conference of 1996/97, to add a new paragraph (u) to Article 3of the Treaty which would read as follows:

- *"(u) a contribution to the promotion of services of general interest."*

Such an amendment, although largely symbolic, would stress the Community's responsibility in this field. However, it would not touch the balance struck in the Treaty between the internal market and free competition objectives on the one hand, and the general interest objectives on the other.

Experience in the different utility sectors confirms the Commission's basic conclusion: the existing Treaty instruments allow for provision of sector-specific policies which take full account of public policy interests in a market economy environment. There is absolutely no need for a Treaty amendment protecting these services. Proposals for such an amendment should therefore be opposed.

14.3 Directive 96/92/EU

Directive 96/92/EEC (on common rules for the EU internal energy market) aims to liberalize the generation and sale of electricity in the Member States according to a reasonable timetable. The provisions stated in Directive 96/92/EEC should come into force by February 1999; exceptions to this timetable are made for Belgium, Ireland and Greece which are given a longer period for adoption[9] due to the existing national systems (Art. 27).

Moreover, the Directive defines national market quotas to determine the degree to which each Member State's imports will be progressively increased

[9] Belgium and Ireland have one additional year, Greece two additional years.

over a period of six years, moving from the threshold of consumption of 40 GWh to 20 GWh after three years of adoption of the Directive and to 9 GWh after six years (see Art.19, 1-2).

Regarding the issue of unbundling, the Directive states that vertically integrated firms should separate their production, transmission and distribution (Art.14.2) in terms of accountability. However, the Directive seems also to suggest separating the activities of the electricity market in terms of management. There is no clear statement about unbundling of management, but it is stressed that the transmission operator (Art.7.6) and the AU (Art.15.1) should operate separately from the other activities.

With the aim of protecting long run investments and the presence of heterogeneous national systems, the Directive leaves two main options open to Member States:

- in the activity of production (generation), the choice between licensing and/or tendering;
- the choice of system for access to the national network.

Moreover, in the Directive there are many points where there are no clear indications for Member States. In what follows I analyze specific Directive provisions on the different activities of the electricity market, highlighting the points that are open to debate and interpretation by individual Member States.

14.3.1 Production

Directive 96/92/EEC does not permit exclusive rights for the production of electricity. Under Art. 4, the building of new production plant to face increases in demand or to replace out-of-date plant can take place through licence and/or tender.

Under Art. 5, licences are to be given on the basis of criteria suggested in the Directive regarding safety, environmental protection, localization and public use of the territory, efficiency of electric power and the firm's economic, financial and technological capacity. Member States adopting a licensing procedure should define and make public information about the criteria adopted (Art. 5.1–5.2).

With respect to tender procedures, the Directive in Section III is quite indefinite: in particular, in that Section, the AU it is never mentioned, although the tender procedure implies the presence of the AU which first acts as the auctioneer and then as the signer of the contract with the winner.

As emphasized in the literature on the "competition for the market,"[10] difficulties in the realization of the tender may arise from insufficient competition on the supply side, definition of the characteristics of the contract, determination of the timing of the contract, and control of performance during execution. However, no precise indications are given in the Directive about the rules for organizing the tender. This is a vacuum that should be filled if the tender procedure is adopted in Member States, given that the results of the tender in terms of economic efficiency are closely linked to the definition of the contract and bidding rules.

14.3.2 Transmission

The Directive states that the transmission system should be

- independent from the activity of generation and distribution "at least in management terms" (Art. 7.6);
- nondiscriminatory with respect to the network users.

It follows that the Directive leaves to each Member State the decision about the transmission system with respect to the large and small customers. The choice here is related to the creation of a single AU at national level or a number of AUs at the local level.

14.3.3 Distribution

Regarding the distribution system, the Directive asserts that the Member States can

- oblige distributors to provide the service to customers in a determined area;
- regulate tariffs to guarantee equal treatment for final customers;

[10] see Chadwick (1859), Demsetz (1968).

- give advantages to production plants using renewable energy sources.

The distribution operator should guarantee the efficiency and the safety of the service in view of environmental issues.

14.3.4 Access to the network

After a long debate over grid access between the Commission and Parliament, embodied in alternative proposals, the Directive states that access to the network is possible through

- a negotiated TPA (Art. 17.1);
- a generalized TPA (Art. 17.4);
- the procedure of AU (Art.18.1).

The main differences among these procedures concern the agents who are entitled to have access to the network and to the determination of the cost of access. In the case of the negotiated TPA, the network operator should make public access prices to the grid and distribution within one year of the coming into force of the directive.

In the case of generalized TPA, operators are entitled to have access to the transmission network at the access prices that have been made public. The transmission network operator and/or the distribution operator may refuse to give access if there are no conditions for access as indicated in Art. 3.

In the case of an AU, a non-discriminatory tariff for access to the transmission network and to distribution should be made public. Qualified customers should be free to contract with producers located in the territory covered by the grid and — given the Member State's permission — with producers located outside. Independent producers contract the access prices with the transmission network and/or distribution operator on a voluntary basis to supply qualified customers external to the network. Refusal of access may be made by the AU under the same conditions as for generalized and negotiated TPAs.

14.4 Privatization of public utilities and competition policy in Italy

The Italian Antitrust Authority (Autorità Garante della Concorrenza e del Mercato) — established in 1990 — acts according to the competition policy guidelines laid down by the European Community. In its 1994 *Annual Report*, the Autorità stressed the need for supervision and investigation of legal monopolies, particularly public utilities, since they represent "a field of primary relevance for the control the Authority should operate on the presence of illegal behavior (...) carried out by enterprises in legal exclusive regimes, behavior that leads to the aim of enlarging their dominant position in contiguous and competitive markets."

In this perspective, the Italian Antitrust Authority usually acts by following two different approaches. The first — which could be seen as a passive activity — begins by pointing out the existence of a problem; the second consists of investigating a specific industrial sector.

As an example of this latter approach, in July 1994 the Italian Antitrust Authority issued a Report on "Competition and Regulation in public utility services" which emphasized that even though in some cases a monopoly may be more efficient than a competitive market, market access should not generally be restricted by legislation. In fact, removal of statutory entry barriers in industries that have long been protected from competition favors the transition to a regime in which the scope of monopoly is determined by market forces. Arguably, liberalization of public utility services may also be made wholly compatible with the essential requirements of security, continuity and universality of services.

Moreover, the Antitrust Authority has repeatedly maintained that privatization in Italy may represent an important means of establishing a competitive market structure under circumstances in which mere liberalization of access is not sufficient. Corporate reorganization, carried out prior to privatization of a company operating under a statutory monopoly may, in some cases, make it possible to sell off plants or different activities separately, enhancing market competition. The more competition on the market, the less need there is to regulate firms' behavior.

In anticipation of the establishment of independent authorities responsible for specific sectors, the Autorità Garante operated in the role of substitute (i.e., in airport services and telecommunications).

Italian Law n. 481 (November 14, 1995) set up the Authority for Energy and Gas. This Law specifies that supervision of competition should be carried out by the Italian Antitrust Authority and that the sectoral Authorities have to inform the former of cases of suspected violation of Law n. 297/90 (on antitrust policy). Moreover, the Autorità Garante gives obligatory advice regarding the establishment of concessions, service contracts and other regulatory instruments.

The Authority for Energy and Gas carries out "advisory and informative activity for the Government in the field of its competence with the aim of definition, application and realization of the Community Law" (481/95, p. 4). The basic characteristics of the Authority stressed in the law establishing it are its independent internal organization and the technical competence of its members. The powers given to the Authority are wider than control over network access, determination of tariffs, and control over quality of the service. It issues the directives for accounting and administrative shares, checks the costs of the specific functions, and controls the supply of services through inspection and investigative powers (...)" (481/95, pp. 5-6). Moreover, the Authority for Energy and Gas proposes changes in technical and economic conditions of network access, suspension or repeal of concessions and licences for new power plants to the competent Ministry. This establishes political control over the Authority for Energy and Gas. It should be stressed here that in this context it would be better to give full independence to the sectoral Authority so that the efficiency aim could be fully pursued by the regulator without political interference.

Summarizing, it seems that the Italian Antitrust Authority will maintain its role in those sectors where competition will be introduced (generation and part of the selling process), basing its antitrust activity in the electricity sector on Law 289/90. The Authority for Energy and Gas will set prices in the regulated divisions, check investments in the transmission network and define licences and concessions.

Two problems can arise from the specific nature and the technical competence of the Sectorial Authority. First, it may happen that the subjects under regulation are able to influence the regulator's behavior to further their own objectives. Second, the regulator may abuse his authority with respect to the regulated subject (the hold-up problem). In this respect it would be interesting to set up a new relationship between the Antitrust Authority and the Sectorial Authority. They pursue the same efficiency objective, but with different tools. The Antitrust Authority should be less open to regulatory capture since it is less directly involved in regulation. It follows that the Antitrust Authority could usefully be given the responsibility to settle controversies between regulated enterprises and the Sectorial Authority; moreover, it could inform the Ministry of Industry of the possibility of connivance between regulated enterprises and the Sectorial Authority.

14.5 The privatization of the Italian energy sector

The traditional structure of the electricity sector was one of regulated monopoly, usually owned by the State. In this sector all the typical causes of market failure — sunk costs, elements of natural monopoly, public goods, externalities, uncertainty — were held to be present. It followed that the structure usually adopted was that of horizontally and vertically integrated monopoly, with state ownership to protect the consumer from allocative inefficiency deriving from monopoly power.

The experiences of privatization and liberalization of the electricity industry in different countries (Great Britain, Chile, Norway, Peru, Argentina) have highlighted the introduction of competition in production and sale of electricity along with the aims of safety, continuity of transmission, efficiency and universal access to the power grid. In particular, the British experience involved a division between generation and supply on the one side and transmission and distribution of electricity on the other. Electricity generation undertakings have been shared and privatized. The processes of buying and selling electricity have been fully deregulated with respect to large consumers, while they have remained regulated with respect to small consumers. Regulation has been maintained in transmission and distribution, where conditions of natural monopoly are still present.

Despite the brief period since privatization and deregulation in the British electricity industry and the problems of evaluating the outcomes, the experience appears to have been successful at least in taking the electricity industry out of the control of government ministers and in making it subject to competitive pressure and independent regulation.

In Italy the debate on privatization of state sectors and on liberalization of protected sectors is relatively recent. The legislative vacuum is particularly relevant given the current extent of privatization.

In 1962 the majority of Italian electric power companies were nationalized and grouped into a single state-owned company, ENEL (*Ente Nazionale per l'Energia Elettrica*). The main economic objectives pursued through nationalization were coordination of large-scale investments and control over prices; these objectives are still present in the current reform of the energy sector (Polo and Scarpa, 1995).

Supply of electric power is usually split into generation, transport (dispatch and high voltage transmission), distribution (low voltage transmission) and sale. In the latter three phases ENEL has a monopolistic position, with the exceptions of a few municipal firms that have a vertically integrated structure covering the production and commercialization. ENEL currently controls more than 80% of electricity production and more than 87% of total distribution. The rest is covered by some existing municipal firms (4% and 12% respectively), self-generators with a more than 70% share of self-production and small firms with an annual production below 15 Gwh (Fraquelli and Vannoni, 1996).

Production of electric power in Italy is based on a mix of technologies: among these hydro-geological sources account for about 20% of production, while the rest is based on fossil fuels (5% coal, 55% oil, 20% natural gas). The cost structure of the different phases can be broken down as follows: 60% production, 5% transmission and 35% distribution and sale.

In 1993 the demand for electric power in Italy was 247 Gwh: consumption was more than three times that recorded in 1963 (70 Gwt). Per capita consumption of electricity in Italy is however one third of that in the USA, and about two thirds of consumption recorded in France, Germany and Japan.

The first step toward the privatization of ENEL can be seen in Law n. 333 of July 1992, which transformed public holdings into joint stock companies, concessionaires of their respective activities reserved by law. From the early 90s, the Amato Government — through different laws — set in motion the transformation of public enterprises into joint-stock companies, laying down the main rules for transformation of state participation firms into public enterprises and for the sale of undertakings under state ownership.

In November 1992, the Treasury Ministry presented the Italian Parliament with the Program regarding reorganization of the State share in firm ownership ("Partecipazioni Statali") for some holdings.[11] In this document

[11]Involved in this program were IRI (Istituto per la Ricostruzione Industriale), ENI (Ente Nazionale Idrocarburi), ENEL (Ente Nazionale per l'Energia Elettrica), IMI (Isti-

the privatization process is expected to be concluded within 3 to 4 years, and priority is given to reorganization and balancing of IRI, the largest Italian public holding. Between 1993 and 1995 a minority share of ENEL was to be sold to private owners. The procedure for selling these state enterprises highlights the need for transparency in the process. Public tender is the conventional method proposed, while private negotiations with potential buyers are permitted only in particular cases. In sectors of particular public interest (such as electricity, energy and chemicals, insurance, airlines, civil and industrial plants, telecommunications) the Ministry's Program suggested the establishment of public companies along with clear rules for groups of shareholdings.

In July 1994, a new law approved by Parliament (n. 474) aimed to clarify and simplify the process of transformation of state enterprises, and to speed the transition from state enterprises to joint-stock companies, and at sale of the enterprises themselves. There are potential conflicts between this law and EU competition policy. In particular:

— the control exercised by the State Auditors Department is considerable and persists in the long run;

— the so called "golden share" or "action specifique" gives State institutions special powers of control over privatized enterprises;

— private negotiations between the State and potential buyers could lead to a selling process without real competition,

— the limits imposed on share ownership during and after privatization;

— the role of the Board of Directors of privatized firms regarding the procedure for election of directors.

In November 1994 the previous privatization proposal was discussed with respect to further sectoral reorganization. Support was given for the introduction of unbundling in accounting between transmission and distribution, competition in production and an independent dispatch function.

At a later stage, positions were again confused and the proposal by the Minister Clô once more suggested reorganizing the sector, aiming at a unitary final structure. The Italian Antitrust Authority raised relevant issues against this position. In November 1995, Law 481 laid down the rules for the creation of the Independent Sectorial Authorities for public services, focusing — in particular — on the energy and gas sector.

---

tuto Mobiliare Italiano), BNL (Banca Nazionale del Lavoro), and INA (Istituto Nazionale delle Assicurazioni).

At the same time of approving Directive 96/92/EEC, the Italian Ministry of Industry set up the "Carpi Commission" to prepare proposals for adoption of the EC Directive on the part of the Italian electricity sector. At the end of January 1997, this Commission produced a document foreseeing the transformation of the Italian electricity system. Briefly, the new organization of the Italian energy sector would be characterized as follows:

- unbundling in accounting and management terms for production, transport and distribution: three operative divisions will be created with independent accounting systems;
- in production, competition is to be implemented through the share of ENEL in a plurality of production companies;
- transmission and dispatch are kept together in an independent company managing the network (grid).
- in distribution, the figure of the AU is created as "an independent national agency" including the Ministry of Industry;
- the functions of transmission and dispatch are exercised by the AU;
- two markets for electricity are defined: the "large market" and the "small market." In the former, large consumers are free to choose their (national or foreign) suppliers; in the latter, small consumers are constrained to buy from the AU, which in turn purchases electricity through public tender;
- the creation of a sort of stock market for energy (MEI, *Mercato Elettrico all'Ingrosso*) with the function of coordinating the market for constrained and free consumers: the subject which manages this stock market is the same as the one managing the transmission grid and dispatch activity;
- definition of a unified tariff system for the whole country, even if this leads to rigidities particularly in distribution;
- a slight increase in the number of actors in the electricity system, with an increase in the number of producers and local firms;

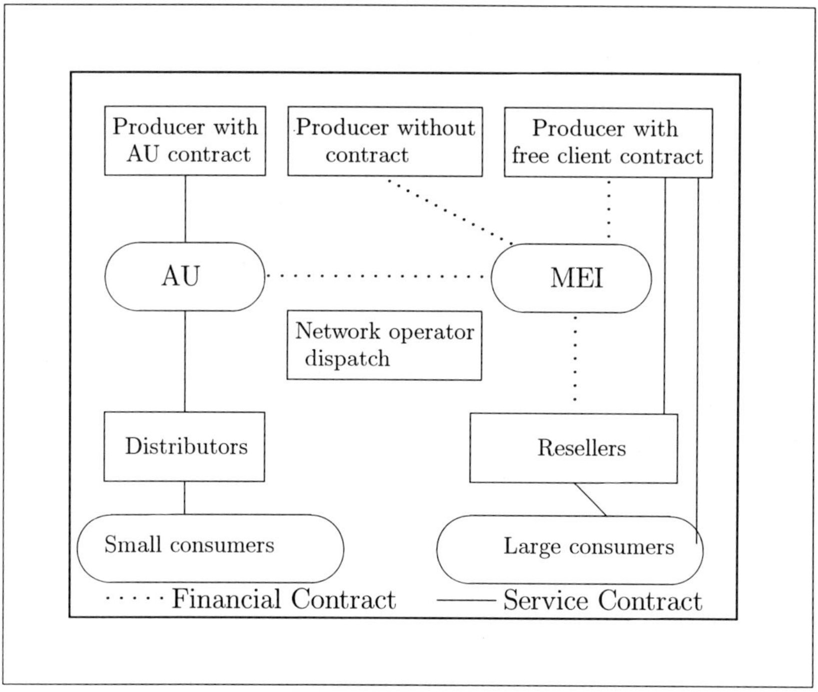

P = producer; IP = independent producer; T = transporter; D = distributor; c = small consumer; C = large consumer; MEI = wholesale energy market.

Figure 14.5: Italian model proposed by the Carpi Commission

- in buying electricity produced by third parties, priority is given to renewable sources.

Focusing on functional privatization of ENEL, this process would lead to an independent firm managing the transmission and dispatch network and to the creation of a number of production firms of sufficient size (at least 10,000 Mw, if 5 firms are envisaged) through the splitting up of ENEL, in order to guarantee competition at national level and the ability to operate at international level; the possible creation of a public hydroelectric firm; the establishment of pluralism in distribution, in a form to be defined, including however the obligation at least to overcome the present overlapping of ENEL and municipal firms in some areas.

Figure 14.5 shows the Italian electricity system as proposed by the Carpi

Commission. This proposal has given rise to a large amount of criticism from trade unions and from ENEL's top management, in particular with respect to management unbundling. Disagreement is mainly related to disinvestment driven by the reduced size of the resulting operating firms and to alleged larger transaction costs.

Given the approval of Directive 96/92/EEC and the above description of proposals of reorganization of the Italian energy sector, the process of privatization of the Italian energy sector presents many points of analysis.

That the unbundling of management in the Italian electricity sector is not limited to accounting systems alone is consistent with the Directive's positive attitude toward the unbundling of the management of production, transmission and distribution.

Focusing on generation, the low growth of demand in the sector (about 2% over the last five years) dictates the division of ENEL into a number of companies to guarantee competition. Regarding the new companies, many issues should be taken into consideration with the aim of increasing real competition in the sector, among which:

- the amount of shares in each new company that will be sold to private investors;
- the control over the new company.

These issues will significantly affect the future of ENEL in the energy market and are still not settled, as shown by the recent agreement signed by ENI and ENEL for the establishment of a joint-venture in electricity production in the market for large consumers. In this particular case, ENI and ENEL are both monopolists[12] in their main activities, which are close to each other. In fact, this joint venture will produce electricity through turbogas power stations, where ENI supplies almost all the Italian turbogas power stations. The new joint venture will cover about one-third of the market for large consumers: this predicted large market share gives room to investigation of the Italian Antitrust Authority about the real transfer of control over the new joint venture from ENI and ENEL to others. The risk is that the share of ENEL does not give the rise to competition in production and the potential gains from electricity privatization will not be

[12] ENEL and ENI supplies about 90% respectively of the electricity sector and the natural gas sector.

fully realized, as it has been the British experience. Moreover, given that the type of power stations (turbogas power station with combined cycle of production) involved in the joint-venture are more efficient than the other types present in generation of electricity in terms of production costs, the market for large consumers will set lower prices than the market for small consumers. In this respect the Sectorial Authority should strengthen the control over tariff to avoid that the costs from inefficient productions are a burden on small consumers.

Regulation should provide adequate assurances of protection for investors, so that the necessary expansion in the production of electricity will take place, while preserving the benefits of market competition. However, horizontal and vertical disintegration could give rise to the hold-up problem in investments, particularly with respect to transmission. In this context, an efficiently-carried out dispatch activity becomes important. Moreover, these aspects of investment incentives underline the need to keep transmission and dispatch activities together, to obtain a coordinated and efficient allocation of production.

Entry of new production plants using renewable energy sources is encouraged by the Directive. In the Italian context this means that the incentive for such energy sources should be known *ex-ante*, and not *ex-post* as under the current procedures.

Considering the choice between the licence and/or tender procedure to establish new production plants, the latter seems more appropriate for the Italian system (see De Paoli, 1996). However, in this respect there are many issues to be defined and solved, given that the Directive is very incomplete as to organization, timing and control of tenders.

The definition of the AU as a distribution system at the national level or of a number of AUs at the local level remains open. If on the one hand the latter definition would be better in terms of efficiency gains from competition, on the other hand demand characteristics, geographical elements and operators' moral hazard could make the implementation of regulation rules at the local level difficult. Regarding this point, the Italian Antitrust Authority has expressed its hope for the choice of the AU at the national level as a transition solution in the Italian energy sector, and it has proposed moving quickly in the market for small consumers to short- and medium-term contracts among producers and distributors. This means that the Italian Antitrust Authority supports a model of AU with multiple of distributors — see Figure 14.4 — where a number of distributors compete in the market.

Moreover, the Italian Antitrust Authority is not positively inclined toward the idea of a unified tariff system for the whole country, given that issues of allocative inefficiency and income distribution will weigh on consumers' price. In this respect, a larger role should be played by the newly established independent Sectorial Authority for Energy and Gas.

The points of analysis discussed above are particularly relevant in the context of privatization and restructuring of the Italian electricity sector, given that such opportunities resulting from reorganization of the whole sector are rare and should not be wasted.

14.6 Final Remarks

The specific requirements of the public utility sector do not justify their exclusion from the scope of the Treaty principles on competition. Given the inherited state-owned, integrated and monopolistic structure, public service obligations tend to include detailed specifications (obligation to supply, equal treatment of users, continuity of service) of the service to be provided when private sector entry on the supply side takes place.

In the case of the electricity industry, the structures and performance of the generation and distribution sectors are potentially competitive. Because competition is more effective than regulation in promoting efficiency, the separation of the potentially competitive phases of electricity supply from the naturally monopolistic phase (transmission) should be pursued. The details of such reform will vary from country to country, depending on whether the system is government owned, investor owned, or under mixed ownership. Separation implies a restructuring that will affect pricing and investment decisions.

To provide legal guarantees for all operators, the Commission specifies the rights and obligations of those acting in the energy market. Directive 96/92/EEC, approved after a long debate, lays down the common rules for the EU internal energy market. It leaves many issues unsettled. In particular, two main options are left to Member States:

- in the activity of generation, the choice between a license procedure and/or tender;
- the choice of the system for access to the national network.

These issues have been discussed in the context of the current Italian debate on privatization and reorganization of the state monopoly energy sector. Competition in generation, the organization of transmission and dispatch activities, the proposed "Acheteur Unique" model and the unified tariff at national level have been analyzed with reference to EU Directive.

In view of the Directive's priorities, there are four main features that have specific relevance for the Italian situation:

- the sequencing of reforms is critical and the government's sustained commitment is vital to the success of the current reform program;

- the explicit separation of the state's regulatory functions from its ownership and policy responsibilities is essential, to allow state-owned firms the necessary autonomy and to provide fairness in regulation for all suppliers, both state-owned and private;

- effective competition in generation requires that there be a sufficient number of independent companies generating power, free entry into the generating market, and facilities for new operators to deliver their output to the trunk system;

- it is necessary to establish an independent transmission company, with nondiscriminatory access for suppliers, in order to prevent the incumbent supplier from frustrating competition.

14.7 References

Chadwick, Edwin "Results of different principles of legislation and administration in Europe; of competition for the field, as compared with competition within the field, of service," *Journal of the Royal Statistical Society*, Volume 22, September 1859, pp. 381–420.

Commissione Carpi "Bozza di Lavoro della Commissione Energia sul Riassetto del Mercato Elettrico," *Staffetta Quotidiana*, November 27, 1996, pp. 6–7.

Council Directive 90/547/EEC of 29 October 1990 "On the transit of electricity through transmission grids."

Council Directive 96/92/EEC of 19 December 1996 "On common rules for the internal market of electricity power."

Demsetz, H. "Why regulate utilities?," *The Journal of Law and Economics*, Volume 11, Number 1 April 1968, pp. 55–65.

De Paoli, L. "Problemi e suggerimenti per il passaggio ad un nuovo assetto del sistema elettrico italiano," *Economia delle Fonti di Energia e dell'Ambiente*, N.1, 1996, pp.79-146.

Fraquelli, G. and Vannoni, D. "Total productivity performance and regulation in electricity: an international comparison," mimeo, 1996.

Italian Departmental Order 28 December 1995: "Attribuzione all'ENEL SPA, ai sensi dell'Art. 14 del decreto legge 11 luglio 1992, n. 333, convertito con legge 8 agosto 1992, n.359, della concessione delle attività per l'esercizio del pubblico servizio di fornitura dell'energia elettrica nel territorio nazionale."

Italian Law n. 481 (November 14, 1995) "Norme per la concorrenza e la regolazione dei servizi di pubblica utilità. Istituzione delle Autorità di regolazione dei servizi di pubblica utilità."

Mandil, C. "Le reforme de l'organisation electrique et gaziere française," in *Economia delle Fonti di Energia e dell'Ambiente*, N.1/1994.

Polo, M. and Scarpa, C. "La riforma del settore elettrico in Italia: una privatizzazione al buio?," mimeo, 1995.

Competition Policies in Europe - S. Martin (Editor)
1998 Elsevier Science B.V.

Chapter 15

Competition Intensity *vs.* Service Quality: On the Distribution of Para-pharmaceutical Products in Spain

Aurora García[1]
Nikolaos Georgantzís
María Victoria Petit

15.1 Introduction

The implications of location choice for price competition among suppliers have been extensively studied. The symmetric-competition-on-the-circle model (Salop, 1979) is especially useful for analyzing the long-run number of firms. In this model, short-run equilibrium profit-cost margins decline as the number of firms increases. Then in free-entry equilibrium there are as many firms as necessary for the zero-profit condition to be satisfied.

[1]The research presented here was financed by *Fundació Caixa Castelló* (project No. P1A94-10). The paper benefitted substantially from comments by S. Martin, V. Orts Ríos, W. García-Fontes and M.A. García Cestona. All remaining errors are the authors' responsibility alone.

However, there are various real-world markets in which entry depends on the distribution strategies adopted by upstream firms (suppliers) and/or the institutional environment. Furthermore, the introduction of an additional product by highly multiproduct firms usually involves negligible fixed costs and plays a limited role in entry or exit decisions. When modelling situations with these characteristics, entry may not be free.

Models of spatial competition have been extensively used to study the implications of entry and price regulation for the distribution of pharmaceutical products. A variation of the model suggested by Hotelling (1929) is used by Garcia-Fontes and Motta (1997) to study entry and price regulation in the distribution of pharmaceutical products; Jansson (1995) uses the set-up proposed by Waterson (1993) to study alternative scenarios with different combinations of liberalization or regulation of prices and/or entry. Although all these applications of spatial competition models also briefly refer to *non*-pharmaceutical products distributed by pharmacies in Spain, their policy implications are restricted to the distribution of pharmaceutical products.

In this paper, we propose a theoretical framework which yields specific recommendations for measures to be adopted by competition authorities with respect to the distribution of para-pharmaceutical products (cosmetics, alimentary and other products for babies, etc.) in Spain. We compare two alternative scenarios:

- exclusive distribution rights to *pharmacies*.

- *partial, selective* liberalization of distribution.

Partial liberalization refers to the granting of distribution rights to several types of retailers, as for example cosmetic dealers, *para-pharmacies*, and supermarkets. Selective liberalization refers to measures that apply to only to *certain* products or groups of products.

As in many other countries, the maximum density of drugstores in Spain is regulated according to the local population density. The law aims at a greater dispersion of drugstores and the opening of some drugstores in low population density areas.

Furthermore, this policy is justified by the state and defended by the owners of drugstores as a reasonable compensation for the special services offered, including night opening hours, advice to consumers, distribution of medicines under the national insurance scheme, and so on.

In the case of para-pharmaceutical products, distribution restrictions are for the most part the result of the decision of manufacturers of certain products to grant exclusive distribution rights to pharmacies, in combination with the permissive attitude of the state toward such restrictions. Recently, the government has decided to liberalize the distribution of some para-pharmaceutical products. This followed the indications of the Spanish competition authority, the *Tribunal de Defensa de la Competencia* (1993) (henceforth, *TDC*), and systematic pressure by consumers and the owners of all kinds of establishments which could act as alternative distribution points (para-pharmacies, supermarkets, cosmetics dealers, etc.). The experience could serve as a precedent to take into account when assessing the effects of further liberalization of the sector, given that there are still a large number of products — especially cosmetics — which are exclusively sold in pharmacies.

It is worth noting that the liberalization studied here has nothing to do with the recently and broadly debated liberalization of entry as a measure aiming at promotion of competition in the distribution of medicines and against unemployment of pharmacists. Instead, we use the term *liberalization of the distribution of para-pharmaceutical products* to refer to measures aiming at making it possible for any other type of establishment to distribute these products. Furthermore, we use the term *partial liberalization* when referring to measures leading to a larger number of distributors including certain types of establishments — in addition to drugstores — but not necessarily all distributors, and the term *selective liberalization* when the measures aim at (partially) liberalizing the distribution of certain para-pharmaceutical products only. We also make a distinction between *passive* and *active* policies of liberalization. By passive liberalization we mean measures aiming at increasing the number of potential retailers and by active liberalization we mean measures which guarantee that a certain type of product is actually distributed by more types of establishments.

The persistence of exclusive distribution rights of pharmacies, which, in general terms, goes against the basic principles of competition policy in the Europe Union and in Spain, has been defended on the ground that the quality of service in drugstores is superior to that available from other types of outlets.[2] The usual response to this *quality argument* is that the service offered

[2] Drugstores are run, necessarily, by pharmacists whose qualifications — they must hold a university degree — guarantee the possibility of an expert's opinion at the moment of the purchase. Furthermore, drugstores are equipped — as stipulated by law — with the infrastructure necessary for the products to be stored in perfectly hygienic conditions.

by pharmacists rarely includes information which could not be provided to clients by the owners or the employees of other specialized establishments. An experienced cosmetics dealer may in fact be more qualified to give information about cosmetics and their properties than a pharmacist who is inexperienced in the field of cosmetics.. Furthermore, it is often the case that the consumer simply purchases the product, but the choice has already been made by a specialist (as, for example, in the case of infant formula and follow-on formulas, which are recommended to the parents by a pediatrician). In such cases, a drugstore's service quality exhibits negligible differences (if any) compared with the service offered by any alternative distribution points. The use of the quality argument would then be just an excuse of manufacturers (and, probably, pharmacists) to reduce retail competition,[3] taking advantage of the fact that the number of drugstores is (as explained above) restricted by law below the level implied by free-entry conditions.

In this paper, we assess the welfare implications of a restrictive distribution scheme like the one described above. The analysis of vertical product differentiation, together with the usual horizontal differentiation aspect of spatial market, allows us to assess the effect of service quality on social welfare, over and above the usual *intensity-of-competition* and *transportation-cost-saving* effects of firm proliferation on consumer surplus and social welfare.

The paper is organized in the following way: Section 15.2 discusses the main characteristics of the distribution of para-pharmaceutical products in Spain. Section 15.3 introduces the theoretical model. Section 15.4 is dedicated to the discussion of the theoretical framework and its application to real-world cases, proposing a rule which is easy to apply by a policy-maker

[3]We do not deal with the literature on vertical restrictions and market foreclosure. Our main objective is to outline a theoretical framework on the basis of which the state could pursue a broader distribution network or, even, the complete liberalization of the sector. That is, in our framework, the presence of upstream firms is ignored and the state is the only agent whose decisions may affect the number of retailers. However, we implicitly use the well established theoretical fact that upstream firms may have incentives to restrict the distribution network of their products or sell only to high-quality retailers. For theoretical results in this direction, see Rey and Tirole (1986), Tirole (1988) and Martin (1993), chapter 12. Among these results we find that there are, also, conditions under which more retail competition is more profitable for the manufacturer. However, the fact that certain manufacturers of cosmetics and other para-pharmaceutical products prefer to grant exclusive distribution rights to pharmacies, indicates that the profitability of more retail competition for manufacturers should be ruled out here.

whose information is restricted to price-cost margins and prices. Section 15.5 concludes.

15.2 The Distribution of Para-pharmaceutical Products in Spain

As in most countries in the world, the distribution of pharmaceutical products in Spain is an exclusive right of pharmacies. This is considered a guarantee of product and service quality which otherwise would be left to the arbitrary decisions of insufficiently qualified, profit-seeking businessmen (*Real Decreto No. 2259/1994*, 25/11/1994):

> The control of the distribution of medicines and pharmaceutical services is very important to guarantee the pharmaceutical quality. With such a control, we can make sure that the product in the market fulfils the characteristics that are certified by the laboratories. These characteristics determine that the use of the product is safe and effective.

The regulation of the distribution of medicines is one of the many examples of intervention by Spanish authorities leading to restrictions in competition. The most important of the limitations found in the Spanish Law[4] concerning the distribution of medicines are:

- First, the profit margin is fixed, at a level reduced recently to 27%, taking the purchase price of a medicine from the manufacturer or the wholesale store as the unit cost of the product;
- Second, there is a geographic limitation to the location of pharmacies, based on the number of inhabitants (one pharmacy per 4000 inhabitants);[5]
- Finally, there is a limitation of hours of service: the General Council of the Official Association of Pharmacists regulates the opening and

[4] *Ley del Medicamento.*

[5] See art. 1, *Real Decreto 1711/80, 31/7/1980*, modifying the *Real Decreto 909/78, 14/4/1978.*

closing times of pharmacies as well as the frequency of their monthly night opening.[6]

An ongoing debate concerns the controlled-entry regime, according to which a pharmacy licence is denied to potential entrants whose proposed location would violate the population density rule. This is justified on the argument that the fact that pharmacies do not locate too near one another, together with the fact that the profit margins are fixed, guarantees a minimum profit to all pharmacies and especially to those located in lower population density regions. In fact, the resulting scarcity of licences in big cities increases the possibility that pharmacies will open in places with lower population densities.

Further obligations of pharmacies concern the production of small-scale medical preparations of limited profitability for the pharmacist. It is often argued that one way of compensating the for the economic losses of pharmacies from such restrictions and obligations is to guarantee them some protection against intense competitive pressures and, therefore, the erosion of their long-run profits that would result from a free-entry regime.

The high profitability of cosmetics and other para-pharmaceutical products has often been considered as a further compensation of pharmacies for their losses due to the aforementioned limitations in opening hours and product line. In fact, retail profit margins from para-pharmaceutical products — and especially cosmetics — distributed by pharmacies are very high.

According to the recent campaign of the Pharmacists' Association in the Spanish press, pharmacies "...are a very important piece of the health system because they professionally and neutrally give advice to patients, and patients trust them."[7] But according to the results of a recent inquiry made by the Spanish Health Ministry, 60% of consumers claim not to have asked their pharmacist for any medical advice. In the cases in which the pharmacist's advice contradicted the doctor's indications in any sense, 77% of them trusted the doctor.

Moreover, some health experts believe that the role of the pharmacist in modern societies is losing its relevance. One of the main sources of consumer dissatisfaction seems to be that the attention of the pharmacist to the consumer of expensive para-pharmaceutical products has a negative effect

[6] *Orden 17/1/1980.*

[7] A sample of the marketing campaign made by the Spanish Association of Pharmacists can be seen in the *El PAIS* (weekly, 1996).

on the pharmacist's willingness to serve the consumer of necessary but less profitable medicines and medical preparations.

The *TDC* recently recommended measures aiming at creation of national and foreign pharmaceutical chains, an increase in the number of opening hours, an increase in sales of para-pharmaceutical products in supermarkets and other shops, a free-price policy for medicines and, finally, the free location of pharmacies. Although the implementation of such a project is far from what we could expect to see in the immediate future, a general tendency to more competition is observed. Among the main changes in this direction, we mention the recent liberalization of infant milk formula distribution,[8] before which pharmacies had the exclusive distribution of the whole group of baby and follow-on formulas.[9]

The incorporation of the European regulation (Commission Directive, 321/CEE of 1991) on milk preparations into the Spanish law was made effective in 1992.[10] However, such specific laws did not actually regulate the aspects concerning the distribution and sales of infant formula and follow-on formulas. In this sense, the European regulation on the matter does not regulate nor does it impose any kind of limitation for the distribution and sales of those groups of products.

The *Real Decreto 46/1996* marks the end of pharmacies' exclusive distribution rights for infant and follow-on preparations throughout the country. This law allows for the distribution of these products not only by pharmacies but also by any other food retailer.[11]

However, consumers have hardly noticed any significant effect of this liberalization, especially with respect to availability of certain products at alternative distribution points. That is, the brands of infant formula which were distributed exclusively by drugstores before the abovementioned regulation, were not afterwards distributed by any other food retailer.

Recently, the opening of numerous para-pharmacies offers a new, high-quality alternative point of distribution of para-pharmaceutical products. Although there is no specific regulation concerning the qualifications of own-

---

[8] *Real Decreto 46/1996, 19/1/1996.*

[9] *Real Decreto 2685/1976, 16/10/1976* and *Real Decreto 1426/1988, 25/11/1988.* The liberalization, some years ago, of the swaddling clothes is another example of para-pharmaceutical product that was distributed exclusively by pharmacies in Spain.

[10] *Real Decreto 1408/1992, 20/11/1992.*

[11] Following the definition of *foodstuff retailer* included in the *Real Decreto 381/1984*, which regulates the Spanish feeding retailer trade.

ers or employees of para-pharmacies, most of them are run by pharmacists or employ a pharmacist. This seems to be a reaction of the market to the efforts by the state to liberalize the distribution of para-pharmaceutical products. Despite this, the manufacturers of certain para-pharmaceutical products still grant exclusive distribution rights to pharmacies and some pharmacies will not distribute a product which is also distributed by a para-pharmacy. This can be easily understood, given the importance of para-pharmaceutical products for pharmacies in Spain (50% of the total sales).

The state should take measures to guarantee the actual liberalization of the sector, having in mind that, following the Spanish regulation on the matter, "the *pharmacy* is the sanitary store which offers assistential pharmaceutical activities and services as well as public care services in the cases and circumstances already determined or to be determined."[12] This means that the new para-pharmacies should not be seen as a threat for pharmacists but as a guarantee that pharmacies will recover their social role.[13]

15.3 A Model of Para-pharmaceutical Distribution

The model is constructed to allow for vertical quality differences as well as the horizontal differentiation aspect of standard location models. Other characteristics of the specific case under study are also taken into account.

Firms are uniformly distributed along the periphery of a circle. More specifically, we assume that drugstore density is exogenously given and constant along a circle, whereas alternative distribution points are a multiple of the number of drugstores. We allow consumers to have two different reservation prices for the same product, one if purchased at a pharmacy and one if purchased elsewhere. Furthermore, given that (especially in the case of milk for babies, in which the child specialist prescribes the brand to be bought) the consumer always buys the product from one establishment or another, we assume that, in any case, reservation prices are high enough so that, in equilibrium, all consumers are served.

Let n drugstores and mn alternative distribution points be uniformly distributed along a unit periphery circle, so that $(m+1)n$ firm locations are

[12] See art. 1, *Orden 17/1/1980.*

[13] See Beunza (1996).

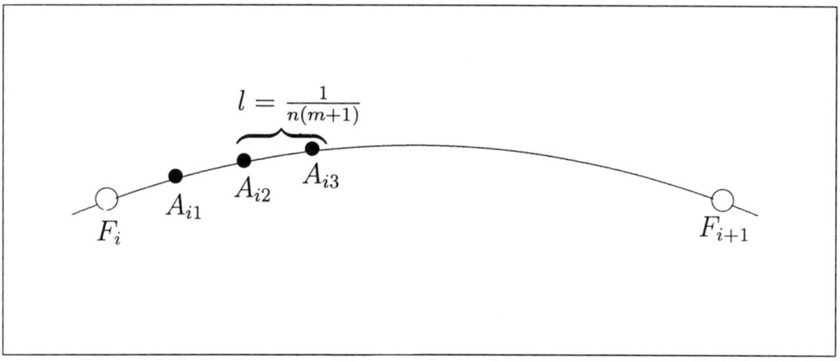

Figure 15.1: Equidistant arrangement with m alternative distribution points $(A_{i1}, A_{2i}, ..., A_{im})$ between two pharmacies $(i, i+1)$ on a unit-periphery circle with n equidistantly-distributed pharmacies.

equidistantly distributed around the circle. Then, we use $l = 1/n(m+1)$ to denote the distance between two adjacent distribution points (see Figure 15.1).[14] Consumers are uniformly distributed around the circle with a density $d = 1$. Each consumer buys one unit of the product, which is homogeneous except for a *subjectively* perceived characteristic that is represented by the distance along the circle from the consumer's location to the purchase point[15] and an *objectively* perceived difference in service quality, reflected by different reservation prices for purchases effected at locations of drugstores and those of alternative distribution points.[16] Then the purchase of a unit of the good

[14]The symmetric (equidistant) arrangement of drugstores along the circle and of alternative distribution points between two drugstores is a special case of a much larger number of arrangements with non-symmetric drugstore or alternative distributors location. However, the symmetric setup can give insights on those arrangements too, by varying the relative (constant) density of the two types of stores.

[15]Which is interpreted, here, as an abstraction of the physical space, rather than the usual interpretation of a product space representing a continuum of product characteristics.

[16]An alternative way of modelling quality differences can be found in Bresnahan (1981), who assumes that consumers have different marginal rates of substitution between the quality of a good and all other goods. Given the partial equilibrium nature of our model, the reservation price for purchasing a para-pharmaceutical product from a pharmacy or from an alternative distributor, reflects the total surplus that the consumer is willing to shift from other goods to the purchase of the product from one distributor or the other. Then, our framework could be seen as the *inelastic demand* analogous of the marginal rate of substitution approach suggested by Bresnahan (1981).

by a consumer located at X will yield a utility

$$U_X = R - P_i - T_{XF_i} \tag{15.1}$$

if she purchases the good from a drugstore F_i, and

$$U_X = r - p_{ij} - T_{XA_{ij}} \tag{15.2}$$

if she purchases the good from an alternative distribution point located at A_{ij}, where P_i and p_{ij} are respectively the prices charged by the drugstore and the alternative distributor and R, r are the corresponding maximum levels of expenditure that the consumer would accept to pay for a unit of the good (depending on whether this is bought in a drugstore or elsewhere). Furthermore, $T_x = tx$ is a linear[17] transportation cost function. It will be convenient to denote locations with capital letters and distances with small letters. Drugstore locations are denoted by F_i and locations of alternative distribution points between drugstores F_i and F_{i+1} are denoted by A_{ij}, with $i \in \{1, 2...n\}$ and $j \in \{1, 2, ..m\}$.

Furthermore, given a set of prices $S = (P_i, p_{i1}, ..., p_{im})$, if the consumer location between a pharmacy and the first alternative distribution point as we move clockwise on the circle is such that

$$U_{X,F_i} > U_{X,A_{i1}} \tag{15.3}$$

the consumer will buy one unit of the good at the pharmacy. If inequality (15.3) is reversed, she will purchase the good from the alternative distribution point A_{i1}. By analogy, a consumer located between the two alternative distribution points A_{ij} and A_{ij+1} will purchase the good at A_{ij} if

$$U_{X,A_{ij}} > U_{X,A_{ij+1}} \tag{15.4}$$

and at A_{ij+1} otherwise. Then, from (15.1), (15.2) and (15.3), we can calculate the distance $x_i = XF_i$ between the location X of a consumer who is indifferent between a pharmacy and the first alternative distribution point as we move clockwise on the circle:

$$x_i = XF_i = \frac{R - r + p_{i1} - P_i}{2t} + \frac{1}{2(m+1)n} \tag{15.5}$$

[17]Similar results can be obtained, assuming a quadratic or linear-quadratic transportation cost functions. However, the analytical expressions of equilibrium magnitudes are far more difficult to derive and interpret than those obtained here.

and, from (15.2) and (15.4) the distance $x_{ij} = XA_{ij}$ between the location of a consumer who is indifferent between two adjacent alternative distribution points A_{ij} and A_{ij+1}:

$$x_{ij} = XA_{ij} = \frac{p_{ij+1} - p_{ij}}{2t} + \frac{1}{2(m+1)n} \tag{15.6}$$

Finally, by analogy, we obtain the distance $x_{i-1m} = XA_{i-1m}$ between an alternative point A_{i-1m} and the adjacent (moving clockwise on the circle) pharmacy F_i:

$$x_{i-1m} = XA_{i-1m} = \frac{P_i - p_{i-1m} - (R-r)}{2t} + \frac{1}{2(m+1)n} \tag{15.7}$$

Given that consumer density around the circle is constant and equal to 1, the profit of each type of firm can be written

$$\Pi_i = (P_i - c)\left(x_i + \frac{1}{2(m+1)n} - x_{i-1m}\right)$$

$$= (P_i - c)\left(\frac{2(R - r - P_i) + p_{i1} + p_{i-1m}}{t} + \frac{1}{(m+1)n}\right) \tag{15.8}$$

for pharmacy F_i (equations (15.5) and (15.7)), where c is the constant marginal cost of distribution, and

$$\Pi_{i1} = (p_{i1} - c)\left(x_{i1} + \frac{1}{(m+1)n} - x_i\right)$$

$$= (p_{i1} - c)\left(\frac{P_i + p_{i2} - (R-r) - 2p_{i1})}{2t} + \frac{1}{(m+1)n}\right) \tag{15.9}$$

for an alternative distribution point A_{i1} next to pharmacy F_i (equations (15.5) and (15.6)), and

$$\Pi_{ij} = (p_{ij} - c)\left(x_{ij} + \frac{1}{(m+1)n} - x_{ij-1}\right) =$$

$$= (p_{ij} - c)\left(\frac{p_{ij-1} + p_{ij+1} - 2p_{ij})}{2t} + \frac{1}{(m+1)n}\right) \tag{15.10}$$

for an alternative distribution point A_{ij} between two distribution points A_{ij-1} and A_{ij+1} (equation (15.6)).

Prices can be written as $P_i = c + z_i$ and $p_{ij} = c + z_{ij}$, where z_i is the price-cost margin for pharmacy F_i and z_{ij} is the price-cost margin for an alternative distribution point A_{ij}. Firms compete in prices and Bertrand-Nash equilibrium implies that each firm maximizes its own payoff, taking the prices of neighboring firms as given. This yields a system of $n(m+1)$ equations in the $n(m+1)$ unknown variables (equilibrium prices).

Given the symmetric arrangement of pharmacies around the circle and of alternative distribution points, we can drop the pharmacy-specific subscript. The analytical expression of the solution with respect to m is too complicated to yield meaningful insights. In Table 15.1, we give the numerical values of equilibrium price-cost margins and market boundaries for $m \in \{0, 1, 2, 3, 4, 5\}$.[18]

Furthermore, we calculate (Table 15.2) consumer and producer surplus — CS and PS[19] — for each case and characterize (Table 15.3) the difference of each one of these magnitudes (respectively, CE and PE) from those of the $m = 0$ case (in which distribution rights are exclusively granted to pharmacies).

The overall welfare effect of a decision to liberalize the distribution (for an exogenously given relative density of alternative distribution points) is the sum of the two changes (that is, $TE = CE + PE$). Finally, given the economic meaning of the difference $R - r$ and the frequency with which it appears in the resulting formulas, we write $g = R - r$ for notational simplicity whenever possible. In each case, we have restricted the analysis to those values of g for which all equilibrium margins are non-negative, so that all configurations under study are non-trivial (see line $z > 0$, Table 15.1).[20]

[18] The analysis is restricted to these values of m because the ratio of alternative distribution points of para-pharmaceutical products (cosmetics dealers, supermarkets, para-pharmacies, etc.) per pharmacy fluctuates — depending on the city — between 1 and 4.

[19] The analytical expressions are: $CS = n(\int_{y=0}^{x}(R - P - ty)dy + \int_{y=0}^{l-x}(r - p_1 - ty)dy + \int_{y=0}^{x_1}(r - p_1 - ty)dy + ... + \int_{y=0}^{l-x_m}(R - P - ty)dy)$ and $PS = n(\Pi + \sum_{j=1}^{m}\Pi_j)$ respectively.

[20] With some algebra it can be shown that the restriction is also sufficient to guarantee non-negative shares of all firms on the circle. However, one should bear in mind that due to the asymmetry introduced by a positive $g = R - r$, the condition for a non-negative market share does not coincide with the condition of positive market shares on both sides (clockwise and counterclockwise) of each firm's location. That is, an alternative distribution point may sell nothing on the segment of the circle on which it neighbors with a pharmacy, while having positive sales on the segment on which the firm competes with another alternative distribution point.

	$m=0$	$m=1$	$m=2$	$m=3$	$m=4$	$m=5$
l	$\frac{1}{n}$	$\frac{1}{2n}$	$\frac{1}{3n}$	$\frac{1}{4n}$	$\frac{1}{5n}$	$\frac{1}{6n}$
z	$\frac{t}{n}$	$\frac{t}{2n}+\frac{g}{3}$	$\frac{t}{3n}+\frac{2g}{5}$	$\frac{t}{4n}+\frac{5g}{12}$	$\frac{t}{5n}+\frac{8g}{19}$	$\frac{t}{6n}+\frac{19g}{45}$
z_1	—	$\frac{t}{2n}-\frac{g}{3}$	$\frac{t}{3n}-\frac{g}{5}$	$\frac{t}{4n}-\frac{g}{6}$	$\frac{t}{5n}-\frac{3g}{19}$	$\frac{t}{6n}-\frac{7g}{45}$
z_2	—	—	$\frac{t}{3n}-\frac{g}{5}$	$\frac{t}{4n}-\frac{g}{12}$	$\frac{t}{5n}-\frac{g}{19}$	$\frac{t}{6n}-\frac{2g}{45}$
z_3	—	—	—	$\frac{t}{4n}-\frac{g}{6}$	$\frac{t}{5n}-\frac{g}{19}$	$\frac{t}{6n}-\frac{g}{45}$
z_4	—	—	—	—	$\frac{t}{5n}-\frac{3g}{19}$	$\frac{t}{6n}-\frac{2g}{45}$
z_5	—	—	—	—	—	$\frac{t}{6n}-\frac{7g}{45}$
x	$\frac{1}{2n}$	$\frac{1}{4n}+\frac{g}{6t}$	$\frac{1}{6n}+\frac{g}{5t}$	$\frac{1}{8n}+\frac{5g}{24t}$	$\frac{1}{10n}+\frac{4g}{19t}$	$\frac{1}{12n}+\frac{19g}{90t}$
x_1	—	$\frac{1}{4n}-\frac{g}{6t}$	$\frac{1}{6n}$	$\frac{1}{8n}+\frac{g}{24t}$	$\frac{1}{10n}+\frac{g}{19t}$	$\frac{1}{12n}+\frac{g}{18t}$
x_2	—	—	$\frac{1}{6n}-\frac{g}{5t}$	$\frac{1}{8n}-\frac{5g}{24t}$	$\frac{1}{10n}$	$\frac{1}{12n}-\frac{g}{90t}$
x_3	—	—	—	$\frac{1}{8n}-\frac{5g}{24t}$	$\frac{1}{10n}-\frac{g}{19t}$	$\frac{1}{12n}-\frac{g}{90t}$
x_4	—	—	—	—	$\frac{1}{10n}-\frac{4g}{19t}$	$\frac{1}{12n}-\frac{g}{18t}$
x_5	—	—	—	—	—	$\frac{1}{12n}-\frac{19g}{90t}$
z's >0	$\forall g$	$g<\frac{3t}{2n}$	$g<\frac{5t}{3n}$	$g<\frac{3t}{2n}$	$g<\frac{19t}{15n}$	$g<\frac{45t}{42n}$

Table 15.1: l: distance between adjacent firms; z: price-cost margin; x: distance between indifferent consumer and counter-clockwise firm, z's >0 line; conditions for positive price-cost margins; $g=R-r$.

	CS	PS	CE	PE
$m=0$	$R-\frac{5t}{4n}-c$	(t/n)	0	0
$m=1$	$\frac{R+r}{2}+\frac{ng^2}{18t}-\frac{5t}{8n}-c$	$\frac{4ng^2}{18t}+\frac{t}{2n}$	$\frac{ng^2}{18t}-\frac{g}{2}+\frac{5t}{8n}$	$\frac{2ng^2}{9t}-\frac{t}{2n}$
$m=2$	$\frac{R+2r}{3}+\frac{2ng^2}{25t}-\frac{5t}{12n}-c$	$\frac{6ng^2}{25t}+\frac{t}{3n}$	$\frac{2ng^2}{25t}-\frac{2g}{3}+\frac{5t}{6n}$	$\frac{6ng^2}{25t}-\frac{2t}{3n}$
$m=3$	$\frac{R+3r}{4}+\frac{13ng^2}{144t}-\frac{5t}{16n}-c$	$\frac{17ng^2}{72t}+\frac{t}{4n}$	$\frac{13ng^2}{144t}-\frac{3g}{4}+\frac{15t}{16n}$	$\frac{17ng^2}{72t}-\frac{3t}{4n}$
$m=4$	$\frac{R+4r}{5}+\frac{34ng^2}{361t}-\frac{5t}{20n}-c$	$\frac{84ng^2}{361t}+\frac{t}{5n}$	$\frac{34ng^2}{361t}-\frac{4g}{5}+\frac{t}{n}$	$\frac{21ng^2}{361t}-\frac{4t}{5n}$
$m=5$	$\frac{R+5r}{6}+\frac{43ng^2}{450t}-\frac{5t}{24n}-c$	$\frac{52ng^2}{225t}+\frac{t}{6n}$	$\frac{43ng^2}{450t}-\frac{5g}{6}+\frac{25t}{24n}$	$\frac{52ng^2}{225t}-\frac{5t}{6n}$

Table 15.2: CE, PE: effects of liberalization on producer, and consumer surplus; $TE = CE + PE$; $g = R - r$.

	$CE > 0$	$PE < 0$	$TE > 0$
$m = 0$	$CE \equiv 0$	$PE \equiv 0$	$TE \equiv 0$
$m = 1$	$g < 1.5(t/n)$ $g > 7.5(t/n)$	$\lvert g\rvert < 1.5(t/n)$	$g < 0.3(t/n)$ $g > 1.5(t/n)$
$m = 2$	$g < 1.53(t/n) <$ $g > 6.80(t/n)$	$\lvert g\rvert < 1.67(t/n)$	$g < 0.29(t/n)$ $g > 1.79(t/n)$
$m = 3$	$g < 1.53(t/n)$ $g > 6.77(t/n)$	$\lvert g\rvert < 1.78(t/n)$	$g < 0.28(t/n)$ $g > 2.01(t/n)$
$m = 4$	$g < 1.52(t/n)$ $g > 6.97(t/n)$	$\lvert g\rvert < 1.85(t/n)$	$g < 0.28(t/n)$ $g > 2.16(t/n)$
$m = 5$	$g < 1.51(t/n)$ $g > 7.20(t/n)$	$\lvert g\rvert < 1.90(t/n)$	$g < 0.28(t/n)$ $g > 2.27(t/n)$

Table 15.3: CE, PE, TE: effects of liberalization on producer, consumer, and total surplus; $g = R - r$.

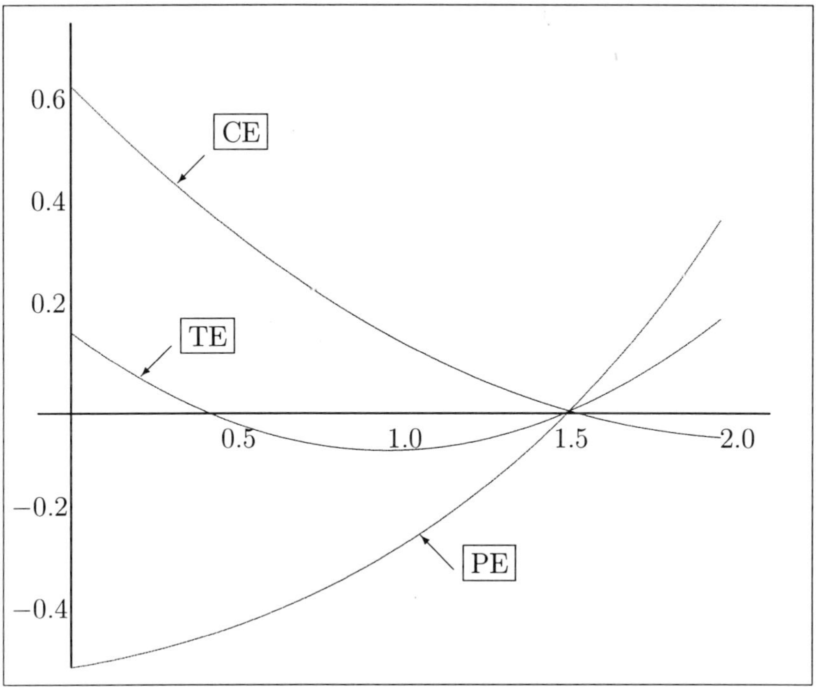

Figure 15.2: Consumer, producer and total surplus effects of introducing $m = 1$ alternative distribution points for $g < 1.5/n$.

We concentrate on the main conclusions drawn from the theoretical model, especially with respect to the effect of a liberalization decision on consumer, producer and total surplus. In all cases, the introduction of alternative distribution points yields lower prices and reduces transportation costs. This result would be expected based on standard spatial competition models.

However, this result has limited relevance in assessing the effects of a decision to liberalize the distribution of para-pharmaceutical products, if the *service quality* argument is to be taken into account. In the presence of a non-negative $g = R - r$, the introduction of alternative distribution points shifts demand from the high to the low quality distributor. Nevertheless, the effect of liberalization on consumer surplus is almost always positive, unless the difference between the qualities of the two types of service is very high and the relative density of alternative distribution points to pharmacies is 2 (see the $m = 2$ case in Figure 15.3, when $1.53(t/n) < g < 1.67(t/n)$).

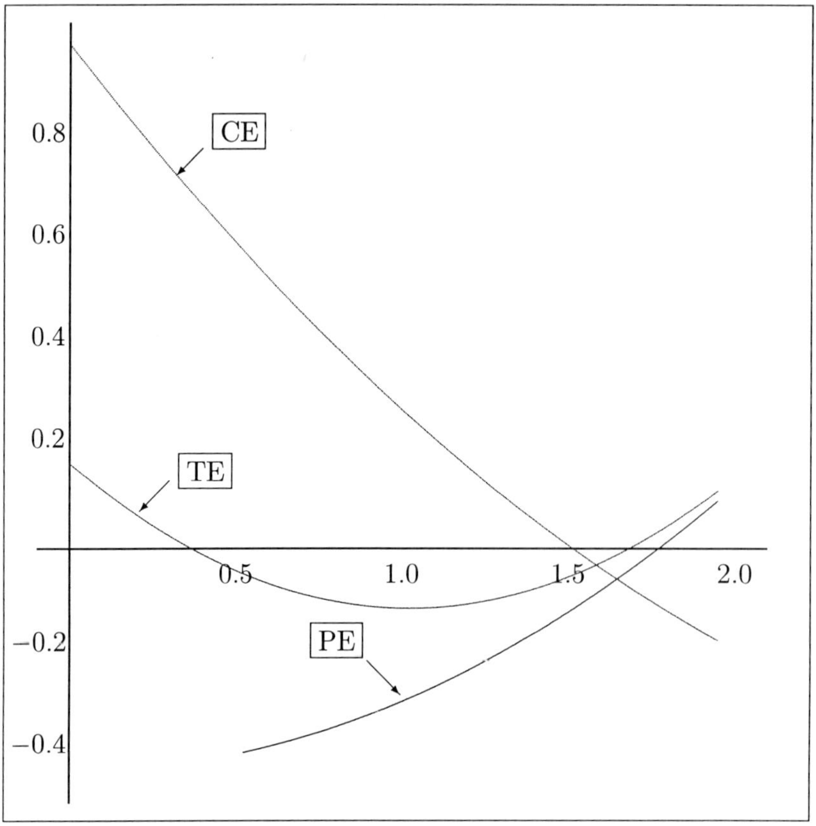

Figure 15.3: Consumer, producer and total surplus effects of introducing $m = 2$ alternative distribution points for $g < 1.67/n$.

In contrast, the effect of liberalizing the distribution of para-pharmaceutical products on producer surplus is always negative. This is so not only because of the usual intensity-of-competition effect of an increase in the number of rivals, but also because demand is shifted to low-quality service and therefore less profitable distributors. However, the total effect of liberalization ($TE = CE + PE$) may be of either sign, depending on the difference between the qualities of the two types of service. We see that in this model the critical value fluctuates between $g = 0.3(t/n)$ (in the $m = 1$ case) and $g = 0.2809(t/n)$ (in the $m = 5$ case).

Figures 15.2–15.6 illustrate the preceding remarks. Furthermore, we can

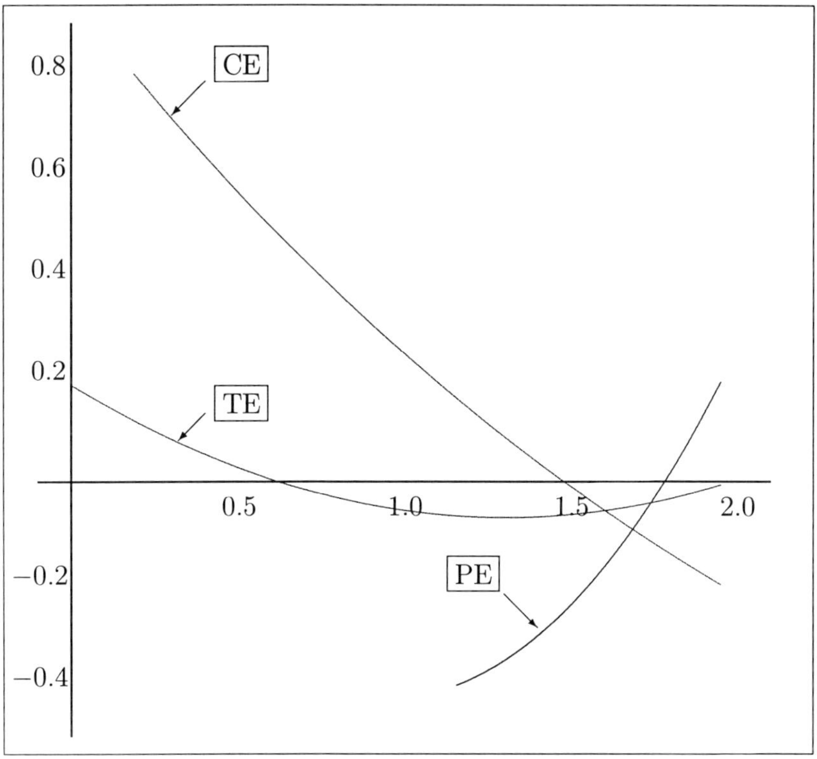

Figure 15.4: Consumer, producer and total surplus effects of introducing $m = 3$ alternative distribution points for $g < 1.5/n$.

summarize other properties of the theoretical framework as follows (which could also be understood by referring to Tables 15.1, 15.2, 15.3), assuming that $g = R - r > 0$:

- Alternative distribution points set lower price-cost margins than do pharmacies and the difference is proportional to $g = R - r$;
- The further an alternative distribution point is from the location next to a pharmacy, the higher the price-cost margin it sets;
- The marginal cost of the product has a negative effect on consumer surplus, whereas it leaves producer surplus and the impact of liberalization on consumer, producer and total surpluses unaffected;

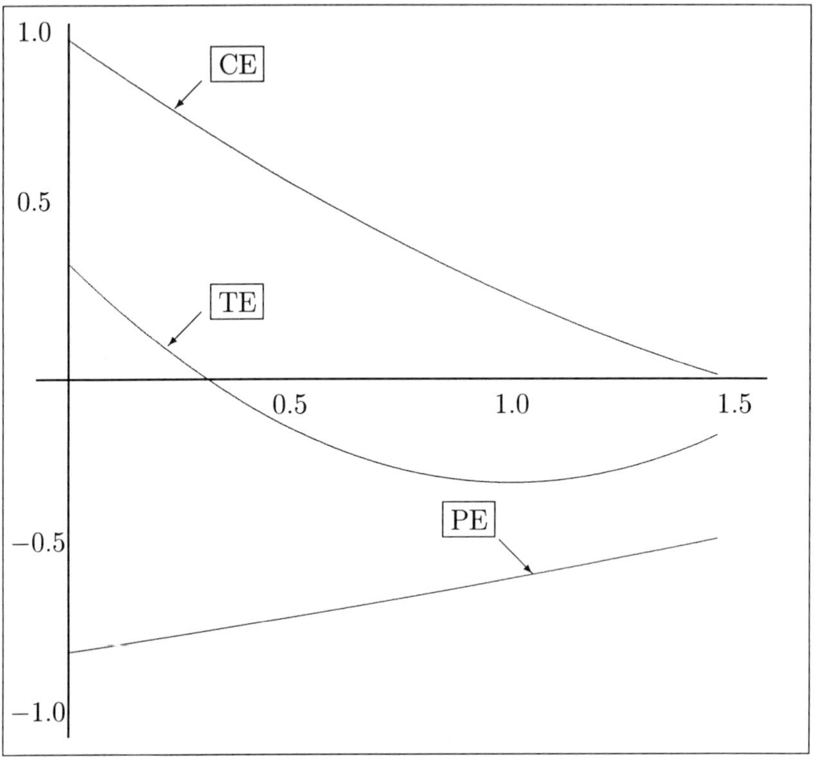

Figure 15.5: Consumer, producer and total surplus effects of introducing $m = 4$ alternative distribution points for $g < 1.26/n$.

- The critical value of $g = R - r$, below which the configurations under study ($m = 1$ to $m = 5$) are non-trivial, behaves in a non-monotonic way with respect to m[21] — and the same is true for the value, below which the effect of liberalization on consumer welfare is positive;[22]
- The critical value of $g = R - r$ below which the total effect of liberalization on social welfare is positive decreases monotonically with m.[23]

In the following section, we discuss the results of the theoretical model

[21]Taking the values $1.5\frac{t}{n}$, $1.66\frac{t}{n}$, $1.5\frac{t}{n}$, $1.26\frac{t}{n}$, $1.07\frac{t}{n}$ for $m = 1, 2, 3, 4, 5$.
[22]Taking the values $1.5\frac{t}{n}$, $1.531\frac{t}{n}$, $1.533\frac{t}{n}$, $1.523\frac{t}{n}$, $1.512\frac{t}{n}$ for $m = 1, 2, 3, 4, 5$.
[23]Taking the values $0.3\frac{t}{n}$, $0.291\frac{t}{n}$, $0.285\frac{t}{n}$, $0.283\frac{t}{n}$, $0.281\frac{t}{n}$ for $m = 1, 2, 3, 4, 5$.

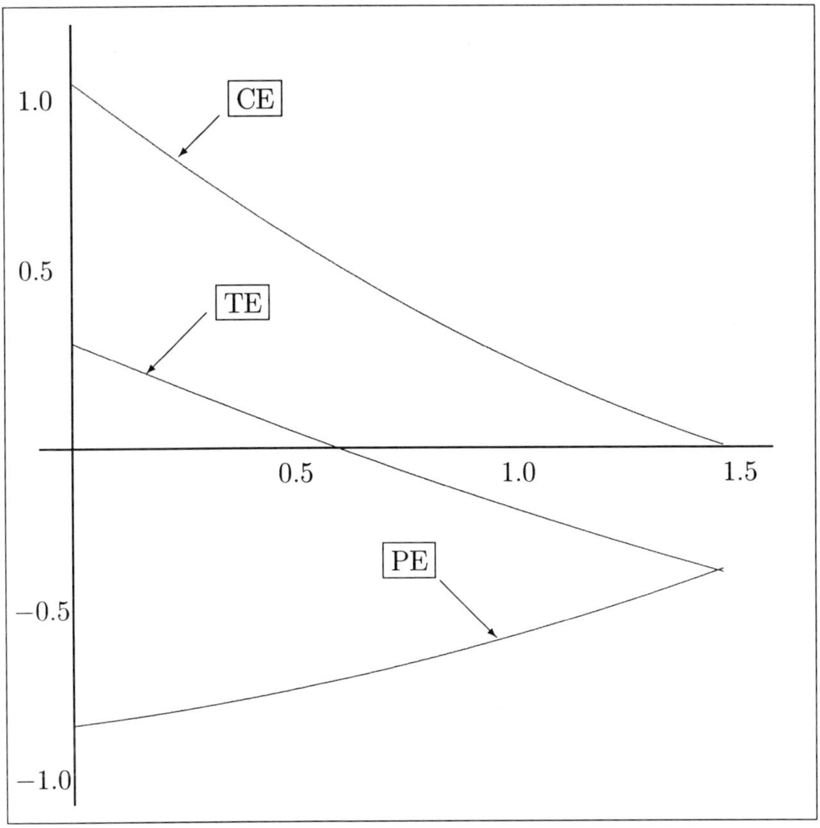

Figure 15.6: Consumer, producer and total surplus effects of introducing $m = 5$ alternative distribution points for $g < 1.07/n$.

and their implications for economic policy.

15.4 Applying the Model in a Real-World Case

The theoretical framework proposed here compares a situation in which fewer firms offer a high quality service with the alternative situation in which the number of firms increases by letting another type of firm, offering a lower quality service, enter into the market. The number of firms is exogenous. This is a reasonable way to reflect the fact that in the case under study the number of pharmacies and other potential or actual distributors of para-pharmaceutical products does not vary with the decision of any type of firm to distribute (or give up the distribution of) para-pharmaceutical products. Furthermore, our intention is to propose a theoretical framework which could help the policy-maker decide whether a free-entry regime or, alternatively, some selective rule (according to the type of product) for partial regulation should be adopted. On one hand, the number of pharmacies is determined by the state on the basis of criteria that have nothing to do with the distribution of para-pharmaceutical products. On the other hand, the number of alternative distribution points depends on the profitability of a large bundle of goods, rather than on the decision of certain manufacturers of para-pharmaceutical products to grant exclusive distribution rights to pharmacists or not.

Our theoretical results indicate that policy-makers should try to quantify the difference between the quality of service offered by pharmacists and the quality of service offered by alternative distributors of para-pharmaceutical products. The perception of this difference by the consumer would be reflected in different maximum levels of expenditure that the consumer would be willing to make in order to purchase a unit of the same para-pharmaceutical product at a drugstore and elsewhere. The relevance of the parameter g in assessing the effects of liberalization on consumer surplus and social welfare has been implicitly recognized by both the consumer and the pharmacists. On one hand, in a recent communication to the authorities, the consumers' association in Spain explicitly refer to their perception of a very small difference between the service they are offered in pharmacies and the service that they could expect to get elsewhere. On the other hand, the Pharmacists' Association in a recent campaign "informs" the consumer of the quality of the service they are offered by pharmacists all over Spain, extending the benefits from such a high quality service to "other products." Therefore, what seems to be the question is *not* whether the difference in service qualities could be sufficient to offset the social gains from more competition. Instead, the problem is how to quantify the difference in service qualities from the information available to us.

15.4.1 An application of the model

In the model, the difference in service quality is common knowledge. In the real world, the difference is implicit in consumer behavior and firms' pricing strategies. Therefore we can approximate g using information on observable magnitudes such as price-cost margins.[24]

Let us first consider an example in order to make our policy recommendations clear. Let us suppose that after the *selective* liberalization of the distribution of a certain para-pharmaceutical product, cosmetics dealers, whose relative density to pharmacies is $m = 1$ (that is, there are as many cosmetics dealers as drugstores), are allowed to distribute the product too. Furthermore, cosmetics shops sell the product 100 pesetas cheaper than do the pharmacies. Write $z(m)$ for pharmacies' equilibrium price-cost margin; $z(0) = (t/n)$. Then, all necessary information on t and n can be obtained from the price-cost margin of pharmacies before liberalization. Let the margin of pharmacies as exclusive dealers of the product be $z(0) = 600$.[25]

Assuming that the difference in prices is due to the difference in service qualities as perceived by the consumer,[26] we can calculate $g = 1.5\Delta P = 150$, where ΔP is the difference in prices (here, $\Delta P = 100$) and, in the theoretical model, corresponds to the difference $z(1) - z_1(1) = (2g/3)$ (see the $m = 1$ column in Table 15.1). From Table 15.3, we see that, if $g < 0.3(t/n)$, the proposed liberalization improves social welfare. In this example, this is true because $150 < 0.3 \cdot 600 = 180$. In fact, there is a critical value $V(1) = 5$, with $V(1) = z(0)/[z(1) - z_1(1)]$, above which the liberalization improves social welfare.

In Table 15.4, we present the critical values of V. Note that for $m = 3$ and $m = 4$ there are two critical values. The first must be used for alternative distribution points directly competing with a pharmacy and the second

---

[24] The literature on prices as signals of quality (Farrell, 1980; Wolinsky, 1983) has very little to do with the theoretical framework suggested here, given that, in the aforementioned literature, the consumer is assumed to have imperfect information on product quality, whereas in our model there is perfect information on qualities. The only informational imperfection appears when we try to apply our model to the case under study and it is the result of imperfect information of the policy-maker about g.

[25] This means that in order to apply our model in real world cases we should make sure that price-cost margins are a decreasing function of the number of firms. With sufficient data on price-cost margins for different para-pharmaceutical products sold in cities with different population and retailer densities, we could estimate the coefficients of the regression: $ln(z) = aln(t) - bln(n)$. For a similar application of the competition on the circle model in the banking sector in Spain, see Fuentelsaz and Salas (1992).

[26] This assumption implies that the cost of the product to both types of distributors must be the same. In other words, we should make sure that the cost structures of the establishments under study are similar. Then, the comparison of cosmetics dealers and drugstores is more likely to give us liable information than the comparison between drugstores and supermarkets.

	$m=1$	$m=2$	$m=3$	$m=4$	$m=5$
V_1	5.0000	5.7372	6.0066	6.1120	6.1615
V_2	—	—	7.0077	7.4703	7.6285
V_3	—	—	—	—	8.0099

Table 15.4: Critical values of $V_j = z(0)/[z(i)-z_j(i)]\ \forall i \in \{1,2,3,...,m\} \wedge \forall j \in \{1,2,3,...,m\}$, above which the introduction of m alternative distributors improves social welfare (note that, in each case, there are as many different values of V as types — regarding their location with respect to the nearest pharmacy — of alternative distribution points per pharmacy). The smaller the difference in post-liberalization price-cost margins and/or the larger the pre-liberalization price-cost margin of the pharmacists, the more likely it is that liberalization is social-welfare enhancing, whereas, the larger the relative density of alternative distributors per pharmacy, the higher the critical value of V above which liberalization is socially desirable.

for alternative distribution points whose neighboring rivals do not include pharmacies. Finally, for $m = 5$ there are three critical values which should be used in a similar way, depending on whether the distribution point under study has a pharmacy as a neighbor (first critical value), or a neighbor of it does (second critical value) or whether neither of the two is true (third critical value). The results indicate that the higher the pre-liberalization price-cost margin of pharmacies and the lower the post-liberalization price difference, the more likely it is that the liberalization improves social welfare. However, the introduction of a larger number of alternative distribution points is less likely to improve social welfare as compared to a policy leading to a partial or selective liberalization introducing a smaller number of alternative distribution points (compare, for example, $m = 2$ with $m = 5$ in Table 15.3). This contradicts the standard result concerning a positive relation between number of rivals or competition intensity and social welfare.

15.4.2 Applying the model when retailers' costs differ

Let us assume that the cost structures of pharmacies and other retailers of para-pharmaceutical products are different, so that C represents the marginal cost of pharmacies and c the marginal cost of other retailers. Then it is easy to show that equilibrium price-cost margins and the critical values presented in Table 15.4 are the same if we replace $g = R - r$ with $g' = R - r - (C - c)$.

Then the critical values presented in Table 15.4 are valid whether costs differ across distributors or not, provided that information on post-liberalization differences in price-cost margins is available. That is, the main difference between the application of the model with and without cost asymmetries is that when costs differ across different types of retailers, we need information on differences in post-liberalization price-cost margins, rather than information on prices.[27]

We would expect that the assumption of cost differences between different types of retailers is more realistic.[28] This would be so, because the wholesale price, the average size of the establishment, the variety of other products sold in it and the qualifications of the employees are likely to differ across different types of establishments.[29]. Unless we are sure that two types of retailers have very similar cost structures — which is very unlikely to be the case here — price-differences may be a misleading proxy for differences in service-quality. Nevertheless, we have seen that the critical values presented in Table 15.4 are robust in cost differences if they are used in the strict sense (that is, differences in price-cost margins are not assumed to be equal to price-differences, unless cost-differences are accounted for).[30]

An example

We assess the effects of the recent liberalization of the distribution of some para-pharmaceutical products, applying the results of the theoretical model presented earlier. Price and cost data are averages from a sample of drugstores, small supermarkets, large supermarkets and para-pharmacies in the Spanish city of Castellón; the sample includes two new para-pharmacies opened at a very small distance from the center of the city.[31]

Given the small data set, which was collected from an area around the center of the city, we cannot test for the relation between price-cost margins and number of firms. Therefore, in the example, we assume that the observed price-cost margins are the result of a mechanism which can be approximated

[27] Which is, generally speaking, easier to obtain.

[28] Which is, generally speaking, easier to obtain.

[29] Which is, generally speaking, easier to obtain.

[30] Which is, generally speaking, easier to obtain.

[31] Given that Castellón is a relatively small Spanish city of approximately 150000 inhabitants, two new establishments mean a surprisingly high rate, especially considering the fact that this type of establishment is very new in Spain altogether.

	Byly	*Dodot*	Sandoz (Mod. 2)
Pharmacy	495	1645	2190
Para-pharmacy	490	1621	2335
Supermarket (small)	—	1545	—
Supermarket (large)	—	1481	—
Pharmacy (pre-librl.)	500	1745	2200

Table 15.5: **Prices** (in Spanish Pesetas)

	Byly	*Dodot*	Sandoz (Mod. 2)
Pharmacy	356	1316	1752
Para-pharmacy	360	1316	1951
Supermarket (small)	—	1285	—
Supermarket (large)	—	1224	—

Table 15.6: **Unit Cost** (in Spanish Pesetas)

by our theoretical model.

We have chosen three products each one of which belongs to one of three large groups of para-pharmaceutical products: cosmetics, foodstuff for babies and other para-pharmaceutical products requiring little if any information or advice by the retailer to the consumer. *Byly* is a deodorant in form of a cream, distributed in tubes of 35 gr. *Sandoz-Modar 2*, distributed in boxes containing 800 gr. of milk in powder is a follow-on formula for babies up to 3 years old. Finally, *Dodot* (package containing 50 units) is a brand of diapers for babies from 8 to 12 months old.

Using our data on price-cost margins, we have calculated

$$V = \frac{z_{pharm}^{pre-lib}}{z_{pharm}^{post-lib} - z_{other}^{post-lib}}. \tag{15.11}$$

The estimated values of V are well above critical levels (Table 15.4), especially for products distributed by para-pharmacies. The distribution of the products under study by supermarkets (small and large) would pass the test too. Nevertheless, in the two latter cases, the small difference between the estimated and the critical values and the small size of our sample indicate that, before reaching a conclusion on the effect of a general liberalization of the distribution of para-pharmaceutical products by *any* type of retailer,

	Byly	*Dodot*	Sandoz (Mod. 2)
Pharmacy	139	329	438
Para-pharmacy	130	305	384
Supermarket (small)	—	260	—
Supermarket (large)	—	257	—
Pharmacy (pre-librl.)	144	429	448

Table 15.7: **Price-Cost Margins** (in Spanish Pesetas)

	Byly	*Dodot*	Sandoz (Mod. 2)
Pharmacies and Para-pharmacies	16	–	8.29
Pharmacies, Para-pharmacies and Supermarkets	–	17.87 6.21 5.95	–

Table 15.8: Estimated Values of V (see Table T10.4)

we should test more carefully for the validity of our theoretical model using data on more products, collected from various cities with different population and retailer densities. For the moment, we could assert that a broader distribution network for para-pharmaceutical products is socially desirable if it consists of — at least — pharmacies *and para-pharmacies.*

15.5 Conclusions and Policy Implications

The addition of a *vertical differentiation* parameter in a model of price competition among firms located on the periphery of a circle may reverse the standard welfare implications of an exogenous increase in the number of firms. Especially when fixed costs are negligible, the relation between social welfare and competition intensity may be negative if the increase in the number of firms is a result of introducing more low-quality competitors. Furthermore, although the model might be applied to other real-world cases in which the policy-maker faces the *competition intensity vs. service quality* tradeoff, the framework exhibits several characteristics which are specific to the distribution of para-pharmaceutical products. In fact, we propose a rule of thumb to be adopted by the authorities when assessing the effects of *total, partial* or *selective liberalization* of the distribution of certain para-pharmaceutical products.

The liberalization of the distribution of certain para-pharmaceutical products in the past can improve our information on the service-quality parameter, given that the quality-service difference is likely to be perceived by the consumer in a similar way for similar products. That is, information about pre-liberalization price-cost margins of pharmacies and post-liberalization price-differences between drugstores and other distribution points in the case of *infant* and *follow-on formulas* is useful not only for an *ex post* policy assessment but also for an *ex ante* evaluation of such policies in the case of other similar products. We have to admit that this leaves unanswered the question of *which* products should be considered as *similar*. Nevertheless, we feel that a rough classification should include four main groups within each one of which the perceived service-quality difference between drugstores and alternative distribution points should not exhibit significant variations. The groups we would suggest are, according to the importance of specialized information at the moment of the purchase (in descending order): *pharmaceutical products without a doctor's prescription*, *cosmetics*, *infant and follow-on formulas* and *other*.

One may wonder why one should assess the effects of liberalization for a product whose distribution has already been successfully liberalized in the past, such as, for example, *infant formulas* or *cosmetics*. The reason is that the state is still too permissive with manufacturers wishing to grant exclusive distribution rights to pharmacies using the service quality argument as an excuse. If the distribution of products like infant formulas and cosmetics by non-pharmacy retail outlets has a positive effect on social welfare — surviving the *service-quality* difference argument — it would be reasonable to undertake general measures which could increase the number of distributors of those products. Especially with respect to certain para-pharmaceutical products whose consumers require little if any information at the time of purchase, any restriction of the distribution network leads to socially inferior market outcomes.

Passive liberalization, allowing the distribution of certain para-pharmaceutical products by alternative distribution points may not be sufficient for *actual liberalization* of the sector to be achieved. This can be easily seen if we compare the number of para-pharmaceutical products sold in pharmacies and in supermarkets. Even after the recent (passive) liberalization of the distribution of infant and follow-on formulas, it is almost impossible to find the same package, same brand of milk on the shelves of a pharmacy and those of a supermarket. In fact, the main difficulty in constructing a data set similar to that used above is that there are still very few products which are distributed by both pharmacies and other distributors of para-pharmaceutical products. The case of cosmetics is even more difficult to justify. A large number of cosmetics are sold with the warning: *"Only in Pharmacies,"* which is supposed to mean: *"More expensive, but better."* Measures of *active liberalization* would include, for example, a detailed examination of the reasons why such a distribution strategy — which challenges the right of cosmetics dealers to exercise freely their main activity — is defended and promoted by manufacturers as a guarantee of quality. If the service-quality argument were shown to constitute a valid reason not to liberalize the distribution of cosmetics or any other type of para-pharmaceutical products, a partial liberalization could offer a better alternative than no liberalization. Cosmetics dealers and the recently introduced *para-pharmacies* could offer an equally specialized service.

Finally, if the presence of a pharmacist is still considered an indispensable guarantee of service-quality, the increasing number of unemployed pharmacists could help to fill the gap. In terms of our model, the difference in service qualities could decrease if legislation encouraged the employment of pharmacists by cosmetics dealers or para-pharmacies. Then the introduction of other-than-pharmacy-retailers would be more likely to improve social welfare, given that the service-quality difference — which, throughout the paper, has been considered to be constant — would decrease. This seems to be realized by the owners of para-pharmacies. In fact, most para-pharmacies in Spain tend to employ pharmacists, if they are not run by one. The state could encourage the adoption of this practice by specific measures of active liberalization aiming at the equal treatment — by the manufacturer and the consumer of para-pharmaceutical products — of pharmacies and para-pharmacies, when the latter employ or are run by a pharmacist.

The service-quality difference between pharmacies and other types of establishments is undoubtedly a valid argument against liberalization of the distribution of products with therapeutic properties and complicated indications. In such cases, the information provided by the pharmacist to the consumer is an indispensable component of the product. Nevertheless, an increasing number of consumers in Spain complain about the quality of service in pharmacies, when they ask the pharmacist for a medical preparation (to be produced by the pharmacist within a reasonable amount of time) or any other low-priced therapeutic product. The low profitability of such products, as compared to the high profitability of cosmetics and other para-pharmaceutical products, may be responsible for the fact that the shelves of many modern drugstores look more like the shelves of a cosmetics dealer than like the shelves of a drugstore of ten years ago. It is often argued that when assessing the welfare implications of regulating the distribution of medicines, retailer surplus should be taken into account.. The same argument should then imply that any measure aiming at improving the pharmacists' profit opportunities as a compensation for their service to society should not imply shifting the pharmacist's main interest from medicines to other products. A more realistic theoretical framework should model the joint distribution of pharmaceutical and para-pharmaceutical products allowing for some (negative) effect of the co-existence of the two types of products on the service offered by the pharmacist to the consumer. It is straightforward to see why the results would be more clear-cut than the results of our model, in which the distribution of para-pharmaceutical products is studied separately from the distribution of pharmaceutical products.

15.6 References

Beunza, D. "Mucho más que dispensar: el nuevo papel que la sociedad exige a los farmaceúticos," Conference at the *Foro Farmaceútico de Valencia*, February 28, 1996.

Bresnahan, Timothy "Departures from marginal-cost pricing in the American automobile industry," *Journal of Econometrics* Volume 17, 1981, pp. 201–27.

EEC Commission Commission Directive 91/321/CEE, On Infant and Follow-on formulas, 14/5/1991.

El PAIS (weekly), No. 1025, Sunday, 19/5/1996.

Farrell, J. *Prices as Signals of Quality*, Ph.D. dissertation, Brasenose College, Oxford, 1980.

Fuentelsaz, L. and V. Salas *Estudios Sobre Banca al Por Menor*, Bilbao: Fundación BBV, 1992.

Garcia-Fontes, W. and M. Motta "Regulación de las Oficinas de Farmacia: Precios y Libertad de Entrada," in G. López and D. Rodriguez (editors) *La Regulación de los Servicios en España.* Madrid: Civitas, 1997.

Hotelling, Harold "Stability in Competition," *Economic Journal* Volume 39, 1929, pp. 41–57.

Jansson, E. "La Regulación de la Distribución de Medicamentos," *Actas de las XI Jornadas de Economía Industrial*, 1995, pp. 161–6.

Martin, Stephen *Advanced Industrial Economics*, Oxford: Blackwell Publishers, 1993.

Real Decreto 2685/1976, 16/10/1976.

Real Decreto 909/78, 14/4/1978.

Real Decreto 1408/1992, 20/11/1992.

Real Decreto 2259/1994, 25/10/1994.

Real Decreto 46/1996, 19/1/1996.

Rey, P. and J. Tirole "The Logic of Vertical Restraints," *American Economic Review* Volume 76, Number 5, 1986, pp. 921–39.

Salop, S. "Monopolistic Competition with Outside Goods," *Bell Journal of Economics* Volume 10, 1979, pp. 141–56.

Tirole, J. *The Theory of Industrial Organization*, Cambridge, Mass.: The MIT Press, 1988.

Tribunal de Defensa de la Competencia, *Remedios Políticos que Pueden Favorecer la Libre Competencia en los Servicios y Atajar el Daño Causado por los Monopolios*, Vols. 1–2, 1993.

Waterson, M. "Retail Pharmacy in Melbourne: Actual and Optimal Densities," *Journal of Industrial Economics* Volume 41, 1993, pp. 403–19.

Wolinsky, A. "Prices as Signals of Product Quality," *Review of Economic Studies* Volume 50, 1983, pp. 647–58.

Competition Policies in Europe - S. Martin (Editor)

Chapter 16

Impact of Community Competition Law on Member State Competition Law

Laraine L. Laudati

16.1 Introduction

In a substantial number of the European Union's Member States, antitrust is a relatively recent phenomenon. Prior to the formation of the European Community in 1957, regulation of competition essentially did not exist in any of the countries which were to become the Member States. France and Germany were the only founding nations to have competition laws at the time, but enforcement was virtually non-existent. The market mechanism was not accepted or relied upon as the means of controlling the industrial economy. Rather, the Member States all engaged in heavy interventionism, either through nationalization combined with uncontrolled state aid, or through over-regulation of industry, or both.

An essential corollary to creation of an economically integrated European Community was that the market mechanism would replace state intervention to control industrial economic relations. Thus, the Treaty of Rome incorporated this fundamental principle, and the substantive rules to regulate restrictive agreements, abuses of dominant position, and state aid incompatible with the common market.

Over the last four decades, Community antitrust rules and the integration process have had an impact on competition throughout the Community both because their enforcement has improved competitive conditions directly and because they have served as a stimulus to the Member States to enact competition laws which are consistent with Community law. Today, each of the fifteen Member States has a competition law covering restrictive agreements and abuses of dominant positions, and eleven Member States have merger control laws.

Moreover, many national authorities are rapidly evolving to become mature, professional, competent, and competition-oriented. They are structured to perform their functions with limited political interference and with a mandate to enforce the laws based on competition policy, relying on economic analysis, rather than protection of national champions. Most national authorities have powers to investigate competition matters which exceed the Commission's powers, as well as powers to impose significant remedies. Moreover, most are empowered to enforce not only their national competition laws, but also, with some limitations, Community competition law, and they are interested in expanding those powers. The extent to which they actually enforce their laws at present varies from one Member State to the next. Nonetheless, the evolution of the national competition law systems, in conjunction with increased emphasis on the subsidiarity principle, is likely to change the structure of competition law enforcement in the European Union.

With the growing importance of the national systems, influence also has begun to flow in the opposite direction. Member State authorities would also like to effect changes to the Community competition law system. For instance, the Member States are critical of the manner in which vertical restraints are handled under the Community system. Some Member States also believe that the institutional structure of the Community system should incorporate elements to ensure independence of decision making, and have advocated establishment of an independent European cartel office. Thus, Community/Member State relations have the potential to induce improvements at both levels.

This paper will first address the influence of the Community competition law system on the Member State systems. It will begin with a description of the historical development of the national systems. The "quiet" harmonization of substantive law which has occurred will be described, as well as the state of harmonization of procedures. The influence of the national systems on that of the Community system which has begun to occur will then be addressed. A case study of the regulation of vertical restraints by the Commission and the Member States will be considered. The institutional structure of the national competition authorities, and how they differ from the institutional structure of the Community, will then be discussed.

16.2 The National Competition Law Systems

16.2.1 Role of National Competition Law

Competition law in the European Union is implemented through a dual enforcement system, with both Community and Member State laws playing an important role in the overall scheme. The Community level rules applicable to restrictions of competition and abuses of a dominant position were designed to apply only to situations where an appreciable effect on trade between the Member States can be established. In merger cases, those transactions which satisfy threshold requirements fall within the exclusive jurisdiction of the Commission; others are subject to Member State controls.

Community rules are needed because only they can create a level playing field for all enterprises throughout the European Union, and only the Commission has the tools effectively to review cross-border arrangements. In contrast, national rules apply in situations where markets within the boundaries of a single Member State are involved. The existence of national competition law is also useful to support Community law, because it helps create a consciousness of the benefits of competition throughout the European Union.

Thus, competition law incorporated strong elements of subsidiarity from the outset, providing the basis for the jurisdictional divide between the Community and the Member States (Overbury, 1993, p. 558). The need for a dual system will continue even after market integration is fully achieved, because some markets will remain national as a result of differences in taste, custom and practicality.

16.2.2 Harmonization of National Law

Substantive Law

Article 87 of the Treaty of Rome empowers the Council of Ministers to enact legislation defining the relationship between national and Community competition laws, but this has never been done.[1] Nonetheless, the Member States have been under constantly increasing pressure through the integration process to conform their national competition laws to Community law (Swift and Anderson, 1992, p. 525). The process of harmonization of the Member State systems has been occurring even without employment of the traditional tool of a Community directive, albeit at varying speeds in the different Member States. This process, known as "quiet harmonization," (Hawk, 1992 Supplement, Volume II, p. 1034) has been occurring for several reasons.

First, pressure has been felt as a result of a broadening interpretation of Articles 3g and 5 of the Treaty. Article 3g requires the institution of "a system ensuring that competition in the common market is not distorted;" Article 5 requires the Member States to "take all appropriate measures ... to ensure fulfillment of the obligations arising out of this treaty." This establishes a requirement that the Member States interpret, apply and develop national antitrust laws by taking account of Community law and practices (Stockmann, 1992, pp. 452–3).

Second, the process of integrating their national economies has placed the Member States under ever increasing pressures to align their competition laws and policies with Community competition laws in order to create a level playing field for their enterprises (Swift and Anderson, 1992, p. 525). Absence of convergence between the two levels would imply that one set of rules applies to larger enterprises, likely to be subject to Community law, and another set to smaller enterprises, likely to be subject to national law (Steenbergen et al., 1992, p. 543). The greater the difference between EU and Member State laws, the greater the difference in the competitive situations of the individual states, resulting in a distortion of competition.

Third, greater consistency of approach and coherence is more comprehensible and helpful to business firms, and enables competition authorities to cooperate more easily when dealing with the same firm (Borrie, 1993, p. 340). The need for consistency is greatest in merger control; differences are tolerable in control of vertical restraints, for instance, as long as they do not affect interstate trade.

Fourth, where both systems apply, conflicting legal consequences and duplicative procedures will occur absent convergence (Bechtold, 1993, p. 343).

[1] To some extent, the relationship has been defined by decisions of the Court of Justice (Swiftand Anderson, 1992, p. 525).

To the extent that the relationship between Community and national law remains undefined, national authorities are free to pursue those who violate national rules, provided this would not prejudice the full and uniform application of Community rules.[2] Should a conflict arise between the two, Community law prevails (Steiger, 1992, p. 9). This creates a force for harmonization. As the Court of Justice observed in *Walt Wilhelm:*[3]

> It would be contrary to the nature of [the EC system] to allow Member States to introduce or to retain measures capable to prejudicing the practical effectiveness of the Treaty. The binding force of the Treaty and of measures taken in application of it must not differ from one state to another as a result of internal measures, lest the functioning of the Community system should be impeded and the achievement of the aims of the Treaty placed in peril. Consequently, conflicts between the rules of the community and national rules in the matter of the law on cartels must be resolved by applying the principle that Community law takes precedence.

Absent convergence, an ever increasing number of conflicts in enforcement of national and community competition laws will occur (Held, 1993, p. 319).

Restrictive Practices and Abuses of a Dominant Position

The Treaty of Rome included the achievement of "undistorted competition" as one of the fundamental objectives of the Community, and incorporated basic competition rules as the means for achieving that objective. Competition was seen as a means for promoting market integration, as well as a goal in itself. The Treaty's competition rules are set forth in Articles 85 and 86: Article 85 prohibits cartels and restrictive practices which may distort

[2] *Wilhelm* v. *Bundeskartellamt*, 1969 ECR 1; Bechtold (1993, p. 348); Zekolle (1991, p. 92). If an agreement has been exempted pursuant to Article 85(3), the majority view is that Community law takes precedence, and national law could not prohibit the transaction (Bechtold, p. 346).

[3] Swift and Anderson (1992, pp. 527–8). In *Wilhelm*, the Court addressed whether the Bundeskartellamt could impose a fine pursuant to German national law while the same case was pending before the EC Commission, on the issue of whether a fine should be imposed pursuant to art. 85(1).

competition; Article 86 prohibits the abuse of a dominant position.[4] The Community system is based on the "prohibition principle," under which all restrictions which contravene the competition rules are prohibited. Notification is required of all restrictive agreements with regard to which a party seeks an exemption pursuant to Art. 85(3).

Following the entry into force of the Treaty of Rome in 1957, each of the Member States enacted some form of competition law, or modified already existing laws which had been ineffective. The first wave of Member States to do so, in the late 1950's and early 1960's, was Germany (1958), the Netherlands (1958), Belgium (1960), and Spain (1963). However, German law was enacted in response to politically motivated external pressure from the United States, which insisted on the abolition of German cartels and monopolies, and not by a desire to harmonize with EC law. The German law reflects the influence of American antitrust law (Majone, 1991, pp. 87–9). However, it applies "abuse control," which holds illegal only those restrictions which are found by authorities to constitute an abuse, to abuses of a dominant position and vertical non-price restraints; and it applies outright prohibition to horizontal cartels and resale price maintenance. Similarly, Spain, which was not a Member State at the time, enacted its original antitrust law in response to external political pressure primarily from the United States. Pressure also was exerted by the European Community, with which Spain was determined to work closely in anticipation of accession. Unlike Community law, competition law in the Netherlands and Belgium (both with strong corporatist traditions) were based on abuse control (Stockmann, 1992, pp. 448-49), and were not rigidly enforced.

The second wave of laws was enacted in the 1970's and early 1980's, by Luxembourg (1970), Ireland (1972 and 1987), Germany (1973), Greece (1977), Portugal (1983) and the UK (1976). The law in Luxembourg is inspired by Articles 85 and 86, but applies abuse control rather than prohibition to most types of transactions.[5] The laws in Greece and Portugal were modeled on Articles 85 and 86 of the Treaty of Rome, in anticipation of their imminent accession to the Community. In contrast, the UK enacted a restrictive practices law in 1976 based on abuse control and which followed an

---

[4]Other competition provisions in the Treaty, beyond the scope of the present paper, are Article 90, which controls state monopolies; and Article 92, which prohibits state aid which threatens to distort competition.

[5]Stockmann (1992, pp. 455–6). The only transactions subject to prohibition are resale price maintenance, refusals to deal and discriminatory practices used to enforce them.

approach in stark contrast to that of Article 85. In addition, France amended its already existing law in 1977 and again in 1986, each time bringing it closer to Community law. French law now tracks Articles 85 and 86, and the Conseil de la Concurrence (the French enforcement authority) has emphasized in its statements its desire for harmony with Community law (Stockmann, 1992, pp. 449–50).

The third wave of laws was enacted in the 1990's, and is even more clearly inspired by Articles 85 and 86. A new law which closely tracks Community law was enacted by Italy in 1990. Earlier laws were replaced in Spain (1990), Ireland (1991 and 1996), Belgium (1993), and Portugal (1993), all of which were motivated by a desire more closely to follow Community law. However, Denmark enacted a new law in 1990 which still differs considerably from Community law, retaining abuse control in most areas. The reason is that Danish authorities prefer a flexible approach with high transparency of market processes to control competition problems in their small country, and they believe one group of enterprises suffices in most industries to supply goods or services for the nation (Stockmann, 1992, pp. 457-58). Denmark's 1990 act, nonetheless, moved closer to EU law, acknowledging that competition is the most important means to achieve satisfactory performance of its economy, and eliminating other goals which the previous competition law had incorporated (Stockmann, 1992, pp. 457-58). Further harmonization of Danish law with Community law is expected in the future.

The most recent round of EU enlargement brought three new Member States (Austria, Finland, and Sweden), which traditionally have not been competition oriented. Finland (1992) and Sweden (1993) enacted competition statutes and set up competition authorities inspired by the Community system. Austria (which, like the Netherlands, has a corporatist tradition) enacted a law in 1988 which was strongly influenced by German competition law. It passed a new law in 1993 which still differs in significant respects from Community law. The three new Member States were members of the European Free Trade Area (EFTA), which entered an agreement with the Community to create a European Economic Area (EEA), effective in early 1994. Under the agreement, the EEA had uniform competition rules based on the Community system (EC Commission, 1992, p. 51). Also pursuant to the agreement, the EFTA countries established the EFTA Surveillance Authority, with equivalent powers and similar functions to the Commission in the field of competition (EC Commission, 1991, p. 51).

Thus, at present, nine Member States (Belgium, Finland, France, Italy,

Greece, Ireland, Portugal, Spain and Sweden) have competition laws with respect to restrictive agreements and abuses of a dominant position which substantially resemble those of the Community. German law differs from Community law because it is even stricter in assessing horizontal cartels and resale price maintenance (which it prohibits outright) than Article 85 (which the Commission interprets broadly and allows a balancing of factors), exempts certain sectors of the economy (agriculture, and to a limited extent, energy, banking and insurance) from coverage, and applies abuse control to abuses of dominant positions and vertical non-price restraints (Stockmann, 1992, p. 442). The need to align German law with Community law is increasingly felt in Germany in order to create a level playing field.[6]

Only four Member States (Denmark, Luxembourg, the Netherlands and the UK) still have laws based wholly on abuse control. The Netherlands government has a policy to apply the law to the extent possible in conformity with Community law and enforcement practices (Stockmann, 1992, pp. 456–7). Moreover, modifications are under consideration to harmonize with Community law. Denmark and the UK are the only Member States whose competition laws still differs considerably from Community law (Stockmann, 1992, p. 457). The UK system is a complex patchwork of diverse laws which are weak, largely due to ineffective remedies. UK law does, however, cover some situations which would not be covered by EU law, such as in the area of abuse of a dominant position (House of Lords Select Committee on the European Communities, 1993, p. 52). A 1989 UK White Paper proposed to reconcile UK competition law with Community law. While there is general agreement in the UK that this is needed, it has not occurred because the issue lacks political clout.[7]

---

[6]This pressure is based on a recognition that exemptions under German law are, according to industry, too narrow, that Art. 85 provides a more flexible approach, and that it is unacceptable to apply different standards to merger control in the Community and Germany. The Bundeskartellamt argues that exemptions are obsolete, and that exempted sectors should be covered in light of the Community's increasing activities in these areas. Moreover, harmonization is deemed essential by German authorities if industrial policy plays a greater role, and merger control is less harsh, at Community level (Stockmann, 1992, p. 452). Private practitioners in Germany agree that further harmonization is needed (Bechtold, 1993, p. 343; Goebel *et al.*, 1993, p. 378).

[7]*Antitrust & Trade Reg. Rep.* (BNA), No. 63, at 99 (July 23, 1992); but see House of Lords Select Committee on the European Communities, 1993, testimony of Stephen Burbridge, Secretary, Monopolies and Mergers Commission, pp. 52–3 (stating he that prefers to retain existing flexible system in UK).

Mergers

The Community's Merger Regulation was adopted in 1989, some thirty years after the signing of the Treaty of Rome, and following 17 years of negotiation and much political compromise. It places mergers falling above specified turnover thresholds of the enterprises involved within the exclusive jurisdiction of the Community.[8] It prohibits those mergers within its exclusive jurisdiction which create or strengthen a dominant position.[9]

The thresholds for application of the Community Merger Regulation are very high: aggregate worldwide turnover of all the undertakings concerned of ECU 5bn, Community turnover of each of at least two of the undertakings of at least ECU 250mn, except that if each of the undertakings concerned has achieved more than 2/3 of its aggregate Community wide turnover within one and the same Member State, then the merger does not fall within the Community's exclusive jurisdiction. Perhaps as a result of these high thresholds, the Member States felt the need to enact their own merger laws in order to fill the gap for those mergers not covered by Community law (Steenbergen et al., 1992, p. 543).

As was the case at the Community level, merger legislation generally was adopted by the Member States some years after they adopted laws governing restrictive practices and abuses of dominant positions. Member State merger control laws play an important role in the scheme for the regulation of mergers in the Community.

Several Member States passed merger control legislation before the EU Merger Regulation was passed. These included Germany (1973, Stockmann, 1992, p. 451), the UK (1973), France (1977),[10] Greece (1977), Portugal (1983, Stockmann, 1992, pp. 460–1) and Ireland (1987). A number of Member States adopted domestic merger control laws after the Community Merger Regulation took effect in 1989 (House of Lords Select Committee on Euro-

[8]The Regulation contains two exceptions to the Community's exclusive jurisdiction: Art. 9, which provides for referral of cases to Member State authorities under certain circumstances; and Art. 21, which provides that Member States "may take appropriate measures to protect legitimate interests other than those taken into consideration by this Regulation. ...".

[9]Council Regulation (EEC) No. 4064/89 of 21 December 1989 on the control of concentrations between undertakings, O.J. L395 (December 30, 1989)(hereafter "Merger Regulation").

[10]Stockmann(1992, pp. 449–50). The enactment of merger control legislation reflected a fundamental change in the French government's attitude towards concentrations.

pean Communities, 1993, Howe testimony, p. 102) including Austria (1993), Belgium (1993), Italy (1990), Spain (1989), and Sweden (1993). Portugal revised its law in 1993. Four Member States still have not passed merger control legislation (Denmark, Finland, Luxembourg and the Netherlands). Danish authorities do not intend to include a merger provision in the revisions to their law. Although they recognize that markets are highly concentrated in their country, they argue that this does not necessarily lead to lower competition at home and may lead to improved competitiveness abroad (Stockmann, 1992, pp. 457–8).

Substantive tests for prohibiting a merger in virtually all Member States incorporate not only competition-based factors but also standards other than competition. This differs from Community law, which does not allow derogation from conclusions of a competitive analysis on the basis of public or industrial policy concerns.[11] Nonetheless, harmonization has been increasing, and competition considerations have come to play a more significant role in enforcement policy.

Belgian[12] and Italian[13] merger control laws largely follow the Community test of "create or strengthen a dominant position." German law proscribes those mergers which would create or strengthen a dominant position in a relevant market, unless the merger would also lead to improvements in the competitive structure of one or more markets that outweighs the anticompetitive effects, and allows the minister to overrule this assessment on political/public policy grounds (Hawk, 1992 Supplement, Volume II, p. 1051). Similarly, Greek law proscribes concentrations that would create or strengthen a dom-

---

[11]Overbury (1993, p. 363). However, Article 21(3) of the Merger Regulation would allow the Member States to prohibit a merger which the Commission has approved on a narrowly defined principle of "legitimate interest," but there is no power to permit a merger that the Commission has prohibited (Overbury, 1993, p. 363).

[12]Art. 10 of the Belgian law of August 5, 1991, concerning the protection of competition, prohibits concentrations which create or strengthen a dominant position as a result of which effective competition will be significantly impeded in the Belgian market or a substantial part thereof. However, the Belgian law permits clearance of otherwise anticompetitive mergers where the conditions for exemption specified in EEC Art. 85(3) are present. See Hawk (1992 Supplement, Volume 3, p. 1039).

[13]Romani (1992, p. 482). There are two major differences between EU and Italian merger law: the Council of Ministers of Italy is empowered to introduce general criteria under which transactions might be cleared on non-competition grounds, and the prime minister may prohibit a merger involving firms whose country of origin is believed to discriminate against Italian firms (Steiger, 1992, p. 10).

inant position, but allows the Minister to authorize those which serve an important public interest (Hawk, 1992 Supplement, Volume II, p. 1056). Under Austrian law, a merger which leads to or strengthens a dominant position must be blocked, unless it is necessary for attaining international competitiveness or if there is a positive overall balance of the effects of the merger on competition.

Spanish[14] and French[15] merger control are similar to each other, in allowing the minister to prohibit any merger meeting specified thresholds with harmful effects on competition which are not outbalanced by economic benefits and technological progress.

Portuguese, Swedish and British merger law are substantially different from Community law. ThePortuguese law prohibits mergers likely to have a negative effect on competition in a Portuguese market without bringing any advantages in employment or regional or technological development (Hawk, 1992 Supplement, Volume II, p. 1069). British law prohibits mergers which operate, or may be expected to operate, against the public interest, which is assessed by taking into account "all matters which appear ... in the particular circumstances to be relevant."[16]

Irish law prohibits mergers "likely to prevent or restrict competition or restrain trade in any goods or services and would be likely to operate against the common good."[17]

---

[14] Under Spanish law, a merger likely to create or strengthen a dominant position that has the object or effect of impeding, disturbing or limiting competition on the Spanish market will be prohibited. Authorities also must assess positive "contributions" of the merger, including improvement of production or distribution systems; promotion of technical or economic progress; the international competitiveness of national industry; and the interests of consumers or users (Hawk, 1992 Supplement, Volume II, p. 1073).

[15] Stockmann (1992, pp. 461–2). Under French law, market shares are the most significant factor for the competition assessment; number of competitors and entry barriers play an increasingly important role in the analysis. If competition is restricted, economic benefits, such as gains in efficiency, employment, technology or the international competitiveness of French industry are assessed (Hawk, 1992 Supplement, Volume II, p. 1044).

[16] Hawk (1992 Supplement, Volume II, p. 1080). The Conservative government has concentrated on traditional competition factors, rather than social or industrial factors Hawk (1992 Supplement, Volume II, p. 1061).

[17] Hawk (1992 Supplement, Volume II, p. 1061). Factors to be considered are: continuity of supply or services; level of employment; regional development; rationalization of operations in the interest of greater efficiency; research and development; increased production; access to markets; shareholders and partners; employees; and consumers. Hawk (1992 Supplement, Volume II, p. 1080).

Thus, merger control laws are less harmonized with Community law than laws prohibiting restrictive practices and abuses of dominant positions, mainly due to conceptual differences. Only five Member States have merger control laws which resemble the EU Merger Regulation. This presents considerable difficulties to merging firms, which often are subject to merger control in a number of Member States.

16.2.3 Procedural Law

Convergence is more complicated and less necessary with respect to procedures[18] than with respect to substantive law (Steenbergen *et al.*, 1992, p. 545). Unlike the situation with substantive law, Member States are not limited by Community law in their power to adopt procedures to obtain necessary information and impose sanctions in antitrust cases (Steenbergen *et al.*, 1992, p. 548). Many Member States have retained existing procedures or enacted new ones which go beyond the Commission's procedural tools.

Notifications

The EU system requires notification[19] of all mergers within the Commission's exclusive jurisdiction, and imposes a waiting period, during which an investigation is made and the merger should not be consummated. A similar system is followed in 7 of the 12 Member States with merger control legislation (Austria, Belgium, Germany, Greece, Ireland, Portugal and Sweden). In Italy, premerger notification is obligatory for mergers exceeding specified thresholds, but no waiting period applies (Laudati, 1995, p. 10). Notification is optional in France, Spain and the UK, and may be ordered by authorities in Finland.

Investigations

The Commission has two main tools to investigate potential infringements of the competition laws: information requests and on-site inspections. Only undertakings or associations of undertakings can be the subject of the Commission's investigations, since it has no powers against the individual. The

[18] See generally Laudati (1995).

[19] Regarding notifications of vertical restraints, see the discussion of procedural rules applicable to vertical restraints, below.

Commission may fine a party which refuses to cooperate, but has no power to use force.

The investigatory powers of the Member States exceed those of the Commission in two important respects: powers against individuals and the ability to use police powers (including the possibility to obtain search warrants) in support of efforts to make on-site inspections. Twelve Member States (all except Belgium, Finland and Germany) have powers to direct their investigatory efforts against individuals who are not undertakings and all have powers to sanction individuals for failing to cooperate in an investigation; seven Member States provide for the imposition of a prison sentence for obstruction of an investigation (Finland, France, Germany, Greece, Ireland, the Netherlands, and the UK) (Laudati, 1995, p. 6., pp. 16–17).

Sanctions

The EU and most of the Member States rely substantially on administrative sanctions to ensure compliance with competition laws. They all provide for prohibition orders against enterprises regarding restrictive practices and abuses of a dominant position; the EU and the eleven Member States with merger laws provide for prohibition orders for violative mergers.

Fines, which are provided for under EU law for substantive violations of Articles 85 and 86, are provided for in eleven Member States. EU law does not provide for fines for substantive violations of the Merger Regulation, but five of the eleven Member States with merger laws do provide for such fines. The EU system only allows for the imposition of sanctions against undertakings and associations of undertakings, but fines may be imposed on the individual in six Member States for substantive violations.

Criminal sanctions do not exist in the EU competition law scheme, and only play a small role in that of the Member States: only Austria, France and the Netherlands provide criminal sanctions, and only for restrictive practices and abuses of a dominant position.

16.3 Control of Vertical Restraints by the Commission and the Member States

As discussed above, harmonization of national law with Community law on restrictive agreements has already occurred on paper in nine Member States. However, this does not guarantee that harmonization has also occurred with respect to implementation. In fact, Member State authorities question the Commission's practices for handling vertical restraints as overly formalistic, and distinguish their own practices in this area. During a gathering of Member State authorities in Brussels in 1995,[20] the Member States were consistent in urging that economic analysis should be the initial step in assessing vertical restraints, in order to determine whether a restriction of competition exists under Article 85(1), and before determining whether an individual or block exemption would be appropriate under Article 85(3). They also criticized the practice of determining legality of a vertical distribution arrangement by analyzing clauses under block exemption regulations. Finally, they questioned the necessity of the Commission's notification system with respect to vertical restraints. They have suggested various reforms of both substance and procedure.

This section will discuss the substantive laws applicable to vertical restraints of the Community and the Member States, and set forth the Member States' critique of substantive Community rules. It will then describe the differences in procedures of the Community and the Member States as they apply to vertical restraints.

[20]In April 1995, the Commission organized its first European Competition Forum, a gathering in Brussels of national authorities and judges from all Member States as well as from 20 other countries which have signed treaties with the European Union incorporating, to varying degrees, EU competition laws. The purpose of the Forum was to air views on the Commission's current approach with respect to certain vertical arrangements, including exclusive distribution and selective distribution, in anticipation of the expiration of block exemptions 1983/83 (exclusive distribution) and 1984/83 (exclusive purchase) at the end of 1997, and of the forthcoming Green Paper on Vertical Restraints. The proceedings have recently been published (Ehlermann and Laudati, 1997).

16.3.1 Substantive Law Applicable to Vertical Restraints

Community rules

In furtherance of the Treaty's market integration goal, the Community has devoted great effort to vertical restraints, given the possibility that companies would divide up the single market through distribution arrangements. Thus, policy has been to apply the Art. 85(1) prohibition broadly to vertical arrangements.[21] This has been done by an expansive interpretation of the notion of restriction of competition, finding one to exist if there is a restriction on "economic freedom" of parties, which implies that the parties are restrained in their freedom to act on the market.

Two types of vertical restraints are deemed to violate Art. 85(1) virtually automatically: resale price maintenance schemes and agreements which establish absolute territorial protection for exclusive distributors.[22] For these, not only does Art. 85(1) apply, but Art. 85(3) exemptions are unlikely to be granted.

Other types of vertical restraints may qualify for exemption if they fulfill the conditions of Art. 85(3), which are designed to separate out arrangements which improve the efficiency of distribution but do not harm the Community's market integration goal.[23] Exemptions may be granted individually, or an agreement may qualify for exemption by meeting the conditions established in a block exemption regulation.

Block exemptions define categories of agreements which generally fulfil the conditions of Art. 85(3), and are therefore exempt. Three types of

[21] A violation of Art. 85(1) is established by a showing of a restriction of competition, appreciability, and that trade between the Member States is affected.

[22] Distributors may be allocated exclusive territories in order better to penetrate the market or to make distribution more efficient. However, protection cannot be absolute. Passive sales (i.e., sales by an exclusive distributor in response to orders received from outside the exclusive territory) and parallel trade (i.e., purchases by customers or intermediaries from any distributor in the Community, and sales by those intermediaries in any other market in the Community, particularly in response to large price differentials) must be allowed. In selective distribution networks, this only applies to qualified distributors.

[23] To qualify for exemption, an arrangement must contribute to improving the production or distribution of goods or to promoting technical or economic progress, while allowing consumers a fair share of the benefits, and not imposing restrictions which are not indispensable to attaining these objectives or affording the undertakings concerned the possibility of eliminating competition with respect to a substantial portion of the market in question.

vertical arrangements are covered by block exemptions: exclusive distribution (No. 83/83), exclusive purchasing (No. 84/83), and franchising (No. 4087/88). The overriding concern is not to permit absolute territorial protection. Thus, these block exemptions specify what is permitted with respect to territorial restrictions, purchasing and selling obligations, non-compete clauses, duration of the contract, and customer restrictions.

No block exemption exists for selective distribution. The rules which have been developed through decisions of the European courts and the Commission with respect to selective distribution are that the distributor should be chosen on the basis of objective criteria necessary for efficient distribution of goods. Normally pre- or after-sales service is provided. The distributor may only sell to final consumers or other selected dealers.

Member State rules

Some of the Member States whose restrictive agreement laws, on paper, resemble those of the Community, do not believe it is accurate to characterize their systems as based on the prohibition principle as opposed to the abuse control principle, due to the manner in which they apply the law.[24] In particular, they undertake economic analysis in order to determine whether the arrangement is prohibited, rather than considering such analysis only at the exemption stage, as the Community does. For instance, the Italian authority carries out a rule of reason analysis both to determine whether a restriction exists and whether an exemption should be granted, relying heavily on economic analysis, especially the economic impact of the agreement in the relevant market. Market access, market position of the parties, duration of the agreement, and cumulative effect of the network of distribution systems are considered. The Italian authority stated in its comments on the Member State survey:

> What is to be considered a restriction of competition under Article 85 of the Treaty as well as under the corresponding national provisions is in no way a self-evident issue.
>
> Under a traditional, legalistic approach one may consider Article 85 to prohibit some clauses in vertical agreements. Nevertheless, an increasingly shared view is that Article 85(1) should be interpreted as prohibiting vertical agreements only in so far

[24]The discussion in this section relies on findings from Laudati (1995, 1996a).

> as they have an economic impact restricting competition on the market. Notably, in many judgments the European Court of Justice has held that the restrictive nature of a vertical agreement within the meaning of Article 85(1) can be considered only by reference to its economic and legal context. On an economic appraisal, there is ample support for the view that an examination of the potentially restrictive nature (in terms of competition) of a vertical agreement should not be confined to its formal aspects.

Similarly, the French authority distinguished its application of the law from the Commission's on the ground that unlike the Commission, it does not interpret exclusivity in sales or purchasing automatically to constitute a restriction of competition. It stated:

> It is only when vertical agreements have a potentially anticompetitive object or effect that they are prohibited under the 1986 competition law, unless they do not result in a sufficient economic benefit. The provision on abuse of dominant position is based on the same conditions.

Accordingly, the French authority takes a positive view of distribution systems because it believes they contribute to economic efficiency, and holds them in violation of its national equivalent of Art. 85(1) only when accompanied by clauses which may be injurious to competition. The authority decides whether these constitute a restriction of competition on the basis of economic analysis, taking account of the increased competition that, more often than not, is generated by this type of system. Foreclosure and the cumulative effect of a network of agreements constitute principal criteria for assessing whether a restriction of competition is present. The French authority views the presence of a degree of competition as a justification for not finding a restriction of competition to be present, which it contrasts from the Commission's approach, which considers it as a condition for granting an exemption. If the French authority deems a restriction to be present, it analyzes whether the conditions for granting an exemption are present, and this analysis is more strict than the Commission's Art. 85(3) analysis.

Regarding the abuse control Member States, a vertical arrangement may constitute a violation if some type of abuse is present. The criteria used to determine abuse vary among these countries, as follows:

Austria:	The restraint is not economically justified.
Denmark:	A "dominant influence" may be exerted.
Finland:	The agreement affects price formation, decreases efficiency, prevents or complicates the practicing of trade by another party, or is incompatible with a binding international agreement in a manner incompatible with sound and effective competition.
Germany:	The restraint has an adverse effect on competition (for exclusive distribution agreements, exclusive purchasing agreements, and selective distribution systems), or exceed the scope of licensed rights (for license agreements).
Netherlands:	The restraint is contrary to the "general interest."
UK:	The restraint is contrary to the "public interest."

Comments by some of these countries reveal that economic analysis plays an important part in determining whether an abuse is present. For instance, the German authority takes the view that a restrictive organization of distribution does not normally endanger workable competition, but may do so when combined with a degree of market power. Thus, under German law, exclusive distribution agreements and exclusive purchasing agreements are permissible in principle but subject to supervision by the competition authorities in order to prevent abuse.

Similarly, UK authorities place heavy reliance on economic analysis in order to determine whether an abuse is present. Exclusive distribution and exclusive purchasing agreements are investigated on a case-by-case basis if a market share threshold of 25% is reached either by one firm or a group of firms through a network of vertical arrangements. A rule of reason analysis is made, balancing the effect on competition at both the manufacturing and retailing level versus the benefits from efficiency gains. Two main structural conditions are considered when making this analysis: (1) market imperfections upstream or downstream, giving rise to significant individual or collective market power in the short to medium term; and (2) widespread use of vertical restraints in a given product market, affecting a significant proportion of total market sales, with no history of significant entry.

The Member States have limited experience in bringing vertical restraints cases. The survey revealed that the number of such cases which a national authority may handle each year varies from 0 to 25.

16.3.2 Critique of Substantive Community Law by Member State Authorities

The main critique voiced by the Member States of Community policy with respect to vertical restraints is that application of Art. 85(1) to vertical restraints is too broad, due to the over-broad interpretation of the notion of restriction of competition. They questioned this policy on the ground that not all restrictions on contractual freedom of action constitute restrictions of competition, and conversely, that companies may enter agreements which will lead them to materially reduce the level of competitive pressure even though they do not legally restrict the freedom to act. Accordingly, the danger exists that the Commission will conclude that a restriction of competition exists when in fact the restriction has no economic effect on the market, or that no restriction of competition exists when the restriction has a harmful economic effect. The Member State authorities also questioned the Community practice of splitting analysis under Arts. 85(1) and (3):

> The French authority argued that in applying a rule of reason analysis, the Commission should consider whether the restraint impedes free access to markets (which requires consideration of effect on interbrand and intrabrand competition and market position of the manufacturer); duration of the contract in conjunction with the network of agreements; and setting prices.
>
> The Italian authority stated that in applying a rule of reason analysis, the Commission should consider market conditions (market access, market position), duration of the agreement, and cumulative effect of the network of agreements.
>
> The UK authority urged that use of the rule of reason approach is "of the essence" because vertical restraints may be efficiency or welfare-enhancing, but may be harmful when certain market imperfections are present.

These observations are consistent with those of several commentators. For instance, Prof. Barry Hawk, who made a presentation to DG IV officials regarding his views of the problems with the current Community vertical restraint policy, has charged (Hawk, 1995, p. 975):

> The majority of Commission decisions fail adequately to consider whether the restraint at issue harms competition in the consumer

> welfare sense of economics, i.e. effect on price or output. Concomitantly, market power, which should be the threshold issue, frequently is hardly examined (let alone given a central role) or is simply found to exist in a conclusory fashion under the rubric of "appreciability."

The Member State authorities generally agree that exclusive distribution agreements are not, in themselves, anticompetitive, and in most cases improve distribution and efficiency, and enhance competition. They believe that manufacturers should have the freedom to design exclusive distribution systems to effectuate their own commercial policy, such as to penetrate new markets. Some Member State authorities remarked that the Commission's approach in this area is inconsistent with the approach of the European courts in several recent cases.

Here again, the critique of the Member States is consistent with that of some outside observers. Prof. Hawk asserted (Hawk, 1995, p. 975):

> Perhaps the most striking example [of the anaemic nature of the economic analysis under 85(1), and occasionally even under 85(3)] is the Commission's (almost) automatic placement of exclusive distributorships or exclusive supply obligations under 85(1) without any inquiry into actual anticompetitive effects or market power. But exclusive distributorships ordinarily pose no risk of anticompetitive effects where interbrand competition is healthy (i.e. the supplier lacks significant market power) and distributors and consumers have a range of similar products from which to choose. This automatic condemnation is particularly troublesome given the broad variety of efficiencies that can result from exclusive distribution.

Regarding selective distribution, the Member State authorities were critical of the Community's focus on nature and quality of product, as overly formalistic and not giving sufficient attention to economic analysis:

> The French authority observed that significant economic changes have occurred over time which affect how competition authorities should handle selective distribution systems. The nature of goods and services is in a process of change, and products which were

> once considered luxuries or hi-tech are now available to a wider public. This suggests that a more restrictive policy towards selective distribution systems is warranted. On the other hand, the balance of power between manufacturer and distributor has changed. It is now more legitimate for the manufacturer to protect itself against the retailer's power, and to be more sensitive to the image of its product, such as by ensuring the provision of quality service after sales. This suggests a more lenient policy towards selective distribution is warranted. Thus, the French authority urged that the Commission should focus less on nature of the product and more on marketing strategies, such as those responding to concentration of buyer power. It also advocated analysis of the cumulative foreclosure effect of a series of contracts.
>
> The Portuguese authority urged that exclusive and selective distribution cases be handled in a consistent manner, since competition problems may arise in both only as result of the cumulative foreclosure effect of a network of agreements.

Prof. Hawk observed with respect to selective distribution (1995, p. 976):

> Specific provisions appear to be simply catalogued under 85(1) or 85(3) with little economic basis or analysis. There are exceptions, notably the Commission's decision in Villeroy & Boch. The Community Courts have engaged in a more economic analysis of selective distribution, an irony to some given that the Courts are intended to provide judicial review of an administrative body enjoying special antitrust expertise and experience.

National authorities questioned the Community system's heavy reliance on block exemptions. Several suggested block exemptions should be abolished and replaced with economic analysis on a case by case basis:

> The German authority suggested that the current blocks should be replaced by generic regulations specifying black-listed clauses, including export bans and market sharing agreements between competitors.

16.3.3 Procedural Rules Applicable to Vertical Restraints

Community rules

Pursuant to Art. 17/62, the Community requires notification of agreements, decisions and concerted practices prohibited by Article 85(1) of the Treaty, and for which the party seeks an exemption pursuant to Article 85(3). A party may also apply for a negative clearance, certifying that the transaction described in the application does not constitute a violation of Art. 85(1). Once a notification has been filed, the notifying party is immune from fines from the date of the notification until a decision is rendered. If an agreement meets the terms of a block exemption, it need not be notified.

The Commission has sole power to declare Art. 85(1) inapplicable by granting an exemption pursuant to Art. 85(3), subject only to review by the Community courts. Once a notification is filed, the Commission conducts a case-by case examination of the application, and decides whether to open an investigation, then whether to grant a negative clearance or exemption, or to issue a statement of objections.

Following entry into force of Regulation 17/62, the Commission was faced with a very large number of notifications, many of which involved vertical agreements. To help cope with the mass of notifications, block exemption regulations were enacted; in addition, the Commission began the practice of issuing "comfort letter" in most cases. It may issue a formal decision in only a limited number of cases each year, due to limitations of its resources.

Member State rules

Seven of the nine Member States with vertical restraints laws similar to the Community's (Belgium, Finland, Greece, Ireland, Portugal, Spain and Sweden) also have adopted a notification system like the Community's.

France and Italy do not require notification of restrictive agreements. In Italy, a voluntary notification system exists. In France, no notification system exists for restrictive agreements; enforcement authorities rely on other means to learn of violations. The French authority stated:

> French law is based on a postulate opposite to that which holds that agreements or commercial cooperation in vertical relations are prohibited a priori. This is why we do not have an obligatory

> notification system. Such a system does not seem to us necessary since we consider vertical agreements to be a priori lawful.

Four of the six abuse control Member States require notification (Austria, Denmark, the Netherlands and the UK), without regard to whether an exemption or negative clearance is either available or sought. These systems traditionally have required notification to provide authorities with information needed to determine whether an abuse exists. In Germany, notification is required only of those restrictions which limit freedom to set prices or terms of business, which are generally prohibited but may qualify for exemption. Luxembourg has no notification system; Finland requires notification when an exemption is sought but does not provide for immunity from fines.

16.3.4 Critique of Community Procedures

The Member States were critical of the Community's notification system. Several Member State officials suggested that market share thresholds be used as a basis for triggering notification. For instance, the Portuguese official suggested that the notification system be replaced with a system requiring notification only when the cumulative effect of a series of exclusive distribution agreements goes beyond a certain level, perhaps 25-30%.

Some observers believe that the notification system consumes an inordinate amount of the Commission's competition enforcement resources without rendering sufficient benefits, and that it should therefore be abolished.

Prof. Hawk observed (Hawk, 1995, p. 984):

> It was evident as early as the 1960's that DG IV lacked the resources to deal with notifications seeking individual exemptions. This should not be surprising. No competition authority in the world has the resources to examine the vast number of vertical agreements (and licenses) whose enforceability has been called into question by the overbroad application of 85(1). The Emperor wears no clothes. The notification system set up in Regulation 17 has never worked and will never work. Like the 1976 Restrictive Practices Act in the U.K., the notification system serves mostly to increase transaction costs and transfer income from firms to outside antitrust lawyers. It has no redeeming enforcement virtues and should be scrapped.

16.4 Influence of the Member State Systems on the EU System: Institutional Independence

The Treaty of Rome endowed the Commission with independent powers to ensure the application of the competition laws.[25] All final decisions in competition cases are reached through a vote of the Commission.[26] Thus, the twenty Commissioners, who are appointed by their national governments for five-year renewable terms during which they cannot be dismissed, are the ultimate decision-makers in competition cases. Most of them have no expertise in competition law and severe time constraints, making it difficult for them to apply complex laws and economic analysis to facts of individual cases. It is questionable whether the Commissioners are professionally qualified to perform this function. Moreover, it is not clear what standards they apply, as policy areas other than competition are considered, including industrial and social policy.

The Commissioners have a mandate (EC Treaty, Art. 157) to be "completely independent in the performance of their duties," they "shall neither seek nor take instructions from any government nor any other body."

When the Community system was established, it was believed that placing these powers with the Commission would minimize political interference with enforcement. However, experience has shown this not to be true, as the Commission has become a highly political body, and political influences play a considerable role in its enforcement decisions (Laudati, 1996b).

Some national authorities, notably Germany, are critical of this system. They argue that the insufficient independence of the Commission and lesser guarantees of Community procedures will be a permanent source of difficulty and distrust in the relationship between national and EU authorities (Panel Discussion, 1994, p. 111). Many see themselves as more independent than the Commission in three respects: decisions are subject only to judicial review, not review by the government hierarchy; appointments on the independent competition councils are irrevocable; and national competition councils are specialized in competition policy, with no other duties, decreasing the likelihood of undue influences (Fernandez Ordóñez, 1994, p.

[25] *Treaty Establishing the European Community*, Arts. 157, 158 (hereafter "EC Treaty").
[26] Reg. 17, Art. 9; Merger Reg., Art. 8.

112).

The trend in recent years has been to place an increasing level of responsibility with independent authorities in order to isolate competition decisions from political influence. For instance, the Italian competition authority, one of the most recently created, is among the most independent and autonomous from political influence of all Member State authorities. It has the power to investigate, make decisions, and impose sanctions. Its decisions are subject only to review by the administrative court. It has taken steps to subject its decision making processes to more internal controls by separating investigating from decision making functions, and increasing transparency.

Independent authorities also have substantial investigatorial and decision-making responsibilities in Austria, Denmark and Finland. However, their commitment to antitrust is still in its developmental stages.

Some national authorities have adopted a two-step procedure, with assessment of cases on competition grounds done by the independent antitrust authority, and assessment on other grounds, such as social and industrial policy, done by a government ministry. This has the advantages of: shielding those responsible for competitive assessment from political pressure and protecting the competition authority's public image; being more transparent and thereby exposing political decisions.[27] Such a split is made in Germany,[28] Ireland,[29] and the UK.[30]

In the French system, the Conseil de la Concurrence was delegated powers of enforcement and decision-making in non-merger cases under the 1986

[27] Steenbergen *et al.* (1992, pp. 552–3). Some argue, however, that greater transparency would be an improvement only if consumers are convinced that their welfare will be improved by safeguarding competition. This requires a learning process (Steenbergen *et al.*, 1992, pp. 538).

[28] Steenbergen *et al.* (1992, p. 536). In cases involving restrictive agreements and abuses of dominant positions, the Bundeskartellamt is responsible to investigate, decide on competition grounds and impose sanctions, subject to review by the Ministry, which is responsible to assess the "general interest."

[29] In Ireland, investigations are conducted by the competition authority, an independent body whose members are appointed by the minister. The minister may issue prohibition orders; those prohibiting a dominant position must be confirmed by the legislature (Laudati, 1995).

[30] The Office of Fair Trade is empowered to investigate all types of cases, and the Monopolies and Mergers Commission is empowered to investigate cases involving dominant positions and mergers. The Secretary of State, with the consent of parliament, may issue prohibition and divestiture orders for concentrations and abuses of a dominant position. The Restrictive Practices Court may enjoin certain activities (Laudati, 1995).

amendment to the French competition law. The power to impose fines, which previously belonged to the ministry, was also placed with the Conseil de la Concurrance (Stockmann, 1992, pp. 449–50). The Conseil's independence was also enhanced by its attainment of power to select cases in which it will commence proceedings, and ultimately to decide those cases. However, the Conseil is somewhat impeded in its ability to act independently because the powers to conduct investigations, to impose sanctions in merger cases, and to decide merger cases remain with the Ministry.

In the Spanish and Belgian[31] systems, the Ministry holds investigatory powers and independent agencies hold decision-making powers. In the Spanish system, the SDC, a government body, has power to investigate cases and initiate proceedings, and the TDC, an independent body, has the power to decide cases, impose sanctions, grant authorizations, review SDC decisions not to proceed and remand to the SDC for further factual investigation. However, the government retains power to grant exemptions, subject only to an advisory opinion from the TDC, to enact regulatory norms which protect restrictive behavior, and to decide merger cases. The inability of the TDC to initiate proceedings and investigate is viewed by some as an impediment to its ability to act independently. However, some TDC officials believe this separation of functions to be a safeguard which benefits the parties (Panel Discussion, 1994, p. 120).

Not all national systems have incorporated elements to ensure independence. Government ministries (or divisions within them) are still primarily responsible for investigation and decision-making in Greece, Luxembourg, the Netherlands, and Portugal.

Many Member States which have developed independent systems for cases involving restrictive agreements and abuses of a dominant position handle merger cases differently. In several instances, the government ministry is empowered to make decisions on mergers, even where this power belongs to an independent competition authority in other areas of competition. This is the case, for instance, in France and Germany. In France, the reason for this distinct treatment of merger cases is that they are believed to involve restructuring of the economy.

---

[31] The 1993 Belgian law created a separate antitrust authority, the Conseil de la Concurrence, with decision-making powers which had been within the authority of the Ministry under the previous law (Stockmann, 1992, pp. 448–9). A unit of the Ministry retained powers of investigation.

16.5 Conclusion

Many of the Member States have harmonized their substantive antitrust laws controlling restrictive agreements and abuses of a dominant position with Community law. This has occurred to a lesser extent with merger control laws, as tests other than competition are still employed to vet mergers. The process of quiet harmonization continues, as the Member States whose laws differ from Community law are under great pressure to converge. The question remains, however, as to whether enforcement of the laws has also been harmonized, both in terms of intensity of enforcement and in terms of common approaches to the interpretation of the laws on questions such as how to define a market, what constitutes dominance, etc. True harmonization will only be achieved if enforcement is at an equivalent level throughout the Community, by both the Commission and national authorities. The implementation of the law by the Community and the Member States with respect to vertical restraints differs, with the Member States placing greater emphasis than the Commission on economic analysis of the market to determine whether a vertical restraint constitutes a violation. Moreover, the Member States do not include market integration as a goal of their antitrust laws, and thus they do not provide for protection of passive sales or parallel imports, as does the Community system.

As to procedure, most Member States do not employ a notification system with respect to restrictive agreements because they believe enforcement resources can be put to better use in other ways, such as investigating complaints which involve vertical restraints. The absence of a notification system is also consistent with the premise that vertical agreements are a priori lawful. Finally, only a small number of cases involving vertical restraints is brought in these jurisdictions, which is again consistent with the notion that these restraints are a priori lawful.

The Member States have not adopted the institutional structure employed at Community level for enforcement of its antitrust laws. They have instead attempted to incorporate a greater degree of independence from political authority in their systems, allowing competition authorities to decide cases on competition grounds. Currently, they are placing the Community under pressure to change its institutional structure to allow for more independence.

An optimal competition enforcement network throughout the European Union would involve more complete harmonization of the substantive law of the Community by the Member States and more consistency in enforcement practices, and adoption by the Community of some of the procedural safeguards that exist in the Member States (Goebel *et al.*, 1993, p. 378).

16.6 References

Bechtold, Rainer "Antitrust Law in the European Community and Germany - An Uncoordinated Co-Existence?," in Hawk, Barry, editor *Fordham Corporate Law Institute*, 1993, pp. 343–57.

Borrie, Gordon "UK Antitrust Law and Policy: A Retrospective," in Hawk, Barry, editor *Fordham Corporate Law Institute*, 1993, pp. 331-41.

EC Commission *XXIst Report on Competition Policy 1991*, Luxembourg: Office for Official Publications of the European Communities, 1992.

Ehlermann, Claus Dieter and Laudati, Laraine L., editors, *Proceedings of the European Competition Forum.* John Wiley & Sons and Office for Official Publications of the European Communities, 1997.

Fernandez Ordóñez, Miguel A. "Enforcement by National Authorities of European Community and Member States' Antitrust Law," in Hawk, Barry, editor. *Fordham Corporate Law Institute*, pp. 629–37.

Goebel, Roger J., Bechthold, Rainer, Borrie, Gordon, Held, Stefan, and Lever, Jeremy "Panel Discussion: German and U.K. Antitrust Law and Policy," in Hawk, Barry, editor *Fordham Corporate Law Institute*, 1993, pp. 371–84.

Hawk, Barry *United States, Common Market, and International Antitrust: A Comparative Guide*, 1978 and 1992 Supplement.

— "System failure: Vertical Restraints and EC Competition Law," *Common Market Law Review* Volume 32, 1995, pp. 973–89.

Held, Stefan "German Antitrust Law and Policy," in Hawk, Barry, editor *Fordham Corporate Law Institute*, 1993, pp. 311–29.

House of Lords Select Committee on the European Communities *Enforcement of Community Competition Rules: Report with Evidence.* London: H.M.S.O. Session 1993-94, 1st Report, Minutes of Evidence, 1993.

Laudati, Laraine L. *Surveys of the Member States' Powers to Investigate and Sanction Violations of National Competition Laws.* Luxembourg: Office for Official Publications of the European Communities, 1995.

— *Survey of the Member State National Laws Governing Vertical Distribution Agreements.* Luxembourg: Office for Official Publications of the European Communities 1996a.

— "The European Commission as Regulator: the Uncertain Pursuit of the Competitive Market," in Majone, Giandomenico, editor *Regulating Europe.* Routledge, 1996b.

Majone, Giandomenico "Cross-National Sources of Regulatory Policymaking in Europe and the United States," *Journal of Public Policy* Volume 11, 1991, pp. 79–106.

Overbury, H. Colin "Politics or Policy? The Demystification of EC Merger Control," in Hawk, Barry, editor, *Fordham Corporate Law Institute,* 1993, pp. 557–89.

Panel Discussion, "Investigatory Powers, Fact-Finding, Procedural Guarantees, Transparency and Independence of Antitrust Authorities," in Hawk, Barry, editor, *Fordham Corporate Law Institute*, 1994, p. 111.

Romani, Franco"The New Italian Antitrust Law," in Hawk, Barry, editor, *Fordham Corporate Law Institute*, 1992, pp. 479–85.

Steenbergen, Jacques, de La Laurencie, Jean-Patrice, Romani, Franco, Stockmann, Kurt, and Swift, John. "Panel Discussion: EC Member State Antitrust Law," in Hawk, Barry, editor, *Fordham Corporate Law Institute*, 1992, pp. 533–56.

Steiger, Janet D. "Effectively Enforcing Competition Laws: Some Aspects of the U.S. Experience," in Hawk, Barry, editor *Fordham Corporate Law Institute*, 1992, pp. 1–29.

Stockmann, Kurt "Trends and Developments in European Antitrust Laws," in Hawk, Barry, editor, *Fordham Corporate Law Institute*, 1992, pp. 441–78.

Swift, John and Anderson, Rupert "Developments in United Kingdom Competition Law and in its Relationship with EC Law," in Hawk, Barry, editor, *EC and U.S. Competition Law and Policy*, 1992, pp. 505–31.

Zekoll, J. "European Community Competition Law and National Competition Laws: Compatibility Problems from a German Perspective," *Vanderbilt Journal of Transnational Law* Volume 24, 1991, pp. 75–111.

Competition Policies in Europe - S. Martin (Editor)

Chapter 17

Contributors

Svend Albæk: Born 1959 in Dronninglund. Associate professor in economics at the Institute of Economics, University of Copenhagen since 1993; postdoctoral fellow, Institute of Economics, University of Copenhagen, 1992; postdoctoral fellow, CentER for Economic Research, Tilburg University, 1991-92; research associate, European University Institute, Florence, 1990-1991; Docteur en Sciences Économiques, Université Catholique de Louvain, 1991; M.A. in Economics, University of Warwick, 1986. Research interests various topics in industrial organization, including oligopoly theory, vertical restraints, regulation, antitrust economics/competition policy.

Wendy Asbeek Brusse: Graduated in history from the Free University (Amsterdam) and obtained her Ph.D. from the European University Institute (Florence) for a study on the trade and tariff origins of the EEC (published as Tariffs, Trade and European Integration, 1947-1957. From Study Group to Common Market. 1997) She is currently a lecturer in the Department of History at the University of Groningen and is working on a book on post-war cartels in Western Europe.

Pedro P. Barros: Associate Professor of microeconomics at the Universidade Nova de Lisboa. He is also Research Affiliate with the Centre for Economic Policy Research, London. His main area of research is industrial organization, namely competition policy issues in open economies and health economics.

Frank Barry: Holds a B.A. from University College Dublin, an M.A. from the University of Essex and a Ph.D. from Queen's University, Ontario. Currently Senior Lecturer in the Economics Department at University College,

Dublin, he has held visiting appointments at the Universities of Stockholm, California, and New South Wales, and was Trade and Industry Advisor to the Indonesian Ministry of Finance with the Harvard Institute for International Development. His interests are in macroeconomics, international trade and economic development.

Massimo Ferrero: Born in Turn in 1964; he has been working in the Italian Competition Authority from 1992. He first dealt with the economic databases of the Authority, with the statistical analysis of mergers in Italy prepared every year for the report of the Authority, and with quantitative analysis carried out in the judgement of particular merger cases. Afterwards he became assistant of Fabio Gobbo, Commissioner of the Authority. He is author of a study about the evaluation criteria for merger analysis in Italy and in some other countries, published in the Authority series "Temi e problemi."

Aurora García: Born in Zaragoza (Spain) in 1964. She received a *Licenciatura* in Business Administration from the University of Zaragoza, a Diploma in Economic Analysis from the Universitat Autónoma in Barcelona and a Master's in Public Economics from the Institute for Fiscal Studies in Madrid (Spain). She holds an M.A. and Ph.D. in Economics from the European University Institute in Florence (Italy). In the winter term of 1992–3 she spent 6 months at the Commission of the European Communities in Brussels as a *stagiare* of DG IV (Competition Policy). Since 1993, she is a Professor of Economics at the Universitat Jaume I (Castellón-Spain). Her research interests include competition policy, applied game theory, and experimental economics.

Nikolaos Georgantzís: Born in Athens in 1962. He received a B.A.-equivalent in Economics from the University of Piraeus (Greece). He holds an M. Phil. in Economics from the University of Wales (Swansea, U.K.) and an M.A. and Ph.D. in Economics from the European University Institute in Florence (Italy). In 1992 he spent 6 months at the Commission of the European Communities in Brussels as a *stagiare* of DG IV. Since 1993 he is a Professor of Economics at the Universitat Jaume I (Castellón-Spain). His research interests include competition policy, oligopoly theory, experimental and environmental economics. He is married and father of a bilingual son.

Fabio Gobbo: Born in Venice in 1947, he is Commissioner of the Italian Competition Authority from 1990. At the time he was nominated, he was a tenured Full Professor of Political Economy at the Faculty of Economics at the University of Bologna. He is author of many books and scientific articles on a variety of topics ranging from the analysis of industrial sectors; the regional and industrial development; the publishing and broadcasting system in Italy and abroad to the control over prices and tariffs and the regulation policies of competition and public authorities.

Richard Griffiths: Formerly professor of Contemporary History at the European University Institute (Florence) is currently professor of Economic and Social History at the University of Leiden. He has published widely on 19th and 20th century Dutch economic history and on the early development of European integration. With Dr. Asbeek Brusse, he is preparing a book on cartels in Western Europe after World War II.

Ulrich Kamecke: Born 1957 in Bonn; Professor of Economic Policy, Department of Economics, Humboldt-University at Berlin, since 1996; Assistant Professor, Department of Economics, University of Bonn, 1989-1991 and 1992-1995; Postdoctoral Fellow, Department of Economics, University of Pittsburgh, 1991-1992; Ph.D., University of Bonn, 1988; MSc Econometrics and Mathematical Economics, London School of Economics, 1984; DiplomVolkswirt, University of Bonn, 1983. Research interests include game theory and its applications to questions of industrial organization.

Laraine L. Laudati: Has worked extensively as a legal consultant to the Directorate General for Competition of the European Commission. She has practiced law in Washington, DC and is currently completing a Ph.D. thesis at the European University Institute in Florence. She is a specialist in EC competition law and has published numerous studies and articles in this area.

Stephen Martin: Director of the Centre for Industrial Economics at the University of Copenhagen. He was Professor at the European University Institute for 7 years, serving as Head of Department for 3 years. He was successively Assistant, Associate, and Full Professor at Michigan State University, having previously taken his Ph.D. in economics at M.I.T. after surviving 3 years in the U.S. Army. His first university degree was in mathematics from Michigan State University. His research interests include all areas of industrial economics, on which he has published widely, with current emphasis on comparative competition policy and experimental tests of signaling behavior in imperfectly competitive markets.

José Mata: (born 1961 in Lisbon) received his Doctorate in Economics from Minho University, Portugal in 1991. He held teaching positions at the Minho University and New University of Lisbon and is currently a Senior Economist at the Research Department of the Bank of Portugal and a Research Affiliate with the Centre for Economic Policy Research (CEPR) . His research interests which spread over several topics in industrial organization, international economics and business policy has been published in *Economics Letters*, the *European Economic Review*, the *International Journal of Industrial Organization*, the *Journal of Industrial Economics*, the *Review of Industrial Organization*, and *Small Business Economics.* He currently serves on the editorial board of the *International Journal of Industrial Organization* and of *Small Business Economics.*

Peter Møllgaard: Born 1964 in Copenhagen. Associate professor of applied microeconomics at Department of Economics, Copenhagen Business School since 1996; Assistant professor, Department of Economics, University of Aarhus, 1994-96; Head of Section, Ministry of Business and Industry, 1993-94; Doctor of Economics of the European University Institute, Florence, 1993; Cand.Polit. (Masters), University of Copenhagen, 1989. Research interests various topics in industrial organization, including oligopoly theory, manipulation of forward markets, and antitrust economics/competition policy.

Manfred Neumann: Professor of Economics at the University of Erlangen-Nürnberg in Germany since 1969, member of the Advisory Committee to the Federal Ministry of Economics since 1977 and member of the Bavarian Academy of Science since 1988. He served as president of EARIE (European Association for Research in Industrial Economics) from 1985 to 1987. In research his fields of specialization are industrial organization and economic growth and fluctuations.

Francis O'Toole: Received his Ph. D. from Georgetown University. His current position is Lecturer in Economics, University of Dublin (Trinity College). His research interests include economic and legal aspects of competition policy and the economics of compulsory voting. He has been employed on a consultancy basis by a number of leading Irish law firms. He has also made a number of contributions to the area of taxation policy and has been involved in a number of TACIS-supported programs.

Per Baltzer Overgaard: Born 1963 in Randers (Denmark). Associate Professor of Economics at the Department of Economics, University of Aarhus, Denmark, since 1993; Assistant Professor, Department of Economics, University of Aarhus, 1990-1993. Ph.D., CORE, Université Catholique de Louvain, Belgium, 1991; MA(Econ), University of Warwick, UK, 1986. Research interests include game theory, industrial organization, economics of information, and antitrust economics/competition policy.

María Victoria Petit: Born in Castellón (Spain) in 1965. She received a Diploma in Business Administration and a B.A.-equivalent in Law from the University of Valencia (Spain), where, in 1993, she defended her Doctoral Thesis, obtaining the maximum qualification. After working as a professor at the University of Valencia, she joined, as a *Profesor Tutular*, the Department of Private Law of the Universitat Jaume I in Castellón. Her published work includes the monographs *Régimen Jurídico de la Auditoría de Cuentas Anuales* and *La Protección del Consumidor de Crédito: Las Condisiones Abusivas de Crédito.* Since 1988, she has collaborated with the section supervised by Prof. Dr. D. Franciso Vicent Chulía of the *Revista General de Derecho.*

Paul Seabright: teaches economics at the University of Cambridge, where he is Director of the M.Phil. programme. He works mainly in industrial organization and development economics, and is co-author of *Merger in Daylight* (with Damien Neven and Robin Nuttall, CEPR, 1993) and *Competition Policy and the Transformation of Central Europe* (with John Fingleton, Eleanor Fox and Damien Neven, CEPR, 1996.

Leo Sleuwaegen: Teaches managerial economics and industrial organization at the University of Leuven and Erasmus University, Rotterdam. He has been a visiting professor of Economics and International Business at the Stern School of Business, New York University, Bocconi University, Milan, the University of California, Irvine and Université de Paris I, Sorbonne-Panthéon. He is a member of the Academic Advisory Group of DG IV, Merger Task Force, of the European Commission. He also holds the CERA-Bank Entrepreneurship Chair at the University of Leuven.

Saïd Mohand Souam: lecturer at the University of Franche Comté in Besançon (France). He is also a researcher at the CREST (Centre de Recherche en Economie et Statistique, Paris) and CEME (Centre d'Economie Mathématique et d'Econométrie, University of Paris I). He has a B.Sc degree in Applied Fundamental Mathematics (University of Paris 7, 1990), a DEA degree in Mathematical Economics and Econometrics (University of Paris 1, 1993). He is also graduated from ENSAE (Ecole Nationale de la Statistique et de l'Administration Economique, 1993) in Economics and Statistics. He will defend his Ph.D. thesis by December 1997 on Antitrust Enforcement and Merger Analysis. He has contributions on Antitrust Enforcement under asymmetric information and merger analysis.

George Symeonidis: Lecturer in Economics at the University of Essex. He studied at the Universities of Athens and Paris and the London School of Economics, from which he obtained his Ph.D. His research covers theoretical and empirical industrial economics.

Paola Valbonesi:Paola Valbonesi is researcher at the University of Verona. After studying at the University of Padova, she pursued Master of Arts in Economics and Doctorate in Economics at the European University Institute in Florence, specializing on privatization in Central and Eastern Europe. She held visiting positions at the Hungarian Academy of Science and University of York. Her main academic interests are in the theory of the firm and industrial organization; her current research concerns privatization of public utility, regulation and competition policy.

Patrick Van Cayseele: Teaches industrial organization and financial intermediation at the Universities of Leuven (K.U.L.) and Namur (F.U.N.D.P.). He has been a visiting scholar in the Kellogg School at Northwestern University and the M.E.R.I.T.-Institute at the University of Maastricht. He is an expert member of the Belgian merger authority (Council for Competition) and is on the board of one of the major Belgian banks. He published numerous articles in scholarly journals as well as a book on Belgian Competition Policy. He has also been the editor-in-chief of a commercial newsletter on mergers and acquisitions.

Index

Names

Subjects